4-27 23

THE LONG WAR

ALSO BY DAVID LOYN

Frontline

In Afghanistan

Butcher & Bolt

THE LONG WAR

THE INSIDE STORY OF AMERICA AND AFGHANISTAN SINCE 9/11

David Loyn

ST. MARTIN'S PRESS
NEW YORK

First published in the United States by St. Martin's Press,
an imprint of St. Martin's Publishing Group

THE LONG WAR. Copyright © 2021 by David Loyn.
All rights reserved. Printed in the United States of America.
For information, address St. Martin's Publishing Group,
120 Broadway, New York, NY 10271.

www.stmartins.com

Designed by Jonathan Bennett
Maps by Jeffrey L. Ward
Title page photograph by Elmer Laahne/Shutterstock.com

Library of Congress Cataloging-in-Publication Data

Names: Loyn, David, author.
Title: The long war : the inside story of America and Afghanistan since
    9/11 / David Loyn.
Other titles: Inside story of America and Afghanistan since 9/11
Description: First edition. | New York : St. Martin's Press, 2021. |
    Includes bibliographical references and index.
Identifiers: LCCN 2021026568 | ISBN 9781250128423 (hardcover) | ISBN
    9781250128430 (ebook)
Subjects: LCSH: Afghan War, 2001—United States.
Classification: LCC DS371.412 .L696 2021 | DDC 958.104/7373—dc23
LC record available at https://lccn.loc.gov/2021026568

Our books may be purchased in bulk for promotional,
educational, or business use. Please contact your local bookseller or
the Macmillan Corporate and Premium Sales Department at
1-800-221-7945, extension 5442, or by email at
MacmillanSpecialMarkets@macmillan.com.

First Edition: 2021

10 9 8 7 6 5 4 3 2 1

Only one who knows the disastrous effects of a long war can realize the supreme importance of rapidity in bringing it to a close.

—*Sun Tzu*

CONTENTS

MAPS x

INTRODUCTION 7

PHASE ONE
2001-2006: THE DIE IS CAST

I NOT BUILDING A NATION 27

2 THE FOG OF AID 59

PHASE TWO
2006-2009: THE TALIBAN RETURN

3 THE BIGGEST WARLORD 85

4 THE HEART OF THE BEAST 109

5 RACK 'EM AND STACK 'EM 121

PHASE THREE

2009-2011: THE SURGE

6 COIN 141

7 OBAMA'S WAR 165

8 OWNING THE VILLAGES 185

9 THE BELL CURVE AND THE ANACONDA 221

10 THE COUNTERINSURGENCY DILEMMA 241

PHASE FOUR

2011-2014: DRAWDOWN

11 PIVOT POINT 265

12 TRIPLE TRANSITION 291

13 TALKING TO THE TALIBAN—I 311

PHASE FIVE

2015-2021: ENDGAME

14 AFGHANISTAN'S WAR 331

15 ENDURING COMMITMENT 349

16 TALKING TO THE TALIBAN—II 369

17 ELECTION AND AFTER 381

ACKNOWLEDGMENTS 399

PICTURE CREDITS 405

BIBLIOGRAPHY 407

NOTES 413

INDEX 441

THE LONG WAR

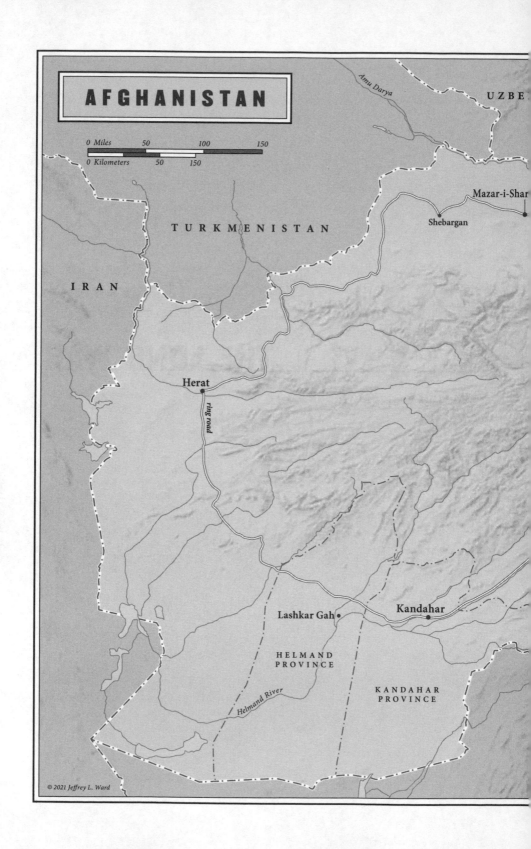

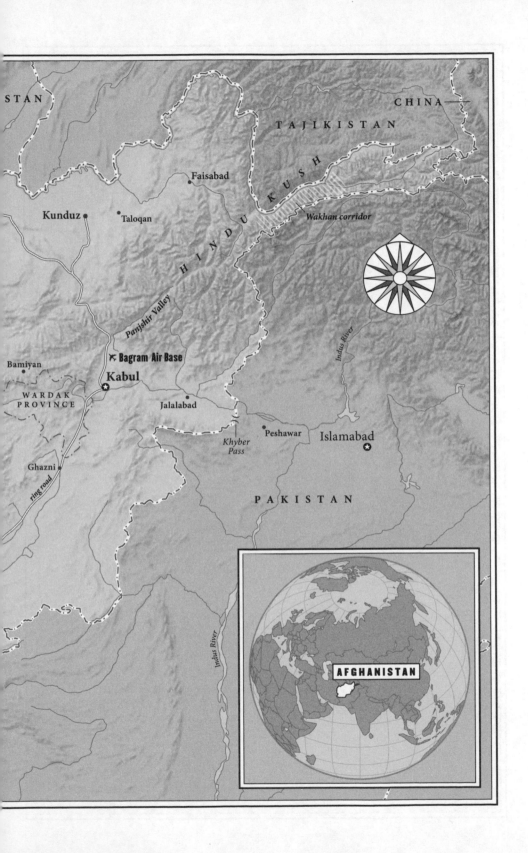

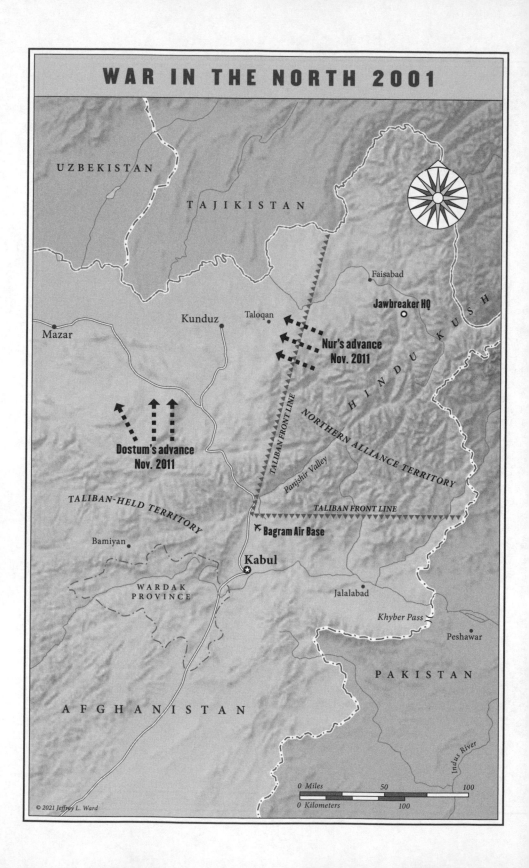

WAR IN THE NORTH 2001

UZBEKISTAN

TAJIKISTAN

Faisabad

Jawbreaker HQ

Mazar

Kunduz

Taloqan

**Nur's advance
Nov. 2011**

H I N D U   K U S H

**Dostum's advance
Nov. 2011**

TALIBAN FRONT LINE

NORTHERN ALLIANCE TERRITORY

Panjshir Valley

TALIBAN-HELD TERRITORY

TALIBAN FRONT LINE

Bamiyan

Bagram Air Base

Kabul

WARDAK
PROVINCE

Jalalabad

Khyber Pass

Peshawar

PAKISTAN

A F G H A N I S T A N

0 Miles   50   100

0 Kilometers   100

© 2021 Jeffrey L. Ward

Indus River

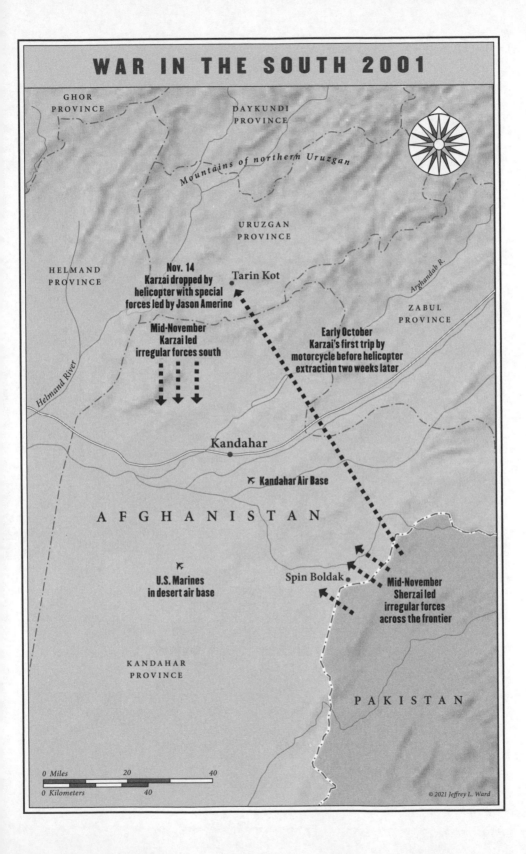

WAR IN THE SOUTH 2001

GHOR
PROVINCE

DAYKUNDI
PROVINCE

Mountains of northern Uruzgan

URUZGAN
PROVINCE

HELMAND
PROVINCE

Nov. 14
Karzai dropped by
helicopter with special
forces led by Jason Amerine

Tarin Kot

Arghandab R.

ZABUL
PROVINCE

Mid-November
Karzai led
irregular forces south

Early October
Karzai's first trip by
motorcycle before helicopter
extraction two weeks later

Helmand River

Kandahar

✈ Kandahar Air Base

A F G H A N I S T A N

✈
U.S. Marines
in desert air base

Spin Boldak

Mid-November
Sherzai led
irregular forces
across the frontier

KANDAHAR
PROVINCE

P A K I S T A N

0 Miles   20   40

0 Kilometers   40

© 2021 Jeffrey L. Ward

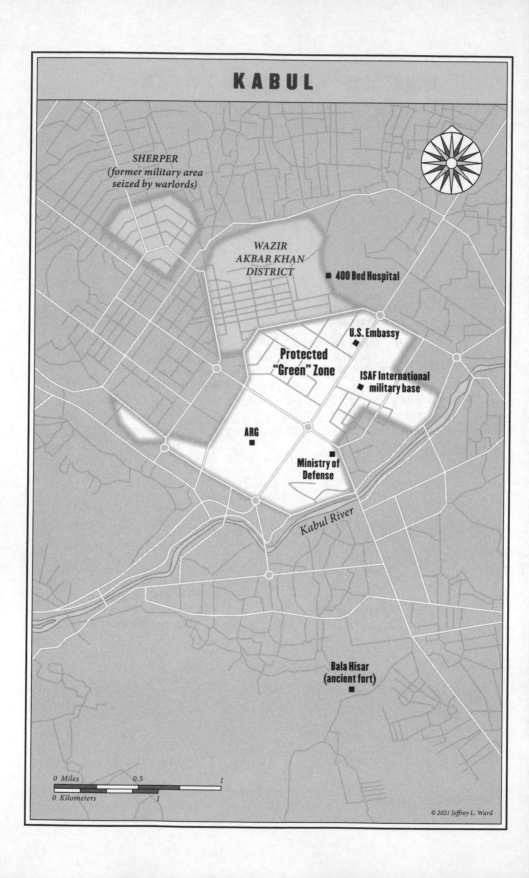

KABUL

SHERPER
(former military area seized by warlords)

WAZIR AKBAR KHAN DISTRICT

■ 400 Bed Hospital

Protected "Green" Zone

■ U.S. Embassy

■ ISAF International military base

■ ARG

■ Ministry of Defense

Kabul River

Bala Hisar (ancient fort) ■

0 Miles   0.5   1

0 Kilometers   1

© 2021 Jeffrey L. Ward

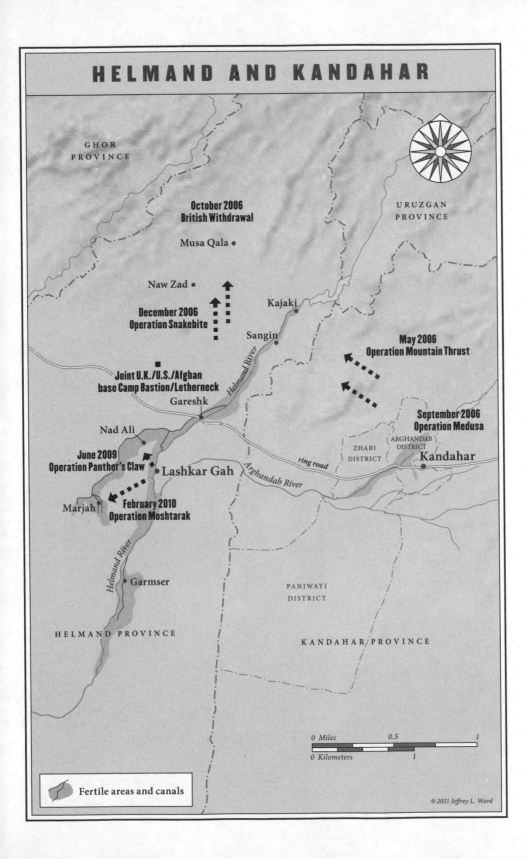

HELMAND AND KANDAHAR

GHOR
PROVINCE

URUZGAN
PROVINCE

**October 2006
British Withdrawal**

Musa Qala •

Naw Zad •

Kajaki •

**December 2006
Operation Snakebite**

Sangin •

**May 2006
Operation Mountain Thrust**

■ **Joint U.K./U.S./Afghan
base Camp Bastion/Letherneck**

Gareshk •

**September 2006
Operation Medusa**

Nad Ali •

ARGHANDAB
DISTRICT

ZHARI
DISTRICT

Kandahar

**June 2009
Operation Panther's Claw** • Lashkar Gah

ring road

Arghandab River

Marjah ▌

**February 2010
Operation Moshtarak**

• Garmser

PANJWAYI
DISTRICT

HELMAND PROVINCE

KANDAHAR PROVINCE

| 0 Miles | | 0.5 | | 1 |

| 0 Kilometers | | | 1 |

◣ Fertile areas and canals

© 2021 Jeffrey L. Ward

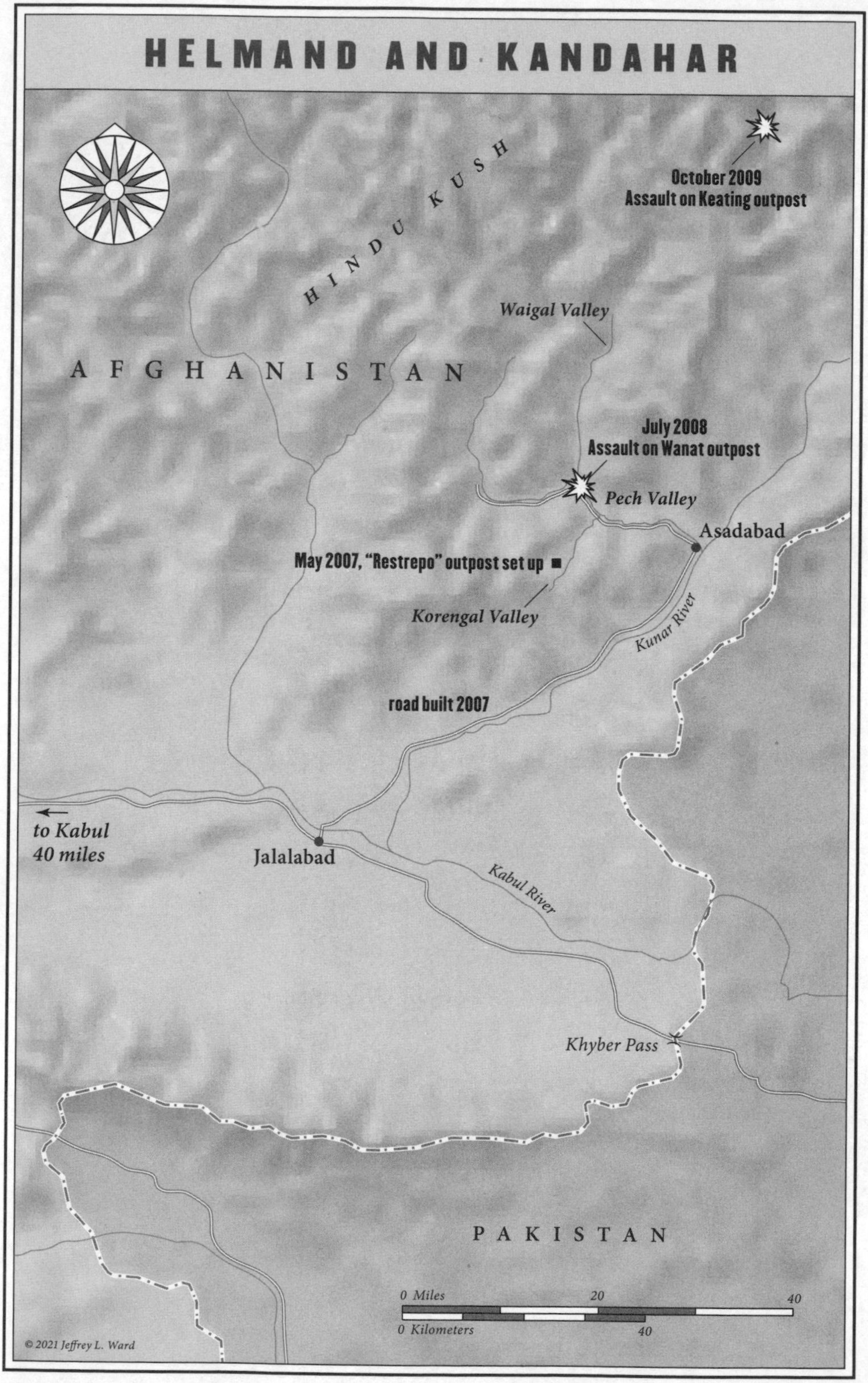

HELMAND AND KANDAHAR

October 2009
Assault on Keating outpost

HINDU KUSH

Waigal Valley

AFGHANISTAN

July 2008
Assault on Wanat outpost

Pech Valley

Asadabad

May 2007, "Restrepo" outpost set up ■

Korengal Valley

Kunar River

road built 2007

← to Kabul
40 miles

Jalalabad

Kabul River

Khyber Pass

PAKISTAN

| 0 Miles | | 20 | | 40 |
| 0 Kilometers | | | 40 | |

© 2021 Jeffrey L. Ward

INTRODUCTION

A SIMPLE GOLDEN CROWN lay in a glass case on the marble mantelpiece in the inner office of the Afghan president, next to a gold medallion. President Ashraf Ghani gestured to these relics of a ruler of Afghanistan's past, "one of the successors of Alexander." Ghani saw himself in a line with the ancient kings and borrowed these symbols of power from the national museum. It was part of his vision of destiny. On his way to file his nomination papers when running for president in 2014, he had sought a blessing from Sibghatullah Mojaddedi, the last representative of a clan who were the kingmakers in Afghanistan's past.

In 1996, when I first entered the Arg, the presidential palace and seat of Afghan power, I had come in with the Taliban. A Taliban tank, festooned with garish plastic decorations from the shops on "Wedding Street" nearby, smashed through the gates. Fighters wandered in and out of the Arg buildings through broken windows and sat in groups on the large lawns eating pomegranates, littering the ground with red-juiced rind. When the Taliban took the capital, two years after emerging out of the desert near Kandahar, my TV crew were the only foreign journalists reporting from their front line. The ruthless speed of the assault surprised their enemies, and when they broke through the defenses of the Sarobi Gorge to the east, thought to be impregnable, the city lay at their feet. These singular fundamentalists were opposed to any depictions of men or animals, and by dawn, they had cut the heads off stone statues of dogs on either side of the staircase in the palace and shot out the faces of men in paintings on the wall.

On one side of the staircase, the walls of a bathroom were covered in blood, where the Taliban had killed the former president Najibullah and his brother overnight. Their castrated bodies hung from a nearby traffic control point on a roundabout, with cigarettes and dollar bills shoved into their hands and mouths—symbols of depravity. Hundreds of Taliban fighters stood around, watching quietly in the dawn.

In 2001, the Taliban were in their turn quickly swept aside in a war from the air with just a handful of mostly American special operators on the ground standing up local militias. What began as an act of righteous revenge for harboring the 9/11 planners turned into America's longest war. Twenty years on, more than a trillion dollars spent, and many lives lost, this book asks why it was so hard.

At the peak, there were 150,000 troops from more than fifty nations under the umbrella of NATO. Those who commanded this first "out of area" campaign for an alliance originally conceived to keep the peace in Europe had a unique task, because of the nature of the conflict and the challenges of alliance warfare. Keeping the coalition together when the predicted peacekeeping and reconstruction mission turned out to be something very different called on unusual skill. The lessons in leadership they learned have an importance beyond the military.

Commanding in Afghanistan raised questions about the ideal division between politicians and the military envisaged by Samuel Huntington in *The Soldier and State*—where politicians decide policy and the military execute it as independently as possible. "The demands of the job made this difficult," wrote General Stanley A. McChrystal. "The process of formulating, negotiating, articulating, and then prosecuting even a largely military campaign involved politics at multiple levels that were impossible to ignore."[1] They had to deal with a fractious and unpredictable host, an ill-equipped coalition, nervous of the worsening conflict, and in Pakistan, a neighbor who proved a duplicitous and dangerous ally. And they were making up a new way of fighting counterinsurgency warfare in the glare of the media. McChrystal and his predecessor as commander, General David McKiernan, would be replaced by President Obama— the first field commanders to be fired since MacArthur in Korea in 1951.

Under Ghani, the traffic control point where Najibullah's body had been displayed was no longer needed. No traffic was allowed near the Arg. A bustling street market had gone, and that roundabout was well inside a new high-security zone behind blast walls. Since 2001, millions of dollars were spent renovating the eighty-acre Arg compound. Scent from a rose garden fills the air where Taliban fighters once sprawled in the dust. But the security threats meant that Ghani lived in isolation, with little contact to the country beyond the manicured lawns of his huge compound. I worked in his office in 2017 and 2018 as a communications adviser and suggested he see a daily news digest, with polling showing his popularity, but did not succeed. He had to fight isolation from reality, living and traveling in a security bubble, the only media in attendance coming from his team in the Arg.

I knew Ghani well before coming to work in his office. He was the country's first finance minister after the Taliban, but soon fell out with the first president, Hamid Karzai, and as a BBC reporter, I interviewed him several times in the years that followed, when he was a strong critic of the international aid effort, and worked as a consultant for several other governments, putting his thinking into a book—*Fixing Failed States.* In office, he consciously saw his administration as completing the reforms begun by King Amanullah, cut short in a coup in 1929 in which rural tribes rose up to oppose their Westernizing progressive king. As part of the renovations Ghani ordered when he took over, he found the desk made for Amanullah, had it restored, and worked at it daily. To him, it was as important a symbol as the Resolute desk in the White House.

Amanullah was lucky to escape with his life. All but one of his successors in the twentieth century were murdered in the Arg. Ghani's election saw the first democratic handover in Afghan history. Facing formidable challenges, he found it hard to fix his own failed state. He trusted very few people, and some he did trust exploited their access in their own interests. Far too much government effort was absorbed in bitter infighting over influence and resources, in a country where control of personnel brings power through patronage networks. Senior government roles come with *tashkils,* allocations of staff, and control of *tashkils* is more important than delivering government services. Soon after Ghani's team came into office, one of his most senior officials fired a gardener, who was useless and deserved to be fired. But absurdly, he had to be reinstated after lobbying by cabinet ministers; firing the gardener had upset a complex web of interlocked interests.[2]

At the other end of the street, about half a mile away from the seat of presidential power, lies the small headquarters compound of the international military alliance, where unlike the government buildings, there was little outside space as accommodation filled every gap. While working in the president's office, I was on a U.S. contract and lived on the base in a converted shipping container. The temporary housing was deliberate, a legacy of the "light footprint" warfare promoted by Secretary of Defense Donald Rumsfeld. Nearly two decades after arriving in Afghanistan, and with the long war not at an end, the maze of alleyways of shipping containers, some residential, some offices, showed how flawed this was.

The Afghan campaign was far less divisive internationally than the U.S.-led invasion of Iraq two years later. Unlike Iraq, Afghanistan had a clear connection to the attacks of 9/11. Even in 2004, when NATO agreed to expand the mission across the country, the Taliban looked finished, and the small international force then in the country took few casualties, so other Western nations were willing to contribute troops for what was seen as a peacekeeping operation, not a war. It turned out to be very different.

The coalition strategy for Afghanistan developed along several lines— the joint civil/military campaign against the Taliban and al-Qaeda and to build Afghan capacity; transition to Afghan control, while building a more long-term strategic partnership; regional diplomacy; and belatedly reconciliation, or talking to the Taliban. The extent that the military operated across these lines of effort depended on the commander at the time, with some more invested in a political strategy than others during a campaign that broke into distinct phases.

Phase One 2001–2006: The operation was improvised with shifting policy goals never adequately scrutinized. The main U.S. effort was against the remnants of Taliban leadership and al-Qaeda, and development spending was uncoordinated.

Phase Two 2006–2009: The Taliban regrouped with far more intensity, sending shock waves across some European troop contributors who had not signed up for a shooting war.

Phase Three 2009–2011: The period of the Obama "surge," a big increase in troops with a clear end date, "one last heave" to hold ground before handing over to Afghan forces.

Phase Four 2011–2014: A period of complex management as hundreds of bases closed and President Hamid Karzai became an increasingly difficult partner. NATO combat operations formally ended at the end of 2014. But the war would not end according to the timetable.

Phase Five 2015–2021: The mission was defined as "train, advise and assist," not combat. But under President Trump the war from the air intensified again. Taliban control grew across rural Afghanistan. President Biden ordered a full withdrawal before there was a final peace deal, with unknown consequences.

Obama was president for the key combat phase and engaged in long discussions over how many troops to keep for how long. The arguments over troop numbers crowded out longer-term policy thinking. Obama's staff felt boxed in by the military, thinking they were always coming back for more, a sense backed by a growing mood in Congress and the media against the "forever war." For their part, the generals felt they were given less than they needed after giving their best advice based on the task set by politicians. In a National Security Council meeting in the summer of 2014, as Obama was trying to set a course to zero troops by the end of his presidency, then two years away, he said, "The fever in this room has finally broken . . . We're no longer in nation-building mode."[3] The truth is that they never were. That was not the plan. But while taking Afghanistan was easy, leaving it secure would be far harder, and twenty years later, the task is not complete.

At the beginning, they neither had enough of the right troops to stabilize the country nor a long-term vision. The nations who sent soldiers, development workers, and cash to Afghanistan after 2001 came with their own national baggage but did not share a contemporary doctrine—way of operating—to deal with the situation they faced, as security gradually spun out of their control. It would be five years after the fall of the Taliban before the U.S. military produced a new counterinsurgency manual—the first doctrine on this scale since Vietnam.

On 9/11 every year in the main base in Kabul, small groups of soldiers carry out a solemn ritual with great reverence, raising, saluting, and then lowering American flags, before folding them in the regulation way and putting each one in its own box. The flags are presented to the families of the fallen, with a note that the flag was flown in Afghanistan on 9/11. Hundreds of thousands of good young Americans, and their comrades from many nations, have served to secure Afghanistan. Their service should not be forgotten.

Sending them weighed heavily on the presidents who bore the burden. After one long meeting to decide Afghan policy in 2009, Obama's first year in office, he walked out to smoke a cigarette by the White House pool, to clear his mind and unknot his shoulders. He contrasted his decisions with those taken by Lincoln and FDR—one to save the Union, the other when America and the world faced a mortal threat. "But in the here and now, the threats we faced—deadly but stateless terrorist networks; otherwise feeble rogue nations out to get weapons of mass destruction—were real but not existential." He wanted analysis, understanding, context, before commitment. In Afghanistan, "resolve without foresight was worse than useless."[4] Eight years into the war, it was already a cliché among analysts that lessons had not been learned, that it was "Year One for the eighth time."

≡ GOING TO WAR

The Americans who commanded in Afghanistan over the two decades after 9/11 were Vietnam-era recruits, although only one, General Dan McNeill, actually served in Vietnam. They were the generation who rebuilt American forces after the destruction of that most controversial of conflicts—hard, sapping work made more so because of the attrition toll the war took on U.S. sergeants, leaving a gap that piled more pressure on young officers. After a couple of years, McNeill could not take it anymore and handed in his resignation, although he was persuaded to withdraw it. Much later in his career, during a meeting where ten of the eleven serving four-star generals in the army were present in person or on a video link, the chief of staff, General Peter Schoomaker, asked how many had handed in unqualified resignations, intending to leave in the years after Vietnam. McNeill was one of eight who put up their hands. He was not surprised. He had witnessed "dramatic missteps" in building a volunteer army after the years of the draft. They had all been "in the trenches building the volunteer force, there was nothing easy about it, nothing easy." Of those who would command in Afghanistan, General Joe Dunford too attempted to resign his commission, two years after first joining the marines. In the 1970s, both the army and the marines fell short of the oath they swore as young officers. They had seen how hard it was to remake their own army—valuable lessons as they built new forces in Afghanistan.

From the moment the planes hit the Twin Towers and the Pentagon on 9/11, the men who later took command in Kabul knew that their world had utterly changed. During those strange days in September after 9/11, McNeill visited every military facility on the Eastern Seaboard, including nuclear sites, to check security. Flying into Washington, the pilot called him up to the cockpit to look at the radar. Theirs was the only plane in the air.

General John R. Allen had the distinction of being the first marine to be commandant of the U.S. Naval Academy at Annapolis in its 150-year history. It is only thirty miles from the Pentagon, and when 9/11 happened, he immediately responded, sending everything from medical support to chaplains to assist in the recovery. The next thing he did was to find the names and photographs of the thirteen USNA graduates who died that day, in the planes or at their desks in the Pentagon, and put them on a prominent board near the mess hall so that the midshipmen now going through the academy would know that the U.S. was now at war. Allen remembered walking past the lines of boards of those who died in Vietnam when he was a midshipman[5] in the early 1970s, and he wanted the new reality to be driven home quickly to a new generation. Unlike his own generation, most of the midshipmen in 2001 did not come from families with a military past.

Allen's father served in the navy through World War II and Korea— eleven years at sea. A picture of USS *Kearny,* torpedoed while he was aboard in 1941, hangs on Allen's office wall. His mother was a nurse in a navy shipyard helping out the war effort. Allen enlisted four months before his seventeenth birthday at the height of the Vietnam War in 1970, inspired by his father's sense that "if you want to make a difference in your country you should pursue a life of service." When he was a midshipman, learning to be an officer at Annapolis, many of his instructors had served in Vietnam, some still recovering from wounds.

While the 2001 generation did not have that background, Allen knew they "wanted to do something bigger than themselves but they didn't know what that meant." The memorial boards were one way of bridging the gap. He watched as the USS *Normandy,* an Aegis-class cruiser, moved into the Chesapeake Bay to extend its missile envelope over Washington. "And we thought, my God, what a different world we're in now. Here's a guided missile destroyer built from the keel up to fight the big, deep blue battle against the Soviets, now providing a missile defense of the capital." But the forces they commanded were not ready for the new environment. They did not need guided missiles but tactics to fight in dusty villages in faraway countries, where poverty and state failure nurtured a deep hatred for the West.

Vietnam cast a long shadow over the military, with its enduring lesson that the U.S. should not engage in counterinsurgency warfare, which meant they did not train for it. Instead, America would only go to war employing massive firepower, for clear goals, with an exit in sight, and then only if backed by clear public consent. These principles were later gathered up as the Powell Doctrine, whose author, Colin Powell, secretary of state at the time of 9/11, knew more than anyone what a bad war looked like. As a major, he had been G-3, the key operational planning role, of the 23rd Americal Infantry Division in Vietnam at the time of the My Lai massacre.[6]

Even without the specter of Vietnam, America had deep-rooted legends that governed the way it behaved abroad. The belief that the U.S. did not do nation-building was deeply embedded in its military and political psyche. Americans came always as liberators, not occupiers, and not to stay. The Bush administration was strongly in this tradition, determined not to follow Clinton's example of engaging in small, complex conflicts that led to the Black Hawk Down humiliation in Somalia. The rhetoric of American exceptionalism defined the U.S. role in overseas military operations not as an imperial invader but a force for good, spreading enlightenment and democracy, and this was upheld as a virtue against the colonial history of the Europeans. Afghanistan and Iraq tested this legend to destruction.

There were other national myths too that informed the American way of war. Officers taught history at West Point and Annapolis, living in a nation with a right to bear arms and memory of the minutemen are far more likely than their European counterparts to encourage local militias in countries like Iraq and Afghanistan. European officers were uncomfortable with the idea and preferred to rely instead on Weber's construct, that to have legitimacy, the state must have a monopoly on the use of force. But Europeans too have their own myths that defined the way they operated. Areas of Afghanistan under Italian control felt more stable than others because deals and accommodations, including payments, would be made with local power brokers.

German troops, schooled since 1945 not to make war, were wary of using force and limited by caveats that restricted their action. The consequence was that when they did need to act—to stop a fuel tanker seized by the Taliban—they could not go out on the ground to investigate since they were restricted from traveling at night. Instead, they called in an air strike, killing dozens of Afghan villagers who had gathered to siphon off the fuel as the tanker was stuck in a riverbed.

British forces were the second largest in the coalition in Afghanistan for most of the war, and while they claimed to be as deployable as Americans, in practice it was more complicated. There were effective caveats on their movement too. General David Petraeus found himself unable to deliver on what he thought a relatively simple request by the U.S. Marine two-star who commanded in Helmand in 2010 to move British troops into two villages. He thought it a tactical decision that did not even need a headquarters sign-off, but it ended up the subject of a late-night conversation with Prime Minister David Cameron, visiting Kabul at the time. British troops went into Iraq and Afghanistan with a confident swagger, believing that centuries of imperial experience made them uniquely well suited to do the complex work required. They were sure of their preeminence in counterinsurgency, buoyed by folk memories of success in Malaya, Dhofar, and Northern Ireland as well as more recent operations in Bosnia and Kosovo. In fact, the U.S. Army was a far more impressive organization in learning lessons and adapting to the new wars.

But they learned from a standing start. Victory was made more difficult by a lack of clarity of how to do military intervention, which led to improvisation throughout. For two decades after Vietnam, U.S. forces had reverted to training for massive armored warfare divisions to take on Russia. McChrystal's father, Colonel Herbert J. McChrystal Jr., served in Vietnam, and McChrystal watched the lessons learned in that conflict being thrown out as the army was remade "culturally, morally, equipment-wise" in the 1970s to face Russia again—constantly exercising with heavy armor configured for symmetrical warfare. Nonconventional conflicts were dismissively known in the jargon as Military Operations Other Than War—the acronym was pronounced *moot-wah*.

"Real men don't do moot-wah," said General John Shalikashvili, chairman of the Joint Chiefs of Staff from 1993 to 1997.[7]

The bloodbath in Iraq that began in 2003, and the collapse of Libya into chaos in 2011—both wrought by U.S.-led attacks—laid bare the myth that the U.S. arriving as a "liberator" would be enough. Could it have been different in Afghanistan? It was always going to be hard. Karl Eikenberry, who uniquely served in Afghanistan in senior roles on the military and civilian side, twice in uniform and then as ambassador, clearly defined the twin challenges. Firstly, Pakistan's support for the Taliban; and secondly, the mercurial President Karzai. "It was not at all clear what sport Karzai was playing, or indeed whether he was even in the same stadium as the Americans."[8] These were precisely the same problems that had bedeviled Vietnam—support for the insurgents across a porous border and an unreliable partner in government.

In Afghanistan, by the time there was a counterinsurgency strategy in place, the U.S. and its allies faced a more intractable problem than when the Taliban fell in 2001. The mistakes were made at the start, when commanders found themselves making it up as they went along, with little understanding by the politicians who had sent them there.

☰ ILLUSION OF VICTORY

The size of the invasion force was too small to stabilize the country. The Bush administration had no doubt about their capacity to take Afghanistan with a small force, but misunderstood what they had done. In April 2002, National Security Adviser Condoleezza Rice declared the Taliban "eliminated," and in July, George W. Bush was already moving on to Iraq, job done: "In Afghanistan we defeated the Taliban regime, but that was just the first step."

Victory was an illusion. Airpower did most of the work in defeating the Taliban, with only a small number of special operations forces in support on the ground, but with no follow-up. General David Petraeus saw this as the founding mistake of the war. "We had not fully exploited the considerable opportunities available in the early years after the invasion in late 2001, before the Taliban and other insurgent and extremist elements regrouped, and returned to Afghanistan, while maintaining sanctuaries in Pakistan. And after they began to return, we always seemed to be shooting behind the target." After the initial operation, the main aim of the war remained the pursuit of the remnants of al-Qaeda, rather than securing Afghanistan. Just as in Iraq two years later, when the country imploded as the U.S. did not replace Saddam Hussein's security apparatus with anything in the early months, so in Afghanistan there was a naive belief that somehow, with the Taliban out of the way, order would emerge.

The policy was a fundamental mistake and prolonged the war by many years. There could have been a different outcome with a larger international force at the start, with zero tolerance of corruption, configured to hold the line and prevent the return of the warlords, and not resistant to nation-building. But neither America nor the allies who rallied round its flag after 9/11 had the capacity, will, knowledge, or forces to fill the gap long enough to stabilize a country.

The kind of force needed would ideally have included troops or civil order police trained in urban stabilization; coast guards to manage the frontier, the main source of legitimate revenue through customs dues, and a potential source of instability through incursion; more ISR assets (intelligence, surveillance, and reconnaissance—the "eye in the sky"); water engineers to fix the shattered irrigation systems that brought snowmelt down from the Hindu Kush; electrical engineers to fix the power grid; liaison units that could join up civilian and military efforts across government and with other international governments; police mentors to ensure the Afghan police did not prey on the people; lawyers to stand up the justice system; large cargo planes, to move these resources around; engineers to quickly restore bridges and do basic road repairs; and so on and so on.

This force, perhaps twenty-five thousand strong, would need protection and the capacity to project a threat, so some paratroopers would be needed, and all of these specialist forces would have the capacity for offensive and defensive operations. Ideally, the core would be units from several nations, with a headquarters equipped and trained to manage international forces engaged in stabilization.

Instead of delivering security themselves, the small initial international force at the start armed and funded warlords opposed to the Taliban. It is not hindsight to criticize this rehabilitation of a warlord elite. A number of foreign correspondents and analysts who had spent time in Afghanistan before 9/11 were surprised at the support for the old warlords, knowing that they were the very people whose corruption and banditry during the civil war of the early 1990s provoked the rise of the Taliban.

The term *warlord* refers to those who rose up in the 1980s, financed mainly by U.S. and Saudi cash, to defeat the Soviet invasion, and then fought among themselves over the spoils of war. Their return to center stage was not inevitable. They were in awe of U.S. power, and were surprised themselves. They expected to face war crimes trials; instead, they were paid to run private militias. The Afghan president Hamid Karzai and Zalmay Khalilzad, the influential U.S. ambassador in the early years (and later peace envoy), were known as the "two Jesuses" for bringing the warlords back to life.[9]

The troops who came into Afghanistan did not immediately identify the type of war that was being fought or the nature of the country. Not only were there not enough troops, but they were not trained for the task. They lacked language skills, understanding of the country, and the ability to operate to make the population the center of gravity of the campaign—the key to successful stabilization.

And when more troops did arrive, they were not necessarily equipped for the task. Managing an unwieldy coalition was another factor in why Afghanistan was so hard to stabilize. Those national caveats restricted the capacity of commanders to employ force in the flexible way they would have wanted. Asked how many nations had troops on the ground that he could deploy anywhere in the country, General David McKiernan put up the fingers of one hand. Many were willing to commit troops to the headquarters and no further, and the numbers in the offices at ISAF swelled out of control, up to 1,200 troops on different rotations, so teams faced a constant churn of different people.[10] General Dan McNeill exploded in a videoconference with Defense Secretary Robert Gates to Washington, "Please no more flags, sir," referring to the dozens of flags across an Afghan map on the screen showing international units. "Unless it's a critical capability like helicopter support, we don't need every country on the map sending a dozen soldiers on four-month rotations so they can tell you that they have contributed to the war . . . If I can be frank, Mr. Secretary, it's becoming more of a burden than it's worth to us out here."[11]

One part of the campaign where ISAF was soundly defeated by the Taliban was in information warfare—a significant failure given the preeminence of strategic communications in modern military thinking.[12] The U.S.-led mission did not communicate itself well to troop-contributing nations, let alone outside, while after 2001, the Taliban were transformed, with messages in three languages across social media, in contrast to their early days when they boycotted all electronic communication. Videos celebrating suicide bombings were slickly produced and widely distributed. The Taliban lied fast and often, while NATO was slow to catch up with the truth.

And beyond the blast walls of military bases, the international intervention itself was not well understood by the donors who poured billions of dollars into the country. There was too much of the wrong sort of aid. This was a reverse problem to the security issue, where there were too few of the wrong sort of troops. This failure was fundamental. Too much aid went outside the state—to international contractors and NGOs. A senior World Bank official talked of an "aid juggernaut"[13] descending on the country, leaving nothing behind. It was as if all that was constructed was elaborate scaffolding. And when the music stopped in 2014 and aid programs wound down at the same time as the troop presence—as they took away the scaffolding they did not leave a building behind.

The large international NGO community built a parallel state. They paid higher salaries to locals than the actual state could, so well-qualified Afghans who returned from abroad found they could earn more as a driver or security guard for an international body than in a senior job in the Afghan civil service. This aid failure made security harder to deliver.

There were deep cultural gulfs across the international presence in Kabul, whose people were drawn from different tribes. Military contractors would stride around the base bearing sidearms, confident in their red-state worldview, keen on making quick impacts on the ground, harnessing development with security, with easy money to spend from the Commander's Emergency Response Program (CERP★) funds. In the embassy next door, USAID officials worried about the stray cats, tended to vote Democrat, and be unarmed. They knew that stabilizing Afghanistan would take longer than the timescale of the quick-impact projects demanded by soldiers.

The cultural gulf extended into how they saw the challenge, as if

---

★ Pronounced *sirp*.

using different calendars. Development officials like to say that while they plan for three years, the military think in terms of thirty days, while for diplomats it's thirty years. "To bring us all down to thirty days is not fair to the country," said one senior worker at USAID in Kabul. "Yes, I want to see immediate results, but when they don't fit into each other, we end up with a bunch of ad hoc half-a-megawatt diesel generators all over the country with no fuel." To her, the large sums available to U.S. commanders through CERP, not coordinated with other development interventions, were "ridiculous overnight spending."

Aid delivered with short-term horizons fueled corruption, and from the beginning, there was a failure to establish the rule of law and institutions accountable to the people that might have checked it. There was a belief that freedom from the Taliban would somehow deliver virtue without any of the checks and balances built into Western systems. Elections alone were not enough without building the institutions of a functioning democracy—courts, legislatures, a civil service—financed by taxation. The system remained dependent on international subsidies. Without institutional architecture giving accountability to the people, elections entrenched the elites in power, a powerful driving force of corruption and instability at the heart of the state. The view that this was a binary war—the government against the "Taliban"—was misplaced. Misplaced aid instead facilitated the rise of a corrupt elite, formed not just from the old warlords but a new generation of business leaders living outside the law, many wrapped into the country's biggest earner, the opium poppy.

Not all aid was wasted. There was a fundamental restructuring of the Afghan government, building of schools and hospitals, and capacity building that delivered new generations of professional people and government officials. But getting the right programs started late. One leading British official said, "We hit on the right strategy in Afghanistan as our patience began to run out."[14]

Afghanistan is in a tough neighborhood that includes China, Iran, and Pakistan—with Russian influence bearing down across Central Asia to the north, just as it did during the days of the nineteenth-century Great Game, when Afghanistan was crushed between Russia and British India. Russia has seen the last two decades as a chance to take revenge for American support of the mujahideen in Afghanistan in the 1980s. And as has been seen in Ukraine, Vladimir Putin is not squeamish about having a bleeding wound close to his border. He would fund the Taliban if that's what it took to give America trouble. America's failure to normalize relations with Iran has had consequences for its conduct of campaigns in both of Iran's neighbors, Iraq and Afghanistan. And throughout the long war, Pakistan wanted a compliant Taliban on the other side of the porous northwest frontier military, so continues to support them. "They were not our allies," McNeill said of Pakistan simply. "They were actively working against us."

A key political failure contributing to lost victory in the long war was unwillingness to talk to the Taliban. At the beginning they were willing to surrender. But Secretary of Defense Donald Rumsfeld did not want that. And it would take a long time before the realization emerged that victory in this complex insurgency would not be as simple as winning battles. After a failed attempt at a peace process for a couple of years from 2010, it was not until 2019 that President Trump's emissary Zalmay Khalilzad opened direct talks with the Taliban in Doha, Qatar. And by then, they were entrenched across large swathes of the Afghan countryside.

☰ AFGHANISTAN BEYOND THE BLAST WALLS

North of the international military headquarters lie 1970s concrete houses, with large gardens, in the symmetrically gridded streets of Wazir Akbar Khan, where many of the streets are now closed to normal traffic by checkpoints mounted to protect the new elites who live there. And to the northwest, on the steep slopes of TV mountain, named for the aerials on its summit, thousands of new houses have been built for the millions of people who have poured into Kabul since 2001. They face constant scrutiny from the large white blimp that sits over the city most days, the eye in the sky that watches through cameras that can see everything, vacuuming electronic material from phones and tablets. But the international community that can see and hear so much knows so little.

There is a new world out there not represented by the old warlord elites or the Taliban but by a population where at least 70 percent are under twenty-five. In an unsettling reminder of the ever-present threat of violence, in 2015, a young woman called Farkhunda was beaten to death, and her body set on fire after an argument with a seller of charms in a mosque. Tragically, it was Farkhunda who was arguing a more orthodox Islamic view, complaining that the man was selling false hopes with his charms. But he was a man, and when he appealed to men outside the mosque, claiming she had violated the Quran, a wave swept in and destroyed the life of this ambitious, principled woman. In the days of outrage and grief that followed, it was a new young civil society who led the protests and filled Afghan social media with the rare openly anti-Islamic statements. The following Friday, when traditional Islamic leaders, including the ayatollah of Kabul, sought to regain the initiative by holding an open-air meeting, they had only a half-hour slot in bookings, which included street theater groups and other young nontraditional protests. It is a new Afghanistan when mullahs are lining up with street actors to take their turn.

Farther north in Kabul, beyond the airport, in apartment blocks that have sprung up since 9/11, a new generation live more or less as young professional people do in the West, not committed to arranged marriages but looking to a different world and sharing a glass of wine behind locked gates. They meet not in the traditional kebab shops, where women are never seen without their husbands, but in new cafés and bowling alleys, and their music and lifestyle is transforming urban life. An inspiring art organization, Artlords, has pioneered a simple stencil technique to cover the monotonous lines of blast walls with color. One of their most arresting projects was to paint a single massive eye on the wall, with a slogan saying that corruption would be found out. The failed aid, constant presence of foreign troops, threat of the Taliban, and old warlord elites hold no interest for this new generation.

This is not a failed nation but a nation that has been failed. Afghans yearn for a different life, proud of a national cricket team that now plays at the highest international level and a soccer team whose victory over India in the South Asian Football Federation Championship in 2013 led to a wild night of celebration. One foreign correspondent encountered a group of Tajik youths whose vehicle was in a headlong collision with Pashtun youths. Both sides were armed, and any other night, there would have been a fight. But the night of the soccer success, they were all Afghans and shook hands instead.

The day before the Afghan soccer league final in 2017, there was a suicide bomb at the national stadium. The final still went ahead—the first floodlit evening game in the history of the country, and crowds, undeterred by the threat of violence, filled the stadium to capacity. A massive national flag was carried across the pitch by soldiers—the black, red, and green tricolor rippling in the evening breeze. This is a nation proud of its flag, army, sports teams, and a new place in the world not mediated by warlords. A video of a well-known female singer set to pictures of the evening game had a massive social media following. She sang the national anthem, which is a recitation of the fourteen acknowledged tribal groups.

This disparate nation, with its many tribes, and complex customs is however
   a nation,
This land is Afghanistan—It is the pride of every Afghan
The land of peace, the land of the sword—Its sons are all brave
This is the country of every tribe—Land of Baluch, and Uzbeks
Pashtoons, and Hazaras—Turkman and Tajiks with them,
Arabs and Gojars, Pamirian, Nooristanis
Barahawi, and Qizilbash—Also Aimaq, and Pashaye
This Land will shine for ever—Like the sun in the blue sky
In the chest of Asia—It will remain as the heart forever.

The Taliban's hold on the nation, though, was profound, and it is a failure of the foreign and military policy of the U.S. and other Western powers that this remains the case. Most of the mistakes were made at the beginning, and the commanders who came later were handed a war that was hard to end because of these failures.

Lacking a doctrine of intervention, obsessed that there should be no nation-building, America was drawn into a long war by the lure of a quick victory. Why was there no course correction? Barbara Tuchman in *The March of Folly* would see this as the nature of humanity—when in a hole, it is very hard to stop digging.[15] Even the searching inquiry by the incoming Obama government that took all of 2009 did not call a pause, or plan for the longer term, but instead announced a surge of troops, more foreign advisers, more aid—it was always the same answer. And optimism bias on the part of those writing reports for consumption at home meant they tended to ignore inconvenient facts.[16] The

Washington Papers, more than six hundred interviews by the Special Inspector General for Afghanistan Reconstruction, released in 2019, showed this clearly. With hindsight, many said they had always tended to put a more optimistic line on official reports than they felt. It was never going to be easy, but it was made harder by mistakes at the start. "There is, at the end of the day, very little that is quick, easy, or inexpensive in the conduct of a comprehensive civil-military counterinsurgency campaign in a context that features the myriad challenges of Afghanistan," said General Petraeus, "though it sure would have helped had we done much more early on than we did."

I have had a ringside seat on the events in this book, as a reporter with the BBC, and later (full disclosure) as a U.S.-funded Afghan government strategic communications adviser. I always found it surprising that Americans—whether military or media—saw this as the "Middle East," putting Afghanistan in the same basket as Iraq and Iran. It was a category error. Afghanistan is the gateway between Central and South Asia, a nation struggling to find a new role in a hostile region. Lumping it together with Iraq in the war on terror was a mistake from the start. Afghanistan deserves better.

PHASE ONE
2001-2006

THE DIE IS CAST

NOT BUILDING A NATION

We are in and out of there in a hurry.

—General John M. "Jack" Keane, vice chief of the army, 2002

☰ "NO MORE BONDSTEELS"

September 11, 2001, Brigadier General Stanley A. McChrystal, chief of staff of XVIII Airborne Corps, was on a routine practice parachute drop at Pope, the airfield at Fort Bragg, North Carolina. They were hooked up and ready to jump when the loadmaster leaned over to tell the commander of XVIII Airborne, Lieutenant General Daniel K. McNeill, that a plane had hit the World Trade Center. McNeill is a compact, solid, square, physically tough, all-American soldier with a reputation for sticking to the rules. Leading from the front, he would be first man out of the plane. "All I could think of was some pilot not doing right." They went on through their countdown and were about a minute away from the jump when low clouds prevented a clear enough view of the drop zone. They remained standing and hooked up, and set off around again until visibility improved enough for a jump.

The aircraft door was already open for the second run, and McNeill had yelled, "All okay, jumpmaster!" meaning his first stick of jumpers was ready, each having tapped the shoulder of the soldier in front to signal he was hooked on, when the loadmaster leaned over again to say a second plane had hit the World Trade Center. It was clear this was no accident.

The role of XVIII Airborne was to be ready to deploy anywhere in the world at any time; they knew they would be called on. The pilot planned to abort the exercise and fly back, but McNeill said the quickest way to the office was down, and jumped out of the plane. McChrystal was close behind him. By the time they hit the ground, mobile phone calls were blocked as the United States entered a new age. "Our feet landed on a nation at war,"[1] said McChrystal. Back at Fort Bragg, Colonel John F. Campbell, the commander of 1st Brigade, 82nd Airborne—the main fighting element in the division—was just coming out of the showers after physical training. Seeing what was happening on TV, he yelled to his sergeant major, and they dressed in the office, watching the events unfold. Campbell, McNeill, and McChrystal would all command at the highest level in the long war that was to come.

McChrystal has sharp features and piercing blue eyes. He is a good listener, with an innovative relentless intellect. He cultivated a mystique for ascetic commitment to duty, pushing himself and his troops hard. Eight months after that parachute drop, he sat at the center of a web of makeshift plywood tables with military-grade laptops open around the hangar at Bagram Air Base in Afghanistan—a world he would re-create time and again, deploying abroad for all but seven months of the next seven years. The first base at Bagram was the most austere, deliberately so, for U.S. troops were not staying. That, at least, was the plan. The small headquarters staff, just three hundred at the start, were not set up for war fighting. The way McChrystal saw it, "It wasn't clear whether there was any war left."[2]

Until their arrival in 2002, Bagram was an unconventional base, its culture determined by the shaggy beards and irregular clothing of the small bands of special operators, who had landed soon after 9/11, and were still chasing al-Qaeda, "bear-hunting" they called it. McNeill changed all that. Uniforms had to be worn and officers saluted. "How many people were killed at the Pentagon?" he asked anyone who opposed the change. "We haven't stopped saluting at the Pentagon."[3] He was given one simple order for Afghanistan: "No more Bondsteels," a reference to the enormous permanent base in Kosovo, housing seven thousand U.S. troops, built in 1999 after Kosovo's independence struggle with Serbia.

Troops were housed in tents, sleeping bags covered by the fine talcum-powder dust that blew into everything across the shattered landscape—rudimentary accommodation for a temporary mission. Before first light every day, lines of fifty to a hundred men and women formed for the few showers. The only intact building was the yellow-painted square stump of the control tower, and even that was damaged in the last stand of the

Taliban. The airstrip was crudely patched with matted metal strips, left by Soviet forces after their invasion in 1979 at the start of Afghanistan's long wars. They were not the first foreign forces in the area. Alexander the Great's winter quarters on his way to conquer India were nearby at Charikar, in the harsh splendor of the Shomali Plain, between Kabul and the forbidding barrier of the Hindu Kush mountain range to the north, flanked by endless snow-covered peaks to the frontier with Pakistan to the east.

The Taliban held the airfield during their five years of rule. Just north of it, broken shipping containers marked the front line between the 90 percent of the country under the Taliban, and the small area in the northeast that held out against them. War made this a dangerous landscape. A couple of years before the American arrival, while walking with Taliban fighters to that front line, I heard a small explosion, like a firework, and a farmer emerged from the bushes, his leg shredded by an antipersonnel mine near the path we had just walked down.

Afghanistan was to be a short war. "We are in and out of there in a hurry,"[4] General Jack Keane, the army vice chief of staff, told McNeill. General Tommy Franks, commander at Central Command (CENT-COM) in Tampa, Florida, was obsessed by the Soviet experience in Afghanistan—more than 600,000 men, armored divisions bogged down for a decade, before an ignominious departure costing 15,000 Soviet dead. "There's nothing to be gained," he told Defense Secretary Donald Rumsfeld, "by blundering around those mountains and gorges with armor battalions chasing a lightly armed enemy."[5] Rumsfeld set the initial ceiling at 5,200 U.S. troops.[6] He was pioneering a new way of doing war: massive use of precision airpower with special operators as the only boots on the ground. In and out quickly, and definitely no nation-building.

This meant plans were improvised in a way McChrystal felt "dangerously ad hoc."[7] The mission needed many more troops to succeed.[8] Because of the troop cap, they had to leave behind some logistics staff in Uzbekistan, so they were stretched on the ground.[9] But already by the time they arrived in 2002, the Afghan war was seen as "mission accomplished"—a sideshow while the Bush administration concentrated on Iraq. Only half of XVIII Airborne's headquarters staff came to the Afghan theater, the others staying behind at their home base, Fort Bragg, to prepare for the impending war against Saddam Hussein. Franks was asked to prepare an Iraq war plan as early as November 2001, before the Taliban stronghold of Kandahar in the south had fallen.[10]

McNeill saw that Iraq was consuming all available oxygen in Washington in his only meeting with President Bush during this first command in Afghanistan. He had little notice, first briefing the defense secretary and senior generals. "That's fine," Rumsfeld said. "Keep it to forty minutes when you do it for the president tomorrow." All Bush wanted to know when they met was whether McNeill could keep a lid on Afghanistan so he could concentrate on Iraq. When Rumsfeld's deputy, Paul Wolfowitz, visited Bagram and found officers talking about building for the longer term in Afghanistan, he told them, "You don't get it. Iraq is what we're after." Afghanistan was to be "an economy of force operation."[11] Across the administration, and at CENTCOM, where it was treated as part of the same war, Iraq already had the best people working on it, a year before the Iraq war started.[12]

This meant that instead of a force large enough to provide stability as well as firepower, Afghanistan had a half-strength headquarters with an unclear mandate. Ironically, a policy designed to be short term meant the war was prolonged by many years. If America were willing to stay in such locations for five years, knowing it might be up to ten, that would be far better than believing "We are in and out in a hurry" and then staying twenty years.

Most of all in those early days, the forces who arrived in Afghanistan lacked knowledge. McChrystal recognized that for Western diplomats and military forces, "Afghanistan was a maze of mirrors, and we too easily framed actions through our own lenses."[13] The belief that if the Taliban were removed, somehow order would be restored without further stabilization forces, was the fatal flaw in Rumsfeld's light-footprint plan—and the main reason this became America's longest war. The plan required a local partner, and those backed with cash and weapons by the small teams of CIA officers and special operators who dropped into the country after 9/11 were the very forces whose criminal excesses in the early 1990s had provoked the rise of the Taliban in the first place.

The American intervention did not promote an anti-Taliban opposition with widespread support. Rather, it took a side in a vicious civil war. The Taliban had brought a reign of terror on Afghanistan, imposed a social order that restricted women, enforced ignorance, and harbored international terrorists. They were small-minded and brutish. But they were not an alien force from outer space. They were formed in reaction to the chaos and banditry of mujahideen fighters, who fought each other after defeating Soviet invaders in the 1980s, backed by America and Saudi Arabia.

Before the Taliban, mujahideen warlords destroyed much of Kabul in vicious street-fighting, including random attacks with rockets. And it was not the Taliban who first insisted on burkas being worn by women but these mujahideen.[14] They became America's allies in the first conflict after 9/11.

☰ THE WAR IN THE NORTH: OCTOBER–DECEMBER 2001

In the makeshift office in a mud-walled house for Operation Jawbreaker, the first CIA move into northeast Afghanistan after 9/11, were four large cardboard boxes. "They became a bench to sit on or a place to rest a coffee cup or water bottle," wrote the team leader, Gary Schroen. "They also proved to be an ideal spot to stretch out for a nap or relax and read."[15] Handwritten on the duct tape sealing each box was a figure of around $2 million. Bills totaling a further $2 million were kept in a nondescript black suitcase. This was the second delivery of cash a month after the arrival of the Jawbreaker team who landed in Afghanistan just two weeks after 9/11. They had already burned through $3 million, handed out to potential allies in the fight against the Taliban. On the night of October 7, they sat on the roof watching "a bright yellow flash in the clouds in the direction of Kabul." Schroen pulled out cigars and handed them round. The bombing had begun.[16]

There was no one better than Schroen to reestablish links with the mujahideen leadership. He had been the last station chief in Kabul before the embassy closed in 1989, and had seen Ahmed Shah Massoud, the main leader of the anti-Taliban opposition, as recently as March 2001. Massoud said he was distancing himself from some of the worse elements of the old mujahideen to build a broader-based political alliance. His death, at the hands of two Arabs with a bomb in a TV camera two days before 9/11, deprived the anti-Taliban opposition of one of its most effective commanders. It was Massoud's hold of the narrow sliver of land in the northeast, from Bagram airfield to the northern Tajik border, that gave the ground war against the Taliban a launchpad. The Jawbreaker team set up base there.

Instead of Massoud, America was faced with his replacement, a more sinister manipulator of raw power, Muhammad Qasim Fahim, a stocky bull of a man with a neck as wide as his head. Under the rolled-wool hat, the *pakhool,* he always wore, Fahim had an unbroken line of thick eyebrows across his forehead, and a squat broken nose. He was known as *Marshal Fahim,* Afghanistan's only field marshal, and was a big backer of *buzkashi,* the wild Afghan game where horsemen fight for possession of the carcass of a calf. Schroen gave him $1 million at the beginning, as well as large sums to other commanders.

Fahim led an unruly coalition of factions known as the Northern Alliance. There was a dispute within the CIA over how much backing to give them. On the ground, Schroen was impatient for progress and wanted relentless bombing of Taliban positions to assist Northern Alliance operations. But the station chief in Islamabad, Robert Grenier, argued that if Fahim's Tajik troops, with Uzbeks and other allied tribes, seized Kabul, it would unite fighters from the Pashtun south and east against them, making it harder to tackle the Taliban. He thought the Taliban could be fractured, allowing negotiation with "moderates."

Grenier had another concern. Strengthening the Northern Alliance would upset Pakistan. Until 9/11, Pakistan gave little help to the U.S., even after al-Qaeda threats became real with the 1998 bombing of U.S. embassies in Africa. Only two days before the attacks of 9/11, General Mahmud Ahmad, the head of Pakistan's intelligence agency, the ISI, was in Washington telling the Americans they had misunderstood the Taliban, who were Afghan nationalists and no danger to women's rights. After lunch with the ISI chief, CIA director George Tenet wrote, "The guy was immovable when it came to the Taliban and al-Qaeda. And bloodless, too."[17]

The attacks on America changed all that. The military dictator Pervez Musharraf agreed to all of America's demands, and the ISI did make a few arrests of prominent Taliban, although not touching their massive support structure across Pakistan. The U.S. needed Pakistan as an ally for overflights, landing rights, and access to bases, although it was unreliable, duplicitous, and occasionally dangerous as a partner. Grenier recommended the U.S. should work with Pakistan to build a broad-based "government-in-exile," leave the Taliban front line north of Kabul untouched, "and go slowly with our bombing over the next several weeks,"[18] until they had a government ready to take over.

Grenier was swimming against the tide. Hank Crumpton, who headed the CIA Counterterrorism Center, thought he had a bad case of "clientitis," and Rumsfeld was contemptuous. A pause in the bombing reminded him of Vietnam.[19] But Grenier succeeded in the early days in limiting U.S. bombing to air defenses and Taliban "political" targets, mainly the homes of senior leaders. This felt like a halfhearted way to go to war and conceded too much to Pakistan. Momentum and constant disruption are essential features of successful military campaigns. The cautious approach risked losing the advantage of early wins and disheartening defectors from the Taliban.

The Jawbreaker team faced daily questions by Fahim over when the bombing of the Taliban front line north of Kabul would begin. His forces were skeptical, wondering if this airpower was really as good as they said. If there was no willingness to employ conventional U.S. troops, Fahim was the only show in town. He had been given a lot of money, winning him prestige and bolstering his position; now was not the time to have reservations. Schroen's tactical air operators had clearly mapped the GPS coordinates of the Taliban front lines. Three weeks after the bombing began, things were about to change.

On a cold night at the end of October, Fahim arrived in a decades-old Mercedes to a remote corner of the Dushanbe airport in neighboring Tajikistan and climbed the side steps into the belly of a C-17. Waiting for him was General Franks himself, who wanted to meet America's new ally. Fahim circled the main northern towns—Mazar-e-Sharif, Kunduz, and Taloqan—with a gold mechanical pencil, then drew arrows south toward the Bagram front line, to lay out his priorities. They bartered over money, with Franks storming outside at one point, smoking a cigarette in the dark under the plane, after Fahim demanded $7 million a month. They settled on $5 million to take the north. Franks was left wondering, "I didn't know whether we had traded a horse or bought a carpet."[20]

The other leaders in the north were also familiar players from the jihadi years, who had fought against each other in the early 1990s in shifting alliances after the fall of the Soviet-backed government. They included the Tajiks Atta Muhammad Nur and Ismail Khan, the Uzbek Abdul Rashid Dostum, and Pashtun Abdul Rasul Sayyaf. Along with the Jawbreaker team, small groups of Green Berets, A-Teams, attached themselves to each of the militia leaders to coordinate the battle.

Dostum and Nur quickly broke Taliban front lines at Mazar-e-Sharif, the key northern town and gateway to Central Asia, backed by A-Team tactical air operators spotting targets on the ground. Dostum's troops were mounted on horseback, and the battle had the unique pairing of a cavalry charge backed by close air support—the oldest and newest forms of warfare on one battlefield. Precision bombing meant there was not much fighting on the ground. Franks was exuberant. "These Green Berets used maneuver and air power," he wrote, "to destroy an army the Soviets had failed to dislodge with more than a half million men."[21]

This wholly misunderstood the context. Most of the commanders now backed by the Green Berets *were* "the army the Soviets had failed to dislodge" in the 1980s, apart from Dostum, who had been the main commander of the north *for* the Soviet-backed Afghan forces. As for the Taliban—they did not exist when the Soviets were in Afghanistan.

A more important lesson from the Soviet years that should have damp-ened early exuberance was that winning tactical engagements was never a problem in Afghanistan, especially with airpower. Holding ground was far harder, as America and its allies were to discover after the stunning early victories. With the Taliban defeated, submerged rivalries came to the surface. Nur reached the center of Mazar first, staking his claim as the main commander of the north, diminishing Dostum's capacity and limiting him to an area outside the city. Dostum retreated to his tradi-tional fortress at Shebargan in the northwest. Their rivalry weakened the chance of stabilizing the country.

Despite the support for the Northern Alliance forces in the battle for the north, there were reservations about allowing them to enter Kabul. Fahim knew this when he traded with Franks in the C-17 meeting in Dushanbe. Looking him in the eye, he said, "We will not enter Kabul until you give permission."[22] It was enough to change the calculation, and despite Grenier's reservations, a relentless bombardment of Taliban front lines at the beginning of November left the capital defenseless.

≡ THE WAR IN THE SOUTH: OCTOBER–DECEMBER 2001

The Islamabad CIA chief, Grenier, believed the new leadership of Afghanistan would emerge from the millions of Afghan refugees living and meeting in the camps and markets of frontier towns. He resurrected and financed a number of former Pashtun warlords in the east and south, who were "pleased to reestablish contact with the CIA after a lapse of some ten years."[23] The policy of standing up former warlords may have been pragmatic, but with more American boots on the ground, such unpalatable choices would not have needed to have been made. Grenier justified supporting one notorious drug dealer in the southwest by saying, "We could not afford to be too selective."[24] These areas would be the hardest to stabilize in the long war that was to come.

The risks were real. A highly popular Pashtun tribal leader, Abdul Haq, tried to rally opposition forces in his home region in the east of Afghanistan. He had cut a deal with a prominent faction of the Taliban who wanted the return of the Afghan king. But he was opposed by the ISI, whose influence meant he had no American backing. He was seized by the Taliban and shot.

Two men eyed their chances in southern Afghanistan. Even before Haq was killed, the braver of the two, Hamid Karzai, wearing nondescript local clothing, made a hazardous journey on the back of a motorbike, crossing Taliban-controlled territory into the mountains in Uruzgan, a province to the west of the main southern city, Kandahar.[25] He rallied some support, but the going was tough. At one point, he and his small band of followers were sleeping in goat sheds, and walking, as he had no transport. He had one U.S. weapons drop. But as the Taliban closed in, the CIA swooped down in a helicopter to take him back to safety in Pakistan. He soon returned to Afghanistan, this time with support from the CIA and an A-Team of Green Berets commanded by Captain Jason Amerine, who brought in air strikes against several large, determined Taliban attacks as the convoy of Karzai supporters grew until it was a traveling circus of four-wheel drives, tractor trailers, "jingle trucks" trailing lines of colored foil, with some followers riding alongside on donkeys.[26]

Karzai was little known then, but would soon become internationally recognizable with an astrakhan hat covering his bald head, neat silver beard, and green-striped tribal cloak across his shoulders, signifying he was a revered elder—garb he wore by chance on arrival in Kabul and never altered. He is shrewd, courteous, with a quick wit, beautiful command of English, and a love of poetry from his education in India. He has a deep knowledge and connection with tribal politics and family links—the invisible thread binding Afghanistan. He was a Popalzai, the ruling clan of Afghanistan in the past, and his father had been a senator.

He was well known to foreign diplomats in Pakistan, and was a frequent visitor to the U.S. embassy before 9/11.

The other man waiting on the frontier with pretentions to power was Gul Agha Sherzai, the former governor of Kandahar, who persuaded the CIA and many journalists that he was the true voice of anti-Taliban opposition in the south. With American funding, he staked his claim through the then new soft power weapon of the sat phone to broadcast to the world, and crucially through the BBC Pashto service, then the main news outlet in Afghanistan. Anyone whose understanding of Afghanistan did not begin on September 11, 2001, would know that he was one of the warlords whose excesses were most responsible for provoking the rise of the Taliban in the first place.

Sherzai, a giant, brutish Jabba the Hutt look-alike who calls himself *Bulldozer,* could not be more different in manner and background to the courtly Karzai. His father bred and trained fighting dogs—a popular pastime in rural Afghanistan. I once went to see him with a German journalist, and he enthusiastically told her what an admirer he was of Adolf Hitler. The Taliban's first major victory when they emerged from the dust of the countryside in 1994 was to force Sherzai out from his corrupt brutal hold on Kandahar, and they won the backing of local businesses and many tribal leaders for this action alone.

Grenier had already been funding Sherzai for a year before 9/11,[27] but his enthusiasm was not shared by the CIA's counterterrorist center. Seeing an opportunity to build up his credibility when Franks came to Islamabad to meet tribal leaders, Grenier wanted Sherzai and another potential leader dressed for the part. "Turbans. Make damned sure they're wearing turbans," he said.[28] He should have worried more about Sherzai's acceptability to southern Pashtuns and ability to govern than what he wore.

In the middle of November, two weeks after meeting Franks, armed and financed by the CIA, Sherzai was heading toward Kandahar from the east, while Karzai came in from the north. Both were supported by U.S. Green Berets. American bombers made short work of what little resistance Sherzai met on the way before he reached the airport on the road to the east of Kandahar, now in the hands of the largest conventional U.S. force on the ground in Afghanistan, Marine Task Force 58, commanded by Brigadier General Jim Mattis (later commander of CENTCOM and secretary of defense).

As American airpower changed the balance in the south, hundreds of Taliban fighters defected, joining Karzai or Sherzai. And there was talk of a more formal surrender of Kandahar itself. Another potential leader of the south, Mullah Naqib, at some risk to his life, was negotiating with the senior Taliban leadership, trying to persuade them to order a surrender in return for immunity from prosecution and a promise to withdraw from politics. Naqib was a hero of the war against the Soviet Union, with deeper connections as a tribal leader than Sherzai, and the two had contested the control of Kandahar before, in the early 1990s before the emergence of the Taliban. Naqib was an old-fashioned Afghan power broker who had consented to the Taliban while they were in power and was trusted by Karzai as an intermediary. But in 2001, the power brokers were the U.S., who had no interest in negotiating terms with the Taliban.

☰ ONE DAY IN DECEMBER

December 5, 2001, was the day that decided the future course of Afghanistan. Karzai was named the interim leader of post-Taliban Afghanistan by a swiftly convened international conference in Bonn, Germany. It brought together the Northern Alliance and a number of groups of Afghan exiles, including one representing the former king Muhammad Zahir Shah.[29] The leaders of the U.S. delegation, Jim Dobbins and Zalmay Khalilzad, were keen to deliver Karzai as leader, but it took tough talking, mostly in exhausting sessions that went on through the night, as the Afghan delegates were fasting during the daytime for Ramadan. The Northern Alliance delegation staked their claim as the people actually doing the most fighting and only agreed to support Karzai in return for their hold on three key ministries—Defence, Interior, and Foreign Affairs. After overnight talks, delegates were called in at dawn on December 5, and Karzai's voice on a poor sat phone connection from southern Afghanistan came through a loudspeaker in the conference hall to thank them for agreeing to make him interim leader.

Karzai's appointment was almost cut short less than an hour later. A targeting error caused by a system reset on a battery change brought a two-thousand-pound American JDAM bomb, designed to penetrate caves, onto his position.[30] Three of Amerine's special operators were killed and twenty injured. Many of Karzai's Afghan supporters died. Amerine was injured, and his swift departure from the battlefield weakened

Karzai's cause with the Americans on the ground, as the replacement team had not established the same bond with him. His face cut by flying glass, it was little wonder that Karzai became skeptical of the claims of accuracy of American airpower. This would be the biggest source of friction during his years as president.

Later that same morning, Karzai met a Taliban delegation brought by Mullah Naqib to discuss the surrender of Kandahar. After several hours of talks, a deal was done—and district by district across the province of Kandahar, Taliban fighters came over to Naqib, named by Karzai as the new governor. Recognizing that Karzai's forces were ill provisioned, the Taliban delegation sent 2,500 naan—the flatbread that is the staple diet of Afghanistan. The Taliban group included Tayyib Agha, who ten years later would be the Taliban negotiator in their first face-to-face talks with the U.S. But in 2001, the U.S. was not in the mood to negotiate. When rumors of a potential deal reached Washington, Rumsfeld said his cooperation with the anti-Taliban opposition "would clearly take a turn south" if Taliban leaders were let off without facing justice.[31] The Taliban heard him, and so did the American backers of Sherzai.

Karzai called Sherzai and ordered him to stay outside the city of Kandahar, appointing him director of the airport. Sherzai insulted him, shouting down the phone, "I don't take orders from Hamid Karzai. I don't know Hamid Karzai . . . Kandahar is mine," telling the media that Karzai's negotiator Naqib was a Taliban sympathizer. Amid isolated fighting between his and Naqib's troops across the city, he seized the governor's palace. Karzai had to be restrained by the new commander of his Special Forces support team, Lieutenant Colonel David Fox, from sending his troops to take him on, Fox telling him, "You are on the verge of starting a civil war."[32]

Sherzai's media campaign had worked. He was framed by American reporters as the rightful inheritor, while Naqib was described as "relatively obscure."[33] One of the better reporters to arrive in Kandahar in that first wave, Sarah Chayes, wanted to report the complexity but was told by her editor at NPR just to send color on Mullah Omar's house. The story had to be binary. America had won, and their allies were good, while the Taliban and anyone who wanted to negotiate with them was bad.[34]

This misunderstood and misrepresented the nature of Afghan warfare, where local allegiances change frequently. Battles are fought not between armies in uniform but to win tribal influence and support. The

Taliban was not a sealed unit but an idea that emerged in reaction to banditry in the early 1990s, and Taliban fighters and commanders could easily change sides. "The Americans were such amateurs," said Akrem Khakrezwal, who would become the Kandahar police chief. "Anyone Sherzai or his interpreter told them was a Talib, they would take it on faith, and act on the accusation."[35]

Naqib, who had tried to make peace and was named by the internationally approved head of state as governor of Kandahar, now called his son to tell him to run away, as their house was likely to be bombed by the U.S. military.[36] This was not about combating international terrorism—the reason for the war. It was using U.S. air strikes to settle scores between rival warlords. The nature of what happened was not well understood in Washington. As late as 2017, the congressional research service wrote that when the Taliban fled in 2001, Kandahar was left "under Pashtun tribal law," a curious description of the CIA-backed imposition of a notorious warlord.[37]

In 2002, McChrystal had three British officers in his team in the hangar at Bagram, among them Colonel Nick Carter, who would later have several senior command roles in Afghanistan, before becoming head of British forces as chief of the defence staff. Carter said it was a mistake to believe Sherzai. "He made us flatten a whole load of people he wanted to get rid of. He claimed they were all Taliban and we believed him. And the upshot of that is that we drove people into the arms of the insurgency."[38] For Carter, this was one of the most important lessons of the Afghan war: "If you get involved in campaigns like these, you really do need to have some insight and understanding."

The main focus for Sherzai, where he named his enemies and demanded air support against them, was Mullah Naqib's home base in the fertile Arghandab Valley west of Kandahar, which became one of the hardest areas to secure in the years of fighting that followed, as tribes targeted by the Americans on the word of Gul Agha Sherzai sent their sons to join the insurgency. "My suspicion," said Carter, "was that some of those who purported to be Taliban would have been easier to govern with than Gul Agha."

☰ STABILIZATION LITE

Karzai did not remain in Kandahar, flying to Kabul in an American helicopter. He was greeted at the airport by Fahim, who asked, "Where are your troops?" since no self-respecting leader would arrive without them. Karzai replied disarmingly, "You are my troops." Karzai had a complicated relationship with the 1980s warlords like Fahim. He had been deputy foreign minister to the unstable mujahideen government in Kabul in the early 1990s, until he resigned after a dispute with Fahim and others.[39] When the Taliban emerged, he was close to them, and his name was put forward as an ambassador, but that never materialized. He fell out with the Taliban in 1999 after his father was shot dead by two Taliban fighters in Quetta, Pakistan. The former mujahideen leaders mistrusted him and thought he was too close to America.

Fahim had inevitably ignored the promise he made not to enter Kabul, seizing military bases across the city. Wais Barmak, who later became interior minister, was the local head of the UN and effectively handed over the city to the Northern Alliance after the Taliban fled. He saw that Fahim's troops knew exactly where to go—their occupation was clearly planned.[40] What was not noticed by the small international presence at the time was that Fahim's militias took large areas of land and property for themselves, including the large military training ground at Sherpur, which they designated prime building land in the center of town, close to one of the most desirable residential areas, and parceled into plots, which were quickly covered with giant garish houses. Their power grab severely complicated the chances of Afghan reconstruction, and in particular weakened the potential for foreign-educated Afghans to play a role in post-Taliban Afghanistan.

Jim Dobbins, the veteran diplomat President Bush appointed as his special representative for Afghanistan, came straight from Bonn with a small advance diplomatic team, who camped in the U.S. embassy. The American flag, lowered when the embassy was closed in 1989, was found locked in a vault, with a message written by marine sergeant James M. Blake to those he knew would return. "For those of you yet to enter Kabul, it could mean a lot to you."[41] It was raised again in a simple, moving ceremony.

Watching Kabul from his dusty bunker in the embassy, Dobbins saw the takeover by the militias as inevitable, as there were no international boots on the ground. This was unprecedented in his long experience. "The idea that Afghans could adequately secure their country after a twenty-three-year civil war struck me as naive and irresponsible." He

had been the senior U.S. representative in Clinton-era interventions—
Bosnia, Kosovo, Haiti, and Somalia—and had never previously encountered "a mind-set that excluded local security as a post-conflict mission
for U.S. forces."[42]

Fahim maintained that his troops should still be able to occupy all the
military land they held. After all, he argued, when they met over a large
map of the city, Dobbins could not be suggesting that the Afghan army
should abandon the Bala Hissar, the ancient citadel of Kabul.[43] There was
an uncomfortable atmosphere in the room as Fahim's power grab was
against the international agreement that "all military units" should be
withdrawn from Kabul. For residents of the capital, Fahim did not represent the Afghan army; he was just another warlord. They had suffered
as he fought the rival warlord Gulbuddin Hekmatyar for control of the
Bala Hissar in the early 1990s, before the Taliban came.

Fahim's takeover was inevitable, as there were no international troops
to stop him even if there had been the political will. International amnesia about the years before the Taliban was total. The Bonn meeting
that nominated Hamid Karzai to head an interim Afghan administration
described in unusually florid and sentimental terms those in the pre-
Taliban government as brave Afghan mujahideen "who over the years
have defended the independence, territorial integrity and national unity
of the country and have played a major role in the struggle against terrorism and oppression, and whose sacrifice has now made them both
heroes of jihad and champions of peace, stability and reconstruction
of their beloved homeland, Afghanistan." The mujahideen president
before the Taliban, Burhanuddin Rabbani, was allowed to return to the
palace ahead of the handover to Karzai's interim administration.

This was a one-sided interpretation of a vicious civil war. The mujahideen had indeed defended Afghanistan and successfully repelled the
1979 Soviet invasion, taking a decade, and at a cost of more than a million lives, an extraordinary achievement. But with the Soviet forces defeated, they fought among themselves until pushed back by the Taliban.
Far from being universally acclaimed as the beloved leader of a nation,
cruelly deposed by the Taliban, Professor Rabbani was a deeply divisive figure—an Egyptian-educated Islamist, close to the Muslim Brotherhood, who played a significant role in the radicalization and spread
of extremist thinking among Kabul students in the 1970s. He initially

fled the country for Pakistan in 1973 in a crackdown against Islamists, emerging as the leader of one of the mujahideen factions after the Soviet invasion in 1979.

After the Soviet military withdrawal in 1989, it took the mujahideen three years to oust the Najibullah government, which remained propped up by Soviet money. Fighting between rival mujahideen groups took precedence over defeating Najibullah. When they finally took Kabul in 1992, they signed the Peshawar Accord, which installed Rabbani as interim president, after an initial two-month transition under another leader. The aim was a revolving presidency, with each of the mujahideen factions having their turn. The accord stated Rabbani would hand over power four months later. For clarity, the agreement read, "The above mentioned period will not be extended even by a day." In 2001, he remained "president" only because vicious fighting between the mujahideen factions that broke out soon after the agreement made any handover impossible and destroyed much of Kabul. Rabbani's troops were as bad as any in this wanton destruction.

The Russians had hardly touched Kabul during their occupation, but the city was shattered amid rape and lawlessness in the civil war years in the early 1990s in fighting between those described at Bonn as "champions of peace." I first came to Kabul at this time, sleeping in the basement with a shovel, as there was random rocketing and we might need to dig ourselves out at any time. Fahim's occupation of the Bala Hissar reminded Kabul residents of those dark days.

ISAF IN KABUL

President Bush made opposition to prolonged military intervention part of his election campaign in 2000, when he ruled out "having some kind of nation-building corps from America."[44] His first national security adviser, Condoleezza Rice, wrote contemptuously about the use of U.S. soldiers to protect children on their way to school in the Balkans. She said the U.S. military should not engage in nation-building. "It is not a civilian police force. It is not a political referee. And it is most certainly not designed to build a civilian society."[45]

This was moral failure. Military intervention is a drastic step that comes with the obligation to manage its consequences. After the fall of the Taliban, there were interventions made by troops on the ground that had a profound impact, altering what happened next. But unlike the Iraq war two years later, there was no hesitancy over the Afghan intervention, no "Pottery Barn Rule" for Afghanistan—the shorthand used by the media to explain Secretary of State Colin Powell's caution over war against Saddam Hussein: "You broke it, you own it." Instead of shouldering the responsibility to deliver stability, the decision to support the old warlords was, literally, irresponsible. It was also shortsighted—creating conditions that meant there were still U.S. troops on the ground nearly twenty years later.

Politicians resolutely opposed to nation-building missed the history of America. Stabilization is after all the norm not the exception. Only eleven of the hundreds of conflicts since the foundation of the Republic have been "conventional" state-on-state wars—the others were all stabilization operations. In the 1990s, the decade before 9/11, the U.S. was engaged in a stabilization role somewhere in the world on average every two years.[46] This was acknowledged in the manual that emerged to deal with the insurgencies of Afghanistan and Iraq. "Contrary to popular belief, the military history of the United States is one characterized by stability operations, interrupted by distinct episodes of major combat."[47] The new manual came out in 2006, but by then, the challenges were far greater than at the start. Forest fires were raging in both Afghanistan and Iraq that would be hard to extinguish, and with different policies may not have been lit in the first place.

While political understanding of the stabilization task may have been absent, there were some in the military who could see that both the shape and scale of the commitment were wrong from the start. General David McKiernan, who commanded the advance into Iraq in 2003 and would later command in Afghanistan, believed that the failure to mobilize the right-size force at the start after regime change in both countries was a fundamental mistake. His sweep across Iraq—one thousand miles in sixteen days, the longest and fastest armored assault ever seen—was an outstanding success in delivering its task of defeating the Iraqi army and ending the rule of Saddam Hussein. But his armored divisions were not configured for stabilization, nor followed up with a different force. There was no plan for what to do on the second day after the fall of Saddam Hussein. McKiernan could see that the same mistakes had been made in Afghanistan:

The argument that I'm not sure has been accepted among political leadership is, sometimes it takes more ground presence *after* major kinetic operations, than it did *during* the major kinetic operations. When you want to control the environment, when you want to protect population, when you want to restore services, when you want to protect infrastructure, when you want to get basic conditions, and some form of government back on its feet . . . somebody has to do it. Usually, those are people in a uniform for an extended period of time until security conditions allow it to be transferred to a civilian presence.

The Bonn agreement approved an international security force for Afghanistan, but the Pentagon watered this down to rename it the International Security *Assistance* Force, to avoid any suggestion that international troops would provide security themselves.[48] And so ISAF was born, amid U.S. opposition to any extension of its initial mandate to patrol in Kabul. The U.S. military mission at Bagram in Operation Enduring Freedom remained focused on chasing the remnants of al-Qaeda and the Taliban leadership. There was even a question over whether they would come to the aid of ISAF troops if in trouble. The UK was the most enthusiastic nation for the peacekeeping operation, and Prime Minister Tony Blair talked personally to President Bush to secure a guarantee of support.

American concerns about being bogged down by the logistical demands of a large ISAF force were legitimate. Few countries had the expeditionary capacity to engage in such a remote location. The U.S. had 250 long-range transport planes; the UK had four. At the time, no other NATO member had any.[49] Even by the end of 2003, when German troops moved to the north, ISAF had only three helicopters of its own in the country and leaned on what was by then a far larger U.S. war machine for support. When NATO secretary-general George Robertson appealed for NATO countries to send more helicopters, none responded.

When the first ISAF troops arrived in January 2002, under the command of a British general, John McColl, they had to negotiate access to the city with Fahim, insisting they would patrol without an escort from his forces. McColl thought he would need five thousand troops to secure Kabul, with a further twenty thousand for the rest of the country. When

Dobbins proposed these figures to Rumsfeld, "his manner indicated his displeasure at the notion."[50] President Karzai had been requesting more boots on the ground since Bonn, a demand widely supported across the country as reassurance against the predatory warlords who had returned. McColl said, "Every week delegations were coming to Karzai to request that ISAF deploy outside Kabul."[51] Bush's appointee as coordinator of the Afghan campaign, Richard Haass, lost the argument for more troops. He wanted a force of up to sixty thousand, half from the U.S. and half from other countries.[52] What Afghanistan had instead was a small expeditionary war-fighting force, with a half-strength headquarters, and an unclear mandate.

☰ WAR OF THE CAVES: DECEMBER 2001 AND MARCH 2002

The light-footprint plan failed its biggest test in the one chance to capture or kill Osama bin Laden after 9/11 in Afghanistan. Intelligence reports placed him, with up to three thousand al-Qaeda fighters, in the Tora Bora cave complex he built during the Soviet war. The caves were in the high northern wall of a ridge at the top of a square valley, six miles wide and deep, close to the Pakistan border. Mountains rising to fifteen thousand feet made air support difficult, so there would need to be a significant ground force.[53] The light footprint demanded they find local militias to do the ground fighting, backed by small CIA and Special Forces teams. Schroen had now been replaced as head of Operation Jawbreaker, by Gary Berntsen who was given one clear instruction by Crumpton. "I want you killing the enemy immediately." Berntsen had been tracking bin Laden as long as anybody in the U.S. system. He was sent to Tanzania in 1998 and walked through the charred remains of the American embassy destroyed by an al-Qaeda bomb.[54]

It was clear to Berntsen that they needed a significant U.S. ground force to assault Tora Bora. He had a stand-up row with the head of Special Forces in Afghanistan, Major General Dell Dailey, who said too many U.S. soldiers might offend their allies. "I don't give a damn about offending our allies," said Berntsen. "I only care about eliminating al-Qaeda and delivering bin Laden's head in a box!"[55] Ground troops could have conducted a block-and-sweep operation, dropping troops at al-Qaeda's back door then pushing them from the front.

But the orders were that this was a war of Afghan liberation, backed up by special operators. Two local commanders were found for the assault on Tora Bora, drawn by significant payments. The more effective, Hazrat Ali, had been a commander in Massoud's forces in the mujahideen. The other, Haji Zaman Ghamsharik, who had also fought in the mujahideen, was a drug dealer the CIA persuaded to return from France when the Taliban fell. "The thinking was that this would show Afghans fighting their own war," wrote Mattis,[56] who watched frustrated from Kandahar airfield. He had 1,000 marines on the ground, the largest formation of international troops in the country, and another 3,500 on ships a short flight away.

The marines bore the code name Task Force 58, the same as the force that took island after island in the defeat of Japan in 1945. Mattis had Harrier attack jets and enough CH-53 helicopters to drop troops forward, equipped with cold-weather clothing. As the days passed before the offensive, he became more impatient that they were not called. "At one point in early December, I was blunt; some described my presentation as highly obscene . . . But I was shouting against the wind."[57] Because of their size and particular history, the marines sat outside the standard CENTCOM reporting lines, and Mattis could not penetrate Franks's obsession with fighting only with local allies. Even an appeal to Bush failed. Crumpton, the CIA counterterrorism chief, told the president, "We're going to lose our prey if we're not careful." Bush asked him about the Afghan forces. "Are they up to the job?" Crumpton replied, "Definitely not, Mr. President."[58]

Rather than calling on the nearby marines, or flying in Rangers from the U.S., the decision meant there were fewer than one hundred international troops on the ground—outnumbered by journalists. Reliance on local militias cost the battle of Tora Bora. They did not have the same motivation as those who had already defeated the Taliban in the cities in the north, Kabul, or Kandahar. Instead, they were being asked to fight in December, high in the snow-covered mountains, in an area where there was considerable local support for al-Qaeda, including among the fighters on the American side.[59] There was fighting between the two militias. It was also the fasting month of Ramadan. The small bands of special operators fighting with them could not persuade them to stay and hold ground they took in the evening, as they needed to come down and break their fast, meaning the same ground had to be retaken every day.

There was certainty that bin Laden was there; his voice was clearly heard on a captured al-Qaeda radio. When word came that he was cornered in the late afternoon on December 10, four days into the battle, special operators moved up for the kill, only to find that their local allies had abandoned the position to return to eat, leaving two Americans surrounded by al-Qaeda.

The following day, the former drug dealer Ghamsharik said he had persuaded al-Qaeda to surrender, and there should be a pause in the bombing to allow them to emerge. The air assault had been around the clock, including the first use since Vietnam of a fifteen-thousand-pound daisy cutter bomb, so large it had to be rolled out of the back of a plane. It had a devastating impact, one radio intercept revealing the horror as the wounded were brought out, before the cry came, "Cave too hot, can't reach others." Because of this, Ghamsharik said, the remaining fighters would give up. Special operators were suspicious, but finally allowed an overnight pause, resuming bombing in the morning when no one surrendered. Hundreds of al-Qaeda fighters are believed to have escaped that night, having paid a bribe to Ghamsharik to order the pause. Even after that betrayal, bin Laden was still there and wrote a new will, sensing the end. He was overheard on the radio, gathering fighters together for a prayer. The CIA then intercepted "the sound of mules and a large ground of people moving about. Then the radio went dead."[60] When the reluctant commander Ali was finally persuaded to leave his men in place overnight, and special operators could move on the caves twelve days after the fighting started, bin Laden was not among the twenty or so fighters who were taken captive. He had made his escape.

The battle for Tora Bora revealed the basic flaw in Franks's war plan. Even when the political stakes were as high as killing bin Laden, he would not change his mind, despite the presence in Mattis's marines of a highly motivated U.S. force large enough to do the job.

There was one other battle in the caves of the east three months later, when a valley in Paktia Province, on the Pakistan border south of Tora Bora, was discovered to be a stronghold of Taliban and al-Qaeda fighters, but intelligence officers had "only the vaguest idea of the enemy situation," according to one official account.[61] There were believed to be 150–200 fighters, and the expectation was that they would flee when attacked. But there turned out to be more than 1,000, with reinforcements pouring in, dug into a complex cave system with entrenched firing positions, and willing to fight. The intelligence failure to discover the scale of the threat was just one of the weaknesses exposed by the ad hoc operation, with a force drawn from the improvised, supposedly temporary nature of the Afghan intervention.

Operation Anaconda was planned to last three days, but it took two weeks of tough fighting that left eight Americans dead. Unlike at Tora Bora, conventional forces were employed for this operation. It was planned and executed by the 10th Mountain Division, who had initially deployed to the transit base in Uzbekistan and were scrambled into Afghanistan in mid-December 2001 to be the eyes on the ground for the main command headquarters in Doha, Qatar. They "found themselves planning Anaconda, the largest U.S. military operation since Desert Storm,"[62] according to a U.S. Naval War College investigation. The mission was titled CJTF-Mountain, a combined joint task force—*combined* meaning multinational, and *joint* employing land, sea, and air assets. Only three people in Lieutenant General Franklin Hagenbeck's headquarters had been in a joint environment before; they were far away from their original mission of providing base security. It was "hardly the proper size" for the staff of a CJTF,[63] "not properly trained, manned or equipped" to handle the operation involving more than 1,400 troops from nine nations, and lacked intelligence and logistics functions that had been left behind. Some key components were not told they were involved until too late. The aircraft carrier USS *John C. Stennis* played no part in the first day of fighting, as it was not given the plan. All flights had been canceled that day, and the warplanes stowed away, as the flight deck was full of sailors enjoying a "steel beach" picnic.[64]

Fortune never favored Operation Anaconda. Poor weather prevented reconnaissance of enemy positions ahead of the operation; the first American to be killed died under misdirected fire from an AC-130, America's most fearsome aerial weapons platform—slow-moving but bristling with weapons, including a 105 mm howitzer. In the days that followed, the U.S. troops encountered the most intense fighting in Afghanistan to date. Four Apaches engaged on the first day, but all had to return to Bagram, having taken so much incoming fire they were no longer safe for combat missions. Most of the fatalities happened while attempting a rescue operation of a Navy SEAL, who slid on oil from hydraulics spilled

from a pipe that burst when hit in withering fire and fell from the open
back door of an MH-47 helicopter onto the snow below.

There were some Afghan militias working with the coalition at Anaconda. In the one joint mission, a Tajik militia band broke off early to
loot an abandoned village, another group went ahead of the air strikes,
lighting an enormous bonfire on top of a hill to keep warm, preventing
the planned use of a daisy cutter bomb. After the failure of local allies
in the first battle of the caves at Tora Bora, there might have been some
adjustment. But the war planners under Franks did not see the military
and political reality of the opposition forces they were depending on.

☰ THE BIG TENT

It was a formative time for the new Afghanistan. The U.S. paid for a big
tent to facilitate a Loya Jirga in the summer, a grand council of elders, the
first opportunity for Afghanistan to meet and discuss its own future without
interference since the Soviet invasion in 1979. The area where the Loya
Jirga tent was erected, in the west of the city, the part most devastated by
the fighting between rival mujahideen in the years before the Taliban, now
filled with the warlords who had caused the destruction, each accompanied
by gangs of armed men. In contrast, the new Afghan army was able to field
just one battalion (1 BANG—the First Kandak, or Battalion of the Afghan
National Guard) to provide some security, wearing uniforms provided by
Turkey, after intensive specific training for the event by British troops.

There was an electric atmosphere in the tent as the conference was
opened by Zahir Shah, the king whose ouster in a coup in 1973 had
begun the country's decline into war. His presence gave hope of the
rediscovery of an Afghanistan lost in the tides of war. He had returned
from exile in Rome and would die in Afghanistan soon afterward, to be
buried with full honors alongside his father, Muhammad Nadir Shah,
who had saved the country from another civil war in the 1920s. The
Loya Jirga was the first opportunity for Afghans who had been close to
the Communists, and the rival mujahideen, as well as returning exiles
to sit and discuss their future. A notable exception in this broad national
representation was of course the Taliban.

The Loya Jirga set the country on a path to elections for a president
and the writing of a new constitution, but Afghanistan had not turned its
back on violence. Inevitably, McNeill was drawn into matters that went

well beyond strict military tactics. Soon afterward, a prominent leader
from eastern Afghanistan, Haji Qadir, was gunned down in Kabul. In
Washington, there was a fear that he had been targeted by the Tajik warlords who had retrenched themselves and that President Karzai might also
be in their sights. McNeill was sent to issue a warning to Marshal Fahim.

In the usual Afghan way, when McNeill arrived, the leader was sitting
on an ornate chair at one end of a room of heavy sofas with lines of
hangers-on and petitioners waiting for a word with the chief. McNeill's
message was that the U.S. was keenly interested in Karzai's health. Fahim
quickly realized what he was being told and asked McNeill if he wanted
to speak alone. The room was cleared of all but Fahim, McNeill, and an
interpreter, Amrullah Saleh, a man of considerable influence himself, a
CIA asset in the Taliban years, who would later head the Afghan intelligence service and become vice president.

After a long pause in the grand empty room, McNeill broke the silence by saying that he represented a group of freedom-loving nations
and they wanted to move forward for Afghanistan's benefit and that Karzai was essential to the stability that was needed. Fahim moved his big
square body forward and said, "I'm no threat to Karzai." McNeill asked
him if he would run against Karzai as president, and he said, "When it
comes, I'll ask around, and if I think I have support I'm going to run
against him. But you also need to know that only a Pashtun can run this
country, and Karzai is probably as good as we can do in the Pashtuns."

Less than a year later, thirty ISAF military vehicles surrounded the
Arg, when there were new rumors of a Fahim-led coup.[65] His northern
Tajik tribe was smaller than the Pashtuns, who were mainly in the south
and east, but the defeat of the Pashtun Taliban gave the Tajik warlords
of the north the upper hand. U.S. military understanding of the Afghan
tribal balance was then in its infancy. And because there was a strong
sense that the war was over, few bothered to learn. The EU ambassador,
Francesc Vendrell, said, "Because there was a feeling that things were still
going to become normal, it was not thought necessary for us to understand the tribal system."[66] McChrystal's conclusion was crisp. "The West's
effort was poorly informed, organized, and executed ... We were like
high-school students who had wandered into a mafia-owned bar, dangerously unaware of the tensions that filled the room and the authorities
who controlled it."[67]

Many Afghan civilians wanted no part of either the Taliban or the returning warlords but were caught up in the war nonetheless. In July 2002 came an incident that, more than any other, would sour Afghanistan's mood about the American intervention—a turning point from which there was no going back. Several two-thousand-pound bombs were dropped on a wedding party in Uruzgan in the southwest of the country—local estimates said forty-eight people were killed, and more than one hundred injured. Most of those killed and injured were women and children. As was customary, there was celebratory firing into the air at the wedding party, mistaken as hostile fire by U.S. warplanes not familiar with local customs. It preyed on McNeill's mind, although he had not personally ordered the attack. This was to become a constant challenge during the near two decades of the Afghan war; because there were many troops outside their command on the ground in Afghanistan, all the commanders of the international force faced the problem of explaining civilian casualties inflicted by forces not under their control.

Karzai felt these civilian losses deeply, weeping on television. It was not the first such attack in Uruzgan, although it was the worst to date, and the president had a special affinity with the province where he had been protected on his hazardous journey to power the year before. Not for the last time, McNeill found himself having to apologize in private to the president and in public to the nation. The press conference he did with the Afghan foreign minister Abdullah Abdullah he thought "as difficult" as anything he had done in his life.

There were other incidents as well. A group of elders were bombed on their way to President Karzai's inauguration, and many were killed, as their convoy was mistaken for the Taliban. Heavily armed militiamen were taken out of their vehicles and beaten up by German peacekeepers when they refused to stop at a checkpoint on their way to the Loya Jirga. The bomb on the wedding party was of a different order. Without a significant ground presence of specialized forces configured for stabilization, and without access to far better intelligence, such incidents were bound to happen.

☰ THE WARLORDS DIG IN[68]

Cash had not stopped flowing since Schroen's first suitcase-full two weeks after 9/11. In the early weeks of the war, I hitched a ride across the snow-covered Hindu Kush mountains in an ancient Russian helicopter over the Taliban front line toward Bamiyan in the center of the country. The Taliban had conducted a reign of terror against the Hazara minority there and committed their worst cultural crime just six months before 9/11—destroying giant Buddhas carved into the solid sandstone wall of the mountain. I dug into giant plastic-wrapped parcels loaded onto pallets in the helicopter to see what they contained. Inside were bales of new Afghan banknotes, going to pay the Hazara forces, lubricating the wheels of war. A group of soldiers from Britain's Special Air Service set up at a remote airfield near Ghazni in the center of the country, armed with briefcases full of cash, offering $1 million each for Stinger antiaircraft missiles still in circulation after being given to the mujahideen in the 1980s to shoot down Russian helicopters.

But the money available for information *after* the Taliban fell was given out in a way that damaged the capacity of a new nation to emerge. The old warlords found that all they needed to do was to give a list of names of suspects to the CIA in exchange for hundreds of thousands of dollars; inevitably, many used this to settle disputes with their enemies. While there was supposed to be cross-checking against other information, intelligence-gathering was rudimentary,[69] and being named an al-Qaeda sympathizer was a one-way ticket to Bagram or Guantánamo for those not immediately killed.

The warlords were weak when the Taliban fell and expected to be questioned for past crimes. They were in awe of the power of the U.S. capacity to deliver precision death from the air, and that could have been leveraged at the time they were down. It was known as the *B-52 effect*. Dostum sought legal advice, fearing he would be carted off to face a tribunal in The Hague. As the sky filled with warplanes, McChrystal saw that "Afghans imagined American power to be infinite."[70] This could have been leveraged far better than it was. But the opportunity was lost. Instead of using this advantage to give Afghanistan a breathing space, the way was left clear for the very people who had brought ruin to much of the country in the early 1990s. They now found themselves wealthy enough to entrench the authority they had quickly grabbed when the Taliban fell. Twenty of the first thirty-four provincial governors appointed after the Taliban were former warlords. Forty warlords took seats in the first Afghan parliament in 2005 (along with twenty-four leaders of criminal gangs and seventeen drug traffickers).[71] One of the first acts of the new parliament was to pass a general amnesty for past war crimes, celebrated with a huge gathering of warlords in the soccer stadium where the Taliban once executed people at halftime during matches.

The level of democratic failure this revealed was illustrated by a poll recording 94 percent support for war crimes trials.[72] The political system that emerged did not represent the nation. "Security has been put in the hands of those who most threaten it," wrote Human Rights Watch. In the relatively sophisticated western city of Herat, the return of the warlord Ismail Khan meant life was in ways *worse* than under the Taliban.[73]

U.S. actions lacked coherence in terms of confronting the demons of 9/11, let alone in terms of the future security of Afghanistan. One of those who became rich rather than being arrested, Abdul Rasul Sayyaf, was later named by the 9/11 Commission as the mentor of the mastermind of 9/11, Khalid Sheikh Mohammed. If this war were to prevent another 9/11, he was at least as much a suspect as the many minor figures who ended up in Guantánamo. Standing for president in 2014, he did not deny that he had worked with Khalid Sheikh Mohammed. "I met him, I met Osama bin laden. I met bigger than them also."[74] He was accused of ordering appalling human rights abuses in a massacre of Hazaras in the Afshar suburb of Kabul in 1993.[75] An exhaustive investigation found there had been mass rape and murder as Sayyaf's men went house to house. Witnesses described lines of heads being left along the top of walls. Some of those he trained went to Indonesia to found the country's most ruthless Islamist group, called Abu Sayyaf in his honor.

Jihadi leaders like Sayyaf were little better than the Taliban in their appalling treatment of women and in some ways worse. Restoring their power would make the fight for equality far harder in Afghanistan. He was in favor of women remaining at home, wearing burkas if they ventured out, and being educated only to the most basic level. But he was safe, as he was in the anti-Taliban coalition.

☰ THE LONG WAR TAKES SHAPE

By the summer of 2002, the template for the long war was set. U.S. forces based in Kabul were training Afghan soldiers, while troops from several nations patrolled the streets. Combat remained mostly a Special Forces affair, and American troops controlled Bagram and the huge ex-Soviet airfield in Kandahar in the south. Although the mission already broke Rumsfeld's ceiling of 5,200 troops, at the time McNeill was talking up an early withdrawal. "If we continue into a transitional government that is a success, if the Afghans are taking control of their own destiny and we don't see the enemy for me to prosecute, you then reach a point where you begin to have an argument over why we need to have this joint task force."[76] If you had asked him the same question when he left a year later, he had changed his mind and believed the U.S. would be there for many years.

One reason for the change was a sense of idealism among some in the Bush administration about the new Afghanistan. There were two contradictory impulses in the White House—hardheaded opposition to nation-building ran counter to a mood of wanting to spread democracy and leave the world a better place. Given the struggles he was having for resources and attention, out of the blue in March 2002, that first envoy Dobbins was surprised to be called by the White House to be asked if it would be appropriate for the president to cite the Marshall Plan for European reconstruction after World War II as a model for Afghanistan.

There were substantial differences in the two situations, beyond the scale of the reconstruction commitment at the start. West Germany was rebuilt with a major military stabilization force, putting American, British, and French military teams into every corner of German life, and a widespread amnesty for former Nazis except the leadership. But in the speech at the Virginia Military Institute, where General George Marshall once taught, Bush talked of clearing minefields, building roads, improving medical care, and developing a new economy, invoking Marshall, who "knew that our military victory against enemies in World War II had to be followed by a moral victory."

The principal legal authority for the war in Afghanistan, the Authorization for Use of Military Force, swiftly passed by Congress after 9/11, was limited to action against people connected to the 9/11 attacks, "in order to prevent any future acts of international terrorism against the United States." But this gave no clarity over what would happen in Phase IV of military operations, stabilization and reconstruction.† So it

---

† Phase I: Deter; Phase II: Seize Initiative; Phase III: Dominate; Phase IV: Stabilize and Reconstruct; Phase V: Enable Civil Authority.

was improvised with two trends pulling in opposite directions—military action against terrorists and an increasing move toward something like nation-building, although it could not be called that.

There was no pause for discussion of goals, timelines, strategy, or tactics for Afghanistan, no single decision that led to the long war, but instead a series of small changes that led to incremental increases in troop numbers, with policy makers always believing that just a few more troops would make the difference—culminating in the force close to 150,000 ten years later. The light footprint was designed to satisfy the tax-paying public who had limited patience for long-term foreign military engagement, but as it failed to stabilize the country, it set the very conditions to make that long-term engagement inevitable.

In June 2002, the first ISAF troops were going home. McColl was replaced by a Turkish lieutenant general, Hilmi Akin Zorlu, whose troops refused to move in until British military engineers had built a better barracks and cookhouse.[77] McColl's force had successfully patrolled Kabul, and apart from "some gunfire exchanged with criminal gangs," there had been no security challenges.[78] Inevitably, the pull to extend ISAF beyond Kabul became too great to ignore, requiring a larger U.S. presence to provide logistics and airlift support. From these origins, ISAF grew incrementally into a nationwide peacekeeping operation.

The bear hunters of Bagram under Operation Enduring Freedom (OEF) were now supplemented with significant conventional forces from thirty-seven nations, including 1,700 British Royal Marines, a substantial part of the fighting strength in 2002. Even if nation-building was off-limits, McChrystal encouraged McNeill to travel widely to talk to Afghan leaders, since the operation up to now was "poorly prepared."[79] Coordination was becoming essential, as the last piece of the jigsaw was placed—a provincial reconstruction team (PRT) in Gardez in the east— not far from the mountains where Operation Anaconda was fought against al-Qaeda in the spring. The idea of nationwide PRTs that could help link the population to governance followed a visit by the British colonel in McChrystal's HQ, Nick Carter. He observed that the U.S. Special Forces team in Gardez had a good rapport with local people, partly because among them were a doctor and a vet, who were reservists. The vet was particularly popular, and this contact clearly built local trust that might deliver intelligence. Civilian contractors were unable to leave Kabul because of security restrictions, and the PRTs would give them protection. McNeill agreed to try small military teams, with development experts on-site, to provide reassurance and the beginnings of reconstruction, to connect provinces to the center. By the fall of 2002, ten teams of six were deployed across the country to assess humanitarian need.

In the south, the light footprint had been replaced by battalion-size operations, around five hundred soldiers dropped from helicopters for two- to four-day fights to support special operators chasing al-Qaeda in the frontier mountains. Colonel Campbell's 1st Brigade, 82nd Airborne, did these operations from Kandahar for six months. "We were just going out there to find bad guys," he said. "There wasn't a whole bunch of reconstruction efforts going on." They were making it up as they went along. Later units would have cultural awareness training, including the need to find groups of elders to hold *shuras,* meetings to secure agreement. That was not part of training for Campbell's soldiers in 2002. "We didn't do shuras, we had no clue what that was."

Sarah Chayes, who first came into Kandahar in 2001 as an NPR reporter and stayed as an aid worker, brought some elders into the air base. One had a heart attack and was treated by U.S. Army doctors, which Campbell said helped to win support. But he admitted that "we probably helped build some of the corruption in there," in contracts for construction and transport. Geraldo Rivera from Fox News came in and signed autographs for soldiers, going out on a couple of operations ahead of a one-hour live show from inside a hangar surrounded by the machinery of war. It was the night before the air attacks on Baghdad that began the Iraq war in March 2003, and Rivera tried to make out that the two campaigns were complementary and coordinated, which Campbell knew was not true. Already Afghanistan was the other war—the backdrop to Iraq.

The new PRTs were staffed from the very small civil-military element in OEF, cobbled together at little notice, backed up by a Georgia National Guard unit. The commander, Brigadier General David E. Kratzer, had no civil affairs experience, which he saw as an advantage, allowing him to "approach the new command with a fresh perspective."[80] After a four-day planning session, he set out for Kabul.

Even this small operation was viewed with concern by senior commanders, still intent on the light footprint. Interviewed for the army's official history, Kratzer recalled his pre-deployment meeting with Franks, who "told me directly, with his finger in my face, that I would not get involved in nation-building."[81] It was a disorganized and unfocused way to run an intervention in the affairs of a complex and unstable country. But with no stabilization doctrine, they were literally making it up as they went along. It would be another year before trained civil affairs officers would command this part of the operation.[82] The development activities by the military were like a vehicle engaging drive with the brake on, drawn to assist as well as fight, and *not doing nation-building*.

In the winter of 2001, while Kratzer set up his HQ in a Kabul villa borrowed from the British government development agency Department for International Development (DFID), in the parallel universe of development, donors were lining up major commitments. Coordination became an increasing challenge, with humanitarian agencies jostling to manage the operation, suspicious of military involvement in development. The civil-military teams "added to the crush of . . . nongovernment organizations (NGOs), donors, and private sector organizations" arriving in Afghanistan.[83]

THE FOG OF AID

What's the only entity in Afghanistan that does not have any money or troops?

Answer: The government.

—Kabul "joke" in the early years of U.S.-led intervention

☰ UNINTENDED CONSEQUENCES

Haji Mohammad sits every day with a wheelbarrow, waiting to get casual laboring jobs in the market area in Herat. Bearded, turbaned, and toothless, he does not know his age; but he remembers clearly how he lost his farm. It was 2002, the year after the Taliban fell. "I could not make any money because the price of wheat came down, and there was a lot of wheat from outside for sale. No one bought our wheat." He had to sell a pair of oxen, donkeys, and a cow. There were good rains after three years of drought, and Afghan farmers had a record harvest. But the price collapsed by 80 percent because the country was flooded with food aid.

Even without the war, Afghanistan would have needed food aid in that terrible winter after the Taliban fell in 2001. Hundreds of thousands of people left their homes in the mountains in western Afghanistan and moved to a makeshift camp in the inhospitable Maslakh desert outside Herat. They were displaced by fighting, but also by hunger caused by the long drought. Those who remained behind in the mountains were reduced to cooking weeds and grass.[1] The initial international response was chaotic and uncoordinated. Many people died even once they reached Maslakh, because the camp was so badly managed. Food aid came by road from the north, through mountain passes that filled with fresh snow every morning. There was no traffic marshaling, and several trucks fell off the road into the ravine below. Much of what came through this hazardous pipeline did not reach the hungry. It was stolen, and sacks emblazoned with the words *Gift from the American people* emerged on the market in Herat, the beginning of the flood of food that suppressed prices.

"We were importing food," said Andrew Natsios, the head of USAID at the time. But by the spring, the fields were full of grain—the first good harvest for years. "If we'd bought the food locally from that surplus, the prices wouldn't have collapsed."[2] He later calculated that if he had bought local grain to give away as food aid, rather than shipping in U.S. corn, he would have needed around 250,000 tons, which would have absorbed the surplus and stabilized the Afghan market.

The collapse of the domestic wheat price that year caused by the flood of food aid had another effect—farmers had no option but to return to planting poppies. In the last two years of their rule, the Taliban had successfully banned the growing of opium poppies. But after the U.S. intervention, this changed quickly. In the Herat countryside, after the collapse in the wheat price, Jalil Hamad, a farmer, said that when it came to plant again, the decision was easy. "We grew only as much as we needed to eat, but grew poppies on the rest of the land."[3]

America's generosity saved lives that winter. But an unintended consequence of generous food aid was that it led directly to some poor farmers losing their land and others returning to plant opium poppies. Lacking an agreed doctrine for intervention, and amid confused political direction, the improvised response fueled corruption, while failing to construct a sovereign independent state able to pay for itself. Poorly delivered aid fed into a negative cycle that worsened security, giving an opening to the Taliban. Afghanistan desperately needed aid, but wrongly applied, it contributed as much to the growing instability as the failure to put in enough troops to stabilize the country.

Those consequences could have been foreseen from previous interventions. But just as the military had no doctrine for foreign intervention, so development donors lacked an agreed way of moving forward. "Washington tended to treat each new operation as if it would also be the last, making little effort to capture the lessons,"[4] wrote Jim Dobbins, the first emissary to Kabul after 9/11. Even after the frequent U.S. military interventions during the Clinton years in the 1990s, there was no accumulated knowledge to manage stability operations because America did not do nation-building. In Afghanistan, "new people" were sent "to face what should have been familiar problems."[5]

☰ WITH US OR AGAINST US

The world wanted to help in Afghanistan, amid unprecedented global sympathy and solidarity for America after 9/11. Within twenty-four hours of the attack, in a stunning show of support, NATO invoked its Article 5 for the first time in the fifty-two-year history of the alliance. This regards an attack on one member as an attack on all and commits all NATO members to assist. For many countries, 9/11 marked the biggest loss of their citizens in a terrorist attack. After Americans, the highest number of casualties were British, and Queen Elizabeth ordered "The Star-Spangled Banner" be played at Buckingham Palace for the Changing of the Guard ceremony on September 12. But President Bush mistook sympathy for consent to go to war. The formulation of the response to 9/11 as a global war on terror, with a binary choice of "with us or against us," and the swift pivot to war on Iraq, caused political nervousness across otherwise friendly countries, particularly in Europe. Rarely can a nation have squandered goodwill so quickly. There was rising concern about U.S. intentions in Iraq as NATO members found the nature of the alliance redrawn to serve the narrow interests of the Bush administration.

Two weeks after the unprecedented invocation of Article 5, Deputy Secretary of Defense Paul Wolfowitz, on a visit to Brussels, redefined the purpose of the alliance—claiming its only relevance now was to support the U.S. counterterrorist effort. And after the Taliban fell, he said contemptuously, "We didn't need most of NATO in Afghanistan." NATO was "useless," according to Secretary of Defense Donald Rumsfeld. "At no point has General Tommy Franks even talked to anyone at NATO."[6] A senior NATO official, Edgar Buckley, who was instrumental in delivering the quick response to invoke Article 5, called this "a fundamental misjudgment about the nature of the Alliance that devalued the importance of strategic solidarity."[7]

President Bush's formulation of an "Axis of Evil," widening his target to include Iran, Iraq, and North Korea, in the State of the Union address in January 2002, raised further European concerns. Throughout 2002, while ISAF peacekeepers patrolled Kabul, the streets of European cities were filled with protestors opposed to the impending war with Iraq. The German chancellor Gerhard Schröder had to apologize after one of his ministers compared Bush to Hitler. As the political temperature on Iraq rose, with France and Germany still strongly opposed to the war against Saddam Hussein, there were contemptuous sneers in Washington about "old Europe" and nonsense about french fries being renamed "freedom fries." It was the "gravest crisis" NATO had faced, according to Henry Kissinger. If France and Germany did not back the Iraq war, "a legacy of distrust will continue to weigh on Atlantic relations."[8] It was in this toxic atmosphere over Iraq that Afghanistan became the "good war," in a reassertion by NATO's European members and Canada of its relevance and the value of cooperation.

☰ NEW AFGHAN ARMY

In October 2002, Major General Karl Eikenberry began the herculean labor of creating a new Afghan army. He was shocked by the unsanitary conditions both for American trainers and Afghan recruits at the huge training ground to the east of Kabul in December—the "Valley Forge of the Afghan Army."[9] The training ground was littered with the stripped-out hulks of armored vehicles, and a freezing wind blew through the broken windows of unheated buildings. It was unsurprising that desertion rates were so high. Marshal Fahim, now defence minister, made no effort to pay soldiers from central funds—he and his allies were content to operate with militias who owed allegiance to them; they had no interest in building a competing national army.[10] He kept his tanks lined up north of Bagram on the Shomali Plain. In the looking glass world created by the warlords, the first post-Taliban Afghan Defence Minister did not want the state to have effective security forces, as they would threaten his mujahideen militias.

Most of the soldiers trained by American soldiers in the first year immediately deserted, leaving the Afghan army at around two thousand. Fahim's behavior underlined the central flaw in the light footprint plan. "At the end of the day," General Franks wrote, "it would be the Afghans who would determine the success of our operations. If they were provided for, Phase IV (Reconstruction) would be accelerated immeasurably."[11] But warlord militias not connected to the state rode roughshod over this expectation.

America took on responsibility for military training at an international summit in Tokyo hard on the heels of the Bonn summit at the end of 2001. Other tasks were carved up between a number of willing countries. The UK took on counter-narcotics; Germany, police; Italy, justice; and Japan, DDR—disarmament, demobilization, and reintegration of militias. There was no liaison with Afghan partners about these priorities and no overall coordinator, which could result in one province "being pushed to eradicate poppy fields, disarm militias and remove its police chief all at the same time,"[12] said the analyst Emma Sky. Inevitably, the U.S. military was drawn into these other areas of responsibility in a chaotic and uncoordinated manner.[13]

The missing element was building Afghan institutional capacity to govern itself and provide a counterbalance to the power of the warlords. The main government buildings lie near each other in the center of Kabul, mostly surrounded by open green space and trees—a memory of a gentler age. The presidential office in the Arg sits in more than eighty acres of parkland, quadruple the size of the White House estate, and more than twice the size of Buckingham Palace. Nearby lie the rolling lawns and parade grounds around the Ministry of Defense, set on a large site going down to the Kabul River. Major General Sher Muhammad Karimi had been called by President Karzai to reestablish the MOD under Fahim. He had a hard time dealing with his American advisers. "Unfortunately in those days they didn't listen much to us Afghans."[14]

Karimi is an outstanding officer with a remarkable military career, serving every Afghan administration, including the Taliban, since he became an officer more than fifty years ago. He graduated from the British officer academy at Sandhurst in 1968 and later passed out of Ranger school in the U.S. Apart from eighteen months in jail during the dark days before the Soviet invasion in 1979, when he was badly tortured, he worked for the Afghan army all his life. Soon after his release from jail, he went back to the MOD, now under Soviet control, and even though he had been a senior officer in that regime, the mujahideen called him to work for them in the early 1990s, as did the Taliban in their turn, such was his reputation for competence. He found the Taliban poorly educated and cruelly unpredictable, and was asked to teach their defense minister, Mullah Obaidullah, how to do the job.

Karimi grew watchful and began to notice other staff officers disappearing. He stayed in a different house every night, and when he left, he planned his escape carefully, under the guise of visiting his family in Khost Province in the east, neighboring Pakistan. Once there, he made his way across the frontier and spent some time in exile in Peshawar, translating documents for Nancy Hatch Dupree, a remarkable American who lived in Afghanistan for nearly all her life and was now trying to recover looted Afghan artifacts—many of which her late husband, Louis, had dug up as an archaeologist.[15] So the only time Karimi left the country he served for so long was briefly in the later years of Taliban rule.

This most experienced of Afghan officers found that the new American arrivals did not ask his advice. He is a proud member of Afghanistan's largest ethnic group, the Pashtuns, prominent across the east and south, where the Taliban first emerged. The first two U.S. officers he worked with as the MOD was repopulated after 9/11 insulted Karimi by saying, as if in a joke, in their first meeting, "If you are Pashtun, you must be Taliban."[16] He was bitter and explained that while the Taliban were Pashtun, not all Pashtuns were Taliban. "This is the first mistake you are making. The majority of this country are Pashtuns. I am proud to be Pashtun, but not a biased, prejudiced Pashtun." To Karimi, his new allies came in with fixed views that had to come from Pakistani intelligence, the ISI. "They were seeing everything through the eyes of the ISI, not through the eyes of Afghans."

Worse, they had no sense of financial accountability, but were building the new army from the bottom, battalion by battalion, without institutional framework at the center. The soldiers being trained would get equipment, weapons, vehicles, fuel as they needed, with no one counting the cost. To Karimi, this was the wrong way around. He wanted to build a headquarters and then an army. But when he objected, he was told by his new American allies, "We must go up from a battalion all the way to brigade, to corps. Then when we have a corps, we will have MOD general staff headquarters." This made it easier for Fahim to manipulate the system, as without a central structure, he could ensure the new force remained weak.

Disarmament did not start until 2003—far too late to deal with the post-Taliban return of the warlord militias. It lacked teeth, according to the first EU envoy to Kabul after the Taliban, Francesc Vendrell. To work, it would have needed a "weaponized military force telling people 'disarm or else.'"[17] There was no attempt to verify disarmament with biometric data, although this was available. The UN agencies had a database of more than a million Afghans they collected to verify returning refugees. But the warlords obstructed its use in the disarmament process. Before the Taliban fell, when Vendrell asked Fahim's predecessor as Northern Alliance leader Ahmed Shah Massoud how many troops he had available, he answered twenty thousand. But Massoud's successor Fahim claimed sixty thousand when it came to receiving incentives for disarmament.[18]

Everything was the wrong way around: too much food aid damaged the rural economy; too few troops meant many more had to come later; building the army from platoon upward left it without a central structure; no disarmament at the start left a virtual monopoly of violence in the hands of one faction. And finally, Bush's vague desire to "help a democratic government emerge"[19] meant there was a move toward a constitution and elections without any of the institutional architecture that made them work. This was in reverse sequence to what should happen. The priority should have been for institutions not individuals, disarmament not democracy—building a system that would have made it easier for democracy to emerge, rather than ensuring it would be founded on corruption. When Afghan elections happened, those in government were accountable not to their taxpayers but international funding. This was representation without taxation—the opposite of the Jeffersonian ideal.

☰ NEW BLOOD

Afghanistan did not lack attention at the top level. More world leaders came to visit in the months after the Taliban fell than in any period of Afghanistan's history. The UN official who had "handed over" Kabul to Fahim, Wais Barmak, thought it an emotional response. People knew about the Taliban, or thought they knew, and wanted to visit. When the UN secretary general, Kofi Annan, came to town, Barmak was asked to make a speech as the senior Afghan on staff and was encouraged to speak as an Afghan, not an international official. He appealed for support to "build government institutions to be able to serve the people of this country who have suffered for decades," instead of funding the UN and international NGOs. "We are so happy that Afghanistan has been freed, and there is no Taliban rule in this country. We are moving for the first time in our history towards having democracy and democratic rights here in this country."

He was soon removed from his post, and saw other colleagues who knew about Afghanistan sidelined and replaced by a new leadership of people from across the UN system with no Afghan experience. When he asked why there was such a widespread replacement of people, risking the loss of institutional memory, he was told that staff who knew Afghanistan were "resisting new ideas"; the UN now "needed new blood."[20] There was competition among UN agencies for postwar reconstruction, as they relied on the overhead payments to run their offices in Geneva or New York. Barmak went to work in the Afghan Ministry for Rural Rehabilitation and Development, where there was no furniture or phones and staff sat in cold rooms on thin mattresses on the floor. The available budget to spend on rural development in the ministry's first year after the fall of the Taliban was fifty dollars.[21]

Across town, in the Afghan seat of power, the Arg, President Karzai's chief of staff, a former San Francisco lawyer, Said Tayeb Jawad, was struggling to do basic tasks. He had brought his own laptop with him and would have the president check documents on it before going to an office supply shop to use their printer.[22] At the beginning, there was no money to pay the civil service, nor for basic reconstruction in the Arg, which had been badly damaged by the Taliban. The international community did not step in with practical assistance to work with Afghanistan as it was but instead came in with a variety of competing grand plans, with overlapping conditions, budgets, priorities, and target dates. The president did not need a plan, he needed a printer.

It was a fundamental misunderstanding of many aid organizations and the U.S. military that Afghanistan was a clean slate, where they needed to do everything from scratch. Aid workers took to referring to it as *Ground Zero*.[23] They would have done better from the beginning to build on what was there, frail as it was. The institutional structure of the Afghan state survived both the chaos of the mujahideen years and the Taliban. With a little attention, it could have been stood up. When the Taliban regime collapsed under sustained U.S. bombing, civil servants forced by the Taliban to grow beards and wear *shalwar kameez,* the baggy cotton pajamas that are universal across the region, went to the barbers for a shave, took their Western-style suits and ties out from under the mattress, and reported for work. But they were told to go home to wait for the new administration—a mistake as serious as the de-Baathification program that damaged the prospects for post-Saddam Iraq.[24]

There are curious elements to this institutional continuity. In the entrance halls of some ministries, including the Ministry of Finance, is a line of pictures of ministers. After the Communists in suits and mujahideen in robes comes a bearded and turbaned Taliban minister. When I worked as an adviser in President Ghani's government in 2017, one of his legal team quoted a precedent from 1998 in a meeting to construct a new policy. I asked, "Are you sure about the date? That was when the Taliban were in power." He said, "It's a decree—as legitimate as any."

Material that could have informed a better policy was available. In the remarkable archive of modern Afghanistan collected by Louis and Nancy Dupree, and now housed in its own center at Kabul University, I came on a report written in 1988 that looked back over U.S. assistance to Afghanistan from 1950 to 1979, the year of the Soviet invasion. U.S. support was only a quarter that of Soviet assistance to Afghanistan in that period, but was still substantial, including major investment in Helmand Province in the southwest to build hydroelectric dams and irrigation canals. The report contains much that would be familiar to those in the international community who dealt with Afghanistan post-2001. It found that "over-confidence in American expertise often meant that too little attention was paid to local circumstances." It would have been better to work with the grain, rather than against "Afghan cultural and institutional factors."[25]

One of the biggest failures in the post-Taliban years was in delivering a better life and opportunities for women. Agreements since Bonn have been full of language about a "broad-based, gender-sensitive, multi-ethnic" settlement for Afghanistan. This led to quotas so the Afghan parliament has a higher proportion of women MPs than many Western countries, but the reform needed was far deeper. Fundamental issues would not be resolved by slogans. Most women in jail were arrested for "running away," leaving abusive husbands; not officially a crime but customarily regarded as one. Despite all the rhetoric, this appalling abuse has not changed. It required robust international action to stop it, not well-meaning and well-funded workshops that made donors feel good. Child marriages, low access to education, and limited employment opportunities continue to make Afghanistan an unequal place. And this remains one of the most dangerous places in the world to have a baby, despite some improvements in health. The best protection for women would be an end to the fighting and equal access to jobs—far more important than platitudes about gender equality. But rights were always prioritized to the exclusion of everything else. When the Afghan government put a request for economic empowerment of women among the advance papers for an international conference as late as 2014, they faced significant pushback from the UN. In the *Alice in Wonderland* world of international agreements, emphasizing economic opportunities for women was seen as undermining the fight for women's rights.

☰ MONEY TO BURN

In December 2002, in the fading gray light of a Kabul winter afternoon, stocky Mongol-featured Uzbek workers wrapped in padded jackets were burning money. One after another, they pushed wheelbarrow loads of old blue Afghani banknotes and hurled them into large braziers, each six feet across and ten feet tall. The notes had been swapped one for one for a new currency, and the old money needed to be quickly destroyed, under tight security, so it was not recirculated. There were two currencies previously in circulation, and barring tiny irregularities, the one issued since the 1990s by the Uzbek warlord General Abdul Rashid Dostum in the north looked identical to the central currency, but was deemed only half its value for exchange purposes.

Bales of notes were tossed up through the air and fell into the braziers—each shooting a stream of sparks as it tumbled down into the fire. The cash swap was a radical tool that could be wielded only once, to reclaim control of money supply by replacing a failing currency where the largest denomination notes—ten thousand Afghanis—were worth just twenty-five cents.[26] There was far more money in circulation than expected, as for many years there had been chaotic distribution of new notes with no reference to the stability of the economy. The cash swap felt like a clean break with the past, although much of the money burned was brand new, coming directly from container loads of cash seized by warlords when they entered Kabul.[27] The cash had been ordered by the Taliban, and the warlords who swept into the city refused to hand it over to President Karzai's government. This was money laundering Afghan-style, where once again the warlords stood to benefit the most.

The currency reform was introduced under the finance minister, Ashraf Ghani, later president, one of a new generation of politicians who had spent most of their lives abroad—in his case, the U.S. He was impatient for change from the start, criticizing the West for failing to support Afghanistan with what it needed when it needed it. It would be another three years before USAID put forward a coherent plan for reconstruction. "We had a strategy in three months," said Ghani. "Why is it one has to go to parallel strategies?"[28]

From his work at the World Bank, Ghani knew that capital was essential in the recovery of fragile states—both financial and human capital. But in 2002, humanitarian aid was the main focus of donors rather than funding for infrastructure, and Ghani could not change that. He did not win support to fund a scheme to zone Kabul with services laid out before the city expanded. The result was that the capital city grew to five times its size over the two decades after 2001, with chaotic layouts of houses, climbing hillsides across town, with no access to utilities. Nor could he and reformist colleagues like Muhammad Hanif Atmar persuade donors to build an advanced Afghan business school to turn out MBAs. "They could have trained armies of civil servants with masters' degrees to serve their country," said Atmar, who later became the foreign minister. "For twenty years they planned every time for a year . . . They were always planning on short-term time lines, saying we just have a year to do this."

In response to President Bush's call for more aid when he referred to the Marshall Plan that rebuilt Europe after the Second World War in his Virginia Military Institute speech in 2002, the U.S. budgeted $1 billion for the following year under the title Accelerating Success. Even if the change in tone was only to ensure troops could depart without leaving chaos behind them, the U.S. now turned on an aid spigot that would not be turned off for a long time. Two decades on, international donors, with the U.S. by far the largest, have spent the equivalent of the Marshall Plan, *adjusted for inflation*.[29] And to put it simply—we have not got Germany out of it. So what went wrong?

After decades of trial and error, development economists are now broadly in agreement that the best way to fund stability in poor countries is to put money through government budgets.[30] If governments are weak, that is hard to do. America wanted to see quick improvements after dislodging a tyrannical government. Since there was no understanding of potential Afghan institutional capacity—this was aid for Ground Zero—the money went to fund programs outside the state—a substitute, not support, for government. The opportunities for corruption were substantial.

By 2004/5, the off-budget cash for Accelerating Success was three times the size of the Afghan state budget. In the unregulated freewheeling world of post-Taliban Afghanistan, with the international community unwilling to provide security or develop institutions to manage the country, off-budget cash was like throwing gasoline on a fire, where the warlords were in the strongest position to take advantage. William Byrd, the World Bank representative in Kabul, said the off-budget aid was like an "aid juggernaut" that descended on the country, rolling over everything, and leaving nothing in its wake.[31]

In those early high-rolling days, it was easy for almost any Afghan who spoke a little English to get rich quick. A former driver for Wais Barmak at the UN became a millionaire virtually overnight by picking up American contracts, where international clients were paying far more than they should have done. The differences in figures were eye-watering. For example, a house would be renovated for $500, but the Americans would pay the contractor $20,000. It was a problem that was never solved. As late as 2014, Barmak rented a large building in the Sherpur district of Kabul for the Afghan government department he then headed. The rent he negotiated was $6,000 a month; the building had previously been rented by an international organization for $45,000 a month.

Like Dante's hell, there were several circles of corruption in Afghanistan after 2001. The first was the grinding petty indignity of the police demanding bribes at checkpoints, or the passport or identity card office, where every official took a cut, but there was also the corruption involved in contracting, where so much was sliced off along the way in substandard subcontracting that the quality of the final work was no good. In between was the vacuuming power of the big international presence in Kabul, that sucked in the best people, so the new money did not grow a new state. This too was corruption. The average salary of 280,000 Afghan civil servants was $50 a month, while 50,000 Afghans working as support staff in the parallel state of the UN and international NGOs could earn $1,000 a month—a disparity that crippled the capacity of the state to recruit talent.[32] "Failure was built in from day one," according to one of Ghani's closest advisers, Scott Guggenheim, because of "a flood of people coming in here, with contractors and NGOs making fifteen times what a civil servant does."[33]

As I entered the World Food Programme compound in Kabul one day in 2006, the security guard told me his story. Like so many Afghans, his family were refugees. Living in a camp in the Northwest Frontier in Pakistan, he secured a university degree, and on his return to post-Taliban Afghanistan, wanting to contribute to building a new country, he worked in the Ministry of Higher Education. But he quit, as the salary for a security guard in an international agency was far higher than a graduate-level job in government. With two children, he made a rational choice.

The report card for the $1 billion spent on Accelerating Success was not good. Just one in ten of the new schools budgeted for were completed.[34] Many spending promises were never fulfilled and were not followed up as attention turned to Iraq. Money was spent on building capacity in a number of ministries, including health and education, but the programs did not deliver much. Staff quality was variable, and it was hard to get people willing to stay in Kabul. USAID had three directors in 2004, its agricultural program had five technical officers. Relatively junior staff were handling huge sums of money. Typically, the spending handled by each staff member in an overseas mission is $1.2 million. In Kabul in 2004, it was $27.5 million.[35]

Much of the spending was as if a mirage—on a balance sheet as aid to Afghanistan, but not getting near any Afghan. In some programs, less than 10 percent of the budget was actually spent on the ground, as the bulk of the funding went to computers, vehicles, salaries, travel, accommodation, and in particular security for Western staff. In an old Afghan proverb, it was like a "cow drinking its own milk."[36] When USAID did provide international consultants to the president's office, the chief of staff, Jawad, fired one who could not write a basic letter.[37]

The road from Kabul to Kandahar, a prestige early construction project, would become notorious for high cost, bad management, and poor quality of the final road—built using foreign contractors and thus not

putting money into Afghanistan. The temptations of "cost-plus" contracts, where bills were paid with little scrutiny, proved too great for the
company Louis Berger, which would settle with U.S. authorities for $69
million in 2010, with a further $17 million in 2015, as several senior staff
were convicted of fraud.

☰ ON BUDGET

There were ways of putting money on budget, through the state, without it fueling corruption. The World Bank created the Afghanistan Reconstruction Trust Fund (ARTF), which turned out to be a simple and
effective way of tracking donor money to limit corruption, funding
salaries, and delivering better roads, schools, and health facilities. Some
technical assistance programs were successful, delivering outcomes that
helped Afghanistan to stand up for itself. The Ministry of Finance was
transformed by externally funded advisers, who worked with the civil
servants who were there, rather than replacing them with highly paid
foreign-educated substitutes. This made it easier to bring modern com-
puting into an existing system, and it delivered results. By 2012, the analyst William Byrd, who once railed against an aid juggernaut, could write
that Afghanistan's capacity to manage public finances "far exceeds other
fragile or conflict-affected low income countries."[38] An initiative to increase the number of people and businesses who paid tax exceeded its
targets. Lines formed at new public taxation offices for people to register.

So not all aid was wasted. The National Solidarity Program was a popular and successful way of building local projects, which turned out to
be a corruption-resistant way of delivering development and building up
confidence in the state. Village committees decided how to spend grants
of around $20,000—small sums compared to other development spend-
ing. They would typically request a bridge, well, generator, or school.
Spending was transparent, and accounts were published on the wall of
the village mosque. At a meeting to decide how to spend the money, in a
village in Logar Province, I asked the backgrounds of those in the meeting. One had been a Communist, another a fighter for the mujahideen,
the next in the Taliban. But they all came together to build the new
Afghanistan and decide on how to manage the small funds now coming
to them. The scheme was wholly funded by international donors and
wholly administered by the Afghan state, but when I asked where they

thought the money came from, they said, "The government." So this was the best kind of international development support, building links between citizens and the state. With conventional USAID-funded schools coming in at around $350,000, and many not built well because of the problems of supervising subcontractors, these local projects were value for money. Fifteen National Solidarity Program schools could be built for the price of one USAID school.

≣ FIVE PILLARS AND A MAGIC CARPET

At the same time as the president announced Accelerating Success to fund development, Rumsfeld announced an end to combat operations, saying the eight thousand U.S. troops then in Afghanistan would move on to Phase IV—stabilization and reconstruction—and one of the most innovative commanders to head the U.S. military in Afghanistan, Lieutenant General David Barno, was appointed to make the change. The new commander of CENTCOM, General John Abizaid, who succeeded the war-fighting Tommy Franks in 2003, took a more nuanced approach to political/military relations. He told Barno to do "big POL and little MIL."[39] Barno expanded from a headquarters staff of six to four hundred in his nineteen months in command. Recognizing that the military were "bankrupt"[40] in doctrine to deal with the challenge of Afghanistan, he dusted off his cadet textbooks on counterinsurgency from West Point in 1974 and put them on the shelf in his office in Kabul when he arrived in October 2003.

Inspired by T. E. Lawrence (of Arabia)'s "Seven Pillars of Wisdom"[41]— Barno introduced "Five Pillars" for the campaign. Beyond defeating terrorism, they extended the reach of the military mission to good governance and regional relations, and most importantly, giving "area ownership" to military units. Until then, the war had been fought by units going out widely from fixed bases. Now troops would live in one area for the whole of their tour and get to know the local leaders informed by a slide that became known as Barno's "magic carpet,"[42] spreading about a dozen activities under the Five Pillars, mostly not involving the use of force. "Afghans' biggest concern," he said, "is not Americans and Westerners overstaying their welcome; it's the fear of abandonment." The memory of America leaving Afghanistan to the warlords and civil war after the defeat of the Soviet invasion was still fresh.

Barno proposed a series of guidelines to ensure that if American troops needed to raid a house, they would do it with least offense—using local troops, getting permission from elders, not separating women unless there were American women in the raiding party. These became known as the *Karzai Twelve*, although Karzai complained they were "never implemented."[43] To Barno, changing the mission 180 degrees from chasing terrorists to a counterinsurgency was like "tuning the car while you're going down the highway."[44] Visiting a battalion close to the Pakistan border, he asked, "How did you get your platoon leaders and company commanders and first sergeants and platoon sergeants to be able to shift gears here midstream and go from one to the other?" The colonel replied, "Easy, sir: booksamillion.com." They were reduced to sourcing what they could find on the internet, as they had had no training for the new kind of warfare.

Barno began to make the first real inroads into the tanks and artillery still held in some force by warlords across the country. Renewed conflict between the two northern warlords, Dostum and Nur, had been looming since Nur had taken the main town Mazar-e-Sharif. A total of 20,000 troops faced each other, supported by tanks and artillery pieces. A small force of 150 British soldiers in two PRTs succeeded in talking them down and persuaded Nur to hand over his heavy weapons, leaving him in control of the province—a result their commanding officer, Colonel Dickie Davis, said gave the PRTs "almost rock star status,"[45] leaving Dostum bruised but still armed. A similar robust approach by U.S. troops in the west reduced the arsenal in the hands of Ismail Khan, and by 2005, Fahim was persuaded to hand over some of his tanks and artillery as well, although disarmament still had a long way to go.

To ensure a coordinated strategy, Barno set up an office inside the U.S. embassy within twenty feet of the ambassador and spent part of every day there. This was welcomed by the new American ambassador, Zalmay Khalilzad, who arrived in Kabul soon after Barno in the fall of 2003. "Zal" is an imposing figure, with a large head and aquiline nose, and the demeanor of a senator in ancient Rome, updated in a charcoal-gray suit. He has deep brown eyes and a ready smile, and a reputation for finding a way through intractable situations, useful when he was appointed to do a peace deal with the Taliban in 2019.

Khalilzad has a unique place in the modern history of Afghanistan.

Born and brought up in Kabul, he had a scholarship to the American University of Beirut—moving to the U.S. before the Soviet invasion of Afghanistan in 1979. As a young academic, he wrote papers that were influential in hardening the resolve of the Reagan administration to support the mujahideen and was a State Department official in the peace talks in Geneva in 1988 to end that war. He was a hawk on Iraq, closely connected to neocons Richard Perle and Paul Wolfowitz, and was sent to Iraq days after the fall of Saddam Hussein but was pulled out soon afterward to serve as ambassador to the country of his birth. He spoke the two main Afghan languages, knew many of the key players from childhood, and had more nation-building ambition than some in the Bush administration. Coordinating with the U.S. military commander fitted his agenda.

Khalilzad saw progress as most likely coming through the private sector, bringing over a group of business leaders to improve coordination of development efforts. It was not seamless. Khalilzad's "cabinet" were given lead responsibility in areas such as energy, banking, governance, and infrastructure, duplicating the effort of USAID officials in his own embassy, who complained that none of the cabinet had been to Afghanistan before and would hold meetings with Afghan ministries without telling USAID colleagues. The ambassador's new team focused their "efforts on criticizing USAID rather than providing constructive advice," according to a Government Accountability Office (GAO) report, which went on with straight-faced understatement, "As a result animosity developed."[46]

There were some in USAID who wanted to do the big infrastructure spending requested by Ashraf Ghani, but they were overruled. Afghanistan had a number of dams and hydroelectric schemes from prewar days, all needing substantial repair. Insecurity and poor contracting decisions meant that it would take nine years after the fall of the Taliban before new turbines were in place for Kajaki—the power station in northern Helmand that supplied the south. Twenty years later, the power station was still not delivering full capacity, after $750 million had been spent on it. Meanwhile, a World Bank proposal for a $1 billion scheme to bring power lines from the north in 2002 was not funded, with the consequence that Kabul continued to rely on expensive diesel generators. USAID attempted to buy one-megawatt generators to power villages, but when the Iraq war started, they were not available, so they leased them instead at inflated prices—leaving no capacity behind when they pulled out.[47] Like the food aid that crashed wheat prices, the best intentions of longer-term development programs faced unintended consequences.

☰ NATO LEANS IN

Other forces as well as the Americans were beginning to move beyond Kabul. After Britain set up in the main northern city Mazar-e-Sharif, a month later, Germany opened a PRT at Kunduz in the northeast.[48] By the end of 2003, there were seven PRTs across the country, and another twelve opened the following year.[49] Germany wanted to repair relations with the U.S. badly torn by Iraq, and this fitted Rumsfeld's view that stabilization was what Europe and Canada did.[50] Old Europe leaned into the good war. There was never a coherent military decision to make a long-term commitment. It developed piecemeal, building one short-term decision on another, with rapid turnovers of people, until the Afghan campaign became a matter of organizational routine, built into the planning cycle across NATO.[51]

In handing over ISAF command from Turkey to Germany in February 2003, Lieutenant General Hilmi Akin Zorlu made a comment repeated often in the many handovers to come. He could see the time when troops could pull out of Afghanistan, but not for "two or three more years."[52] This was a plausible horizon, just beyond reach, requiring another rotation of troops, so that rather than decisive action at the start, a series of gradual increases built a huge military force, always there for "two or three more years."

ISAF command was handed over to General Rick Hillier from Canada in 2004, who, like Barno, believed international forces should be nation-builders. While preparing for the post, he met President Karzai, who told him the biggest threat was not the Taliban or al-Qaeda but Afghanistan's inability to function as a state. Karzai had seen plans come and go and complained of the incoherence of international assistance, telling Hillier, "The greatest way to help us overcome the threat to us is to help us build our ability to govern ourselves."[53]

Hillier liked to draw diagrams to find solutions, and on the way home, on an enforced layover of six to seven hours at the U.S. transit base in Uzbekistan waiting for delayed transport, he found a whiteboard and worked with his closest staff to draw up a plan that would become the

Strategic Advisory Team. His idea was to task twenty, mostly Canadian, officers to work across the Afghan government, giving technical support to help them to write laws and construct budgets—"basically teaching them the ABCs of responsible government."[54] He had no permission from NATO to do this, although it differed wildly from the street-patrolling that General Gerhard Back, the German head of NATO Joint Force Command at Brunssum in the Netherlands, thought was all they should do. Hillier derided Back as a "typical Cold War bureaucrat," and boasted of shouting matches with him on the phone.[55]

As Hillier saw it, the military should respond to the demands of the leader of the nation they were supporting. But with no coordination, the effect was limited. While Hillier was putting in his team, the UN was building links across the Afghan government for their reconstruction approach, and the U.S. government had a series of overlapping schemes, often with as little coordination within the American system as with outside agencies.

These initiatives lasted only as long as the commander who brought them in, as they were not part of an overarching plan. The straight-talking Canadian Hillier found that the Strategic Advisory Team did not survive his time in office; the French, Turkish, and Italian ISAF commanders who succeeded him had no interest in it. Hillier visited Kabul again the following year as Canada's chief of defence staff, and Karzai asked him to reboot the idea, which he did, using Canadian officers, with the support of an enthusiastic Canadian ambassador, Chris Alexander. But it was finally closed in 2008 when Ottawa pulled the plug and said they did not want the military doing what looked like civilian work. Hillier encountered one other obstacle in his command that all the commanders would face, and would worsen as the fighting intensified. Troops from individual countries, even his own, were not really under his command. He referred to the Canadian Battalion, code-named CANBAT, as *Can't Bat*.[56] If he asked Canadian troops to carry out a task, they sometimes needed seventy-two hours for approval from Ottawa. In Hillier's experience, only the UK and Norway were willing for him to use their troops flexibly.

The weak Afghan government system had now faced two activist, politically engaged military commanders in Kabul in Hillier and Barno, a U.S. aid system that was mostly contracting for its own ends, outside the state, with an ambassador's "cabinet" running different policies, and a myriad of other consultants writing assessments of need. Other big donors, Japan, the UK, and the World Bank had their own schemes and reporting structures, while there were various fiefdoms in the UN with contracting authority. The consequence was that in those early years the Afghan bonanza did more to perpetuate the warlord elite than build the state. Issues that really mattered to ordinary Afghans, in particular justice and property rights, deteriorated as corruption took hold. This gave an opening to the Taliban, who promoted themselves in reaction to the corrupt elite and began to recruit again with the promise of swift justice, clean government, and a nation free of foreign troops—a consistent message over many years to follow.

☰ BACK TO BASICS

The crucial decision that regularized command and control of the Afghan war, and the role of its commanders, was taken at NATO's Istanbul summit in June 2004. It put most forces in the country, including much of the U.S. combat strength, under ISAF command. The decision was taken in the face of American concern over the quality of NATO nations, seen as unwilling and ill equipped to fight. Retired general Barry McCaffrey, visiting Kabul to report progress to Abizaid, had a grim warning, referring to the worst moment in recent NATO history, when eight thousand Bosnian men and boys were murdered by Serb fighters in 1995 after a small Dutch force were disarmed and failed to defend them. "NATO-ISAF expansion to include the West and the South of Afghanistan would pose the immediate and real risk of another Srebrenica disaster with the population unprotected by an incapable or incompetent NATO force."[57]

Even after ISAF took over, there remained significant exceptions to this unified command, in the continued deployment of Special Forces and the twelve thousand conventional U.S. troops in Operation Enduring Freedom, on missions against the Taliban and al-Qaeda. This perpetuated an opaque military structure, and the public image of these different entities were never resolved for the whole of the long war. It would not be until four years later, under General David McKiernan in 2008, that all U.S. troops would come under ISAF. CIA operations remained unaccountable to the commanders in Afghanistan even then. Two commanders after McKiernan, General David Petraeus said "Lines of authority were confused in some cases ... when you're looking at SOF [special operations forces], and you've got black SOF, white SOF, coalition SOF, some U.S.-only SOF, it actually matters. You have to know what hat a guy is wearing at a particular time." This had a damaging effect when special operating forces carried out raids on the ground, leaving conventional forces to pick up the pieces although they had no control over the raids.

There would be one more American commander before the U.S. handed over strategic ownership of the Afghan war to NATO. Karl Eikenberry, who had been tasked with training the Afghan army in 2002, returned to Kabul, now with his third star as a lieutenant general, and took a very different view to Dave Barno. On arrival, he took one look at the Five Pillars and said, "That is ridiculous. That is like the Soviet Five-Year Plan."[58] He went back to basics, moved his office out of the embassy, tried to fire three heads of PRTs, and dismantled many Barno initiatives that went outside the conventional military lane.

This ended one of the most promising attempts to harness customs revenues for the state. Like many undeveloped economies, the biggest Afghan taxation stream was from customs revenues. There were seven main customs posts, much of whose revenue was captured by regional warlords. In an effort to reach a compromise as finance minister, Ghani pleaded to have access to the revenues from just two for the center, but was rejected.[59]

The border area at Herat between Afghanistan and Iran should be the most lucrative customs post in the country, because of a trade in used Japanese cars, shipped to the Gulf and then traveling overland across Iran and Afghanistan, toward Pakistan. In the early years after the fall of the Taliban, it was a lawless zone of bazaars. Ismail Khan, the warlord restored in the west in 2001 with U.S. support, had captured much of the revenue collection. Trucks driving through had to drop fuel into an underground tank, which was Ismail Khan's personal slice. Barno's British deputy, Major General Peter Gilchrist, ran a simple scheme to rebuild border fences, close down the bazaars, empty the fuel tank, and crucially to replace the border guards with a trained team from another province. Revenue collection immediately doubled. He wanted to roll it out nationwide, which could have transformed the revenue-earning capacity of the government, but it was scrapped by Eikenberry.

Back in Washington, Barno found his experience ignored. Although he had been the youngest lieutenant general of his generation, Afghanistan marked the effective end of his career. He was given a relatively mundane job and left the army a year later.[60] The relatively permissive security environment in the early years was deceptive. The Afghan conflict was about to enter its bloodiest phase: casualties among international troops were relatively light, but the Taliban were actively targeting development workers, killing eighty-one in 2005, mostly in isolated rural projects.[61] The West had backed the losing side in an ugly civil war. The winners of that civil war in the 1990s, the Taliban, had not gone away.

☰ THE PLACE OF THE SOLDIERS

Lieutenant Colonel Henry Worsley‡ stood in the Helmand town of Lashkar Gah in January 2006 and said quietly, "We've come here to police aid, but there's no aid to police." There were more reporters than soldiers on the street outside the base, as Britain wanted to signal its move into a wider role in Afghanistan; every soldier on this choreographed first street patrol was wearing a remote microphone. Britain never publicly acknowledges its special operators, but Worsley was a commander in the Special Air Service—the SAS.[62] He had been in Afghanistan for some months, gauging the temperature ahead of the arrival of British troops for the first time in the south and outlining the triple aim of providing security, governance, and development to village meetings, *shuras*. But from the beginning, he could see that governance and development would be starting from scratch. The presence of British soldiers would be like "stirring up a hornets' nest."[63]

Helmand is Afghanistan's largest province, about the size of West Virginia, with mountains in the north and a giant arid desert bordering Pakistan to the south—and always an unruly place. Although bordering the Taliban spiritual home in Kandahar to its east, they found it hard to control, only securing it in their last two years in power. During Taliban rule, their grip on order meant it was safe to travel across most of Afghanistan, except Helmand. Local rivalries between warlords meant that in the Taliban's early years, this was the only province you still needed

---

‡ Colonel Henry Worsley died in January 2016, within days of the end of an attempt to make the first solo unassisted crossing of the Antarctic by foot.

local armed guards in the car, changing at a checkpoint every twenty miles or so, and that "protection" of course came at a price. That's one of the reasons they could not outlaw poppy growing until close to the end of their regime, when they secured enough control of Helmand, the source of most of the world's illegal heroin. The main populated zone runs down the center of the province—a wide cultivated area on either side of the Helmand River, extended by the complex canal system built by U.S. engineers in the 1960s. The water from 40 percent of the land-mass of Afghanistan drains through this area.[64]

That first platoon was the advance guard of a deployment of more than three thousand troops as the UK took over the PRT in Lashkar Gah. The name of the town means "Place of the Soldiers." They were coming to a place with a long history of warfare.

Worsley was struck by the forcefulness of the elders he met. One said they did not want development but security. "I want to be safe, I want to be able to go to my local policeman and tell him I have a problem, because my house has been robbed . . . and I want a safe country."[65] The old man remembered Russian forces coming and they too promised development; he demanded to know if the British had the patience to see it through. The policy loop connecting security to development and diplomacy was about to be tested to destruction.

PHASE TWO

THE TALIBAN RETURN 2006–2009

THE BIGGEST WARLORD

What would Haji Nazar Muhammad think of it?
—President Karzai's appeal to remember the typical Afghan tribal elder

☰ THE BREEZE OF CHANGE

May 29, 2006. Kabul erupted in rioting, unnerving in its intensity. It began with a traffic accident. A U.S. military truck with poorly maintained brakes ran out of control on a hill way up in the north of the city, hitting several Afghan vehicles late in the afternoon when the streets were full of people. An angry crowd quickly gathered to confront the American soldiers, who shot five civilians dead to disperse them. As if on a secret command, the whole city rose up in anger, dragging foreigners from cars and beating them. A USAID guesthouse was burned to the ground. Crowds gathered around embassies, foreign-run offices, and residential accommodation, firing random shots, and thousands massed near ISAF headquarters. Kabul had grown since the fall of the Taliban five years before. Maybe five million people were now crammed together in makeshift mud housing clinging to the sides of the high mountains that surrounded the city. It was poor, and in the teeming alleys, Kabulis were quick to anger.

Gunmen broke through roadblocks to reach the heavily protected Pashtunistan Square outside the Arg, taking random shots at the seat of Afghan power. Afghan police were outgunned and isolated when the mobile phone network, their only communication system, became overloaded. An uncounted number of civilians died in the chaos before order was restored by Afghan and NATO troops firing live rounds.

Besieged and lonely in the Arg, President Karzai repeatedly watched footage of the riots, fearing this was the beginning of a coup.[1] But the mob were not acting on orders; they had risen spontaneously, sharing impatience with the pace of reform, the indignity of corruption, and a growing sense that international intervention had brought neither development nor security. And in the countryside, the Taliban were steadily gaining ground, exploiting the growing discontent.

Karzai was more rattled than at any time in his presidency. Frightened by the power of the mob, he told the U.S. ambassador Ron Neumann,[2] in the evening gloom as the riots died down in the streets outside, "If the people don't want me, maybe I should step down." The CIA station chief with Neumann told the president in brisk and undiplomatic language that his place was in the palace, and walking away would let down those who had died to put him there.[3]

The large rooms of the Arg, draped in red damask and lined by the ornate gilded stuffed chairs favored by Afghan dignitaries, told a tale of fading splendor. Karzai liked to remind foreign visitors of the fate of leaders who had tried to change Afghan society too radically. Many had died violently in that building. He was particularly keen not to be likened to Shah Shuja, installed by British force in 1838 and deposed in a general uprising three years later. The knowledge that he owed his position to America gnawed at him, challenging his sense of authority, even after he won his first presidential election in 2004.

Karzai's old-fashioned good manners disguised a deep sense of insecurity. Constantly needing reassurance, he held court daily in the Arg with tribal leaders from across the country. With his staff, he would test new policies by asking, "What would Haji Nazar Muhammad think of it?," conjuring a mythical village elder whose consent would be needed for reform. He did not focus on policy detail, nor military briefings, but wanted to keep his finger on the pulse of the Afghan village. It was this preoccupation that led to his growing differences with America.

At the start, Karzai was strongly in favor of the international military presence. In the 1990s, he had visited Washington on behalf of the mujahideen faction he supported, and welcomed America's reengagement in Afghanistan. He enthusiastically communicated the views of the many Haji Nazar Muhammads who wanted ISAF troops to go beyond Kabul. "People would visit me from all the provinces of the country and ask me to send them ISAF forces and to free them from militia forces, from warlords."[4] But this changed as he saw former Taliban fighters being arrested or killed when they were trying to make peace. "He felt embarrassed, as he could not give them protection," according to Jawed Ludin, who worked closely with Karzai in a number of roles, including as chief of staff and deputy foreign minister.

After 2004, when the ISAF mission changed and did begin to spread beyond Kabul, the number of civilians killed by American bombs and intrusive night raids darkened Karzai's mood. "The breeze of change began to blow: slowly, slowly," he said, "because of some of the bombardments that the Americans did on civilians; because of the bursting into people's homes at night; because of the disrespect of Afghan sovereignty that began to emerge."[5] The Afghan president's consent could no longer be assumed.

☰ "THREE YEARS AND WITHOUT FIRING A SHOT"

May 4, 2006. General David Richards, from the UK, took command at ISAF in a decisive year when it would move out to take on the whole country. He would be the first non-American officer to command U.S. troops in combat in NATO's first Article 5 operation, a mission he knew came with high political stakes. Embroiled in Iraq, President Bush quickly accepted Tony Blair's offer for Britain to take the lead. Richards came to Kabul with a headquarters staff who had been training for the task for a year,[6] far better prepared than any command group that came previously. But the improvised nature of the growth of the operation meant there was a lack of clarity of command as the war moved into a new phase.

When he arrived in May, there were four distinct regional theaters of operation. The west, where Italian troops were centered in Herat, and the north, with the Germans in Mazar-e-Sharif, were both relatively stable and under full ISAF command. The east, which would be last to come under ISAF in October 2006, was the main effort for the U.S. military and again had been relatively quiet until now, with patrols taking few casualties and attempting to win hearts and minds by operating mobile clinics in remote mountain villages. The fighting here intensified in the spring of 2006 as more Taliban fighters came across the porous mountain frontier with Pakistan—sending a grim message for the 2006 fighting season. The south was also still outside ISAF and under Operating

Enduring Freedom until 2006, answerable to a U.S. major general, Ben Freakley, at Bagram. So when the first three thousand British troops of 16 Air Assault Brigade arrived in Helmand Province in the southwest in the spring, they were not under the command of Richards, the most senior British officer, at ISAF. These tangled command lines would lead to confusion over priorities and tactics—adding to the hazards when the shooting really started that spring.

The essential contradiction at the heart of the Afghan war—between the U.S. counterterrorism mission, and NATO's plan for nation-building and reconstruction—was now laid bare. Brigadier Ed Butler, a former commander of the SAS, wrote simply, "The ends, ways and means of the two missions were diametrically opposed."[7] He thought the British mission to Helmand under-resourced from the start. Politicians never clearly articulated what the war was about and clearly had different views of it across NATO and within governments.

Butler commanded the incoming British brigade in the lead-up to Afghanistan, but was now moved up to overall command of the UK contingent in Afghanistan because it was decided he could not serve under a Canadian brigadier general commanding the south as they were the same rank. He had been of the small number of British Special Forces troops fighting alongside the U.S. against the Taliban in the first days of the war after 9/11. He had spent a year planning the Helmand operation, and contemplated resigning when he lost direct field command, a decision he felt "went against sound military judgement and previous good practice."[8] This lack of coherence in command felt designed for confusion and misunderstanding, and so it proved, just at a time when the Afghan war became far more violent, with rising casualties on all sides—among international forces, insurgent fighters, and, in far larger numbers, the Afghan people wretchedly caught in between.

Britain's initial plan had been to send troops to Kandahar, not Helmand, and NATO had hoped that Canada would send its three thousand troops to a multinational mission in the west alongside Italy. But Canada was intent on running its own war in the south. This was where its troops had been for a year during the far more peaceful days of 2002. Now that NATO was gearing up for a very different type of conflict, the Canadian Army wanted to show it could fight. Moreover General Rick Hillier, the ISAF commander in Kabul at the time the decision was taken in 2005, was now Canada's chief of defence staff and had a personal interest in the deployment. He had a forceful personality. Canadian forces "had rediscovered their mojo under Rick," said Richards. Britain stepped aside and took on Helmand.

The British government made this look like a coherent policy. Tony Blair had volunteered to take the international lead in combating opium poppy growing in the carve-up of roles at the 2001 Tokyo summit, and Helmand was the hotbed of the opium industry. So far, there had been little fighting in the south.

Butler saw it differently. In his pre-deployment report, he wrote, "The nature of the fight is likely to become a classic insurgency with a number of players, all with very different agendas."[9] There was no understanding of this in London, where he thought the government naive and their campaign plan "at best, a collection of essays, with no reference to theater."[10] An official told another senior officer in that first British brigade, Lieutenant Colonel Stuart Tootal, that he "didn't anticipate there being any trouble from the Taliban in Helmand." Butler and Tootal had talked to the SAS soldiers who had been into Helmand in 2005 to see the lay of the land ahead of the arrival of a larger force. Tribal elders pleaded with the British soldiers not to send more force. One SAS officer told the British author James Fergusson there would be a reaction from people who the SAS described as not necessarily Taliban, but "the community's warrior class who always defended their community against outsiders . . . The Taliban, in that sense were an enemy of our own creation." The SAS officer sent a memo to John Reid, the defence secretary, saying, in effect, "If you want an insurgency here you can have one."[11]

Reid ignored the advice, and the divergence between the expectations of the soldiers who would lead the mission from those who sent them, led to the most ill-judged comment by any foreign politician during the Afghan war. Reid, on his first visit to the region in 2006, made the remarkable observation that British troops "would be happy to leave in three years and without firing a shot." He meant they were there to back up development efforts—to police aid.

The comment followed a breakfast briefing in Kandahar. Reid told Butler he had been told in London this was a development support mission; no one in London talked about counterterrorism or counterinsurgency. Butler said that "three years and without firing a shot" was the sort of thing Reid must have been told by London officials.[12] Reid missed Butler's mocking contempt for the view. Wanting to promote nation-building, he seized the line for himself, taking it out to the press immediately after their meeting. Far from not firing a shot, by the end of their first tour, British soldiers had fired more than a million bullets.[13]

Butler, the plain-speaking ex–Special Forces fighter, put it simply: "The Task Force entered Helmand in April 2006 within a policy vacuum, which further undermined the ability of the ground commanders to provide clear direction to their troops." A later British commander in Helmand, Brigadier Andrew Mackay, said British troops first arrived in the province "with their eyes closed and fingers crossed."[14]

☰ "CLOUT, DON'T DRIBBLE"

David Richards is a short, charismatic man with a ready smile, who likes to bend the rules, calling the bluff of authority. He earned a green beret after completing the UK Royal Marine commando course precociously young after leaving school. Before leaving for Afghanistan, he lost two arguments. He did not have his own aircraft to move around the vast terrain of Afghanistan, and more importantly, he failed to get a reserve force. Fighting any military campaign without a reserve broke the most fundamental rules of warfare; it was such basic military doctrine that he was surprised he had to make the case, telling his superiors that "if you come up with a plan as a cadet at Sandhurst and you haven't got a reserve, you will fail the course." The problem with fighting without a reserve is that it assumes the best-case scenario all the time, which is unrealistic. At NATO, he reported to General Back, the Cold War throwback whom Rick Hillier had crossed when he was in Kabul. NATO headquarters at Brunssum still did not see this as a war-fighting operation. Back rejected all of Richards's demands.

To Richards, neither the military nor political leadership grasped the nature of the operation he was undertaking. In London, when he went for a pre-tour briefing, he was given a plan by a senior civil servant. He told her that it was different from the NATO plan he had been working on. She said, "Oh, don't worry about that. You're a British officer." To which Richards replied, "No, you've got it wrong. I'm a NATO officer.

I happen to be British and I will be implementing the NATO plan and you need to know what that plan is, because that's what we've signed up to as a nation."

Apart from the late decision as to where to send the troops, there were also questions about what equipment they should have. Richards was very sure that they needed to be able to demonstrate significant strength. The "biggest lesson coming out of Afghanistan" was the need to commit enough troops to deliver effect. A saying he liked to use was "Clout, don't dribble." Mass matters. He argued for artillery and Apache attack helicopters after Defence Secretary Reid approached him, with no officials present, to ask if they were needed. "We ended up having a clandestine breakfast meeting in Berlin when Reid was there for a NATO summit."[15] The lack of clear policy direction, a confused command structure, allies unwilling to take risks, misunderstandings about what was the UK and what was NATO, the separate U.S. mission, the late decision to go to Helmand, and secret meetings between ministers and generals—it felt like a very dangerous way to run a war. And what made this lack of understanding tragic was that the Afghan conflict was about to enter its bloodiest phase: casualties among international troops were relatively light until the end of 2005 but would rise steeply in the years after that.

≡ MOUNTAIN THRUST

When Richards arrived in May, a major U.S. military operation was underway in Helmand to shape the area before British troops moved out into the province. The decision to carry out Operation Mountain Thrust was taken by Major General Freakley at Bagram, an old-school conventional warfare infantry officer. He called Butler in to inform him of the decision. With British troops already moving into Helmand, Butler opposed the war-fighting plan, preferring more of a counterinsurgency approach, engaging with the population. He was concerned that a full-scale assault would only make things worse, alienating local people and stirring up the Taliban. And he knew that the UK force did not have the manpower to hold the areas that would be cleared.

Butler thought Freakley did not understand his role as commander of a national contingent, instead interpreting his reluctance to commit British troops to the clearance operation as "both insubordination and lack of commitment to the task force." Butler wanted talks with the

Taliban, which Freakley thought "worse than dealing with the devil."[16] Tempers rose when Butler talked of British superiority in past counter-insurgency conflicts. According to Freakley, although Butler later denied it, Butler said that Britain did not need to learn any lessons from the U.S. "We fought in Northern Ireland. You did Vietnam. We've got this." Freakley was "as mad as hell at that arrogant bastard."[17]

In practice, although he had been cut out of field command, Butler was part of a complex command loop for British forces in Helmand, guided by the British permanent joint headquarters in a James Bond–style underground complex set among redbrick suburban streets at Northwood, by Heathrow Airport in northwest London. But Butler was not in direct command of British troops, Freakley was. It was a recipe for confusion, misdirection, and resentment. Butler crisply described it as a "misalignment of the strategic levers of power."[18]

The American 10th Mountain Division troops, sent by Freakley from the east with the intent to disrupt the Taliban in advance of the UK troops arriving, were on the road for fifty-two days, covering more than five hundred miles, much on dirt roads or desert. They had almost no notice for the operation and withdrew from frontline positions in the east under cover of night so they would not signal any reduction in troop levels to the Taliban. Their commander, Lieutenant Colonel Chris Toner, said that from the moment they arrived in the south, they encountered a very different atmosphere from the east. Although fighting had been more intense in 2006 in the east than before, they felt they were still operating with consent. They continued to do medical clinics in remote villages to win confidence and received good intelligence in return. In the south, it was very different. From the moment they turned right from Highway 1 into the desert to head up to northern Helmand, every-one they met was hostile. Toner said that once they reached the town of Sangin, "There were just men, no women, no children. We should have realized we were going to have a fight."[19]

They set up base in the desert north of Musa Qala, the name meaning "Fortress of Moses," a town that would acquire totemic significance well beyond its size or local importance in the months and years to come. The Taliban were onto the Americans every time they moved. If a ve-hicle broke down, an ambush would be staged within twenty minutes. Toner said it was the weirdest place he had ever been. Lone Afghans on motorbikes emptied their weapons in the direction of the Americans and their Afghan army allies with no warning. It made them suspicious of everyone, corroding their relations with local people.

When they first arrived in the area, the Taliban did not attack; they were waiting. On the second day, Freakley came to see progress, and Toner took him to a meeting with local Afghans in the district center to talk about reconstruction, road building, and so on. The streets were teeming with men. "What I did not realize at the time was that I drove him through about three hundred Taliban fighters. I don't know why they didn't do anything. Maybe they were as surprised as we were." It changed the next day. In the fifty-two days of the operation, Toner's team fought twenty-two major firefights. The Taliban would lose men but still fight on. Toner remembers a fight where he had more than twenty U.S. vehicles firing heavy machine guns, but they were still put under pressure. "Nobody had ever seen that boldness or ability to maneuver or act from the enemy."

The British move into Helmand was already delayed by the delay of Dutch troops into the mountainous region of Uruzgan to its northeast. The Netherlands, backed by Australia, finally arrived after much indecision caused by the increased intensity of the threat. They deployed only after Australia effectively agreed to provide security for their base. Afghanistan was an increasingly hot war, and Richards knew that many countries who had committed to the new NATO/ISAF mission had a very low threshold of risk. He said, "I've often speculated that if they had known in 2004 what they knew in 2006, whether those people would have said yes to George Bush's request. I have an idea many more would have said no."

The delay in the British move to Helmand after Mountain Thrust meant the Taliban had more time to prepare. When British troops finally arrived in Helmand, three months late, the poppy harvest was about to begin, and more men would be available to fight once the harvest was in. What is extraordinary given the level of hostility encountered by 10th Mountain on their shaping operation is that British troops were still sent out into small forward bases—"platoon houses"—during the next few months. Richards was certainly opposed. "We are being bequeathed the proverbial dog's dinner," said Richards when he finally took command of the south, and so the whole country, in July, "a resurgent Taliban, a disillusioned population and corrupt, poppy-driven local administrations."

≡ HELMANDSHIRE

Before the troops arrived, Britain had already intervened by removing the governor of Helmand Province, Sher Muhammad Akhunzada—known by international troops as SMA, a significant power broker, and related by marriage to the president.[20] He was replaced by Muhammad Daoud, "a technocrat, not from the south," said Richards, "who didn't really know much about Helmand." Instead, pressure could have been put on SMA to be more moderate. "He did have the means through his own militias to have kept a lid on a lot of the problems that subsequently visited the British." Daoud was the right man at the wrong time—a technocrat with none of the skills to take on the warlords.

Removing SMA was done very crudely. Troops raided his office when they knew it would be full of sacks of raw opium resin. Like so much else in the country, defeating the narcotics trade lacked coordination. NATO was reluctant to make confronting this part of ISAF's military mission, and Richards strongly agreed because of the sheer scale of the challenge and because it distracted from the aim of securing the population. Destroying poppy fields hurt only poor farmers. But the year before, the U.S. had unilaterally decided to engage in large-scale eradication, contracting out the work to DynCorp, who employed a fleet of tractors fitted with chains rigged to the back to destroy poppy fields. SMA made a show of supporting the eradication, which he was able to channel onto fields planted by his competitors. As part of his desire to please, he stored caches of opium resin seized in raids ahead of widely publicized public burnings. British troops raided his compound knowing it to be full of one of these stores, ignoring the governor's protestations that he was holding it for the American eradicators. It was this "evidence" that enabled them to force Karzai to remove him from office, a decision he bitterly opposed.[21]

The defining feature of Helmand Province is the river that runs down the center—the populated zone along it widened by a latticework of American-built canals from the 1950s. This narrow area would see the most intense fighting of the Afghan conflict, and the names of its towns and villages would become familiar to the mainly American and British troops who would fight there. From Kajaki Dam in the north, running through Now Zad, Musa Qala, and Sangin, to the hamlets of Garmser in the south. Between north and south lies a wider populated zone around the provincial capital, Lashkar Gah, and smaller towns Gereshk and Nad Ali, where the canals provide irrigation to a far larger area. The original British plan had been not to move out of this main populated zone in central Helmand. But when the Taliban began to attack this settled area, Butler believed British forces needed to take the fight to the enemy. His first objective was Sangin—up the valley north, since it was the main launchpad for Taliban attacks. This move came despite a failed attempt by a British unit to establish a base in Sangin during Operation Mountain Thrust. The troops needed to be extracted again by helicopter without even staying one night, so intense was the firefight.

Despite this setback, British troops moved into platoon houses in a string of isolated Afghan towns after Freakley's shaping force withdrew to the east. These were set up in Afghan district centers, typically a large meeting room, with light perimeter defenses, in the string of towns up and down the Helmand River from Musa Qala in the north to Garmser in the south. In the months to come, Butler watched as they came under constant attack, unprecedented for the modern British Army, an "extraordinarily high-intensity period of 24/7 fighting not seen since the Korean War."

Richards knew that Lieutenant Colonel Tootal, the commander of the main British infantry unit 3 Para, was not keen on extending beyond the main town, Lashkar Gah, because Britain did not have enough force. But Richards had no say in this, because he did not have command of the south until July. He watched, frustrated, as British soldiers were thinly spread across a wide landscape and began to take casualties. They had even gone as far as Kajaki in the northeast of the province, where the hydroelectric scheme needed urgent repair work.

The most optimistic reading of the plan was that the troops would stabilize a town and provide security for development and government to return, spreading good governance across the landscape like ink on blotting paper to join with similar ink spots elsewhere. It was classic counterinsurgency strategy, based on the ultimately successful British operation in Malaya in the 1950s.[22] But rather than spreading the writ of the government in Helmand, in each small base, a few dozen men were pinned down in the suffocating heat of the summer, fighting for their lives. To Richards, it seemed "an arid strategy in that we weren't achieving any of the psychological enhancements—the security, the development, the slight whiff of growing prosperity that was so vital to the long term campaign. They were just fighting themselves to a standstill." Richards felt that his own government had a "little England" approach, that could not see Afghanistan beyond "Helmandshire," an Afghan province coopted as if a British possession.

The arguments between the American headquarters and senior British soldiers, and between national governments and their own troops on the ground, made Helmand feel dysfunctional in 2006—a series of private wars conducted by officers seemingly with their own agenda, strategy, tactics, and internal chains of command. Why was Freakley so keen to send an operation to disrupt the Taliban in Helmand? How could Butler have allowed British troops to be stretched out so thinly? Why did the government in London have such a slender grasp of the reality in Helmand that they thought they might leave "with not a shot fired"? Some of the answers lie in how little attention Afghanistan was receiving outside on the world stage in 2006, and the natural confusion of alliance warfare. When casualties increased in 2006, and it was clear that troops were not "policing aid," the response of the British Ministry of Defence was to restrict media access, apart from short, carefully shepherded trips, further obscuring the picture, and delaying rational decision-making. The military concentration on Helmand would continue in later years, when the deployment of U.S. Marines there formed a large part of the surge of troops ordered by President Obama in 2009.

Mike Martin, a British soldier who learned the Pashto language and worked as a political adviser, said that the battle in Helmand should not be seen in simple terms as between "the Taliban" and "the Afghan government." Instead, it was a series of interlocking tribal disputes, where foreign forces were unwittingly being used to settle old scores. "Taliban" was a badge of convenience against foreign invaders, but nothing more. On one occasion, he explained this to an incoming commanding officer but was told to keep quiet, since that was not how London saw it. The British Ministry of Defence tried to ban Martin's book explaining the complex terrain, preferring their simplistic analysis rather than facing the truth.

A British captain, Leo Docherty, resigned from the army at the end of the mission in protest at the move of British troops beyond the populated zone around the provincial capital. He watched as soldiers were scattered across Helmand "in a shallow, meaningless way ... where the only way for troops to survive is to increase the level of violence so more people get killed. It's not something I want to be part of."[23]

☰ OPERATION MEDUSA: THE "MAIN SET-PIECE BATTLE"

September 2006. Richards's focus moved from Helmand to neighboring Kandahar Province, where Canadian troops faced the first major battle of what would become quite a different war in Afghanistan. The need to take on a major Taliban command center in Panjwayi, south of Kandahar, became a pressing priority, since it was believed that the Taliban were now massing to attempt to retake the provincial capital, the spiritual heartland of both the Taliban themselves and the Durrani Pashtun tribes. There had already been one battle at Panjwayi on the Arghandab River, during the shaping and disrupting operations of the summer, but the Taliban were back in force. Their strength there went back to the decision to reinstate Gul Agha Sherzai in 2001, who directed major bombing operations against Mullah Naqib's supporters in the Arghandab Valley, turning the area into a hotbed of Taliban sympathizers.

Richards saw the operation, code-named Medusa, as the "main set-piece battle" of his time in Afghanistan. But during the planning phase, in contacts with his political masters in Europe, he did not mention the assault, fearing that political nervousness would get in the way of what he saw as clear military necessity—"Don't ask, don't tell, just do it." He was already being criticized by his superior officers in London for writing memos demanding extra troops and hinting at the risk of additional casualties if another battalion was not sent. "I felt I was being criticized for telling the truth, for fear of it upsetting our political masters."

He reported up a number of command chains in NATO, the U.S., and the UK. Most immediately, there was Brunssum, NATO's operational command center in the Netherlands. But there was also the NATO political center in Brussels. And he kept in contact with the Supreme Allied Commander Europe at the SHAPE headquarters in Mons, Belgium, as well as CENTCOM in Tampa, Florida, and the layers of military decision-making at his own Ministry of Defence and at the Northwood headquarters in the UK. The arguments he had on his way out to Afghanistan, about a reserve in particular, led him to believe that none of the bodies above him in the military hierarchy were really behind him. "I suppose in my mind it reinforced this determination of, bloody well just do as I felt was right, and sod those back up the chain of command ... they thought it was a walk in the park."[24]

He had to cajole nations to contribute troops to what he knew would be a tough fight. "The fact is that ultimately the nations decided, as opposed to the military commander. You had to construct a plan around that." Britain could not spare any troops for Medusa, pinned down as they were in Helmand, nor did the French offer troops.

The planning process for Operation Medusa forecast a bloody battle, with a cost that would be unacceptable in the capitals of most troop-contributing nations. According to Richards, "there was no guarantee that it would go that way, but the calculations were pretty well done." It was a situation that tested his judgment. "It's a command decision, not a medical decision, as to whether you accept the risk of casualties that are being predicted."

He succeeded in improving that grim calculus by employing more air-power and artillery, but even then, the strict requirements of the doctrinal template, analyzing the correlation of forces and determining the minimum size of an attacking force, were never met. The Taliban had a superiority of six to one, in a well-defended position, and even with airpower, that was not a comfortable ratio. Richards had to make the decision to go ahead without meeting the basic requirements of military doctrine. He owned the risk himself. This sense of planning for life or death set apart military command from any other executive office. It defined the difference between a CEO and a general.

Canadian troops were untested in a complex battle, although in the weeks before Medusa was launched, they faced a number of fierce Taliban assaults. Their commanding officer, Brigadier General David Fraser, wanted to delay the operation until October, when they would have Leopard tanks available, but both Richards and Freakley insisted they could not wait; there was a genuine fear that Kandahar could fall to the Taliban, and the presence of a Taliban stronghold so close to a major city had to be confronted. There were several hundred, possibly thousands of Taliban in well-defended positions on ground they knew well, and they could reinforce with fresh recruits with ease.

Zero hour for the ground offensive in Operation Medusa was

Sunday, September 3, after two days of artillery and airstrikes, including a confirmed hit on a group of senior Taliban leaders at a meeting. It was brought forward at the last minute by Freakley, after intelligence revealed that Taliban were seen to be leaving because of the intensity of the bombardment. He called to say, "They're leaving, you're letting them out of the bag."[25] Richards watched initially from Kabul as a battle began that would determine so much and was in the end "a very close-run thing."

The Taliban were confident of the strength of their position, but that, according to Richards, "was their undoing," giving them a false sense of security. They were dug into "an old-fashioned defensive position with three lines of trenches, and underground shelters straight out of a military manual." There was even a fully equipped field hospital in the complex of trenches and tunnels dug through the tight-packed mud walls of vineyards. Dotted among the tunnels were hardened bunkers with steel joists for blast protection. Thick fields of marijuana up to eight feet high hampered thermal imaging capability because of the heat-absorbing capacity of the plant. The Taliban converted raised sheds, built for drying grapes, into firing platforms, shooting through the ventilation holes, while protected behind thick mud walls that were as good as modern armor. They had sown substantial numbers of pressure-triggered IEDs in the ground ahead of them and widened a canal to make it harder for vehicles to cross the steep sides.

The assault began with virtually the whole Canadian battle group attacking across a wide riverbed. The Canadians made good ground but took significant casualties, four dead and eight wounded. Richards worried when they stopped at nightfall and returned across the riverbed, impatient that they might lose momentum. "It was for resupply, but normally you wouldn't give up ground." He had a virtually sleepless night.

Next morning, eating breakfast in the half-light of dawn before making a fresh assault, Canadian troops were targeted by an A-10 Warthog—whose Gatling gun tore through the unit, killing a former Olympic athlete, Private Mark Graham, and wounding thirty-five others, including the commanding officer of the assault company.[26] The American plane had mistaken which side of the river they were on and mistook their burning garbage for a Taliban campfire. Another A-10, hard on the heels of the first, was called off the raid just in time. It was a bitter irony that it was the heavier airpower Richards had demanded that caused this disaster.

The assault took the main infantry capacity out of the center of the Canadian front line. A sergeant who survived the attack, Brent Crellin, said of the blasts hitting the ground around him, "There were sparks in the dust, like the sparklers you wave on Canada Day." The front lines were so close, and the smoke in the air so confusing, that a Chinook called in to carry out the wounded landed for a few seconds among Taliban fighters and amazingly was not shot at. The incident led to a significant loss of nerve on the part of Canadian officers—one was threatened with being removed from command if he did not get a grip.

Richards wanted to be on the spot and arrived in Kandahar on Wednesday, two days after the A-10 strike, to find the Canadian commander, Brigadier General Fraser, close to calling off the whole operation. He had sent a somber and gloomy assessment home to Ottawa, which Richards thought "hugely magnified concerns about further casualties"[27] and led to the brakes being put on. Richards tried to put some steel back into the battle and, severely worried about the loss of momentum, returned to another almost sleepless night in Kabul, calling Ottawa himself. "I was very worried that NATO was about to be defeated on its first major challenge and I was going to be remembered as the general that lost NATO's first war and first big battle."

In the event, the fighting restarted virtually spontaneously, backed by a determined U.S. assault into the defensive trench system from the south of the Taliban stronghold, where an attack was least expected. The ad hoc force included troops from 10th Mountain, who had just returned to their posts in the east after fighting the intense battles to shape Helmand ahead of the arrival of British forces. They turned round again to head back to the fight when they got the call and, as the situation was so precarious, fought with no sleep after driving all night.

After the new U.S. force entered the trench system from the south, the Canadians' fresh assault in the middle broke Taliban resistance. It was a rough-hewn improvised operation. Canadian engineers had to clear safe routes through the IED-strewn ground and deploy a bulldozer to cut through thick mud farm walls. The Taliban were so confident of victory that they continued to bring in reserves after the start of the battle and took very heavy casualties, possibly as high as one thousand—although the lack of supporting troops beyond those engaged in the operation meant there was no effective cordon, and hundreds of Taliban fighters escaped. The fighting took a week, and civilian casualties were reduced to a minimum by warnings of the impending assault. Before the offensive began NATO forces saw streams of thousands of old men, women and children leaving the battle zone.

Richards was jubilant. He felt that "NATO had come of age." Kandahar had been saved, and many Afghans were in no doubt of its significance. When he returned to Kabul, he "had never been hugged by so many men in beards in my life." Neither President Karzai nor the higher command levels of NATO had realized how narrow the margins were, or how close the Canadian troops had been to losing.

The soldiers who did the fighting, at the cost of five dead and forty wounded on the ground, knew that the Taliban would be back.[28] Canadian troops and their allies could not hold the ground. Intelligence estimates suggested that twelve thousand Taliban fighters came into the south in 2006. "The Taliban flowed in immediately behind the withdrawing troops," according to the commander of the assault force at Operation Medusa, Lieutenant Colonel Omer Lavoie. "Now we must go and retake them again, compound by compound."

But any planned Taliban offensive on Kandahar had been stopped. If the southern city had fallen in 2006, the government in Kabul would have been threatened. Despite the success, Richards knew that his superiors did not trust him. "After all we have achieved against the odds," he wrote in his diary, "bollocks to the pusillanimous, ignorant and cravenly political lot of them."[29] His success in Kandahar would be quickly overshadowed by an impending crisis in Helmand that dominated his remaining months in command.

☰ ANOTHER MAIWAND IN MUSA QALA?

The intensity of fighting for British troops, strung out in isolated posts across Helmand, led to Butler proposing they withdraw, at least from the remotest, Musa Qala in the north. Richards knew it would be used by the Taliban—"another Maiwand," referring to the nineteenth-century defeat of British forces in the same area. The artillery regiment where he began his military service had a "Maiwand Battery" in memory of the battle; every Afghan knew the story of the British defeat. He had been opposed to British troops going up as far north as Musa Qala but now was against them leaving, and was involved in arguments with Butler, who did not want to risk any more casualties after a fierce summer of fighting. The crunch point came when it became impossible to secure a landing site for a Chinook. The Taliban would have greatly benefited from the propaganda value if one had been shot down—not to mention the loss of life it would have entailed. The big twin-rotored helicopters were the workhorses of the Afghan war, but if they could no longer land near Musa Qala, then medevacing the injured would become impossible. One pilot had already been given a medal for touching down only the rear wheels of his Chinook in a space between houses, then hovering with the front in the air, while wounded were loaded on board.

As a fig leaf to cover withdrawal, British forces handed over Musa Qala to local elders, who said they would not allow the Taliban within four kilometers of the center. Richards tried to make the best of this deal, calling it a redeployment, not a pullout. "The security of Musa Qala itself, the town, is now ok. So we don't need to stay there any more, we can use them in other ways."[30] He claimed it was the same kind of deal that U.S. forces had done to bring security to the countryside in Iraq by empowering tribal elders: "I had a lot of intelligent American interest in how you might make this work. President Karzai absolutely knew all about it and encouraged it and it was all being held up as an example of the way things might work out. It was, if you like, an experiment in practice."

No one believed it. No amount of spin would diminish the humiliation, made worse by TV pictures of the evacuation of British soldiers on locally hired "jingle trucks"—with brightly colored silver chains hanging down and flashing in the sun. U.S. forces in the country, particularly those who had fought hard in the operation in June to disrupt the Taliban in Helmand, were contemptuous. Ambassador Neumann met with Richards and got an assurance that no deals like it would be struck again. Neumann felt the political impact when several delegations of worried Afghans came to remind him of how their wily mujahideen commander Ahmed Shah Massoud would do similar deals with the Russians during their occupation. The elders warned him that Massoud would use the breathing space to regroup and build up his forces.[31] "Musa Qala was unimportant in itself," said Neumann. "The problem was political. It sent a message reverberating round Afghanistan that the Taliban were going to end up with safe havens."[32] And Richards knew it. He confided to his diary that Britain was in danger of becoming "ISAF's laughing stock," because of continued failure in Helmand. Officials were going round Kabul claiming that it was some kind of exemplar province, but little of any substance was happening other than fighting. He blamed his own country for being "inward-looking and lacking in vision at both the strategic and tactical level."

☰ PLEASE ASK THE GENERAL

Richards enjoyed his reputation for making his views known and leading from the front. In 2000, he mobilized resistance to a takeover of Free-town in Sierra Leone, going well beyond his stated mission, which was to evacuate the government and British citizens. When reminded of what he had been sent for, he cheerfully said, "Bugger the orders!"[33] Freetown was threatened by a murderous rebel army, the Revolutionary United Front (RUF), which specialized in cutting the hands off civilians, including children, with machetes. The RUF were stopped by a coalition of British troops, foreign mercenaries, and various local militias, including a notorious band called the Westside Boys, who were persuaded to come on the government side. A small UN force also played its part. Richards wanted to apply the full spectrum of tools available for influence, knowing that victory is about perception of power as much as its application. The government stood firm, backed by a small force, judiciously applied, because the people believed they could win. "We started to do what they should have been doing in the first place, but hadn't realized."[34] The key lesson he took away from Sierra Leone was not so much about the application of military force but more about the psychology of war.

In Afghanistan, the need he first identified when he arrived was to im-prove international coordination. He found a system of "ad hoc phone calls, visits, no mechanism for bringing it all together." He proposed a committee to bring together people responsible for development, gover-nance, and security so that efforts would be more effective. Hanif Atmar, a British-educated and reform-minded minister, told him Karzai would never agree, because it gave away too much power. Karzai did things like a traditional tribal elder, not sharing too much because, to him, "information, knowledge, was power." Richards understood these pressures. He knew that Karzai had to balance the influence of the warlords. But as one elder said at a meeting in the palace, with Richards's thirty-five thousand international troops, he was the "biggest warlord now." And he wanted to use that to change things.

His opportunity came early in his command when the sudden rioting in Kabul shifted the power balance. "Karzai was used to the warlords," Richards observed. "But suddenly it was the people as well" exerting a new and frightening power. And in the wake of the riots, he persuaded the Afghan president to agree to a policy action group (PAG) that would bring together key international players with senior Afghan ministers in a coordinating committee chaired by Karzai himself.[35] Karzai found it hard enough to deal with the uncoordinated and sometimes competing demands from different parts of the U.S. system, let alone the burgeoning international presence in Kabul. He would ask his staff, "Which is the real America?"[36] Richards persuaded him to implement the PAG.

For Richards, with his proactive personality, it filled a gap left by the lack of coordination. He felt he had to step in because "there was no diplomatic big hitter" in Kabul. "The military effort was not matched by a civilian one."[37] Unlike some of the later commanders, this was where Richards felt comfortable: playing in the political sphere as well as applying military force. As a schoolboy, he studied the speeches of Winston Churchill and would go off to the woods to practice speeches.

Was he exceeding his authority as a military commander in introducing a political mechanism? Like Hillier, he liked to think that he was someone who "spoke truth to power" and did not ask permission from his NATO chain of command in Europe to do it, realizing that decision-making there took months and would stifle his ability to command in an agile way. The way he extended his reach led to comparisons with the legendary innovator in counterinsurgency warfare, Field Marshal Sir Gerald Templer in Malaya in the 1950s. "I sometimes wonder if I am a politician or a soldier," he wrote.[38]

But he saw one crucial difference—Templer "had all the organs of the state under his command." Unlike British imperial adventures, Richards realized the Afghan government was not under his control, nor did he have flexible command of the troops on the ground. As soon as decisions were referred back by members of the alliance to national capitals, "it was paralysis." There was one lesson from Templer that Richards knew, but was too often forgotten during the long war in Afghanistan—it took twelve years to settle Malaya. Even the most successful counterinsurgency operations take time.

The policy action group ruffled feathers in the small diplomatic community in Kabul. A London summit in January agreed a different mechanism, which met twice a year, too slow for Richards. His was a divisive policy; ambassadors of nations excluded from the group felt it a criticism of what they had been doing. The acronym PAG was mocked as "Please Ask the General" and "President Asks the General." Richards was making his mark.

He was aware that aid organizations also had a role, and he opened ISAF HQ on some Thursday evenings to aid workers and others. Richards had no illusions about them. "Anyone who thinks they're meek and mild and only do-gooders, forget it; you have to see them for what they are, which is, on the whole, very competent organizations who ruthlessly propagate their own intents." He knew too that they could be useful sources of intelligence who were better inside the tent understanding something of the military mindset.

Thursday evenings at ISAF HQ became legendary in the summer of 2006—"like something from the Raj," according to one official, as lines of Afghan ministers, ambassadors, and aid workers rubbed shoulders with journalists and soldiers sitting at tables with crisp tablecloths. To Richards this was vital coordination, helping to forge links. He had his own political advisory team, the Prism group, to keep across what was going on.

All of this was in accord with his commander's intent, written on a single sheet of paper, widely circulated around ISAF, that defined his mission. The language was focused on building a new nation, not defeating the Taliban and al-Qaeda, referring, for example to the protection of water, power, and mineral resources. Richards described his "Main Effort" as not to chase terrorists but to "extend and deepen" the areas where the government, international agencies, and NGOs could safely operate. To him, the mission priority was changing the political narrative, not piling up bodies of the enemy dead.

He made clear in his commander's intent that "where necessary, traditional military force would be required." But it would always be for a "greater purpose" than destroying the Taliban. It was to create the conditions for a new state to emerge that governed with the consent of the people. Richards could see that international forces were not going to "win" in a conventional military sense—insurgencies are rarely quelled in that way. Some of his superiors questioned whether he emphasized the use of force enough, but his plan was consistent with the NATO strategy, and they backed him. Richards knew, though, he would have a problem explaining the emphasis to "many Americans" in Afghanistan "who hitherto had been more focused on just beating the Taliban in a military sense."

He was responding to the same dilemma faced by all the ISAF commanders—how to find the right balance between war fighting and the political aspects of counterinsurgency, and coming down very much for counterinsurgency. But he did not have the force levels needed to engage in the population-centric approach he wanted in such a large country. And he overreached himself in one plan—for Afghan development zones (ADZ), a new application of classical counterinsurgency doctrine again going back to Malaya in the 1950s. Development and governance would move out from centers that were protected by the military.

Richards always saw security as a means to an end—development and governance should provide the lead. More ambitious than the existing PRT idea, the ADZ was a "cohering mechanism that required all those trying to help a province, whether military or non-military, Afghan or international, to work closely together in a common cause." There was opposition to the idea from his European allies, in particular France and Germany, although it was very similar to the "eighty secure districts" plan eventually introduced by General David Petraeus in 2010. Richards never had anything approaching the money or troops that were later available to Petraeus. Distracted by Iraq, policy makers did not put the resources needed into Afghanistan until the situation had dramatically deteriorated and it was almost too late.

☰ WHO IS THE FIVE STAR?

U.S. defense secretary Donald Rumsfeld came to Kabul a few days before the first expansion of NATO's ISAF command in July. As U.S.

troops would be directly under Richards's command, Rumsfeld wanted to meet him. When Rumsfeld asked why things were getting worse in the south, Richards replied that there were not enough resources to make people confident of ISAF intentions, and in too many places, the Taliban were being welcomed back. There were "insufficient troops and insufficient resources. The Taliban have realized this and they are coming back in. We have not met all our promises, so people are a little frustrated." The lack of resources was a constant problem for all the ISAF commanders, and he was voicing the concern to the man most responsible for it, a true believer and the original architect of the light military footprint. Rumsfeld closed the conversation with a curt reply: "General, I don't agree, move on."

Later that day, Rumsfeld singled out Richards among the group accompanying him for a meeting with the president. He asked Karzai, "What do you think of General Richard [sic]." And Karzai replied, "I like General Richard. What do you think of General Richard." Rumsfeld's reply was a put-down, and a clear response to him speaking his mind. "I like General Richard too. There is only one thing I would say about General Richard: he is sometimes confused about who is the three star and who is the five star." At the time, Richards still had three stars as a lieutenant general. His fourth star, and promotion to full general, would come when he took over command of the east, and so the whole country, in October.

Control of the east put Richards in direct command of Freakley, the competent, hard-bitten, and opinionated U.S. two-star general whose commitment to development he doubted. He had no doubt of Freakley's capacity to run a battle, but that was not enough in a senior commander. "If I was in a major fight, I'd want Freakley running it for me, and indeed, I'd probably want him to tell me what to do. His problem was that he was very black and white in his interpretation. As you got more senior, and shades of gray start to affect decision-making, he didn't have much time for that." Richards noted in his diary at the end of June:

> I'm not certain that Ben Freakley yet has his heart in it. Everything about him suggests resentment, and absolute focus on so-called kinetic solutions. He doesn't seem to understand that we're not going to do things in the way the US has done them. Even if we could,

which we can't, I would not want to. Herein lies the source of his resentment. It's combined with the belief that we don't appreciate the strength of the enemy, but even this is not that pertinent. He thinks we can defeat the Taliban principally through killing more of them. I don't share this view, seeing it as just one weapon in the armory, along with much speedier reconstruction and development, a political outreach program, and much else.[39]

And even after he had assumed command of all of Afghanistan, bringing the east under the NATO umbrella, many U.S. troops remained outside that structure, some in Special Forces, and others under the umbrella of Operation Enduring Freedom, the original Afghan mission of destroying al-Qaeda. Fourteen thousand U.S. troops were inside the NATO tent, but twelve thousand were outside, and hence outside his legal command and carrying on their own secret war in Afghanistan. Their commanding officer understood that this might cause problems, and although he could not give Richards opcon (operational control), he coined the term *warcon,* a common-sense arrangement, under which the ISAF HQ was made aware of what the Americans were doing. This meant that Richards was not embarrassed when he had to stand up in front of TV cameras, or the Afghan president, and explain when things went wrong. To the Afghans, it did not matter if a misdirected air strike came from OEF or ISAF—and Richards was the front man for both operations, so warcon was a valuable tool.

To the Americans in Afghanistan, there were advantages in having a senior British commander; it was a counter to the criticism that this was an all-American occupation. Ambassador Neumann was grateful to Richards for telling ISAF headquarters they should listen to him, Neumann, because of America's large role in the country. "If an American commander of NATO had said the same thing, this would have been seen as the American cabal at NATO trying to put everybody else down."[40]

Relations were not always good. In October, the Special Forces HQ gave Richards details of a suspect Taliban group they were monitoring near Musa Qala. Richards believed that they were probably there to talk to tribal elders, and killing them would cause "a huge problem of strategic scale." The U.S. officer replied that if Richards did not "have the stomach to kill them," then Special Forces would bomb them regardless.[41]

4

THE HEART OF THE BEAST

As the sun of civilization rose above the hills, the fair flowers of commerce unfolded and the streams of supply and demand, hitherto congealed by the frost of barbarism, were thawed.

—Winston S. Churchill on the effect of road-building, 1897

☰ METAPHORICAL BULLETS

In 1897, Britain, then controlling India, fought a war on the Afghan frontier to push a road north to Chitral. As a young war correspondent, Winston Churchill saw the road as bringing civilization, opposed by those who depended on the "ignorance and credulity" of the tribes.[1] Just a few miles away on the other side of the mountains on the same frontier in Kunar, 109 years later, Lieutenant Colonel Chris Cavoli echoed Churchill's "fair flowers of commerce" when he noted "surplus crops are growing and being sold" on new roads being pushed through remote valleys. A road that opened up the Kunar provincial capital, Asadabad, to the main ring road to the south for the first time led to the opening of two savings banks and the establishment of the National Solidarity Program, the main Afghan government development initiative. But Churchill would have been surprised by the challenges Cavoli faced to secure support to push these roads through.

Cavoli's commander was Colonel John W. "Mick" Nicholson, on the first of six tours connected with Afghanistan, culminating as the commander of Resolute Support in Kabul ten years later. He was distantly related to another General John Nicholson, a British commander pacifying tribes on the other side of the same frontier in the 1850s.[2]

In 2006, Nicholson was determined to turn the dial toward counterinsurgency for the deployment of 3rd Brigade, 10th Mountain, in Task Force Spartan. This entailed a four-part plan—secure the people, separate them from the enemy, help them choose their own leaders, and connect them to the government.[3] But Nicholson had trouble standing up the political and development support he needed. He had political advisers who could describe what was going on but who had no capacity to build government at a local level, and development advisers who opposed his plans to build a road.

To the military, this is a moral question, particularly if engaged in counterinsurgency, fighting not just to kill terrorists but win over the population. To separate the terrorists from the people, they needed to offer improvement—roads, schools, clean water, and better government. The year before, in the same area of operations, trying to bring development behind their military maneuvers, the commander of 1st Brigade, 82nd Airborne, Task Force Devil, Colonel Pat Donahue, and his deputy Lieutenant Colonel Mike Fenzel, found themselves facing "staggering gaps in communication, cooperation and collaboration between various agencies." USAID officials in the field worked on contracts with "no explicit provisions for cooperation": their "bureaucratic necessities proved universally frustrating."[4] Colonel William B. Ostlund, commander of 2nd Battalion, 503rd Infantry, Task Force Rock, later in the same region questioned why he could expend "millions of dollars on ordnance in an afternoon with no questions asked," but to spend thousands on development needed an agreement that could take weeks. "Dollars are nonlethal effects," he wrote, "metaphorical bullets."[5]

This was more than a turf war between different Washington silos for control. If America wanted to deliver a difference in Afghanistan beyond chasing al-Qaeda, the approach needed coherence. USAID relied on the military for security in the field but took a principled stand against being enmeshed in their agenda. USAID funding was neither coordinated with the military effort nor building a resilient state. Instead, too much American cash went into the parallel warlord economy, making life harder both for the international military presence and the Afghan state. It took until 2009 to reach an agreement that USAID would assist in development programs for what was called *hot stabilization*.[6] But it came with a stern warning that humanitarian assistance "must not be used for the purpose of political gain, relationship-building, or winning hearts and minds."[7]

There are three sections to the Afghan frontier to Pakistan—a mostly mountainous region that hosts one-fifth of the world's terrorist groups. "This is where the war started," said Nicholson. "The heart of the beast of al-Qaeda."[8] The most intense firefights were in the northernmost— "N2K" running from Nuristan through Kunar and Nangarhar down to the Khyber Pass. South of the Khyber Pass is "P2K"—Paktika, Paktia, and Khost. In these two sections, the frontier runs down impenetrable mountain ranges, which is why the few wider areas for movement, like the Pech Valley, are strategically important. In the southernmost section, wrapping round the bottom of Afghanistan to Kandahar and Helmand, the border is in many places an ill-defined line in the sand of the desert.

Nicholson knew that the "Pashtun tribes don't think much of the border." With close family links, the people ignored the legal border. His solution was to focus on the tribes. "If there's infiltration occurring in an area, we don't look at it as a border problem, we look at it as a tribal problem. So we'll go to the elders of that tribe and say look, you are allowing enemy, bad people, to transit your area and attack your government. And you need to stop it."[9]

As so often in the long war, the government on the other side of the frontier made the job of U.S. soldiers far harder. In 2006, Pakistan negotiated a peace deal with the tribes of North Waziristan, across the frontier from P2K, a hotbed of Islamist militancy and the main support network for Jalaluddin Haqqani, responsible for some of the most murderous suicide bomb attacks in Afghan cities. The peace deal had several conditions that were problematic for American forces on the other side—not least the reduction of Pakistani patrols and removal of checkpoints. As cross-border attacks increased Nicholson's response was to engage the elders on his side. The risks were obvious. Three days after one well-known elder signed a contract for business with the American forces, his body was found near the border, with a note pinned to it as a warning.

☰ KORENGAL

Nicholson and Cavoli did succeed in building roads both north and south, connecting the capital of the east, Jalalabad, to Kunar's provincial capital, Asadabad, then pushing west through the wide, flat, densely populated Pech Valley, some funded by USAID and some by military CERP money. After a visit, the counterinsurgency expert David Kilcullen said the achievement was not the fact of the roads but the *process* of construction—engaging the local tribal leadership, employing people, increasing their incentive to protect the road, connecting people to government, and limiting the space for insurgents. This was "political maneuver as a counterinsurgency technique,"[10] fulfilling what he saw as a "moral obligation" to defend people who have made "the dangerous choice to side with the government."[11]

Nicholson's focus on road-building and governance did not mean there was less fighting. During his fifteen months in command, he dropped 75 percent of the bombs dropped across the whole country in this small corner of the northeast. The war in the mountains was becoming as intense a daily firefight as in Helmand at the same time. The area would see some of the biggest losses of American life in single incidents in the long war. The first casualties came in April 2005 before the push of troops into the valleys, when nineteen special operators were killed in a valley whose name, Korengal, would become notorious. A four-man SEAL team was ambushed and killed, and fifteen others died when a rescue helicopter was shot down by a rocket-propelled grenade.

The Korengal Valley is only a few miles long, winding south from the Pech Valley between very steep wooded hillsides. The Korengali people live in stone houses, built against the hillsides. They speak a different language from the people of the Pech Valley, running east-west, and from those in the Waigal Valley, a longer deep valley running north. Fighting in these steep valleys north and south of the Pech was as tough as any in the war. Without enough forces, soldiers set up small outposts on peaks, but there was always a higher slope. In 2007, Captain Dan Kearney led Battle Company of the 173rd Airborne Brigade Combat Team to a hill that had been in Taliban hands overlooking the Korengal combat outpost, and they lived there for fifteen months, calling the new setup of tents and wooden huts Restrepo, after Private First Class Juan "Doc" Restrepo, the platoon medic, killed in the first days of their tour. Kearney said in *Restrepo,* the feature film about their deployment, that they felt "like fish in a barrel."[12] They filled huge Hesco canvas and wire baskets with earth from inside the base, shovel by shovel, to form their only defense. They came under daily attack and found Pakistani cell phone numbers painted onto rocks for potential local recruits to call.[13]

There were mysteries behind every stone. General David McKiernan, who commanded ISAF from 2008 to 2009, knew that the nature of the landscape—deep, wooded ravines and high snow-peaked mountains—bred a people suspicious of their neighbors in the next valley, let alone young foreigners from seven thousand miles away. "It is Hatfields and McCoys times a hundred,"[14] he said, comparing it to nineteenth-century clan wars on the West Virginia / Kentucky border. "There are languages that are spoken, dialects in the east, that are not understood outside that local tribal clan area." Among the people living in the Waigal are two tribes named after the different cheese they produced—determining the ways they managed their dairy cattle and competed for use of pasture.[15] And that was where America's problems began. Since education in this mountain fastness was limited, translators tended to come from the cities and lacked nuanced knowledge to deal with local complexity at this granular level.

After the Taliban fell, "everybody was supporting the Americans," according to the governor of Nuristan province, Muhammad Tamim Nuristani. But as elsewhere in Afghanistan, the focus in the early years of the war on chasing terrorists led to people naming their enemies as supporters of al-Qaeda, using air strikes to settle old feuds. "Whether information was wrong or right they gave $100," and animosity grew as the bombs fell. "Because of that we lost opportunity in the first three years to do anything," said Nuristani.[16] By the time Nicholson's Task Force Spartan arrived, separating the people from the insurgents, in particular in the Korengal Valley, was a hard task.

To deny space to the enemy, Nicholson put troops into 120 small combat outposts, typically with twenty to fifty Americans, alongside as many Afghan troops. But there were never enough to dominate the ground for counterinsurgency; he had one brigade where there would be fifteen in Iraq. Nor did he have enough other capability in other areas like helicopters or intelligence, surveillance, and reconnaissance (ISR). And he was facing a dramatic increase in the number of insurgents using the mountain trails that laced the frontier region. "In 2006," according to Ron Neumann, the U.S. ambassador to Kabul, "infiltration into Afghanistan increased several fold."[17] Pakistani forces turned a blind eye to the traffic across the frontier when they did not actually support it. In this respect more than any other, there was a direct parallel with Vietnam, where America faced an enemy with seemingly limitless supplies of fighters and weapons across a land border.

☰ BATTLE OF WANAT

The worst U.S. losses in the east came after Nicholson's time. In July 2008, nine Americans died in a determined assault on a new U.S. base at Wanat in the Waigal Valley. The lead-up to the incident is disputed, but the officer who had first opened up the Waigal under Nicholson, Lieutenant Eric Malmstrom, could see when he left in 2007 that he had been like a player in a "Greek tragedy," where the very presence of U.S. troops was causing people to get hurt. "The people had turned cold. They wanted us out of their lives."[18] In an incident nine months before the Wanat assault, six Americans and two Afghan soldiers died in an ambush after a local security chief was fired. After this incident, the troops of Chosen Company, 2nd Battalion, 503rd Infantry Regiment, "no longer gave the Afghans the benefit of the doubt," according to a draft of a report by contract army historian Douglas Cubbison. The final report issued by the Combat Studies Institute at Fort Leavenworth, Kansas, is a sanitized version that did not include this line. In one of the interviews that did not make it to the final version, a soldier tells Cubbison that after the ambush there was no longer any interaction with Afghan civilians or security forces. "They didn't come near us and we didn't go near them."[19]

The incident that provoked the attack was the destruction of two trucks by Apache helicopters. The trucks were moving out of an area where Chosen Company were pulling back from three remote bases to a new site at Wanat, farther down the valley. The governor of Nuristan, Tamim Nuristani, said nineteen people died, including the family of the owner of the land leased for one of the bases. The convoy was full of civilians leaving the area because, Nuristani said, they were warned by U.S. soldiers that fighting might break out as the bases were closed. The immediate army inquiry in Afghanistan found "insufficient evidence" that there were civilians on board the convoy, and pressure was successfully put on President Karzai to fire Nuristani as governor. But the task force intelligence officer, Captain Benjamin Pry, told Cubbison that he believed there were civilians on board the trucks, and insurgents forced their way among them.

When Lieutenant Jonathan Brostrom arrived in Wanat to scope a site for a new base, on his first meeting with elders in Wanat, they handed him a list of names of those killed in the convoy. Four days later, with the new base still in a rudimentary state—as local construction workers had not arrived in time to build defenses—it was assaulted on all sides by a well-planned and coordinated dawn attack with hundreds of RPGs pouring in. The assailants had disguised their movement in the night under sound from a diverted stream. The Americans were pinned down. The unit's best weapon, a TOW antitank missile launcher, was set on fire in the first salvos, and soldiers could never reach one mortar position, as it was exposed to murderous fire throughout the attack. Eight of the soldiers who died fell in a separate observation post. They included Brostrom, who ran under fire to relieve his comrades. The Taliban were supported by villagers who joined the attack and almost certainly by local police officers. A CENT-COM investigation forced by Brostrom's father, Dave, a retired army colonel, found failings up the chain of command and recommended letters of reprimand that would have ended several senior careers. But the finding was overruled, so the dead ended up taking the blame.

Chosen Company were in the last days of a fifteen-month tour. These were now becoming the norm for Afghanistan—the first was Nicholson's Task Force Spartan, who had finished their planned twelve months when they were told they would extend in 2007. The ISAF commander, General David Richards, was impressed by the length of the tours. It meant the American military really were "at war," with a commitment not shared by European armies. The muscular military capability of the Americans and their will to engage "made the rest of NATO look rather pathetic." And most Americans were willing to support his intent for an enlightened counterinsurgency strategy, not merely concerned with grinding down the Taliban, although he conceded, "Not all of them agreed with it." The replacement for Task Force Spartan still came out as scheduled—doubling the force in the east, and the first sign of a new focus by the Bush administration on the Afghan war, ratcheting up beyond this being an economy-of-force operation.

≡ PAKISTAN

In an effort to cut cross-border infiltration, Richards unilaterally embarked on a mission to improve relations with the Pakistani leader, President

Pervez Musharraf. This went beyond what might have been expected of a theater commander. There was an unwillingness in Washington to confront Pakistani duplicity because of concern over destabilizing an Islamic state armed with nuclear weapons, and because American trucks full of key supplies for the war needed to cross Pakistan. This was a fundamental plank of U.S. foreign policy with deep ties that took some years to change after 9/11. The alliance went back to the days of the Cold War, when Pakistan received military aid at levels unparalleled anywhere except Israel, as America's only guaranteed friend in the region—and was a launchpad for spy plane flights over the Soviet Union. In the 1980s, U.S. funding of Afghan guerrillas based in Pakistan to fight against the Soviet occupation of Afghanistan left a toxic legacy as Pakistan's intelligence service, the ISI, forged deep links with the most fundamentalist Islamist mujahideen groups who received the lion's share of the funding.

Pakistan's view that its security interests depend on a compliant government in Afghanistan brought it on a collision course with the U.S. after 9/11. It was playing with fire by promising to support America against al-Qaeda, while continuing to train and support the Taliban in Afghanistan, helping them to recover and regroup after their defeat. Afghan foreign minister Hanif Atmar said Pakistan made an "industrial-level effort to reorganize the Taliban," to ensure they still had influence in Afghanistan.[20]

Musharraf had put himself in power in a military coup two years before 9/11, regularizing his rule with an election in 2002. Richards believed it was important to create a relationship with the government in Islamabad at his level, to have the ability to influence them, and even aspired to use his office to bring better relations between Afghanistan and Pakistan. He did not seek approval from General James Jones, who as SACEUR, the Supreme Allied Commander Europe, was responsible for NATO in the Afghan campaign. And Jones did not back the initiative when he heard about it, becoming increasingly concerned about Richards's political maneuvering. Musharraf was keen for the talks to go on, approving a plan for a joint Afghan/Pakistani committee, and asking Richards to be a facilitator. The ISAF commander was flying on his own, but he misjudged the wider effects of his maneuvers. His peace initiative never had any traction in Afghanistan, where Pakistan was seen as being at the root of all the evils that had befallen the country.

Karzai was convinced that Pakistan had been behind the targeted assassination of his father on Pakistani soil, and was never a willing partner in the Richards peace initiative. And the plan to broker a new AfPak deal would not be picked up by the next ISAF commander, General Dan McNeill. But Richards was willing to risk an inevitable suspicion on Karzai's part if he could improve security. "My role was to bring the two nations together as best I could, I felt, and therefore, I had to sort of balance the two. They both were paranoid about each other, and I was there trying my best to keep a balance."

He had no illusions about Pakistani duplicity, confirmed years later when Osama bin Laden turned out to have been living in Abbottabad all along, a town Richards visited as a guest of the Pakistani army. Kickbacks from U.S. funding for Afghanistan had been lucrative for Pakistani military and intelligence officers since the 1980s, and Richards knew there were some "who could not put the habits of a lifetime behind them." He would raise the issue of Pakistan's clear protection for senior Taliban figures living in the Quetta area every time he visited, and a handful of Taliban would be arrested a few days before he came to blunt his criticisms. But he recognized that his regular visits to Islamabad "certainly constrained" his influence back in Kabul. He would try to put Pakistan's case to Karzai, who believed he had gone native and never trusted him again.

☰ LEARNING THE LESSONS

Richards's belief in his ability to influence political events was part of his boundless belief in his own capacity. He saw self-confidence as the "priceless" commodity "that a commander must have if he's to do anything out of the ordinary. And if you haven't got it, you're playing at it." This extended to a strong belief that he could manage the media in pursuance of his broader view that victory was as much a matter of belief as physical power.

In July he was reported as saying the situation was "close to anarchy." In vain he told Jones his comments were misreported—he had been talking only about the problem of international coordination. He received an official warning and was later banned by Jones from further contact with the media. This followed a phone press conference that Richards treated too casually, as the audience were Washington's most vigilant observers of Afghanistan in the Pentagon press corps. A remark he made about the lack of progress in the war was taken as criticism of U.S. government policy. But the gagging did not last. Inevitably, within a few weeks, when there was a vacuum in information from ISAF, Jones asked him to speak to the media again.

Shortly before Christmas 2006, Richards became dangerously ill and was taken to a French field hospital and was then flown out of Afghanistan to a hospital in Germany. He had pneumonia, and while still in Kabul, overheard a request to his protection team for his religious denomination, as there was a priest outside. Richards's robust response was, "You tell the effing priest that I am not going to die." The sheer stress of the job had contributed to his collapse, and in Germany, the doctors tried to stop him going back to Afghanistan. But he insisted, flying first to have talks with Musharraf in Islamabad. His remaining days as ISAF commander were dominated by the British retreat from Musa Qala.

McNeill was due to replace him in February 2007 and did not want to take over with the Musa Qala deal in place. Britain tried to change his mind, briefing him in Washington and London, when he held meetings in late January, shortly before he flew to Kabul. As American concerns rose, Richards was asked to prove that tribal elders, not Taliban, were in control of Musa Qala, or cancel the deal and retake the town before McNeill arrived. Richards developed a series of tests to prove the town's neutrality. "The first one was that police had to be able to go in and out. Then the governor's representatives had to go in, and I insisted that the British were able to patrol through it."

That old thorn in the British side, the governor they had forced out, Sher Mohammad Akhunzada, was conspiring against the continuation of the deal. His scheming bore out the strong view of some Afghan analysts, such as the British soldier turned political adviser Mike Martin, that the conflict in Helmand was not so much between the "government" and the "Taliban" but a far more complex battle for control of opium poppy fields between different tribal power brokers, using Taliban as a flag of convenience.[21]

January 26, 2007. Less than a week before Richards handed over command to McNeill, a missile was dropped on a group of Taliban vehicles just outside the four-kilometer exclusion zone around Musa Qala. Even if technically outside the zone in which both ISAF and the Taliban had agreed there would be no hostilities, it was against at least the spirit of the Musa Qala deal. The intended target was identified by ISAF as a Taliban commander, Mullah Ghafour, but the strike actually killed his brother Mullah Ibrahim and several other fighters. It had been ordered by an American officer in the Special Forces, under Operation Enduring Freedom, the U.S. troops still outside ISAF command, and there was some suspicion in Richards's mind that it was orchestrated to wreck the Musa Qala deal ahead of McNeill's arrival.

In response, Taliban fighters stormed into the town, killed elders who had been loyal to the deal, and bulldozed part of the district headquarters. The Taliban commander Mullah Ghafour was killed in a separate air strike on February 4, the day of the handover of power. Richards left a letter on his desk at ISAF for McNeill, showing that the decision to pull British troops out of Musa Qala had been taken in London, not by him.

Richards returned to his home base in Germany and was disillusioned by the reception he had from the British government. In Downing Street, Tony Blair was warm enough, but the atmosphere in the Ministry of Defence was frosty. Richards found them preoccupied by the British withdrawal from Iraq, and he had to put together meetings to brief people on the Afghan war. It was perhaps a relief to his superiors that he was out of Afghanistan because of his constant demands for more planes and other resources the forces so clearly lacked. Meeting NATO chiefs in Brussels, Richards told them that while progress had been made, Afghanistan was "ours to lose." He would finish his career as the head of Britain's armed forces.

While in Afghanistan, he had visited the battlefield at Maiwand, scene of the epic defeat of British troops at the hands of an Afghan army in 1880. He felt emotional looking across the flat Afghan landscape, wondering if we ever learn the lessons of history. The "biggest lesson coming out of Afghanistan" to him was the need to commit enough troops to deliver effect.

> A politician who has never been on a course, even, to look at how correlation of forces work, is not in a good position to opine about military judgement, and I'm afraid, repeatedly, politicians have almost plucked the thing out of mid-air to say, "Well, I'm not giving you more than 30,000, whatever it is, but I still want you to do this."

Richards took the view that politicians ignored this simple rule and engaged in warfare without adequate resources for domestic political reasons. And the result was that "young soldiers will continue to be put into impossible situations, end up dying, or being very badly injured, because people have gone off at half cock." The greatest regret in his life was "not having the opportunity to do Afghanistan properly." Like many people who go there, Afghanistan got into his blood, and his wife, Caroline, set up a charity to support education in Helmand.

RACK 'EM AND STACK 'EM

Pakistan were not allies . . . they were actively working against us.

—General Dan McNeill

☰ DAY ONE FOR THE SIXTH TIME

The day Dan McNeill took command of ISAF forces in Afghanistan, February 4, 2007, was the anniversary of the death of his brother, Boone, in the Vietnam War in 1969, aged twenty-one. Boone was less than a year older than Dan, and they were often thought of as twins when growing up. He would remember Boone every February 4 and every time—and there were many—that he watched the coffins being ferried out of Afghanistan for the journey home. "I doubt I ever went to a ceremony in Kandahar or Bagram that I didn't think about him or ever a memorial service that I didn't think about him."

When appointed in 2006, he was already a four-star general and commanding the largest part of the U.S. Army at FORSCOM, in Atlanta, Georgia. He had a maximum of one more job before retirement and hoped it would be Iraq, the largest overseas operation and the one with the political attention. He saw Afghanistan as a poor-cousin war. He and his wife, Maureen, were staying with friends on an island off the coast of North Carolina, and he was out cycling when he got the call to come and see Donald Rumsfeld. He protested that he was on leave, and the military executive officer on the phone said, "Secretary knows that. He doesn't care."

They put McNeill on a special flight, and the next morning, he was at the Pentagon. Most of the meeting was about the situation in Iraq. It was only as McNeill rose to leave that Rumsfeld said, "Hey, are you standing up with Afghanistan?" And McNeill said, "Yes, sir, I am." "And what do you think of this new NATO command arrangement?" And McNeill told him he thought it too complex. "I do, too." And that was it. He went back to his cycling holiday and the next day had the call to go to Kabul. David Petraeus got the coveted Iraq post. He had been McNeill's chief of staff and was several years junior to him.

Maureen, normally 100 percent supportive of his life as a soldier, was not happy. McNeill had nothing left to prove after almost forty years in the army. She did not want him to die on this last deployment. He told her he wanted to get back in the fight. Yet they both knew they did not have many more memorial services in them. They felt the loss deeply, and McNeill knew what it was like. His mother wrote a letter to Boone every day until the confirmation of his death, and his father was never the same again.

He would go to every memorial service that happened under his command and remembers one at Fort Stewart more vividly than others. It was for the deaths of four senior soldiers, including a lieutenant colonel, from a unit in the Third Infantry Division that had taken more than fifty casualties in a month.

> Four brand new widows, eight newly fatherless children. It wiped us all out. It was about as hard as anything I've ever done. . . . This one got to us in the worst kind of way, and that's when we started saying, I don't have many more. I'm out of gas, I don't have anything left in my tank. We did keep doing it, and I had some conversations with bereaved ladies that, you know, I said, "Ma'am, I just don't have the words, I don't know what to say." She said, "Just being here is good enough, General." I said, "No, it ain't good enough to me."

In January 2007, a month before going to Afghanistan, he found President Bush as consumed by Iraq as he had been during McNeill's first deployment to Kabul five years previously. Bush told him to "always tell me what you need. You're not going to get it, but you need to tell it to me anyway." The president asked McNeill what he thought he could do, and he said, "There's one thing I believe I can accomplish. I'll get the Europeans outside to wire more into the act, more into the fight."

And the president said that would be good enough. McNeill did not rate the NATO campaign plan. "There was a lot of verbiage. There was no campaign plan. It just wasn't there." He asked several people in Washington what winning meant, but could not get an answer to the question. "Nobody would give me a good definition of what it meant . . . Some people were thinking in terms of Jeffersonian democracy, but that's not going to happen in Afghanistan."[1]

His arrival in Kabul in February 2007 coincided with the targeted strike that killed the Taliban commander Mullah Ghafour near Musa Qala. McNeill immediately picked up a nickname, "Bomber," that he could never shake, although it is not something he likes; his friends do not call him that. (Actually, they call him "Duffelbag.") The strike had been ordered before he assumed command, but that detail eluded those who were looking for any sign that McNeill was going to take a more robust approach to the war and be less interested in development and governance. The concern was widespread. McNeill had a reputation as a fighting general. David Richards noted in his diary that the German general who had come out from NATO command to preside over the change of command, Egon Ramms, "pointedly warned Dan that it was necessary to engage at every level and not just the tactical."[2]

McNeill visited a month before his arrival, and there was a cultural and personality gap between the upper-class Brit and the general who had risen from the North Carolina tobacco fields that went beyond their command style or the disagreement about Musa Qala. Richards found the American general "slightly ill at ease in company" and wondered if he had the "vision and impetus to get above the tactical fray and play his part on the wider stage." For Richards, "the real challenges of a theater command are not necessarily the military ones, but the political ones." McNeill thought Richards's engagement in politics a defect—meaning Richards could not manage his ego. Unlike his predecessor, McNeill was never going to be banned from speaking to the media for talking out of turn. He did not see his role as a peace envoy to President Musharraf of Pakistan. For him, Richards was too much of a "proconsul"; he thought being a general was enough.

He repudiated Richards's approach from the beginning of his tour, telling the handover team that he disagreed with what had been going on—particularly in Helmand. He said bluntly, "We're going to change strategy. The bad guys are all up in the north-east, and we're going to kill them. We're going to stack them up like cordwood."[4] His black and white view of the world was a very different tone and style from the more fastidious British general he had replaced. It is not surprising that critics called it "Day One for the sixth time."

Richards's one political reform, the policy action group, was allowed to wither and die. It was not lamented. Its meetings had often been chaired not by Karzai but instead by the national security adviser, Zalmay Rassoul, so decisions had limited value. Afghan officials went through the motions. They had learned how to perform decisions for the event, but not actually using the meetings for meaningful engagement. The highly opinionated new British ambassador, Sir Sherard Cowper-Coles, was also opposed to the PAG, believing it reduced his influence. McNeill abandoned the Afghan development zone concept, which Richards had never managed to get off the ground. "Right from the get go" said McNeill, "I knew that a lot of resources were going into the ADZs and the Afghans didn't understand it . . . On its best day it was dysfunctional, on its worst day it was non-existent."[3] He did not appoint a political advisory team to succeed Richards's Prism group. And the party scene for NGOs at ISAF was stopped within a few weeks—a decision McNeill found easier to take after he was bitten by a dog belonging to one of the visiting aid workers. He introduced General Order No. 1, banning alcohol for U.S. soldiers at ISAF HQ, an order that was never rescinded.

McNeill immediately noticed significant improvement in Afghanistan since he had been a commander in 2002. But there was no doubt either that the Taliban threat was growing. Whatever progress had been made was threatened. An independent survey in the south and east found that Afghans were "increasingly prepared to admit their support for the Taliban."[5] Almost half of the twelve thousand people polled believed that the international community would lose. More than five years after the fall of the Taliban, this showed how little real progress there had been, despite the surface improvements.

≣ RETAKING MUSA QALA

Karzai was comfortable with McNeill, reminding him of the simpler times in 2002, when "there were just the two of us." One crucial piece of U.S. influence was Karzai's personal relationship with President Bush.

"Mr. Bush treats me like a peer, another head of government, Karzai told McNeill." Five years after they first met, McNeill now saw Karzai as something of a Jekyll and Hyde. He had a compliant, easy, biddable face in public with a ready laugh. But in private and later in public, he would rant about foreign forces, and in particular civilian casualties.

In their first meeting, McNeill raised the issue of Taliban control of Musa Qala. Karzai was keen to leave things as they were, not wanting to interfere in local dynamics. McNeill told him that they could not afford to risk another Panjwayi, where the Taliban secured a strong defensive position close to Kandahar, needing the major offensive of Operation Medusa to clear them out. He would raise the issue five times across the summer, and every time, Karzai dodged it, not wanting another confrontation in northern Helmand. But the problem would not go away, and McNeill would not let it go.

McNeill had been tracking the situation for many months before he arrived and thought that British forces had been wrong to try the "ink spot" strategy, as they did not have sufficient forces. "The Afghans thought it was the nineteenth century all over again," when they were often at war with Britain. He was particularly critical of the British decision to keep U.S. special forces out of Helmand, and to insist that Sher Muhammad Akhunzada was fired as governor. "SMA was dirty but he kept stability because people were afraid of him. It's not good and I am not advocating dancing with the devil, but maybe one of his disciples, and that was SMA." But once British troops had gone as far north as Musa Qala,[6] he thought they were wrong to leave. Ironically, of course, he and Richards agreed on this, but Richards was blamed for the debacle of the British withdrawal. In a cable from Kabul, McNeill wrote, "The Musa Qala deal opened the door to narco-traffickers in that area and now it is impossible to tell the difference between the traffickers and the insurgents."[7]

In the months after McNeill arrived, the need to act became more urgent after a series of operations cleared other parts of Helmand. He knew he had to do something to stabilize northern Helmand, if only to give better protection to a British Royal Marine unit defending the Kajaki Dam, in the northeast of the province, beyond Musa Qala. The marines had moved into Kajaki after Operation Achilles, the first of the series of joint U.S./UK operations against the Taliban in Helmand beginning in March 2007. Their aim was to protect the hydroelectric scheme at the Kajaki Dam.

The project was the biggest part of the infrastructure of the canal scheme built by American engineers in the 1960s, when this part of Afghanistan was known as "Little America." McNeill saw renovation of the power plant as an important part of his mission. This was against the stereotype often portrayed of this general, that he was interested only in killing Taliban. But it would be another year before British forces succeeded in moving a huge new turbine into position—a complex undertaking since it could only be moved slowly along roads under constant threat of Taliban attack—and even then continued insecurity meant the upgrade work to bring the plant into full production could not be carried out.

The opportunity to retake Musa Qala came in November 2007, after a local warlord allied to the Taliban, Mullah Salaam, came over to the government side. Karzai called McNeill and said, "What do you know about Mullah Salaam?" and McNeill said, "I'll kill him if I get the chance." The president said, "I don't want you to do that." McNeill was skeptical when he heard that Salaam had come over, believing him to be "an opportunist of the worst order," one of many small warlords, fueled more by his desire to control the poppy crop than any ideological beliefs. There turned out to be two Mullah Salaams—the one that was the more significant Taliban commander had not changed sides. But that detail did not deter President Karzai, who was now willing to back an operation to retake Musa Qala.

By the late summer, British forces had reinforced positions across a larger part of Helmand, with U.S. military support, making the assault on Musa Qala easier to mount. Operation Snakebite in December was a textbook military success. The British commander in Helmand, Brigadier Andrew Mackay, one of the more enlightened, had conceived a far more population-centric policy than his predecessors, despite the small number of troops at his disposal. He had been concerned when he arrived that officers seemed to have been "making up policy as they went along." He wanted to reduce civilian casualties as much as possible in the battle for Musa Qala. The assault was led by a fast maneuver across the desert by British and American forces. Afghan soldiers tagged along, although ISAF tried to promote the fiction that the operation was "Afghan-led," ensuring it was Afghan soldiers who entered the town first once the Taliban were defeated and put up the Afghan flag on the district headquarters.

The governor of Helmand was now the unwilling and ineffective

Assadullah Wafa, whom McNeill could see "wanted to live in the western part of the United States more than he wanted to be in Helmand
Province." Wafa had been appointed for no better reason than Karzai
wanted Governor Daoud out, because he was the British favorite. The
Afghan president had never forgiven Britain for disrupting things in
the first place by insisting he remove Sher Muhammad Akhunzada,
his brother-in-law, from the post of Helmand governor. And just after Christmas 2007, he expelled two diplomats, Michael Semple and
Mervyn Patterson. Neither represented Britain—Semple, from Ireland,
was an EU official, and Patterson was with the UN. But they were in
the firing line for holding meetings attempting reconciliation with the
Taliban in Helmand, funded by Britain and not sanctioned by Karzai.

Semple was a Pashtun-speaking adventurer who wore local clothing
and claimed to have met "more Taliban field commanders than [their
leader] Mullah Omar." He was able to show that he had informed Afghan intelligence, the NDS, about his initiative. But Karzai's mind could
not be changed, and he did not trust the Tajik-dominated NDS, now
led by Amrullah Saleh, whom McNeill had met five years before when
he was interpreting for the Tajik warlord Marshal Fahim. Expelling the
diplomats was Karzai's way of signaling opposition to a British-backed
plan to introduce a big-hitting international diplomat to coordinate the
international effort. The name of the former Balkan envoy, a British
ex–Special Forces marine turned politician, Paddy Ashdown, was in the
frame for the role, which infuriated the Afghan president.

McNeill was opposed to talks with the Taliban. Fitting his no-nonsense
image as a soldier who did not stray from the military lane, he wanted
to stack them up like cordwood, not negotiate with them. He thought
their strength exaggerated by international media. They were a "ragtag
bunch" who did not "pose a strategic threat to Afghanistan."[8] He met
and gained insights from enough people who were talking to the Taliban, including Semple, but did not want to see them recognized as a
political entity, which would acknowledge their success in returning to
Afghanistan. Unlike Richards, who went sailing with Semple on a Kabul
lake, McNeill met him in his office.

McNeill strongly disagreed with the head of the UN mission, Tom
Koenigs, who wanted the Taliban "accommodated into the political process." He never believed that the Taliban would negotiate freely anyway,

since they were managed from Pakistan. He had no doubt "there were certain people in the Pakistani military that had reasonably close associations with the insurgent leadership." Whatever their protestations to the contrary, significant parts of the Pakistani military and intelligence establishment "were actively working" against the U.S. He did not speak in public about his strong distaste for Pakistan at the time, because of the wider strategic need to keep good relations with Afghanistan's troublesome eastern neighbor. Secretary of Defense Rumsfeld had gagged officers from talking of Pakistani duplicity, along with a list of other heretical views such as the need for more troops, the likely return of the Taliban, issues with the Afghan government, or counternarcotic strategy.

☰ THE PROBLEM OF PAKISTAN

In May 2007, McNeill experienced one of the worst incidents in his time in Afghanistan, with the death of a major from 82nd Airborne, Larry Bauguess, shot at close range with no warning by a Pakistani border guard—supposedly an American ally. Bauguess was from his home state of North Carolina, and McNeill knew the family, Larry's wife, Wesley, and two small daughters.

Bauguess was part of a small group of U.S. and Afghan soldiers and officials who had gone to a meeting in Pakistan at a small border post called Teri Mangal. They were aiming to reduce tensions after several people had died on both sides in a worsening dispute over where the border lay. Bauguess was shot with no warning as they left the meeting, and other Pakistani troops opened fire from inside the building, injuring three other American soldiers. It was clearly a planned ambush, not one rogue gunman. There was an attempt to kidnap another group of soldiers, who had to stop their Pakistani driver at gunpoint, abandon the vehicles, and run to waiting helicopters to escape. McNeill was badly affected by the incident. "There's no good way to die and there's no good day to die either, but that one bothered me greatly, still does."

The initial news reports did not reveal the full story, saying instead that Bauguess had been killed by a "militant." In public at the time, McNeill talked of how hard it was to defeat an insurgency, when there were "sanctuaries for the insurgents that lie just out of the reach of this country,"[9] not naming Pakistan, although he was privately fuming at their deceit. At a Pentagon press conference after he left Afghanistan, McNeill revealed the full story. "If I live to be as old as Methuselah, I'll be forever scarred by one event that occurred, and that was the assassination, and I don't have a better expression for it, of Major Larry Bauguess, a fine officer of the 82nd Airborne Division, spring of last year."

≡ COUNTERINSURGENCY MATH

During McNeill's time in Afghanistan, *Army Field Manual 3–24* was published—the first attempt by U.S. forces to systematize counterinsurgency in the modern age, drawing on lessons identified in Iraq and Afghanistan. Using the manual, McNeill's staff came up with a total figure of 480,000 security forces that would be needed to make COIN work in Afghanistan. Bush had increased U.S. forces at the end of 2006 and increased funding for "military-civilian teams carrying out projects to improve the daily life of Afghans." By the time McNeill ended his term of office, he had 47,000 ISAF troops and, at least on paper, around 150,000 Afghan soldiers and police. Even if all the Afghan forces were where they should have been, the total was still less than half the number needed to run a COIN operation under the new doctrine as his staff calculated it.

McNeill illustrated how he would like the average ISAF soldier to present himself—offering the choice that he could fight or build. "When you look at this soldier, you'd see a shovel in his right hand, an assault weapon of his country's choice—G5, M4, M16, whatever—in his left hand. He'd be standing in front of his Afghan hosts and offering this question: 'I've got the will and capability to use either. Which would you prefer I use, and where would you like me to use it?'"[10]

America was at war, with more willingness to employ the assault rifle than most of the countries in the coalition, who had made the commitment to send troops to Afghanistan when there was far less fighting going on and could not stand the heat of the increased intensity of war, nor were they equipped for it. American trainers found themselves supporting European soldiers, who would arrive without vehicles, electronic countermeasures against IEDs, or any means of supporting themselves in the field.

At some points during the long war, ISAF commanders were grappling with up to eighty different restrictions on their ability to employ the troops nominally under their command, so-called caveats on action. McNeill had a chart of the caveats that each nation imposed on the use of its troops on the wall of his office that he liked to show people.

Of the large troop contributors, Germany was the most risk-averse, refusing to send troops out of "their" area north of the Hindu Kush. They would not go out at night, refused to release aerial footage if it might be used for offensive operations, and they had very few helicopters, so little mobility. The caveats were constantly changing as European parliaments debated an increasingly unpopular war as fighting intensified after 2006. Alongside the reluctant NATO members were countries outside the alliance like Georgia and Macedonia—hanging on American coattails, and doing base security but unwilling to fight.

"Nothing was harder for me than NATO partners putting caveats in place and then denying they had caveats," said McNeill.[11] To him the "extreme limitations" imposed on his ability to employ troops flexibly contravened the basic principles of war set down by Clausewitz—including speed, mass, supplies, security. "You can use any one of them to explain why caveats are not good."

McNeill had a consistent message to his frequent senior Western political visitors, including prime ministers and presidents from across the multinational alliance: he needed more to fight the war, and it was not just a question of troop numbers. He needed more air mobility, and more intelligence, surveillance and reconnaissance systems. Only the American military had the depth of capacity in these areas that were the critical deciding element in modern warfare. Afghanistan tested the resources of other NATO forces, and all were found wanting. Most NATO nations were not equipped for expeditionary warfare. Even if they had been willing to fight, they did not have the equipment, and every military move was subject to political decisions made in dozens of capitals by politicians nervous of rising casualties and reports that security in Afghanistan was getting worse.

When Robert Gates succeeded Rumsfeld as Secretary of Defense in December 2006, he thought the Afghan war was awry. He had worked on the country as deputy national security adviser at the end of the 1980s, admitting that they did not anticipate that international terrorism could emerge from the region. "Our mission was to push the Soviets out of Afghanistan."[12] Returning to the file as secretary, he thought effort was going to waste. There was "confusion in the military command

structure, confusion in economic and civilian assistance efforts, and confusion over how the war was actually going."[13]

Gates was wary of a syndrome in the military identified in Vietnam,
that assessments by those in the field were often more upbeat than analysts in Washington or Brussels and that the military tended to believe
things were going better than their civilian counterparts. The phenomenon was most famously observed in 1963 when President Kennedy
asked, "You two did go to the same country, didn't you?" to Major
General Victor C. Krulak and the retired foreign service officer Joseph
Mendenhall, who came back from a four-day fact-finding tour of
Vietnam with diametrically opposed views of the prospect of success. Gates
sent the undersecretary of defense for intelligence, Jim Clapper, to assess
views in Kabul. "He reported a couple of days later that the disconnect
was worse than we thought; there were differences in assessment between General McNeill's headquarters, Central Command, NATO, and
both CIA and Defense Intelligence Agency analysts in Washington. Not
a good situation in the middle of a war."[14]

As well as not being able to employ NATO forces flexibly, McNeill
did not have overall American military authority in Afghanistan. The
contrast with Iraq could not have been clearer. There, David Petraeus was
the sole commander of the U.S. effort. If Gates wanted a videoconference to discuss Iraq, it was just Petraeus and Admiral William "Fox" Fallon, the head of CENTCOM, on the call. With Afghanistan, every screen
on the wall was full of generals on satellite links, like a scene from a movie.
As well as Fallon at CENTCOM, there was the NATO element with the
Supreme Allied Commander Europe (SACEUR), General Bantz Craddock, and two other Americans as well as McNeill coming in on screens
from Afghanistan—Major General David Rodriguez, commanding U.S.
forces in OEF separate to ISAF, and Major General Robert Cone, training Afghan armed forces. It may have been brilliant IT, but it was not a
good way to run a war. Gates observed dryly, "The military command
problem was the age-old one of too many high-ranking generals with a
hand on the tiller." And it was made worse because Craddock and Mc-
Neill did not get on. "Craddock guarded his NATO turf zealously,"[15]
wrote Gates, and tried to keep McNeill away from briefing European
defence ministers.

In one memorable videoconference at the Pentagon, Gates asked Mc-Neill, down the line from Kabul, "Dan, I'm trying to get a sense if we are making progress. Are we making gains in quelling the insurgency? If we are making gains, by what measure?" McNeill's reply was shocking in its directness. "Mr. Secretary, I was sent here to get our NATO partners in the fight. I can tell you, sir, they are in the fight every day. Some may be fighting more than others, but at the end of the day, we are racking and stacking the Taliban in a big way."[16]

This focus on piling up enemy dead, attrition warfare, where the only metrics that matter are body counts, was the opposite of the population-centric approach demanded by counterinsurgency tactics. It was Mc-Neill's only measure of success in fighting his elusive foe with the limited resources at his disposal. But his rhetoric spoke of a more aggressive fight than many NATO allies were willing to join.

McNeill employed larger concentrations of forces than Richards in "clear and sweep" operations and ordered more air strikes, a decision that coincided with an increase in the tempo of night raids and air strikes carried out by special operators outside his command. Civilian casualties inevitably increased. News releases denying any civilian harm, while announcing precise tallies of Taliban dead, began to cause disquiet across NATO.

In April 2007, two months after McNeill took over, a release reported, "87 Taliban killed, no civilian injuries reported," after two days of fighting in Shindand in the western province of Herat. Those fighting against American forces in the Shindand villages turned out not to be Taliban but local people coming together to defend themselves after American raids on the homes of leading tribal elders.[17] Local people said that fifty-seven civilians died, half of them women and children. The (Canadian) chief public information adviser to the chairman of NATO's military committee in Brussels, Colonel Brett Boudreau, wrote a memo warning that releases focused on Taliban body counts were "damaging" NATO's interests. "It is disingenuous to write 'there were no civilian injuries reported' after 20,000+ pounds of ordnance were dropped in two battles, in multiple locations in about 24 hours worth of pitched fighting."[18]

In July, the NATO secretary-general, Jaap de Hoop Scheffer, said the alliance should use smaller bombs, and new instructions had gone out to hold off attacking the Taliban where civilians were at risk. "If that means going after a Taliban not on Wednesday but on Thursday, we will get him then."[19] The change did reduce civilian casualties for about six months, but they increased again at the beginning of 2008.

There was increasing anger too from the Afghan president, who said, "NATO has no respect for Afghan lives," criticizing them for frequent use of long-range artillery. McNeill said that the increase in violence, was because of an increase in ISAF activity, taking more ground. He denied that the Taliban were any stronger than they had been the year before. "We had a basic operational concept which was get out of the wire, stay outside of the wire, advance against the enemy," he told a Pentagon media briefing.[20] His constant complaint was that too few allies would go on the offensive. He pointed to U.S. success in the east with population-focused counterinsurgency, where units were in country for more than a year, and that had made it more stable than the south.

≣ GETTING SKIN IN THE GAME

In January 2008, General James Jones, now retired as the SACEUR, cochaired an influential independent commission into Afghanistan with former U.S. ambassador Thomas Pickering. He urged the Bush administration to decouple the conflict from Iraq and give it more resources. "The United States and the international community have tried to win the struggle in Afghanistan with too few military forces and insufficient economic aid, and without a clear and consistent comprehensive strategy."[21] McNeill's next appeal for troops was heeded, with the deployment of three thousand extra U.S. Marines to Helmand.

But building up Afghan forces to fight alongside was a slow process. Desertion rates of around 50 percent meant that the new army was disappearing as quickly as it was being trained. Desertion depleted the ranks more swiftly than combat. An avid reader of military history, McNeill was lenient on Afghanistan for poor retention. He knew that at crucial moments in American history—the Continental army at Valley Forge, the 7th Cavalry on the frontier—desertion rates were as bad or worse than in the new Afghan forces. One solution might have been a draft. Karzai would talk in colorful terms of former Afghan kings, who would expect to be able to raise an army by sending messages out to the provinces, calling for troops, but was not willing to try it in his time, fearing a backlash.

McNeill's sense that people should be willing to serve went back to his own experience. His family were dirt farmers scrabbling a living in the tobacco fields of North Carolina, and as a route out of poverty, his father was determined the boys go to college, where it was a condition of his grant to spend two years in ROTC. With the Vietnam War at its height, his father said, with a sense of duty, "Son, I think this Indochina thing is here to stay with us for a while; you might want to consider staying a little longer in ROTC." It would be another thirty-five years before he retired from the army.

McNeill thought the draft would be good for Afghanistan, as it would mean larger numbers of people invested in success. He told the Afghan president that it would be good if more Afghan families had skin in the game. But Karzai dismissed it out of hand. McNeill watched his approach with some frustration. "Karzai could not think in a broader context beyond the model laid out by his father, holding court, reconciling and leading tribal groups. That's not what we needed him to do, that's just the way he wanted it to be. He was what he was, and he thought he would make the most progress by resolving tribal disputes. But he didn't have his father's instincts."[22]

McNeill saw Karzai several times a week. He was keen to get him out to meet people more, and move beyond the tribal elders who courted him, to be seen to be accountable to the people who had elected him. Isolated in his palace the president risked being out of touch. But there were dangers. Leaving the governor's compound in Kandahar, where he had flown in a U.S. plane, Karzai was talking to a young well-wisher out of his car window when shots rang out. The assassin was killed by Karzai's close protection team, and the youth talking to Karzai died in the cross fire.

On another occasion in Kabul, at a rally to celebrate the Afghan victory over the Soviet Union, fire from automatic rifles and rocket-propelled-grenade launchers was directed at the crowd from a nearby hotel. McNeill was sitting alongside Karzai and many members of his government. The Afghan president appeared on state TV an hour later to appeal for calm. But the far more popular channel TOLO TV was carrying long items criticizing him and senior ministers for running from the scene, while McNeill was said to have stood his ground. McNeill tried to persuade the president to appear on TOLO, but he was unwilling. McNeill was interviewed in his place and said that the president had not run away but been moved out of danger by his security team.

☰ "IF THEY CALL ME TONIGHT, I'VE STILL GOT A RUCKSACK"

McNeill's last months in Afghanistan were as the 2008 election campaign was entering its final stages. The Democratic chairmen of the Senate Foreign Relations Committee and Armed Services Committee, Joe Biden and Carl Levin, respectively, sent a letter arguing for a change in tack in the region—to combat the terrorist threat emerging in Pakistan. The letter called the Afghan/Pakistan frontier "the freeway of fundamentalism." Biden came through Kabul in February and articulated what McNeill derided as an "offshore strategy," in which the only focus was on counterterrorism "and the hardcore ideologues who won't change." McNeill disagreed, telling the man who Obama would pick as his running mate only a few months later that his policies would "lead to greater insecurity and instability in the region."[23] But "there was no reasoning with Biden."

Shortly before he finished his tour, McNeill was invited at the personal invitation of President Karzai to a gathering at the Ministry of Public Health. He did not know what it was about and was wary of a political ambush, but went along to discover there were very few other foreigners there and no ambassadors. He found himself sitting next to Sibghatullah Mojaddedi, one of the most senior figures in the Afghan tribal hierarchy; his family had the role of choosing kings in the past. Three Afghan women and several Afghan children came in and sat at the other end of the front row, and Mojaddedi pointed out Karzai's wife and son among them, whom McNeill had never seen before. The event turned out to be an announcement that Afghanistan had climbed a number of places in the world ranking of countries for child mortality. McNeill had discreetly assisted in providing security for a polio vaccination program in the south—although the program was managed by an NGO that was opposed to any links with the military. His presence at the event was in honor of that support.

The costs of the war to civilians affected him too. He had been very emotional at the bedside of a young girl in a hospital in Mazar-e-Sharif. "She said, 'This doctor's taken care of me, has fixed me up.' And, of course, the doctor's trying to tell me in my other ear, 'Whoever did this to her butchered her.'" And he remains troubled that years after he left

Afghanistan, the state of women had not improved. "There ain't a hell of a lot of movement there." He was troubled too that the nation changed its name to become the "Islamic Republic" of Afghanistan. McNeill lived the American constitution and had a deep sense that the state and religion should be kept apart.

Back in Washington, President Bush invited him and his wife, Maureen, to the White House. Like many people who came close to Bush, McNeill thought his public image unfair. One on one, he was direct, intelligent, and informed, unlike his performance at a press conference or TV interview.

Bush asked him to give him an account of Afghanistan, "without varnish," and then said, "OK, what about my man Karzai," and when they were done, reporters came in for a photocall. Gates arrived late, almost at a run, and said, "Mr. President, it's my duty to tell you that Dan's served 40 years as an American soldier, and he's never served a day in Washington DC." Three times McNeill had the papers to go to D.C. for an office job, and every time, he found a reason to avoid it and go back to Fort Bragg. Gates said deadpan, "Nobody else will do it, Mr. President."

Some years after retiring from the army, Dan McNeill finally put his brother, Boone, to rest. The son of one of the other men on Boone's plane made a trip to the crash site in 2012 and recovered what were said to be human remains. DNA testing, not available when the plane went down, established that the remains were not American, and some were not human at all. But now the air force had reopened the case, they polled the families and asked if they would like the mass grave site at Jefferson Barracks National Cemetery, Missouri, to be opened to see if they could identify the bodies using DNA samples.

It was a difficult decision. The fallen had been buried with their comrades forty-six years before. Some wanted to leave them where they were. But most, including the McNeills, agreed that the bodies should be disinterred. In the event, they found 60 percent of Boone's body. For Dan McNeill, it was the "second best possible outcome." The best, Boone walking out of the jungle alive, had not come about. In 2014, air force sergeant Clarence "Boone" McNeill returned to North Carolina to be buried in Warsaw, close to his father and mother. When his coffin came into Raleigh-Durham, the airport was decked in flags, and he was given a hero's homecoming.

Dan McNeill was overwhelmed by the generosity of the reception. "It was a scene of Americana that every American should see—to see how respectful and how nice people were, it was just extraordinary. I don't have better words for it, it was the most extraordinary occurrence." Four air force F-15 jets flew over the funeral, the day after Thanksgiving. One of the jets broke off the V formation, leaving a gap, in the traditional pilots' homage to one of their own.

Dan McNeill may have retired from the army the day he left Afghanistan, but still sees himself as a soldier. "If they call me tonight, I've still got a rucksack, I'd go back tomorrow."

PHASE THREE
2009-2011

THE SURGE

COIN

What is war doctrine? Basically, it's a written guide,
based on historical precedents, of the best fighting
practices for commanders and troops to follow . . .
based on lessons learned in experiments or at great cost
in bloody battles.

—General Jim Mattis[1]

⬚ FIGHTING SMALL WARS

In 2008, the last year of the Bush presidency, Secretary of State Condoleezza Rice said she was "struggling to master the challenge" of counterinsurgency.[2] Since 9/11, Western leaders managing the new wars were on a steep learning curve. Few elected politicians had military experience, and most came from cultural backgrounds with no contact with military affairs. This led to an inevitable time lapse between changes in the highly technical business of military practice and the awareness of it by politicians, the press, and the public. In her last week in office in January 2009, just before Obama's inauguration, Rice signed a joint State/ Defense agreement on a new counterinsurgency guide with Defense Secretary Gates. Until this late feel-good moment, most in the Bush administration were wary of COIN, counterinsurgency's catchy new acronym; it sounded too much like nation-building. Rice's deal was drawn up with little reference to troops on the ground,[3] and given the timing, was more of a gesture than a serious redirection of policy.

There was in fact nothing new about COIN. The U.S. Army had been fighting insurgencies since its early days against Native Americans on the frontier; its first manual on counterinsurgency doctrine, *General*

Orders 100, was drawn up to deal with Confederate bushwhackers in 1862.[4] In 1935, the U.S. Marine Corps produced *Small Wars Operations,* based on twenty years fighting "banana wars" in Central America. Revised as the *Small Wars Manual* in 1940, it has been reprinted since and was referenced in Vietnam and Iraq. But development of the doctrine was piecemeal and lacked consistency of support both in training and during conflict. The principles did not change, although some of the guidance in the manual was of its time, for example: "It is quite unbecoming for officers who accept the hospitality of the native club for a dance, whether local ladies and gentlemen are in evening clothes or not, to appear in their khaki shirts."[5]

The manual was not updated, because counterinsurgency was never given the attention it deserved. Time and again, after each of the small wars and insurgencies they faced, the army and Marine Corps defaulted to the routine norm of training to fight symmetrical enemies in big wars. Gates was keen to change course and despaired that he had to fight entrenched interests to put counterinsurgency doctrine at the heart of planning, training, and procurement: "The military's approach seemed to be that if you train and equip to defeat big countries, you can defeat any lesser threat."[6] The military default was to train for conventional operations, and promotion to senior ranks continued to depend on expertise in large-scale mechanized warfare.[7]

In trying to change the way America fought, he found he needed "to fight the Pentagon itself," a system geared to preparing to fight conventional nation-states. Institutional inertia blocked training for the full spectrum of conflict, including counterterrorism and small wars like Afghanistan. The Pentagon—supported by major defense contracting lobbies, Congress members with pet programs, and most senior military commanders—saw Afghanistan and Iraq as "unwelcome military aberrations, the kind of conflict we would never fight again—just the way they felt after Vietnam."[8] Procurement requests went into what Gates called the "Pentagon Black Hole."[9]

By 2007, insurgents sharing information between Iraq and Afghanistan had found a way of making roadside mines—IEDs—that would destroy armored Humvees, until then the troop carrier of choice. Gates hustled the slow bureaucracy of government to rush mine-resistant vehicles, MRAPs, into service, after first hearing about their capability not through the Pentagon but an article in *USA TODAY*.[10] It turned out in the post-9/11 wars, soldiers did not need more tanks but better-protected minivans.

☰ FOCUS ON THE WATER, NOT THE FISH

Since those early pioneering days on the frontier, America's capacity to engage in counterinsurgency warfare developed along three lines: first, training and adapting by troops on the ground; second, doctrine; and third, direction by politicians; and the three were never quite in sync. In 2006, before the Bush administration had politically signed up to counterinsurgency, the army turned to Lieutenant General David Petraeus, a storied officer with glittering Iraq experience, to devise a new doctrine. At the time, Petraeus commanded the army's main powerhouse of learning, the Combined Arms Center at Fort Leavenworth, Kansas. His orders from the chief of staff, Peter Schoomaker, were clear: "Shake up the Army, Dave."

Petraeus's lifelong interest in counterinsurgency came when, fresh out of West Point, he encountered French paratroopers at jump school in his first posting with the 509th Infantry Regiment in Vicenza, Italy. Among them were veterans of France's colonial wars of the 1950s and '60s, Vietnam and Algeria. He said, "I became fascinated with the conduct of French operations in, as they said *Indochine,* and then of course in Algeria, and read avidly the various books about various leaders, about various operations and sought to learn what I could from that." He briefly served at Fort Stewart, Georgia, where Stanley McChrystal was also stationed, before becoming ADC to the incoming commander of 24th Infantry Division, Major General Jack Galvin, the most important influence in the development of General David Petraeus.

Galvin encouraged him to study, and two years after they first met, on a break from Princeton, it was with Galvin that Petraeus saw his first small wars in action. Galvin was now commander of SOUTHCOM at a time the U.S. was supporting right-wing governments in a number of conflicts across Central America. In El Salvador, when Petraeus showed up at the house of the U.S. commander, "his wife greeted me, ushered me to the guest wing . . . and handed me a loaded MP-5 submachine gun to keep me company."[11] In contrast to Vietnam, Petraeus saw more willingness in Central America for the U.S. military to coordinate activities with civilian officials. But he recognized that this was not the norm across the army: "Civil-military integration efforts . . . seem to be an example of success in spite of the system, not because of it."[12]

Back at Princeton, he wrote a paper arguing for more specific training to fight insurgencies. He identified a paradox that while Vietnam had made U.S. generals more cautious about engagement in counterinsurgency warfare, training for them was essential since "involvement in small wars is not only likely, it is upon us."[13] He wrote to Galvin, "I think the next big debate will be about counterinsurgency operations—whether the U.S. should get involved in them, and if so, how."[14] And he recommended that Galvin produce a new army manual for counterinsurgency, to replace the "rather poor" field manual then in circulation.

This thinking was gathered together in his final Ph.D. thesis in 1987. It took apart the conventional wisdom that had grown up since Vietnam, that the U.S. should not intervene unless with substantial force, clear public support, and a clear end in sight. The officers at the top of the military in the late 1980s were seared by their experiences as platoon and company commanders on the ground in Vietnam. They were influential advocates for the prevailing cautious approach to warfare, summarized by Petraeus: "When it comes to the use of force, contemporary military thinking holds, the United States should either bite the bullet or duck, but not nibble."[15] The consequence of this, he argued, was that the U.S. did not put enough resources into training for smaller wars and insurgencies.

When 9/11 happened, Petraeus, now a brigadier general, was in Bosnia as assistant chief of staff for the NATO stabilization force. It was here that he first encountered special operations forces close up as they chased war criminals from the Bosnian conflict. He accompanied them on several night raids in civilian clothes. When their mission changed to tracking down Islamist terrorists in the region after 9/11, he became deputy commander of a new interagency task force on terrorism. This stood him in good stead in the wars to come.[16]

Petraeus kept a photo on his wall of the French general Marcel Bigeard, and the two corresponded until Bigeard's death in 2010. Bigeard was taken prisoner in Vietnam in the French defeat at Dien Bien Phu in 1954 and was the model for the hero of *The Centurions,* a novel by Jean Lartéguy, which Petraeus likes to quote from. In the book, the Bigeard character learns the guerrilla way of war from his captors, including one deceptively simple idea: "You've got to have the people on your side if you want to win a war." This was initially turned into doctrine by David Galula, another French officer who also learned the hard way, in captivity.

Galula was alone on an operation in China in 1947 when he was taken prisoner by Mao Zedong's Communists as they swept the country. Watching Mao's forces, Galula gained the insight that the priority in a counterinsurgency should not be targeting insurgents but protecting the population—winning the support of the people was more important than taking ground. "Revolutionary war is 20 per cent military action and 80 per cent political." It was Galula who popularized Mao's maxim that guerrilla fighters are like fish and the people the water they need to survive.[17] If the people are won, the guerrillas are left high and dry. Although his *Counterinsurgency Warfare: Theory and Practice* was first published in the U.S. in 1964 by the RAND Corporation, it was not picked up by mainstream military thinking, nor applied in Vietnam, which was just then morphing into a full-scale war.

☰ LEARNING ON THE GROUND

At different levels, the army and Marine Corps are sinuous institutions, often good at learning from experience, with internal networks where officers share best practice. Some officers recognized the need for counterinsurgency techniques in the early years of the post-9/11 wars. Sent to hold Mosul after the invasion of Iraq in 2003, Petraeus moved quickly to stabilization, not wanting to lose momentum gained. He saw "money as ammunition" and filled not just the security but the administrative vacuum left by the collapse of the Saddam regime—arranging the wheat harvest, fuel supplies, negotiating with elders, ensuring payment of officials. It was a rare pivot. Elsewhere, and particularly in Baghdad, Iraq descended into chaos. Shocked by the lack of a follow-up plan when he commanded the marines who took Baghdad in 2003, a year later, Lieutenant General Jim Mattis ensured counterinsurgency training for the marine's second tour of Iraq. "Never again" he wrote, "did I want to invade a country, pull down a statue, and then ask, *What do I do now?*"[18]

Preparing to return the year after the invasion, Mattis made the *Small Wars Manual* required reading for the marines, who also had rudimentary

Arab language training. Mattis added "First, Do No Harm" to his mantra of "No Better Friend, No Worse Enemy" as a reminder of the need to protect the population. His chief of staff, Brigadier General Joe Dunford (later to command ISAF and finish his career as chairman of the Joint Chiefs of Staff), said the 2004 Mattis plan was to "establish a relationship with the people, establish an intelligence network, and begin to get after what are associated with counterinsurgency tasks."

Marines wore soft hats and patrolled block by block to win back the people in the insurgent hotbed of Fallujah, growing mustaches to blend in. Mattis discussed the plan with Major General Stanley McChrystal, then commanding special operators across Iraq and Afghanistan. "Neither of us thought simply being in soft caps would win Fallujah," wrote McChrystal. "But Mattis, early on, understood that perceptions were at least as important as any tactical gains."[19] Mattis wanted to continue the counterinsurgency plan after the bodies of four U.S. contractors captured in a convoy were hung from a bridge. To him, the Iraq war was "an extremely violent political campaign over ideas," where counterinsurgency tactics would be more effective and sustainable than those of conventional war.[20] But he was overruled. Not for the first time in the post-9/11 wars, the military judgment was second-guessed from Washington, as TV images of the burned bodies rattled politicians, and they ordered an all-out assault—only to order a humiliating halt when the human cost became clear, leaving the Sunni insurgents claiming victory. McChrystal called it "the worst day for the Coalition since the invasion."[21]

In 2005, Colonel H. R. McMaster (later a lieutenant general and President Trump's national security adviser) was seeking to avoid a repeat when retaking the town of Tal Afar—a battle billed as "the next Fallujah." He arranged concentrated training sessions in Fort Carson, Colorado, with exercises that included soldiers sitting in mock houses, learning to recognize signs that showed whether the occupants were Shia or Sunni, and attempting to secure information, which they were given "only after they had sat down three or four times, accepted tea, and asked the right questions."[22]

Afghanistan too saw counterinsurgency principles adopted before the 2006 manual, particularly under Lieutenant General David Barno. Many officers heading for the mountains of eastern Afghanistan read Lewis Sorley's 1999 revisionist account of Vietnam, *A Better War,* which argued that even late in that war, counterinsurgency tactics introduced by General Creighton Abrams could have prevailed if politicians had understood what he was doing and given him more time.[23] Old British warriors from the two colonial conflicts where counterinsurgency was regarded as successful, Malaya in the 1950s and the Dhofar rebellion in Oman in the 1970s, were consulted alongside Vietnam veterans.

Winning hearts and minds—the term popularized in Vietnam to describe the change in priorities needed to conduct counterinsurgency warfare—drew on an old British colonial phrase.[24] Making the population the prize required troops to understand local context and perform functions different from conventional war fighting to persuade people that their government is better than that offered by insurgents. And it took patience sometimes to stand back and allow local solutions, rather than try to impose perfection—a principle the new Petraeus-Mattis doctrine explicitly derived from T. E. Lawrence: "Better the Arabs do it tolerably than you do it perfectly."[25]

☰ NO MORE POLISHED CRAP

"Dave, you and I can do this," Mattis told Petraeus when he called him for support in turning their experiences into a new counterinsurgency doctrine. "But let's keep it between our two commands. If we take this to the Pentagon, it'll take forever. We need to move fast."[26] Mattis now headed the marine equivalent of Leavenworth at Quantico, Virginia.

They knew they would need to build alliances beyond the military to combat strong institutional opposition. To launch the process, 135 experts came to a meeting, drawn from a wide circle, including prominent human rights advocates who were skeptical of the U.S. military. As they gathered, the army historian and Petraeus's West Point classmate Conrad Crane handed round bowls containing around one hundred small, highly polished green stones called coprolites. He explained that these pretty stones were actually fossilized dinosaur excrement.[27] It was a graphic display designed to show that this time it would be different— the new doctrine would not be polished crap.

The new doctrine required a fundamental rethink of military priorities to make protection of the population, not destroying the enemy, the main mission of any campaign. Counterinsurgents needed to focus more on the water than the fish. And the Petraeus–Mattis COIN doctrine drew further lessons from Mao, who had outlined three phases of protracted insurgent warfare—defensive, stalemate, and counteroffensive. If they understood this, then soldiers were better able to counter different insurgent tactics in different locations in Afghanistan: major conventional attacks in one place, guerrilla strikes in another, and attacks on civilians in a third. The doctrine demanded flexibility and adaptability, since what worked this week "might not work next week," and it warned troops against being lured into complacency by winning single battles—tactical success was easy with unchallenged mastery of the air, but it was not victory. Troops needed to accept more risk, get out on the ground, understand the value of nonlethal action, and promote political solutions. All military operations are part offense, part defense, and part stabilization. The way Petraeus saw it, the key to understanding COIN was that "the stability operation component is much more prominent than in conventional warfighting operations."

Local civilian engagement did not come easily for modern soldiers trained and equipped to fight in a different way. Karl Eikenberry, the former lieutenant general, appointed as the U.S. ambassador to Kabul in 2009, used a memorably earthy phrase to describe the challenge: "The typical marine is hard-pressed to win the heart and mind of his mother-in-law; can he really be expected to do the same with an ethnocentric Pashtun tribal elder?"[28]

No one thought change would be easy. The illusory power of the full-spectrum dominance of the most sophisticated war machine in the world blinded it to the value of simple human contact. But change was essential if there was to be a way out of the quagmire both in Iraq and Afghanistan. General Bigeard's deceptively simple idea that "you've got to have the people on your side if you want to win a war" was not rocket science, but as one of the modern exponents of counterinsurgency, John Nagl, put it, "if it were, western militaries would be better at it."[29]

"WE COULDN'T KILL OR CAPTURE OUR WAY OUT OF AN INDUSTRIAL-STRENGTH INSURGENCY"[30]

The catalyst for the change that began to synchronize training on the ground, military doctrine, and political will on counterinsurgency was the success of the Democrats in the midterm election in November

2006. This was the worst year of the Iraq war so far in terms of U.S. casualties, and the loss of confidence in Rumsfeld inside the military establishment had come out into the open in the "Revolt of the Generals," when six former commanders in the army and the marines said he must go. Chastened by the November drubbing at the polls, Bush moved to replace his contentious defense secretary with Gates on the day of the election results.

Not only had Rumsfeld opposed counterinsurgency, he had even bridled at the use of the word *insurgent,* believing it conferred political legitimacy on terrorists. He insisted that troops in the field talked of their enemy as AIF (anti-Iraq forces) or AAF (anti-Afghanistan forces). But even with Rumsfeld out of the way, the path to the acceptance of the new Petraeus-Mattis doctrine was not obvious. The generals who "revolted" were not a coordinated group. They were not pushing for counterinsurgency warfare; their beef was that if there had to be an invasion of Iraq, which some thought a bad mistake anyway, the initial invasion force was far too small.

There were other strong voices arguing against counterinsurgency. Ahead of the publication of the Petraeus-Mattis doctrine, there was a report by the Iraq Study Group, a group of grandees jointly chaired by former secretary of state James A. Baker III and former congressman Lee Hamilton. They recommended a more conventional path to withdrawal from Iraq—a surge of forces, but not to engage in counterinsurgency. Instead, their plan called for a surge to improve the capacity of Iraqi forces, for a quick handover and full withdrawal.

Shelving the Iraq Study Group report, President Bush came down instead on the side of the new counterinsurgency doctrine after a briefing by a group of outside experts who had war-gamed Iraq options. Prominent among them were the trusted bow-tied academic Eliot Cohen, ubiquitous and on the inside track of thinking about America's new wars, and retired army chief of staff General John M. "Jack" Keane, a New Yorker with the build of a quarterback, who had worked his way up the army, beginning as a paratrooper in Vietnam, and was one of Petraeus's mentors.

This group arrived in the Oval Office from a three-day exercise run by the American Enterprise Institute, involving experts including officers who had recently served in Iraq. Retired lieutenant general Dave

Barno, who had trialed a version of counterinsurgency in Afghanistan as early as 2004, was part of the exercise. They proposed a new approach to "stop the bleeding" and halt the slide to what they saw as a "primitive civil war."[31] They argued that thirty thousand troops be sent to Iraq to conduct a full-scale counterinsurgency along the lines of the new doctrine. Bush agreed to the change of direction, but institutional resistance continued. Gates was turned down when he tried to write the need for training for nonconventional wars into the National Defense Strategy in 2007.

Promoted to full general with a fourth star, and appointed to command Operation Iraqi Freedom in February 2007, Petraeus needed to find ways to bypass these institutional obstacles to implement his newly minted counterinsurgency doctrine. Minding his back was the formidable figure of Jack Keane, well connected at all levels in the administration, and alongside a handpicked team of military officers with Ph.D.s, he took with him to Baghdad a group of maverick academics, some not even U.S. citizens.

The shift to counterinsurgency, and its first real tryout in Iraq, would make 2007 a landmark year. Events that year would shape Afghanistan's destiny—four out of the next five commanders of ISAF in Afghanistan would serve in Iraq as Petraeus rolled out his counterinsurgency plan. Apart from Petraeus himself, Lieutenant General Stanley A. McChrystal was now in his fourth year commanding the Joint Special Operations Command TF-714, which ranged across Iraq and Afghanistan, and was based in Baghdad. John R. Allen was promoted to major general in January 2007, in his second year as deputy commander of the region, including the restive Al-Anbar Province, where the insurgency would be decisively turned round that year. And John F. Campbell, then a brigadier general, was deputy commanding general in Baghdad, which had the lion's share of the surge troops, as insurgency doctrine and practice began to catch up with the wars actually being fought.

≡ THE OTHER WAR

In June 2008, the month General David McKiernan replaced Dan McNeill in Kabul as the commander of ISAF, U.S. fatalities were higher in Afghanistan than Iraq for the first time. These were "the most dramatic years" of the war, according to Kai Eide, then head of the UN mission in

Kabul, and Washington was beginning to notice. Until then, the relative priorities of the two theaters of war were clear and defined simply by the chairman of the Joint Chiefs of Staff, Admiral Mike Mullen—"In Iraq we do what we must, in Afghanistan we do what we can." But by 2008, the success attributed to General David Petraeus in turning the tide on what he called "an industrial-strength insurgency" in Iraq led to modest troop withdrawals, allowing Afghanistan, "the other war," to claim some share of the available oxygen in the corridors of power. McKiernan knew the system well enough to know it could focus on only one war at a time. He gave a downbeat assessment five months after his arrival that confirmed the growing view in Washington that things might get worse in Afghanistan before they got better. "I won't say that things are all on the right track especially in the South and the East . . . in large parts of Afghanistan, we don't see progress."[32]

McKiernan avoided time in the Pentagon for almost all his military career, preferring to lead in the field. Unusually for someone who achieved the highest military rank, he is a quiet, reflective introvert, who likes to remind people "There's no *I* in teamwork." He did not go the West Point route but studied history at William & Mary in Virginia, one of America's oldest colleges. When appointed as the commander in Afghanistan, he wanted to learn what he called the "non-military variables," preparation lacking in the Iraq war. In 2003, commanding the armored assault into Iraq, he knew he did not "have a good appreciation of history, of religious variables, of ethnic fault lines, of economics." Preparing for the Kabul command in 2008, he sought out two sociology professors who had been traveling to Afghanistan since the 1980s to brief him.

In contrast to the sizable group Petraeus took with him to Baghdad, McKiernan came to Kabul with just three people: two executive officers and a personal security guard. He trusted the system to provide, but found a dysfunctional operation. The number of soldiers in the ISAF headquarters had swollen to two thousand as more nations jostled to show they were alongside America, while not willing to expose their troops to danger beyond the walls of the HQ. McKiernan thought the work done by the headquarters staff was "largely irrelevant" because he could not issue commands that would be obeyed uniformly. "Each regional command had a different environment, different problems, different troops, and different national guidance." His senior aides were of varying quality. His chief of staff, the most significant senior role, running operations and plans, was an Italian, who although competent enough, did not speak good English, so orders were delivered through an interpreter. His G-2, senior intelligence officer, was Turkish, and McKiernan despaired, "There are reasons why we don't share all our intelligence with the Turks." Any relevant headquarters staff work was largely accomplished through key staff officers from the so-called Five Eyes countries—U.S., UK, Canada, Australia, New Zealand—who share the highest levels of intelligence.

There was *nobody* in the headquarters responsible for the media, public affairs, or strategic communications. When McKiernan queried this, a retired Greek general, who had never been in Afghanistan nor had any experience of media relations, was sent out. McKiernan put him straight on the next plane home, ruffling feathers across the alliance, and instead appointed Skip Davis, a competent American colonel.

National vulnerabilities were revealed even more strongly down the command chain, as McKiernan saw for himself, traveling often outside the artificial bubble of Kabul. The biggest command challenge was in the south, where British forces were dug into "Helmandshire," with Dutch troops under very tight restrictions imposed by their government, protected by an Australian detachment, in neighboring Uruzgan. There were Romanian troops assisted by Americans in Zabul, and a Canadian force in Kandahar with the regional HQ. Four different national campaigns in just one highly volatile region, where McKiernan knew the Taliban were not similarly restricted by provincial boundaries or caveats.

In the months before McKiernan arrived, McNeill had failed to put the crucial southern headquarters under American command, winning instead a concession that its NATO command staff would do nine-month tours to improve continuity. No other armies were willing to do the yearlong tours then standard for U.S. troops—with many on longer fifteen-month tours. The problem with short tours was that it would take any new staff at least a month to settle in, and their effectiveness was reduced for at least a month as they wound down on leaving. Added to that, each nation rotated its troops in and out at a different time, and most took a two-week break in the middle of a six-month tour, further reducing the effectiveness of multinational regional command centers.

Even those few European nations whose troops were capable and willing to fight were faltering as the body bags came home. In August, ten French soldiers were killed in a well-planned Taliban ambush in Sarobi, east of Kabul. Several hundred Taliban fighters stopped an armored convoy of one hundred French and Afghan troops and encircled their rear in a classic pincer move. Only intense close air strikes called in by U.S. special operators traveling with the convoy stopped the Taliban attack. The French were leading their first patrol after taking over from an Italian contingent. Italian troops preferred to pay locals for information and were not fastidious about who took the money—effectively paying the Taliban for a quiet life. French troops who wanted to operate differently and get out on the ground faced determined opposition from insurgents backed by locals who had lost a source of income. McKiernan had an uncomfortable meeting with the French president, Nicolas Sarkozy, who flew straight to Afghanistan after the incident.

The incident was only the latest in a series of attacks testing the nerve of European troop-contributing nations—highlighting the gap between the peacekeeping operation they had signed up to support and the war they were actually fighting. The way McKiernan saw it, "many countries that contributed troops felt they were somehow 'bamboozled' by America to get into such kinetic fighting in parts of Afghanistan. That's not what they really thought they were signing up for."

≡ GOOD AND BAD TALIBAN

To try to win some breathing space, McKiernan revived links across the frontier with Pakistan, going to their army headquarters in Rawalpindi after the attack. McNeill had not been there since the fall of 2007 and had not met the new head of the Pakistan Army, General Ashfaq Kayani, who had been long in the shadows as the head of the Pakistani intelligence agency, the ISI. He succeeded General Pervez Musharraf as head of the army, regularizing command.

Musharraf had held on to the role after seizing power in a military coup in 1999. It is an analyst's cliché that Pakistan is not a country with an army but an army with a country, so Kayani's role was critical.

Given Pakistan's role as safe haven for the Taliban, it is remarkable that it hardly featured in McKiernan's pre-deployment briefing, "I wasn't given any regional guidance." The lack of coordination is even more surprising given the number of other U.S. agencies involved in dealing with Pakistan. McKiernan wanted to reset military-to-military relations. "There's no war that's contained within the borders of one country. In the case of the dilemma in Afghanistan, it will not be solved, nor will there be lasting effects, without Pakistan being in the equation."

McKiernan's cross-border initiative came less than a year after a significant turning point when the Pakistani army mounted a full-scale military assault on the so-called Red Mosque in the heart of the capital, Islamabad. The emergence of the Red Mosque insurgents—Islamists now fighting against Pakistan—was a classic case of blowback, the violent unintended consequences of a state acquiescing in the dirty business of terrorism against its neighbors. Pakistan had armed and financed guerrillas fighting in India and Afghanistan for so many decades that some now turned inward. The mosque was being used to store weapons and train militants for attacks on the Pakistani state.

The shock of the battle at the Red Mosque led to the beginning of a realization of the dangers of harboring the vicious bacteria of Islamist militancy. In the summer of 2008, an increase in violence against music shops, singers, and dancers in the northwestern Pakistani city of Peshawar caused unease across the country, making it easier for McKiernan to suggest that the Pakistani military should take a more robust approach to Taliban crossing the frontier into Afghanistan.[33] As a reminder of the alternative, there was a sustained U.S. artillery campaign across the frontier against militant strongholds in Waziristan.[34]

McKiernan established close relations with Kayani, watching "a growing recognition on the part of the Pakistani leadership that they had an existential insurgent threat within their borders." The two met about every six weeks, usually in Kayani's headquarters in Rawalpindi, once going to a retreat in the hills. "Did we see the problems in Afghanistan differently? Yes. But as two military professionals, we had a pretty good relationship." The Pakistani commander was a chain-smoker and mumbled indistinctly; McKiernan found he "really had to focus to get through the smoke and the mumbling." Kayani became emotional when McKiernan told him he was leaving his post, "and he was not an emotional guy."

The two established a unit to coordinate investigations into cross-border incidents and disrupt safe havens. McKiernan set up a joint operations post at Torkham, the main border crossing between Afghanistan and Pakistan at the Khyber Pass, with a live feed of pictures from a Predator drone flying along the frontier, and shared radio frequencies and access to intelligence.[35] And in November 2008 came another reminder of the threat to the region from Pakistan's willingness to support cross-border terrorism, with the deaths of 164 people at the hands of the Lashkar-e-Taiba group in the Indian city of Mumbai, launched from Pakistan and coordinated by phone throughout by Pakistani controllers.

Despite McKiernan's overtures, Pakistan continued to support the Taliban and their allies in the Haqqani network who operated freely from safe havens across Pakistan. The links of Pakistan's security establishment with the Taliban went deep and would not be easily uprooted. On May 27, 2009, more than thirty police officers were killed by a suicide bomb attack that blew out the back half of a handsome redbrick colonial-era building in Lahore, Pakistan. Sitting in the unscathed front office, behind a handsome pillared porch, and speaking the cultured old-fashioned English of the Pakistani elite, the police chief condemned the TTP, the homegrown Pakistani Taliban, who had carried out the attack. "But of course," he said, "I still support the Afghan Taliban in their fight for their country."[36] It was the clearest display of the Janus-faced hypocrisy of Pakistan's establishment—a division between "good" and "bad" Taliban.

☰ CHEMICAL BILL

McKiernan made little progress combating Afghanistan's drug economy—a major driver of violence and criminality. Encouraged by the American ambassador, William Wood, a chain-smoking veteran of U.S. drug wars in Central America, the military now gave logistical support, including transport planes, to the Drug Enforcement Agency. Wood, known as "Chemical Bill" because of his enthusiasm for spraying crops, did not convince McKiernan, who saw this would damage only the farmers themselves—the poorest people in the supply chain. He reached his conclusion after personally going on a raid in a DEA helicopter.

> We were probably the second aircraft in, and we sat down outside of a village, and went in where the lead guys had gone in, and found a stash of wet opium that the local farmer was going to sell to somebody who was going to sell to somebody else, and eventually it was going to be converted into heroin and money. I watched this

unfolding, and they found a significant amount—probably not in the totality of drugs that were available, but a significant amount. But the intelligence network of the Afghan villagers was such that they probably knew they were coming, and all the villagers had left the village and were sitting up on the side of the hill just watching this. And I thought, this isn't going to do it. Who we're hurting right now, making an effect on, is the farmer, and the farmer's not the problem. The farmer's trying to grow a crop and scrimp together enough to live on, and there's not enough interdiction missions we can do that will change that dynamic.

McKiernan saw that a second-order effect of what they were doing in the dawn raids was to recruit soldiers for the Taliban. "If the farmer that we took his livelihood from that morning was neutral, he might not have been neutral after that day." McKiernan preferred to go after labs, where the raw opium was processed into heroin. "When I say lab, I don't mean a lab we would find in Boston; a lab might be some fifty-five gallon drums of water, some fire, and a couple of precursor chemicals that are easily obtained and heated up. Didn't take an advanced degree to do that." But despite pursuing better intelligence on the labs, and stepping up attacks, the effects on production were marginal.

There was coincidentally a cut in opium poppy production in 2008 for the first time, but not caused by drug raids or eradication. Farmers in several areas had decided not to plant poppies after religious leaders were persuaded to preach against it, with stronger leadership by several provincial governors encouraged by development cash if they could prove their provinces poppy-free. The UN head, Kai Eide, also noted a more basic reason: "Drought had contributed to bad harvests, especially in the north and northwest . . . we could not take it for granted that the same positive trends would be seen next year." Eradication from the air, or from chains dragged behind tractors, had limited effect. It was also hugely expensive—$36,000 a hectare, compared to $1,000 in Colombia.[37]

ISAF was not responsible for much of this eradication activity, and when McKiernan arrived in Kabul, he was not even in command of many American troops in the country, in Operation Enduring Freedom under a three-star U.S. general at Bagram airport an hour's drive north of Kabul, who reported directly to CENTCOM—not the ISAF chain of command to NATO in Europe. McNeill had put in place some mechanisms to deconflict operations, but there was still the potential for dangerous misunderstandings in overlapping campaigns without a single chain of command, especially after President Bush decided in July that U.S. forces would, in the future, carry out raids in Pakistan without informing the Pakistani authorities first. The decision was not announced at the time, but it was hard to keep such raids secret.[38] On September 3, Navy SEALs landed several miles across the border and killed several Taliban and al-Qaeda fighters. Pakistan called it a "gross violation"—claiming that sixteen civilians, including women and children, were among the dead. The operation was not under McKiernan's command. In the resulting furor, NATO had no option but to issue a clear statement distancing ISAF troops from the incursion and saying they were "not authorized to enter or land in Pakistan."[39] It made McKiernan's job harder. His lack of operational knowledge of the OEF counterterrorist campaign was a significant contributory factor in a decisive shift in the mood of President Karzai, who strongly moved against American intervention after the summer of 2008.

☰ MR. PINK AND MR. WHITE

The turning point came in July 2008, at Deh Bala in Nangarhar in the east, when once again warplanes mistook celebratory gunfire at a wedding party for hostile action: forty-seven died, thirty-nine of them children and women, including the bride. Karzai was struck by the question of one elder when he visited the scene: "Mr. President, for how long will you be attending these funerals?"[40] He returned to Kabul resolved to change the situation, and the opportunity would come in another attack a month later. A trusted senior adviser, Nematullah Shahrani, came into the Arg with a blanket containing body parts of children, which he threw onto the table in front of Karzai. The Afghan president became very emotional, crying out, "Call the general to see for himself, are these fingers of Taliban or fingers of children?" The final death toll in the killings at Azizabad, in the western province of Herat on August 21, was ninety-two, including many children. The body of the last victim to be found, a baby, was uncovered in the rubble ten days later.[41] McKiernan had only the military account to work on, which held the line for some days that there were few if any civilian casualties in a successful operation to kill a local Taliban commander, Mullah Sadeq.

McKiernan's equable temperament worked against him on these occasions. His calm, professional manner infuriated the Afghan president, who had preferred the openly emotional McNeill, who would shed a tear with village elders when faced with evidence of civilian casualties. "McNeill was a man who had feelings, who would understand, who told the Afghan people that he was a good Christian," Karzai said. "McKiernan was a quiet person; he would never speak." McKiernan stayed inside his military lane and stuck to the account he had been given, since that is what he had been told by U.S. investigators. Not for him the approach of some other ISAF commanders, who wore Afghan army patches on their uniform and told the president they were "his" commander.

The raid did not just affect U.S. relations with the president. It would cause one of the most serious rifts with the UN during the years of the Afghan war. When the first news of the attack emerged, McKiernan was in a meeting in Kandahar at the launch of a new initiative on Afghan local government. The head of the UN mission, Kai Eide, was at an adjoining table, and the two sat huddled separately with their staffs trying to understand what had happened in Azizabad. When Eide sent a senior official out of the room with a press release expressing deep concern about the reports of civilian casualties, she was obstructed by an ISAF officer who insisted it had been a successful attack against a Taliban leader.[42]

The version put forward by the U.S. military, that there were only a handful of civilian casualties, was corroborated by, of all people, Oliver North, the former marine officer once notorious for his part in the dirty war that siphoned arms from Iran to right-wing Nicaraguan guerillas in the 1980s. He was in Afghanistan for his program on Fox News, *War Stories with Oliver North*. Embedded with special operators who raided the village, he reported it as a successful operation to kill a Taliban commander and twenty-five fighters, and seize an arms cache. He emphasized that U.S. troops rescued a wounded woman and child. He put the reports of civilian casualties down to a "very effective propaganda campaign" by the Taliban and their supporters.[43]

There was a dispute about whether U.S. troops had investigated on the ground after the raiders left at dawn. McKiernan was told that they searched the village and found up to thirty-five bodies of military-age

males and five dead women and children. But local people told the veteran *New York Times* reporter Carlotta Gall that no American soldiers had
visited. In a report two weeks after the incident, Gall said that she saw
cell phone images of around eleven dead children and heard credible
accounts of more than forty fresh graves.[44]

Relations between the UN mission and ISAF were now strained to
the breaking point. Eide found his staff under attack from the American
media and from the administration in Washington. "We were not talking
about two versions that varied slightly, there were two very different stories. I wondered at one stage if we were talking about two different attacks."[45] He refused an offer by McKiernan to a joint UN-Afghan-ISAF
investigation, since he believed the vested interests of each party would
cloud their judgment. After sitting alone late into the night, counting
pictures of dead children, he called in McKiernan and the U.S. ambassador, William Wood, separately to view the video footage assembled by
UN investigators, and neither said much in response.

Eide stuck to what he believed to be true. He had been facing intimidation since his appointment. When he first met the U.S. ambassador
to NATO, Victoria Nuland, she warned him there should be "no surprises" about civilian casualties—she repeated it as he left her office: "No
surprises." It was as if the publicity were more serious than the civilian
casualties themselves. Secretary of State Condoleezza Rice told him he
should have consulted U.S. forces before reporting his findings at Azizabad. A Western diplomat in Kabul told him he was "serving the Taliban"
by highlighting the incident.

Eide's firmness was strengthened by the aftermath of the earlier shooting at the wedding party. There was no dispute about the casualties on
that occasion, but the UN was made to look "weak and indecisive"[46]
when he delayed releasing UN findings at the request of U.S. forces, who
took some time to issue their own report.

Eide condemned what he called "spin and deception" on the part
of the U.S. It was for them an "automatic reflex" to issue an immediate
denial of civilian casualties, then later have to admit they were wrong, resulting in a "loss of face every time it happened."[47] U.S. officials pointed
out that on any given day, there were more civilian casualties in Iraq than
Afghanistan, without the same uproar.

One difference with Iraq was the "flash to bang time" in reporting the incident to the president himself was instant, as tribal elders would phone the palace while raids were on. McKiernan knew that in this new world, the military needed to be more proactive with the near-universal owner- ship of smartphones. "You have to be very quick with the truth and with evidence, and I think that's something that leaders are going to have to grapple with because that's going to be the nature of war in the twenty- first century." This most methodical of commanders introduced a new policy to track civilian casualties and quickly investigate reports of them. There was no consistent system until he established the Civilian Casualty Tracking Cell, which recorded every suspected casualty caused by ISAF. He would routinely call in investigators from the UN and the Interna- tional Committee of the Red Cross (ICRC) to review military findings.

Eide sought to repair relations; he did not want to undermine the U.S. military and had some sympathy for McKiernan's predicament—arguing a case that had been given him by investigators into an incident that was not under his command. When it was clear that some civilians had died, McKiernan went to Azizabad and faced a meeting of elders. Karzai in- sisted on new rules to limit civilian casualties, and by February 2009, he had secured an agreement signed by McKiernan and the Afghan defence minister, Abdul Rahim Wardak, to improve coordination between U.S. and Afghan forces. McKiernan also offered to share potential targets with Afghan intelligence officials, giving the right of veto to President Karzai ahead of any operation.

It would take more than ten years and a legal action against the De- partment of Defense to reveal the full story of the casualties at Azizabad. The investigation by Brett Murphy of *USA TODAY* in 2019 uncovered one of the strangest and most tragic incidents of the whole war.[48]

The tip-off that there were senior Taliban present at Azizabad came from two sources code-named Romeo and Juliet. The military-age men who were killed were not Taliban but security guards for the nearby ISAF air base, and the weapons seized had been supplied not by the Taliban but by the U.S. for the security contract. According to the DOD inquiry uncovered by *USA TODAY*, the tip-off was as a result of a turf war between two local warlords to secure the lucrative contract. Armor- Group, who ran the contract, code-named the two warlords "Mr. Pink" and "Mr. White"—the names of the feuding thieves in Quentin Taran- tino's *Reservoir Dogs*.

The civilians in Azizabad on the night of the raid had gathered for a memorial for Mr. White, who had been shot dead by Mr. Pink. To clarify who was on who's side—the U.S. sources Romeo and Juliet were known associates of Mr. Pink, and the Taliban commander was Mr. White's nephew.

They were "the two most corrupt families in Afghanistan," according to the district governor, Lal Muhammad Umarzai. But the American forces never asked for his advice.[49] The Americans were used, as so often, to settle a local dispute by people claiming their enemies were Taliban—with the added irony on this occasion that those killed were actually contracted to provide security for NATO troops.

After the killings at Azizabad, the damage to relations with Karzai was permanent. Eide said his "increasingly confrontational approach . . . shocked visiting ministers as well as ambassadors in Kabul."[50] Rumors of his mental state swirled around; many observed that a nervous tic in his left eye seemed to be getting worse. America's concern about the negative publicity and his highlighting of the Azizabad incident were strongly expressed in a phone call by Condoleezza Rice. He claimed that she threatened to cut off U.S. aid. Karzai angrily responded, "If you continue to be this way, we will treat you like we treated the Soviets. We treated the Soviets as an invader."[51]

☰ A DINNER TO REMEMBER

The Afghan president's opposition to civilian casualties was rational. "When you hurt normal civilians they become Taliban," said his chief of staff, Muhammad Umer Daudzai.[52] But Karzai's increasingly unpredictable moods made it difficult for the military and international donors to deal with him. He was mocked in private by senior Western diplomats as "the mayor of Kabul," with limited influence beyond. As he set his face against cooperation, he was further undermined by news that Western diplomats were sounding out other credible candidates to run in the presidential election scheduled for the following year.

In November 2008, he faced the most radical shift in his relationship with the West with the election of President Obama. President Bush had treated him as an equal, a fellow president—"My man Karzai"—and they talked on a videoconference twice a month. "Bush conducted himself with Afghanistan with dignity," said Karzai. "In conversations, he would understand my point of view."[53] He was used to getting his own way with U.S. officials who knew he could appeal to the president. Karzai thought Bush "treated Afghans with respect; he would have tea with us, he would have coffee with us, he would have our food, he would meet the Afghan leaders." This easy access was abruptly cut when he faced the chill blast of the skepticism of Obama, who barely acknowledged him.

A month after the U.S. election, in the depths of the Kabul winter, Obama sent his newly elected vice president, Joe Biden, on a tour of the region to reset relations. Biden came in a very different mood from a trip in early 2002, when he had been one of the first international politicians to visit the new Afghan president. "Whatever it takes we should do it," he said then, and warned that history would judge America harshly if they "failed to stay the course." By 2008, he was warier of long-term commitment and became the standard-bearer in the Obama administration for cutting troops and pursuing only a limited policy of hunting down enemies of America, not rebuilding Afghan forces or developing government institutions. In a bipartisan gesture, Biden was accompanied by Senator Lindsey Graham, an air force reserve colonel, and close friend of the defeated Republican candidate John McCain. They had what Graham called "a dinner to remember"[54] in the presidential palace.

It began cordially enough with a one-on-one meeting between Biden and Karzai, and they then went into a large hall with the whole Afghan cabinet sitting at a dinner table. With the U.S. economy in meltdown following the crash, Karzai was told that American voters would no longer sign a blank check. Voices were raised on both sides—Biden repeated the "mayor of Kabul" gibe and complained about corruption, referring to the ornate homes of many of those at the dinner that were on display in central Kabul. The breaking point in the conversation came over civilian casualties. There was a growing American sense that while the vast majority of Afghan civilian deaths were at the hands of the Taliban, those killed by international troops were given undue prominence by the president's very public complaints. Karzai pleaded that Afghans should be "partners and not victims." The U.S. ambassador, William Wood, vainly tried to intervene, but failed, and when Karzai said, "We are just poor Afghans, nobody cares," the evening abruptly ended when Biden threw down his napkin, and stalked out of the room, saying, "This is beneath you, Mr. President." On his return to the embassy, Wood was flooded with phone calls from distressed ministers asking what was going on. In the Afghan context, the tone and manner of Biden's abrupt walkout was as important as the substance—no friend would treat a friend this way. His treatment of the president would have been a snub in any country; here it was interpreted as a hostile act.[55]

Karzai felt increasingly cut off. No personal contact with Obama, insults from Biden, the businesslike demeanor of McKiernan, and then to cap it all was the appointment of the forthright Richard Holbrooke in a new role as representative to both Afghanistan and Pakistan. The proposal for the diplomatic role linking the conflict was one of the recommendations made by McKiernan in his initial review, feeding into a growing awareness in Washington that they should take a tougher line on Pakistan. Holbrooke's abrasive personality won him few friends. Karzai gloomily told the emollient UN head, Kai Eide, after Holbrooke's first trip to Kabul, "He wants to get rid of you and me." In Washington, Karzai was increasingly seen as an obstacle. To Gates, he was the most troublesome ally since De Gaulle. "Both were nearly totally dependent on the United States and both deeply resented it."[56] And Karzai had lost his privileged access to the top.

7

OBAMA'S WAR

Changing the commander is not the silver bullet that's
going to change all the dynamics in Afghanistan.
—General Dave McKiernan

☰ COIN OR CT

In the "Yes, we can!" optimism of the change of power in Washington, D.C., in January 2009, a profound rethinking of "Bush's wars" was one of the top priorities. The defeat of the Vietnam War hero John McCain by Barack Obama, the first president too young to have faced the draft, was more than a generational shift at the top. Afghanistan was no longer the "other war" but the "good war," Iraq the unnecessary "war of choice." While both wars were to be ended, the administration was not united on how that should be done.

Obama hedged between values and interests in foreign policy, idealist promotion of democracy against realist focus only on U.S. economic and security concerns. Recognizing that American interests with the Middle East were sundered by the Iraq war, he made a speech in Cairo promising a "New Beginning."[1] But he was wary of deeper involvement. Counterinsurgency was fashionable, but few in the administration were committed to the number of troops that would be needed to make it work. The leading realist, Vice President Joe Biden, argued that America should not throw any more money or lives into the maw of Afghanistan other than the bare minimum in adopting counterterrorist tactics (CT), pursuing the remnants of al-Qaeda with drones and Special Forces.

Far older than most in the administration, Biden was first elected to the Senate in 1972, aged just thirty, when he ran on an anti–Vietnam War platform. He had been on the other side of the argument from the soldiers who had joined up then and were now the generals commanding America's wars. In Afghanistan, his stripped-down counterterrorist plan was derided by many in the army as unworkable. "To defeat a network, you have to attack the network," said McKiernan. "It's not just about getting the top guy; it's about attacking somewhere, and developing intelligence that leads you to somewhere else to defeat the network." Military thinkers going all the way back to Sun Tzu have known that force should be the last resort, and the use of force has unintended consequences that are hard to calibrate. In the complex post-9/11 wars fought among poorly educated rural people, understanding the context—history, religion, tribal dynamics—was too rarely achieved. Precision bombing, the main CT tool, had a deceptive simplicity in dealing with one problem, while causing others.

> If I approve a strike by our special operators to go in and target, kill or capture a bomb maker in a village in rural Afghanistan, and I don't ask the question of, what are the second and third order effects of that, besides killing the bomb maker or capturing him, and what if I find out, well, he's the son of an influential tribal elder. So is there another way of taking him out of the picture in the bomb-making capabilities, besides going in and killing or capturing him? What's the effect on the population? I might create a far greater threat by allowing that raid to happen, and find out, well, this is maybe not the individual that we really wanted to go out and kill.

It is a well-tested military maxim that to win, insurgents need only outlast the will of those fighting them—contained in the much-quoted line said to be used by the Taliban, "You may have a watch, but we have the time." Unlike conventional armies, insurgents can face tactical defeats, losing every battle, and still prevail if they have enough support from the population.[2] Counterterrorist tactics alone would not deliver the minimum result required of the campaign—that it prevented Afghanistan again becoming a haven for people planning attacks on the homeland. This was the Afghan dilemma the Obama administration never resolved.

By 2009, the Petraeus-Mattis COIN doctrine was more widely accepted across the U.S. military. McKiernan was employing it in

Afghanistan. "I'm a war fighter, but the nature of the war in Afghanistan is such that you have to use counterinsurgency ways and means to achieve your ends. At the same time, you have to use counterterrorist ways and means to defeat terrorist networks that operate in the region . . . It's not COIN versus CT; it's COIN and CT . . . you have to do both. You can't do one or the other and have lasting effects." Fighting, training local troops, and building up the Afghan government were all parts of a virtuous circle, where security would sustain better governance, building a stable economy to provide jobs, to make it easier to encourage those insurgents not deterred by tough military action to lay down their weapons.

That was the theory at least. But a properly resourced counterinsurgency would take more time and more money than the Obama administration was prepared to commit. Afghanistan had "one of the lowest soldier-to-inhabitant ratios in a modern post-conflict setting," an enthusiast for a bigger security footprint, the former envoy Jim Dobbins, pointed out.[3] And Biden's minimalist approach had significant traction in Obama's Democrat support base inside and outside Congress, who feared being sucked further in. It cost $1 million a year to keep a soldier in Afghanistan.[4] In the year of global financial meltdown, spending more on the long war was a hard sell.

≣ BOXED IN BY GENERALS

When the Obama team came into the White House for transition talks, they faced an outstanding request from McKiernan for thirty thousand more troops, on the table since his first review in July. Bush handed the decision to the incoming administration for final approval. Obama's national security adviser designate, retired general James Jones, said they would hold off for now.[5] At CENTCOM, General David Petraeus, commander since October 2008, backed the troop demand. He was a powerful voice to tilt resources from Iraq to Afghanistan.[6] His deputy General John Allen shared McKiernan's alarm. "What was clearly happening was that the Taliban, having now licked their wounds for some period of time and rested and refitted for a number of years, were now coming into the battle space in '08 and '09 in a very big way." Better trained and led, the Taliban were fighting in larger formations than previously, flexibly adapting to circumstances, and employing weapons for more lethal effect. Training camps in Pakistan, run by the ISI, were functioning more effectively than ever.[7]

Obama was more receptive to increasing force levels in Afghanistan than in Iraq, a war that "distracts us from every threat we face."[8] But in his first meeting to discuss Afghanistan, in the White House Situation Room on the Friday of his inaugural week, he decided to hold off, pending a review. It was the beginning of a process to reexamine the war from first principles that would not be completed until December. Obama was skeptical of McKiernan's demand, which would effectively double the number of troops in Afghanistan. On the way out of the meeting, Biden grabbed him by the arm and, in what Obama called a stage whisper in his book *A Promised Land,* told him he thought the generals were trying to jam him. "One thing I know is when these generals are trying to box in a new president."[9]

On February 24, in a low-key decision announced by media release, the new president agreed to an increase of seventeen thousand troops, not the full thirty thousand requested by McKiernan seven months previously. Four thousand more were added soon after to bolster training of Afghan forces. It set the tone for Obama's relationship with his generals. They would put in a request based on what they needed in order to fulfill the task they had been given, and it would be pared back. McKiernan saw this approach as "not optimal" to achieve the task he had been sent to do. He had "insufficient combat power to gain momentum while the center of gravity is being developed, and that's the Afghan National Security Forces." The U.S. Army definition of a center of gravity is "the source of power that provides moral or physical strength, freedom of action, or will to act."[10] In 2009, Afghan forces fell well short of that.

The problem of the piecemeal approval of troops was not just about numbers but effectiveness. McKiernan's troop request was not an arbitrary figure but one that drew on a sophisticated process of planning to turn the war round and reverse what he called the "sky is falling" narrative.[11] Delivering military power is a complex jigsaw with matériel delivered on the basis of "time-phased force deployment," where sequencing matters almost as much as the amount of force. This model has more application in a conventional campaign than long-running wars such as Afghanistan, but without it, military resources were always behind the curve, commanders improvising as things arrived out of sequence, and combat power was reduced. McKiernan remarked dryly that the way troops were sent was "not what military commanders would prefer."

Surges of troops in response were "treating the symptom, not the illness." McKiernan had watched Iraq slide into violence after his successful operation to take the country in 2003. The consequences were "ethnic strife, Sunni extremism, ISIS, and other things, and it's disheartening." The same mistakes were now being made in Afghanistan.

> I really dislike the term "surge" . . . American people think surge is some sort of military strategy—"surge." Well, we surged in Iraq and we surged in Afghanistan, because in both places, there was insufficient combat power to achieve our objectives. So, it was a reactive approach to ways and means, not a proactive approach to ways and means . . . It is really an admission that we don't have enough combat power, we're at risk of mission failure, so let's surge; let's put more forces in there for X period of time, and then bring them out. I don't think we've learned that lesson. You can try to do war on the cheap, and I think you'll pay more in the long run than you would if you had overwhelming combat power at the very beginning.

Faced with a politically driven arbitrary head count of soldiers, commanders contracted out logistics and engineering tasks to non-uniformed contractors, who were not in the crucial military head count. This was the most expensive way to run a conflict, as contractors come at a higher cost than troops. Lieutenant General Stanley McChrystal, then director of the Joint Staff in the Pentagon, knew of the dangers of "incremental escalation." A voracious reader, he drew a clear lesson from history. "Trailing an insurgency typically condemned counterinsurgents to failure."[12] The approach handed politicians a strategic military power they did not know they had. Democratic control of the military is of course essential, but the ideal is that elected officials define the task they want done and ask the military to do it. Partial increases of troops in Afghanistan tipped the balance of decision-making too far in the direction of politicians, and to seasoned military observers, there were too few people in the Obama administration with the right skills to make these decisions.

Defense Secretary Robert Gates, a surprise holdover from the Bush administration, watched the new team in the White House with concern. Gates believed they mistrusted the motives of military commanders. "The suspicion would only fester and grow over time."[13] It was a clash of cultures that would have serious consequences for Afghanistan. On the one hand were soldiers trying to fit troops to task and wanting politicians to state the task, and on the other, politicians and officials desperate to avoid mission creep, believing that whatever they provided, soldiers would always ask for more.

McKiernan's figure of thirty thousand was not plucked out of the air. He wanted to break the stalemate in the east and south. He needed two battalion-strength task forces for the provinces around Kabul to stabilize the east, and a brigade combat team for the south equipped with Stryker armored vehicles. He knew that high-tech assets—Predator drones, electronic surveillance planes, and so on—were a finite resource. In Iraq, there were then around sixteen Predator lines. He had only two and wanted some moved across. He needed more medics, more troop-carrying planes, and more route-clearance vehicles to combat IEDs, the increasingly sophisticated and lethal roadside bombs that were causing many casualties.

McKiernan also wanted a significant increase in training, with two more brigade-strength training teams—around ten thousand troops, to put U.S. troops alongside Afghan units to mentor and advise them as partners on operations as well as training. He knew that building the Afghan army, in particular its leaders, would take time. It had taken the U.S. a generation to rebuild the army from the force broken by Vietnam he had joined in the 1970s, to what was available to him in taking Baghdad thirty years later. "It takes us twelve to fifteen years to grow a first sergeant of a company . . . Why would we think that we'd have great first sergeants in Afghan companies, when we can't produce them any faster?"

☰ WRONG ENEMY IN THE WRONG COUNTRY

Other troop requests would have to wait for the result of a yearlong rethink. "In my entire career," wrote Gates, who served eight presidents, "I cannot think of any single issue or problem that absorbed so much of the president's and the principals' time and effort in such a compressed period."[14] The Bush team handed over an in-depth review on Afghan policy by deputy national security adviser, "war czar" Doug Lute, called because of a growing recognition that Afghanistan suffered from strategic neglect under the shadow of Iraq. "I think we may have lost sight of our national objectives in Afghanistan, our strategy to achieve them, and who's in charge," said Vice President Dick Cheney, launching the review process in the fall of 2008.[15] A series of different campaigns had developed without coordination or single command. Lute focused on Kandahar in one slide in his presentation—counting ten different wars in the same battle space. From the CIA counterterrorist pursuit teams, JSOC "black SOF" raids, "white SOF" Green Beret operations, and U.S. conventional operations, the slide included other NATO conventional operations, training teams with the Afghan army and police, provincial reconstruction teams (PRTs), Afghan conventional operations, and the campaign across the border in Pakistan.

The lack of coordination between these different units was having damaging effects on the mission. Afghan civilian casualties caused in night raids by special operators had to be dealt with by conventional forces on the ground who had no idea they were coming. "The sun would come up, and there would be a burning compound," said Lute. "A conventional infantry unit would have to go and figure out what happened, make amends with the locals, and it just went on and on."[16] Without more coordination between the ten wars, Lute thought the war lost. He recommended a crackdown on corruption, more coherence in the military and civilian campaign, and better training of the Afghan army.[17]

The one unit in the U.S. armed forces that was specifically tasked to train indigenous forces was the Green Berets, set up by President Kennedy to train the Montagnards in Vietnam. In Afghanistan, they delivered the best trained Special Forces in the region. But, Lute said, "it turns out they are still the only formation in the American force structure, organised, trained and equipped to enable and promote indigenous forces." Most training and advising of Afghan units was conducted not by Green Berets but rather by soldiers and marines untrained for the task. During a visit to Afghanistan for his review, he encountered an ad hoc unit from the National Guard training Afghan troops. They did not have any specific Afghan training. "We had soldiers who were completely misfit for the advising job we gave them." He asked them who was the intelligence adviser, the member of the team who would advise the Afghan intelligence chief. One answered, "Oh, that's me, Sergeant First

Class someone." Lute said, "OK, what's your intelligence background?" "None, sir. I'm a supply clerk."

Lute is a large, amiable man with an easy laugh and an appetite for process. Obama asked him to remain in his post, another holdover from the Bush administration, valuing Lute's capacity to make things happen, delivering alliances across competing parts of the administration. He retained his military rank as lieutenant general, only retiring from the army in 2010, and was influenced by General John Abizaid—the Arabic-speaking commander of CENTCOM until 2007, who was opposed to more American boots on the ground. Lute's military friends said he "never saw a surge he didn't like."[18] He would be an influential voice against increasing troop numbers.

But in the early days of the Obama administration, the most influential voice on Afghan policy was Bruce Riedel, who had been with the CIA in Pakistan's northwest frontier in the 1980s struggle against Soviet rule in Afghanistan. After the new president appointed him to lead yet another review, Riedel stunned the first meeting of the team involved. As soon as they had been round the room to introduce themselves, he said he would have a first draft by the end of the week. The result would clearly be little more than a copy-and-paste job from a pamphlet he had written at the Brookings Institution about al-Qaeda. His cochairs were the veteran diplomat Richard Holbrooke—whose experience went back to Vietnam and the successful Dayton Accords ending the Bosnian war—and Michèle Flournoy, the new undersecretary of defense for policy. "Michèle hadn't even formed her own team yet," said Lute, "she hadn't had time to visit Afghanistan, she hadn't had a chance to talk in depth to the commanders and suddenly Riedel announced, 'I'll have the first draft of our report by Friday.'"

Riedel's analysis fitted the growing consensus that Pakistan was a strategic risk to the mission, actively training and supporting the Taliban. In the early days of cross-border drone strikes, the location and targets were shared with Pakistani intelligence ahead of time, but "This changed," according to Riedel, "when it became apparent that some if not all of the targets were being tipped off."[19] By the time of his 2008 review, Lute had concluded that America had no vital national interests in Afghanistan. Their only vital national interests in the region were both in Pakistan—the security of Pakistani nuclear weapons and the location of the main commanders of al-Qaeda. Holbrooke agreed, putting it succinctly: "We may be fighting the wrong enemy in the wrong country."[20]

☰ COIN-LITE

Obama made his first speech linking the two countries on March 27, describing the situation as "perilous" in a low-key appearance in the Executive Office Building.[21] There were more than forty references to Pakistan, two-thirds as many as to Afghanistan. More than $8 billion of the $11 billion in U.S. aid to Pakistan since 9/11 had been in military aid,[22] but there were to be "no more blank checks." He unlocked $1.5 billion a year in aid to Islamabad, enraging the military establishment there by making it strictly nonmilitary. As for Afghanistan, the world faced an "international security challenge of the highest order," and America "must no longer deny Afghanistan" what it needed. But this did not extend to more troops beyond the twenty-one thousand already announced.

McKiernan became increasingly frustrated. "We didn't have enough Western security . . . we didn't have enough NATO and other troop-contributing national forces to establish the security conditions that would buy time and space to support the growth of Afghan security forces . . . we didn't have enough, period."

The president's solution to filling this gap was a civilian surge. "To advance security, opportunity and justice—not just in Kabul, but from the bottom up in the provinces—we need agricultural specialists and educators, engineers and lawyers . . . I'm ordering a substantial increase in our civilians on the ground." It felt like COIN-lite and was the least successful initiative in the war. Some civilians did answer the call, brave men and women who did good work. But they were hard to recruit, and there were too few of them. It was the largest recruitment drive for civilians in conflict since the CORDS[§] pacification program in Vietnam forty years earlier, and even though far smaller than CORDS, the systems to provide such staff did not exist. The State Department had to run some basic courses on things like "applying for a passport."

Once in Afghanistan, tours for the new civilians were too short to make a difference—one year was the maximum contract with frequent "hardship" breaks out of the country. The normal turnover time was

---

§ Civil Operations and Revolutionary Development Support

between May and August, losing continuity at the height of the Afghan fighting season. Leaving aside the more searching questions asked by development professionals engaged in longer-term projects in Afghanistan about whether these experts could do anything to make a difference, there were basic issues of logistics that were never resolved. Apart from not having the "required skills," Gates said, many new recruits "spent their entire Afghan tour holed up in the fortified embassy compound."[23]

The civilians found it hard to communicate with each other, let alone Afghanistan. State and Defense had different computer systems, one frustrated official reporting that "in the time it could take for an email to pass through the various firewalls of the different systems, he could print off the email and walk it across the embassy to a colleague's office."[24] There were agricultural experts available and ready to go, but the Department of Agriculture did not have a budget to send them to Afghanistan, and when they asked for help from the Department of Defense, the money could not be transferred. The new recruits were hugely expensive to deploy, requiring protection, but hampered by security restrictions on their capacity to make a difference, limiting contact with Afghans.

Michael Waltz, who worked for part of the war as a policy adviser to Vice President Dick Cheney and part as a Green Beret commanding special operators in eastern Afghanistan, told of one incident where an American agricultural specialist could not get to the rural college where he should have been teaching.[25] After his first day at work, the college asked him not to come back because the heavily armed convoy that brought him and stayed while he taught made the center a Taliban target. The district police chief, whose son was a student, promised local security if the American adviser came in a civilian car, a solution rejected by the State Department security officer responsible for his safety. Ignoring this, Waltz arranged lower-profile U.S. vehicles to take the adviser to the agricultural college before dawn—on random days, varying the route. "To me, it was a much bigger risk to have an expert in agriculture sitting on his rear end doing nothing a stone's throw from people who wanted his help."[26] He knew he would have lost his job if harm had come to the civilian expert. But he had been in enough meetings in Washington where Pentagon officials berated the State Department and USAID for not providing civilian assistance, and thought it a risk worth taking.

☰ FRESH EYES

In June 2009, Obama fired McKiernan, taking the advice he was given that he stood in the way of introducing COIN—the new map out of the labyrinth of the U.S. war in Afghanistan. The decision was a recognition "that we have to apply some fresh eyes to the problem," according to Obama.[27] Petraeus had not backed McKiernan, and Petraeus's mentor Jack Keane had been working behind the scenes to oust the Kabul commander since the inauguration, telling the new secretary of state, Hillary Clinton, that McKiernan was "the wrong man for the job. Too old school."[28]

Gates had approved McKiernan's appointment to Afghanistan in 2008, but in his memoir, *Duty*, written with the benefit of hindsight, he said his confidence waned several months before he made the decision to remove him. "To this day it is hard to put a finger on what exactly it was that concerned me, but my disquiet only grew through the winter."[29] He thought McKiernan lacked the capacity to innovate—and was not quick enough to change plans when things did not work out. "McKiernan was a very fine soldier but seemed to lack the flexibility and understanding of the battlespace required for a situation as complex as Afghanistan."[30] He had seen the ISAF commander close up in the twice-monthly video-conferences down the line that linked Presidents Bush and Karzai, free-ranging discussions that demanded a lot of the general. The video-conferences did not play to McKiernan's strengths. "I'm not sure things change as rapidly as you'd think they change every two weeks in Afghanistan," he said.

To Gates, the administration was short of the quality of analysis needed to sort through the blizzard of different reports on the state of the Afghan campaign. He constantly challenged the differing analysis of those on the ground and those in Washington. CIA reports remained constantly less positive than those from the military in Kabul. In a video-conference with McKiernan in Kabul, Gates exploded, "You guys sound pretty good, but then I get intelligence reports that indicate it is going to hell. I don't have a feel for how the fight is going. I don't think the president has a clear idea either of exactly where we are in Afghanistan."[31]

As early as 2007, Gates had signaled a different shape for the army by bringing Petraeus back from leading the counterinsurgency fight in Iraq to head the promotion board, deciding which forty colonels went on to their first star as brigadier generals. Those promoted were those who showed counterinsurgency flair, a quality not highlighted by promotion boards until then, among them H. R. McMaster.[32]

McKiernan was a man out of time. He was one of the best armored-maneuver commanders in the world, with a background training on the German plains to combat Russia. He spent seventeen years in Germany altogether, five tours during his army career, where he met Carmen, a German national working for the U.S. military, who became his wife. In the 1980s, once a month, as part of Operation Lariat Advance, they moved into position to defend against a Russian attack. Tanks would be armed for combat, and the men inside them did not know if this was a training exercise or for real. At the end of the day, they would drive to an agreed rendezvous point, "And we'd all look at each other and say 'This probably is not going to happen. We're not going to reconstitute. It's going to be a fight right along the border, and there's not going to be any combat power left.'"

The move into Baghdad that McKiernan commanded with such panache in 2003 would be the last big moment for the heavy army. The light army's time had come, as infantry and counterinsurgency skills were more rewarded. Brigadier General Austin Scott Miller created a new career stream, turning out "Afghan Hands," counterinsurgency experts who spoke the Afghan languages, Dari and Pashto. (Miller was a legend among special operators for commanding the team on the ground in the Black Hawk Down incident in Somalia in 1993, and would later go to Kabul as the commander of the coalition.)

McKiernan's fate was sealed after the undersecretary for defense, Michèle Flournoy, returned from a trip to Kabul in early April. She told Gates of her concern that civilian casualties were not being managed well enough, and he decided it was time for a change. Petraeus and the chairman of the Joint Chiefs of Staff, Admiral Mike Mullen, quickly agreed. General George Casey, the army chief of staff, and McKiernan's only ally at the top table, was a rare senior voice of dissent, saying it was a "rotten thing to do."[33] He called McKiernan and said, "Have you talked to the chairman lately?" And McKiernan said, "Not for a few days." It was the first indication he had there might be a problem.

Mullen called McKiernan the day before he was due to go on his first leave for ten months; Carmen was waiting to meet him in Germany, and they were planning a week's holiday in Oman. There was no reference to other NATO allies in making what was an American political decision. McKiernan knew he did not have a choice in whether to stay but only how he left, and when Mullen said he could "retire and go quietly," McKiernan turned him down. He argued that he should be allowed to remain until the spring of 2010. He knew he would not be able to look at himself in the mirror if he walked out; he had made commitments to his team and to people in Afghanistan, telling them he would be there for the long haul, see the job through. "I basically said, 'If you want to replace me you're going to have to fire me,' and naturally, they fired me."

McKiernan did not lack understanding of the doctrine—he lacked the troops he needed to apply it to make a decisive difference. At a press conference in the Pentagon, he made a strong case for extra troops. "We're into a very tough counterinsurgency fight there and will be for some time."[34] He had thought deeply about counterinsurgency before assuming command, and issued his own guidance when he arrived in Kabul in June 2008, defining his "operational imperative" as "protecting the population while extending the legitimacy and effectiveness" of the Afghan government—as good a definition of modern counterinsurgency as there was, and straight out of the manual. He put civilian protection ahead of defeating the enemy as the main goal of military action. "Success in Afghanistan will not come from the sole pursuit of a security line of operation by military forces. Claims that ISAF does only security have no place in this campaign. These lines of operation are interdependent and are intended to be complementary and comprehensive; failure in one means mission failure in all."[35]

In his guidance he outlined the phases of "Shape, Clear, Hold, and Build," the building blocks of successful counterinsurgency operations as defined in the new doctrine—*Shape,* meaning to understand and prepare the ground; *Clear,* eliminate insurgent activity; *Hold,* ensure sufficient force to establish security; and *Build,* deliver economic benefits to extend the effective reach of the Afghan government. Each of these phases needed to be in partnership with Afghans, and with them in the lead if possible, and the military did not have all the answers. McKiernan told his troops on his arrival in Afghanistan, "There is no purely military solution to the situation in Afghanistan."

One of the concerns expressed by Flournoy in the visit that sealed McKiernan's fate was that she believed he did not engage at political levels in Afghanistan. For those who knew him, this was far from the truth. It was only that he did not shout about it. He was constantly on the ground in Afghanistan, comfortable working at lower levels. One of his advisers, a former navy pilot, Paul Farnan, wrote:

> I have seen our focus in Afghanistan shift from kinetic military op-
> erations to one of engaging the population, building the capacity
> of the Afghan government, and ensuring that the military's top pri-
> ority is the training and mentoring of the Afghan army and police.
> Integrated strategic planning with the United Nations and the Af-
> ghan government is now the rule rather than the exception, as it
> was when McKiernan arrived last June. The general has travelled
> around the country and has held countless forums, known as shuras,
> with Afghans in various localities. He has engaged local and provin-
> cial leaders one on one to hear their concerns and ensure that they
> understood the intentions of the international coalition. All of our
> Special Forces operations combined cannot win the support of the
> Afghan people the way these shuras do.[36]

COIN also required a sophisticated communications strategy, particularly in the new world of the near-universal availability of smart-
phones in Afghanistan, which caused McKiernan such problems managing civilian casualty incidents. And he understood the need to grasp it particularly at lower tactical levels. "When you're in an environment of counterinsurgency, and trying to support the growth of a government, and dealing with population," a successful communica-
tions strategy "is a vital ingredient to what the commander has at his disposal to create effects." It was in pursuit of COIN principles that McKiernan was close to completing a new partnership deal with the U.S. embassy to encourage civil/military coordination when he was forced out of his post. If David Petraeus's new way of doing war was to work, it had to be embraced by commanders with a conventional background like McKiernan, not only the charismatic mavericks like

McMaster now on the ascendant. But a new administration wanted a new general for a new policy.

≡ RAMPANT TRIBALISM

The only specific disagreement Gates had with McKiernan was over a decision in October 2008 to bring all U.S. troops in the country under him, including those on Operation Enduring Freedom (OEF). Instead of the unified command, Gates wanted to appoint a three-star lieutenant general under McKiernan to be "totally focused on the fight,"[37] taking command of day-to-day operations—"down" and "in." This would leave McKiernan's focus "up" and "out"—strategic command of the conflict and liaison with President Karzai and the hydra-headed international political and military structures with an interest in Kabul. But McKiernan wanted to end what he saw as "rampant tribalism" between different forces on the ground in Afghanistan. And so Gates agreed to change the structure, extending McKiernan's command to the fifteen thousand or so American troops deployed under OEF—mostly in the frontier region in the east, as well as most special operations forces, although CIA operations remained outside his control. The lack of overall command had led to many arguments between President Karzai and ISAF commanders unsighted on operations that caused casualties. The move meant that for the first time since 2001, nearly all U.S. military assets in the country were under one command. The ISAF commander was held accountable by Afghan politicians for everything that international forces did in the country; he needed to be responsible for it as well. NATO allies were opposed. They felt the U.S. had "sucked them into Afghanistan as an alliance project" before wanting to put it all under an American again.[38] They feared they would be implicated in American black ops.

McKiernan returned to Kabul from negotiating with Gates in October, confident he now had the mandate he needed for the new combined command role. But while in Washington, he missed the importance of key changes in the administration of the army. In August 2008, McChrystal was brought back from five years commanding special operations in Iraq and Afghanistan to become the director of the Joint Staff at the Pentagon. This was Gates's move against what he saw as the inertia of a large bureaucracy that was comfortable planning wars but not geared to fighting them.

The chairman of the Joint Chiefs of Staff, Admiral Mike Mullen, told McChrystal to "attack and destroy the network," and the network he was talking about was the Pentagon itself. "Tear it down and rebuild it to be faster, more transparent, and more effective."[39] Petraeus, the other force used as a creative disruptor from the inside, arrived back from Iraq to the center of things three months after McChrystal, in October 2008, as commander of CENTCOM in Florida. And Petraeus was one of the architects of the plan to split the Afghan command that McKiernan opposed. It was not just McKiernan who felt the heat of the administration's impatience with progress in the wars. To get to CENTCOM, Petraeus elbowed aside Admiral William "Fox" Fallon, who had fallen out with the administration over Iran, where he was more cautious than the Bush White House.[40]

McKiernan's whole career was in the field—Germany, Korea, the Balkans, Iraq, and Afghanistan—apart from a brief spell in the Pentagon, where he was called in just after 9/11 to be G-3 of the army, responsible at the highest level for operations and planning of America's response to the attacks on the homeland. He never did the more political jobs that were available. He had not been a general's aide, or stalked the corridors with a mission to dismantle the bureaucracy or shake up the army—the roles given to the disruptors McChrystal and Petraeus. McKiernan's distance from the political machine was more than physical—he inhabited a different world, where virtue was demonstrated by delivery, not by shouting about it. "Ambition is looked upon favorably in life, and I'm not sure I would hold it in that high a regard." Where once quiet competence may have been enough, it was not now.

McKiernan remains disappointed with the decision and angry that it has often been reported that he was relieved of command. "When you're relieved of your command in the military, it's for an error. I was not relieved . . . I was replaced." Gates came to speak to McKiernan in Kabul two weeks after Mullen's call and said, "He acceded with extraordinary dignity and class."[41] McKiernan called in all the general officers then in Afghanistan, about a dozen, for a dinner, and told them that while it was not how he would have wanted to go, he was not bitter. "I've had these incredible experiences serving my country. This is just the way it is."[42] The decision shocked the military establishment—it was the first time a commander had been replaced in the field since Douglas MacArthur in Korea in 1951. The day before he met Gates in Kabul, McKiernan appeared on *Time* magazine's list of the one hundred most influential people in the world. General Wesley Clark, who had been McKiernan's superior officer in Iraq and Kosovo, wrote the citation for the magazine. "He's extraordinarily calm under stress, a clear thinker, tough and morally courageous . . . McKiernan is not afraid to stand up and ask for what he needs."

The issue that had caused him trouble throughout—civilians killed by U.S. air strikes—also reemerged that week. There were riots by rock-throwing protestors in Farah in the deserts of the southwest, one of the poorest provinces in Afghanistan, after the deaths of at least sixty-three women and children in an air strike—one of the worst death tolls in a single incident of this kind. A B-1 bomber dropped munitions in two waves after dark, destroying a mosque. As so often, the American military had good reason to respond at first to a request by Afghan troops who came following the public beheading of three villagers by the Taliban. The air strikes were called in after intense fighting in which both U.S. and Afghan troops took casualties. But investigators later found that the bombing hit compounds where women and children were sheltering sometime after the shooting stopped, against McKiernan's commander's intent.[43]

≡ NO NEW STRATEGY

Dave McKiernan retired to Marblehead, Massachusetts, where the only intelligence briefings he gets are from *The Boston Globe,* and there is nowhere he would rather be than a ski slope. At his retirement ceremony, Secretary Gates said he had "handled everything the Army and his commander in chief have thrown at him with supreme professionalism, intelligence and dedication to our nation, and the men and women under his command." In the June sunshine at Fort Myer, across the Potomac River from Washington, his last event in formation in uniform, McKiernan said he was "dismayed, disappointed, and more than a little embarrassed" to be standing there, while encouraging those who sympathized to spare their condolences "for those who truly need them—the families, friends and comrades of men and women who either will not return home or whose lives have been permanently scarred by war."

Like many in the military, his children followed his career. His son,

Captain Michael McKiernan, served in the military police, advising Afghan police in Gardez in 2009, and his daughter, Lieutenant Stephanie McKiernan, trained as a helicopter pilot in the 1st Cavalry, his old division, and flew her father in Kandahar in 2013 on a return trip to the country.

McKiernan had made a virtue of avoiding the political game, admitting that "visits in Washington, press conferences, or briefings to the civilian leadership, that's not my comfort zone." It meant he did not watch his back and had no notice of the growing concern about him in a new administration seeking to stamp their mark on the Afghan campaign. The foreign and security policy team around Obama thought they now grasped COIN—the shiny new policy that would change the course of the war—and thought that McKiernan did not. It was politically convenient for the Obama administration to promote a story blaming him for standing in the way of the policy.

Encouraged by Pentagon briefing, a characterization grew of McKiernan as an armored warfare expert who did not understand the nuances of the new war: "solid but uninspired," according to David Ignatius of *The Washington Post;*[44] "an excellent general in the old mold,"[45] wrote Fred Kaplan at *Slate* magazine. This characterization was not recognized by those who served with him in Afghanistan. One senior Canadian officer wrote, "For the first time in the ISAF mission the coalition had a strategy that was not just working well, but was delivering results that exceeded expectations."[46]

His successor was General Stanley McChrystal, and Gates moved swiftly on the plan to split the command role opposed by McKiernan, appointing his own military assistant, Lieutenant General David "Rod" Rodriguez, to return to Afghanistan, where he had been the year before, to command the day-to-day fight. Gates had plucked the two commanders who were in his sight in the Pentagon every day to run a war that was now more in the public eye than ever, and they would be under the oversight of the regional commander and godfather of counterinsurgency, David Petraeus at CENTCOM.

On May 12, alongside Mullen at the Pentagon, Gates said, "We have a new policy set by our new president. We have a new strategy, a new mission and a new ambassador [the former lieutenant general Karl Eikenberry], I believe that new military leadership is also needed."[47] Those around McKiernan said there was no new strategy. All he lacked was the resources to do the task. One of his senior planning officers said McKiernan "had done the ground work, but Gates did not know that."[48]

In his last encounters on the ground in Afghanistan before he was fired, in the south of the country, McKiernan revealed to the assembled elders, "I'm reading a very good book now about this part of the world. It's written in English, but it's all about you—it's the Quran."[49] An elder spontaneously presented him with a fine piece of purple-, red-, and green-colored cloth to wrap his translated copy to give it respect. In separate meetings in Kandahar and Helmand, McKiernan apologized for past mistakes and addressed concerns about night raids and the need to respect women in Afghan homes. He received strong applause for saying the Taliban could not be defeated unless their safe havens across the nearby border were destroyed. U.S. troops would soon be stationed for the first time in these southern provinces close to the frontier, where mainly Canadian and UK forces had been leading the fight until then. McKiernan's visits were deliberately aimed at laying the ground for the increases he had fought so hard for. By the time the troops arrived, he had been forced into retirement.

McKiernan's career was over. He was skeptical of the claims of a "new strategy" made by those who succeeded him. "Changing the commander is not the silver bullet that's going to change all the dynamics in Afghanistan." He had been elbowed aside by the command team of McChrystal and Rodriguez, whom Gates believed had "a unique skillset in counterinsurgency,"[50] as Afghanistan fully became Obama's war.

OWNING THE VILLAGES

They own the villages. That's where this is going to be won.

If we have lost our influence and legitimacy in the villages, we've got a big problem. It happened in Vietnam and it happened in Afghanistan.

—General Stanley A. McChrystal

☰ TEAM AMERICA

Lieutenant Colonel Stanley McChrystal introduced a fitness regime in his first battalion command role in the 82nd Airborne in 1993.[1] Over a four-week rotation, every soldier had to run first four, then eight, twelve, then twenty miles. His battalion wondered how McChrystal himself would fulfill his commitment when a conference was scheduled for the Thursday he was due to run his twenty miles. As they arrived on buses at dawn for the conference, McChrystal ran past them. He had set out after midnight. It was the beginning of the creation of a legend of an obsessive warrior-monk, sleeping four hours and eating one meal a day, a leader totally focused on the fight. His single-minded pursuit of wanting every soldier in the right frame of mind led admirers to compare him to General Matthew Ridgway, who took over from General Douglas MacArthur at the height of the Korean War. Like Ridgway, McChrystal was known to lead by example.

Arriving in Afghanistan in the height of the summer of 2009, McChrystal took on Baskin-Robbins before he turned his attention to the Taliban, attempting to close a string of fast-food outlets at Kandahar and Bagram Air Bases that had sprung up since the days of the austere encampment he

knew in 2002. He banned alcohol for non–American troops still then allowed to drink and saw as an affront the coffee bar in the garden in front of
the "yellow building," the main ISAF headquarters—one of the few places
soldiers could smoke in the cramped alleyways snaking through stacks of
containers that made up the base. The garden and bars were "relevant pieces
of terrain" in McChrystal's sights as he sought to refocus total commitment to winning.[2] He ordered that flags should no longer be lowered to
half-mast for losses, but kept fully raised. "A force that's fighting a war can't
spend all its time looking back at what the costs have been."[3]

To get his senior staff out of siloed single offices, he had a situational
awareness room (SAR) built onto the side of the yellow building—a
large rectangle with desks around three sides of a model map showing
Afghanistan in relief and a bank of screens on the fourth side. It replicated what he had built in his previous role as commander of TF-714
coordinating special operations in Iraq and Afghanistan. To be close to
the campaign 24-7, McChrystal slept and worked out in a small win-
dowless cell above the Kabul SAR, furnished by just an iron-framed bed
and gym equipment. He had given five years to his previous role and
told Obama he would do three in Afghanistan. Alongside him in the
nerve center, he brought a tight team of senior officers mostly from the
special operations world, told not to see this as a tour with an end date:
they would be in Afghanistan "for 18 months, two and a half years, for
the duration, however long it took to win."[4]

McChrystal was skilled at communicating to thousands of people,
valuing input across a flat hierarchy—not the normal military model.
The SAR idea grew from his experience when he arrived in Iraq in
2003. He discovered bags piled up as if trash, full of documents, CDs,
and hard drives seized on raids that had not even been opened—a wasted
resource. Special operators going out on raids nightly had little connection with the analysis of the products they brought back. He moved
the analysts closer to the action to turn the intelligence into real-time
information, and penetrated closed bubbles to get information shared
with his TF-714 special operators across the alphabet soup of U.S. secret
networks—the CIA, FBI, DIA, NSC, and NGA.¶

¶ CIA: Central Intelligence Agency; DIA: Defense Intelligence Agency; FBI: Federal Bureau of
Investigation; NSC: National Security Council; NGA: National Geospatial-Intelligence Agency.

Unnervingly for people used to hoarding secrets, he made the whole Baghdad SAR a top secret–secure facility, so there was no excuse not to cooperate.[5] The wide sharing of information had its downside. The material copied by Chelsea Manning, when she was Private Bradley Manning, onto CDs labeled "Lady Gaga" and sent to WikiLeaks, came from this access. But the upside was swifter analysis of information, turning a hard fight in Iraq to America's advantage. McChrystal repeated the model in Kabul, building a flat network to link as many people as possible across the country into his morning briefing. He was less worried about leaks than troops not knowing what they should be doing. "It's a tradeoff and I think I come down on this side every time."[6]

It would take more than an open-plan office and interconnected communications to build a counterinsurgency campaign. The messy, complex, political and tribal world of Afghanistan could not be analyzed as easily as a terrorist group. For much of McChrystal's military career, he had seen Iraq and Afghanistan through the lens of a Predator drone camera, the prisoner captured at night, the harvest of intelligence. "When our helicopters landed, our operators normally had the benefit of surprise, the cover of night, and intimate knowledge of whom they would find on their objective." Success in Iraq was measurable. "We could both see and feel the impact we were having on Zarqawi's organization." Counterinsurgency did not have such clear metrics. A campaign where progress could not be measured by direct attrition of a terrorist network was harder to do, harder to assess, and harder to explain, both to his own troops and the public, weary of a lack of progress in the long war.[7]

The arrival of McChrystal's retinue of thirty mainly American ex–Special Forces officers, immediately called Team America, brought friction into a multinational headquarters, where McKiernan had been liked. There was "palpable resentment" as one of the new arrivals, Colonel Kevin Owens, admitted. "Frankly we probably reinforced it at times, whether consciously or otherwise."

McChrystal *believed* in counterinsurgency, as the tool that would change the dial so it was no longer year one every year. He knew he came with a reputation as "one of the killers," but had a long-term interest in counterinsurgency, in particular French experiences in Indochina and Algeria. "I'd been fascinated by it when I was young. That was more my DNA than the CT stuff that I ended up doing later." In Iraq, he had watched Petraeus's delivery of counterinsurgency make a difference, as part of a wider national plan, and wanted the same effect in Afghanistan.

There was no difference on paper between his counterinsurgency and the plan adopted by McKiernan. "You know these are not new ideas," the deputy commander of ISAF, British lieutenant general Jim Dutton, sharply reminded Team America when they proposed a new directive to reduce civilian casualties. "We actually put out guidance to this effect several months ago."[8] But beyond the written guidance, to McChrystal, it was a question of *belief* down to every private soldier. He wanted to "change the mindset" in Kabul, where on arrival he found "a creeping, fatalistic pessimism, as though the fight were over, the effort failed."[9] The effort in Afghanistan was not just less than Iraq, it was "junior varsity, B-squad level," starved of both resources and good people.[10]

McChrystal did not blame McKiernan, who had requested more troops that did not arrive until his last days in command. But he thought the problems more serious than had been reported. Failure was inevitable unless there was a radical shift in direction. He put his chances of success at fifty-fifty, "and only then if we made serious changes."[11]

≡ DEFEAT OR DESTROY

It was still no clearer what winning meant. At the beginning, President Bush sent troops to Afghanistan "to destroy the Taliban and al Qaeda,"[12] before drifting into an ill-formed dream of building democracy. The language of President Obama's first speech on the war in March signaled narrower aims: "To disrupt, dismantle and defeat al Qaeda in Pakistan and Afghanistan and to prevent their return to either country in the future."[13] But neither president was willing to commit to the long-term stability that would indeed "prevent their return."

The paradox of not wanting to commit to nation-building but only short-term fixes was that it condemned America to be in Afghanistan for the long term. Obama recognized that because of the wasted years, when the long war was overshadowed by Iraq, "we'd have to start from scratch in Afghanistan. But it nonetheless dawned on me that even in the best-case scenario—even if Karzai cooperated, Pakistan behaved, and our goals were limited to what Gates liked to call 'Afghan good enough'—we were still looking at three to five years of intense effort, costing hundreds of billions more dollars and more American lives."[14] He was wary of committing the resources needed. During the arguments in 2009 over troop increases requested by McChrystal, the president was clear. "I'm not doing ten years. I'm not doing a long-term nation-building effort. I'm not spending a trillion dollars."[15] As a consequence, America would indeed be in Afghanistan for another ten years, spending many billions of dollars, still without a plan for anything other than the short term.

The pity was that rethinking the war in 2009 was supposed to be different—making judgments based on more than the numbers of boots on the ground, the only metric that ever seemed to matter. But it did not turn out that way because of the narrow aperture of the war aim, as if looking down the wrong end of a telescope. If the only target were al-Qaeda, the administration would not commit to a whole of Afghanistan policy, including security, long-term programs for governance, infrastructure, land reform, justice, higher education, a road map for talking to the Taliban, and a coherent approach to the continued threat played by the non-Taliban warlords.

Obama saw the decision he had to make as consequential as LBJ being asked to send ground troops to Vietnam in 1965.[16] By 1965, Richard Holbrooke had been in Vietnam for three years as a foreign service officer; his experience haunted the deliberations over the Afghan surge. Staffers born far later than 1965 were handed photocopied pages from Holbrooke's ghostwritten autobiography of Clark Clifford, the Kennedy and Johnson adviser who opposed the troop increase.[17] Across the administration in 2009, they were reading *Lessons in Disaster,* a book just out about national security aide McGeorge Bundy's missteps in pushing for more troops in 1965. Obama's team were determined to learn from Lesson Five—"Never Deploy Military Means in Pursuit of Indeterminate Ends."

It was unclear what the ends were. McChrystal regretted not pushing Obama to give him clearer guidance when he was appointed. "I should have given him a piece of paper and said, write down what you want me to do, and I will try to do that. It would have forced him to get in his own mind what he wanted me to do, and me to understand it." He was appointed quickly on Gates's recommendation when McKiernan was cast aside, and did not take the chance when he could to insist on a focused conversation about war aims. Instead, his appointment meeting in the White House was little more than a photocall. Obama was unnerved by the lean, muscular intent figure with no small talk. "McChrystal's whole manner was that of someone who's burned away frivolity and distractions from his life."[18]

On arrival in Kabul in June, McChrystal was asked for his strategic assessment, and Gates told him to provide it without any troop numbers attached. The administration wanted to know the full effect of the twenty-one thousand committed at the beginning of the year before sending more. Speaking marine to marine on a fact-finding trip to Helmand, National Security Adviser Jim Jones told Brigadier General Larry Nicholson that if Obama were asked for more troops at this stage, he would likely have a "Whiskey Tango Foxtrot moment"[19]—meaning *what the fuck.*

There were nine long meetings between the president and senior cabinet members before Obama stood in front of the latest cadets in the long gray line at West Point to announce his decision in December, and there were many WTF moments along the way as the White House felt boxed in by generals going public with demands for more troops. At the beginning of September, Petraeus called Michael Gerson at *The Washington Post* to rebut a David Ignatius column saying counterinsurgency would fail in Afghanistan. Far from it, said Petraeus. More troops were needed for a fully resourced counterinsurgency. "We have to get ahead of this, to arrest the downward spiral, to revive momentum."[20]

The comments outraged the White House, and Petraeus, who had an easy relationship with reporters, was forced to tone down his rhetoric. One speech prompted Tom Ricks to write, "Dave does dull." Petraeus sent him an email: "You have no idea how much skill is required to do dull on a topic as emotional right now as Afghanistan."[21]

Afghan experts and think tankers brought to Kabul to inform McChrystal's strategic assessment wrote op-eds on their return saying more force was needed, with bylines associating them to McChrystal.[22] Having his staff contact them to lay off was just locking the stable door. To the White House, it looked like a coordinated campaign. Biden called it "fucking outrageous."[23] Gates called in Mullen and Petraeus with McChrystal in a videoconference call from Kabul, where Petraeus protested his innocence. "We all resolved that we need to again avoid any perception that we are trying to jam the President or that we're trying to go around him to the press."

There were leaks too from officials in the administration attracted to a plan Biden called *counterterrorism-plus.* "*The New York Times* was besieged by unsolicited White House sources offering their views," according to Gates.[24] Under CT-plus, involving fewer than ten thousand U.S. personnel, the U.S. would keep only Kandahar and Bagram air bases, with enough capacity to dominate the skies and human intelligence networks to feed information to Special Operation Forces and CIA counterterrorist teams targeting al-Qaeda.

Doug Lute said the arguments through the fall swirled round the "action verb." What were troops there to *do*? "Disrupt, dismantle and defeat al Qaeda" was what Obama said in his March speech. Steve Coll reported that *defeat* was inserted in place of the original draft word *destroy* only twenty minutes before he stood up. When Mullen told the president *destroy* was a very high bar, he changed it.[25]

At Gates's insistence, the strategic implementation plan, effectively the orders given to McChrystal, had stronger language than the Obama speech. The enemy who should be defeated was not just al-Qaeda but also the Taliban.[26] *Defeat* is defined by the U.S. Army as "rendering a force incapable of achieving its objectives."[27] It may not involve any military action at all, if the political environment could be altered. Defeating the Taliban meant denying them space to operate, so to McChrystal, the campaign "necessarily included building capacity across the government and providing the opportunity for economic development."[28] It set alarm bells ringing, as it sounded like nation-building.

Defeat "scared the hell out of NATO," according to a member of the drafting team for the McChrystal assessment, Colonel James McGrath. "It was a tall order to get our NATO brothers to understand that we're going to call a spade a spade and frankly be very American about it." Many NATO nations had signed up to support development, peacekeeping not war fighting. Germany deliberately did not call it a war, forcing the resignation of a president in 2010 who used the wrong language. McGrath said NATO command at Brunssum had "101 issues" with the word defeat, which was an affront to "NATO sensibilities."[29]

The parrying over language went on throughout the long White House meetings to decide a policy, McChrystal talking at cross-purposes with those promoting CT-plus in some "really contentious" videoconferences.[30] Biden said at one meeting, "Wait a minute, why are you trying to destroy all the Taliban?" McChrystal said that was not what defeat meant. If the Taliban were prevented from accomplishing their mission, they would be defeated, "even if we kill nobody." For the next meeting, he produced a slide with *defeat* in the middle and a series of other words around it, from *degrade* to *eradicate,* to show what he was being asked to do and how it had derived from the March speech and his strategic implementation plan. "It seemed to surprise some of the participants," McChrystal said.

The president came down on his side. "Stan is just doing what we've asked him to do."[31] But later, given how far the options then being considered were from full resourcing for counterinsurgency, Obama said, "We have done a disservice to McChrystal" by not making clear the goal was shifting.[32] Experienced counterinsurgency experts began to despair of the delays and overthinking at a time when there were only two choices—either leave or commit more troops. David Kilcullen likened it to a burning building with firefighters already inside. "It is not appropriate to stand outside pontificating about not taking lightly the responsibility of sending firemen into harm's way. Either put in enough firemen to put the fire out or get out of the house."[33]

≣ MORE FORCES OR MISSION FAILURE

The word *counterinsurgency* was not used in the president's March speech; he took it out of the National Security Council draft.[34] But it was recommended by Bruce Riedel's paper and was at the heart of McChrystal's strategic assessment, a sixty-six-page document sent in September. "We must conduct classic counterinsurgency operations in an environment that is uniquely complex," McChrystal wrote. "Success demands a comprehensive counterinsurgency (COIN) campaign." Like so much, the strategic assessment leaked. The American people could read it in *The Washington Post* before McChrystal had briefed it to senior military commanders—four columns under the headline MCCHRYSTAL: "MORE FORCES OR MISSION FAILURE." It could not have been timed worse, appearing online on the evening of Sunday, September 20, a day the president had been on several talk shows wanting to move on to talk about health reforms and, when asked about Afghanistan, stressed he "did not want to put the resource question ahead of the strategy question." Senior commanders thought the leak a turning point, damaging trust, perhaps irreparably, in the relationship between the president and the military.

The main writer of the assessment was Jeff Eggers, a former SEAL close to McChrystal, who said the sense of impending failure was put in by McChrystal "to stick a finger in the chest of people reading it."[35] McChrystal knew the shock effect of what he was doing. In the military, it's cool to understate and say things are fine. This was not going to be an understated report; its conclusions were deliberately stark. "Failure to gain the initiative and reverse insurgent momentum in the near term . . . risks an outcome where defeating the insurgency is no longer possible." While there were no troop requests in the document, McChrystal wrote, "Inadequate resources will likely result in failure."

Later that week, CBS's *60 Minutes* aired an interview with McChrystal in which he revealed that in his first two months in command, he had spoken to Obama only once on a VTC from Kabul. It made the president look remote, unconcerned.[36] Ten days later, in answers to questions after a speech at a London defense think tank, the International Institute for Strategic Studies, McChrystal was asked if he would support counterterrorism alone, the Biden option, although Biden was not mentioned by name. He said, "The short answer is no." Reducing the mission to drone attacks and air strikes would lead to "Chaos-istan." He went further, in what was construed as an implied criticism of White House delays in taking a decision. "Waiting does not prolong a favorable outcome. This effort will not remain winnable indefinitely." He said he was encouraged by the administration to express his views, but "they may change their minds and crush me someday."

The day after the London speech, McChrystal was called to Copenhagen, where the president was on a stopover, to be reprimanded, and earned a further public rebuke from Secretary Gates, who said advice to the president from civilian and military leaders should come "candidly but privately."[37] The president called in Admiral Mike Mullen and Gates, asking, in controlled anger, "Is it because they figure they know better and don't want to be bothered answering my questions? Is it because I'm young and didn't serve in the military? Is it because they don't like my politics?"[38] He met with America's most respected military leader, retired general and former secretary of state Colin Powell, who told the president, "Don't get pushed by the left to do nothing. Don't get pushed by the right to do everything."[39]

The conversation continued both in lengthy deliberations in Washington and in public. Kabul ambassador Karl Eikenberry's opposition to more troops in a memo to Clinton was leaked.[40] More troops, he wrote, would mean deeper engagement "with no way to extricate ourselves, short of allowing the country to descend again into lawlessness and chaos." He was particularly critical of Karzai as an unreliable partner, and recommended the U.S. take more time before deciding—which Gates saw as "ridiculous" after a yearlong reassessment.[41] The memo made Eikenberry's position in Kabul unworkable since Karzai now refused to see him on his own, and it damaged his relations with McChrystal, who was "completely blind-sided by it. I thought it was just discourteous." He thought Eikenberry was getting his opposition on the record for the history books.[42] The memo arrived in Washington (and inevitably leaked to *The New York Times*) in the last critical weeks of decision-making in November. Eikenberry remained in post for several more months, backed by Biden, although Clinton and Gates wanted him out.[43]

McChrystal's troop request, separate from his strategic assessment, did not leak. His three alternatives depended on what the president decided to do. If all that was planned was a training operation, then eleven thousand troops would be enough. A counterinsurgency would need forty thousand, a more robust counterinsurgency eighty thousand. It was a classic Goldilocks ploy, with the expectation that the middle number would be chosen. There was no mention of CT-plus, the preferred Biden option, which McChrystal saw as "pretty close to the status quo." That was what was not working.

The upper-end figure of eighty thousand did not come out of the air. Working on a low estimate of the Afghan population of twenty-four million, counterinsurgency math would require 480,000 troops.[44] If there were four hundred thousand Afghan troops, then the U.S. could make up the rest. But the math would only go so far. No American administration would fund an Afghan force that large, although Petraeus continued to push for it.[45] McChrystal recognized there were command decisions on risk that could not be run through the computer. "Counterinsurgency doctrine on security force levels was as much art as science."[46]

On December 1, 2009, in a somber atmosphere at West Point, in a

long speech punctuated only five times with applause, the president unveiled his Afghanistan strategy, denying there had been any operational
delay. "Afghanistan is not lost, but for several years it has moved backwards." Just as he had second-guessed McKiernan's request at the start
of the year, approving only two-thirds of the troops requested, so he approved just thirty thousand of McChrystal's forty-thousand request, with
the hope that NATO allies would make up the rest. Again, counterinsurgency was not mentioned, and after months arguing over whether the
mission was to defeat the Taliban or "deny," "disrupt," or "degrade" them,
Obama said the goal was "narrowly defined as disrupting, dismantling,
and defeating al-Qaeda and its extremist allies."

Its extremist allies was ambiguous—and could be seen to refer only to
international terrorists, not the Taliban. In McChrystal's mind, the ambiguity was not cleared up in a six-page amended plan sent to McChrystal
the White House called the "terms sheet"—as if a legal contract. It was
an unusual document, issued as an "order" in the final meeting ahead
of the public announcement, to the surprise of Gates, who had never
heard anyone issue an "order" before at that level. He thought it revealed
"the depth of the Obama White House's distrust of the nation's military
leadership."[47] The leaks and sense of being jammed in by the generals had their effect. Obama wrote, "McChrystal's lengthy timetable for
both installing troops and pulling them out looked less like an Iraq-style
surge than a long-term occupation."[48] So he wanted a clear exit. Bob
Woodward reported that the terms sheet was personally dictated by the
president, based on a memo written by Gates.[49] Doug Lute said it was
quite clear and deliberately designed to limit the mission, both in scale
and duration.

Rather than spreading the surge forces across the country, they would
be focused in less than a quarter of the country in what were called "Key
Terrain Districts"—strategic hubs that would spread stability and join
like ink blots. This was a classic COIN idea. Lute called it a "tailored
or metered counterinsurgency." But the document was "inelegant" in
McChrystal's eyes and lacking clarity, except in what *not* to do. The mission was *not* a fully resourced counterinsurgency, and it was *not* to *defeat*
the Taliban, instead the document used words like *reverse* their momentum, *deny* their access to key population areas, *disrupt* and *degrade* them
to a level manageable by the Afghans.[50] McChrystal was sympathetic

about the lack of clarity; Afghanistan was a tough conflict to define. "I'd watched all these different studies that say what you have got to do, and at the end of the day they reached pretty similar conclusions. But what you've got to do is really hard." The counterinsurgency manuals defined this kind of conflict as 80 percent political. He kept his focus on the political need to stand up the Afghan state and its security forces, but was left with "a lesser level of effort" for the task as he saw it.

There was one more condition attached. This was the last throw of the dice. There would be no more troops for Afghanistan, and the withdrawal would begin in 2011. In a separate videoconference with McChrystal and Eikenberry, the president made this limitation clearer: troops should not go to areas that could not be handed over to full Afghan security control by 2011. McChrystal told Obama he did not agree with the deadline, but would salute and get on with it. "You have made your decision and I appreciate being listened to."

In the president's mind, the troop surge would be on a standard distribution bell curve, out on as steep a slope as they went in. There should be no more policy drift. He wanted troops on the ground at the "fastest pace possible" and tried to shift the start date to the left.[51] The eighteen-month timeline was designed to focus attention in the Afghan government to step up, improve their forces, and take on the fight for themselves, based on Pentagon assessments of how long it would take for the surge to take effect.

The withdrawal schedule was opposed by almost every senior military figure in the land, handing tactical advantage to the Taliban, who would know how long they had to hold out. Immediately, Petraeus and others worked to move the reverse slope of the bell curve to the right, or at least flatten the top of the surge, so troops could stay for longer.

Nine days after announcing the largest increase in troops since the start of the Afghan war, Obama went to Oslo to collect the Nobel Peace Prize. The same day, McChrystal headed out to spend a night next to the Gettysburg battlefield with his wife, Annie. It was a place where he often sought inspiration at important moments in his life. He had just given testimony to Congress and, as always at big moments, went running.

I strongly believed we could succeed, and committed myself completely. As I ran that evening alongside the grass of the battlefield, gray and dry in the wintry early evening, I knew that despite all I'd done, all I'd learned, and all of myself that I was prepared to devote, in war, nothing was certain.[52]

≣ MARINE-ISTAN

Four days after McChrystal arrived in command in Kabul in June, Operation Panther's Claw kicked off a rolling series of offensives in Helmand. More than three hundred soldiers from the Scottish regiment, the Black Watch, were dropped at night from twelve CH-47 helicopters into farmland at Babaji in the west of the main populated zone in Helmand.

Nowhere in the long war can the words *missed opportunity* be used more accurately than for Helmand. Issues of land rights, justice, access to water, as well as security were not dealt with in the years after the Taliban fell. In many places, a predatory police force alienated people from the government and weakened local security, so that when the Taliban returned, they found people willing to support them again. British troops had been outnumbered and pinned down in daily firefights in the three years since they arrived in the province in 2006. Panther's Claw was designed to change that—to allow a British withdrawal to the main population centers around the capital, Lashkar Gah, while U.S. Marines moved in strength to the more scattered communities on either side of the Helmand River in the north and south of the province. This was one of the most consequential strategic decisions of the war. Not only were McChrystal's first six months dominated by the protracted reexamination of the war in Washington, but his ability to shape the war on the ground was limited. The plan was already in place and hard to change. The British protectorate of "Helmandshire" was to become "Marine-istan."

Marine commandant General James Conway had been trying to get the marines out of Iraq and into Afghanistan since 2007 but had been turned down by Gates, who relented "for one-time only" when McNeill needed extra troops for a summer offensive in Helmand in 2008, sending the 24th Marine Expeditionary Unit.[53]

They first took an airstrip built by Saudi falconers to hunt in the southern Afghan desert and then destroyed Taliban forces in the southernmost populated district of Garmser, causing up to five hundred casualties for the loss of one marine. As at Arghandab when assaulted by Canadian troops in

Operation Medusa in 2006, the Taliban were confident they could hold the ground, and reinforcements were sent by the Quetta Shura. It was the "worst defeat in the recorded history of the district," according to a physically brave and intellectually curious State Department political officer who arrived in Garmser in 2009, Dr. Carter Malkasian.[54]

The marines used the Garmser battle as a wedge to lever open the door for a far larger deployment to Helmand. In February 2009, anticipating the first Obama surge announcement, Brigadier General Larry Nicholson went to look around and saw the empty desert next to the main British base in Helmand, in the center of the province, where they had laid down a modern airstrip long enough for civilian airliners. "Who owns that space?" he asked a British colonel, who said, "Fucking you do, if you want it."[55] A huge new marine base, Camp Leatherneck, was built by navy Seabees in the desert, and ten thousand marines began to arrive in June, comprehensively equipped with their own artillery, air capacity, and other assets. This was most of the effective fighting strength of the twenty-one thousand troops Obama agreed ahead of the 2009 assessment—plans on track when McKiernan was abruptly moved out.

Given a clean slate, McChrystal would have secured Kandahar first, "get that squared away, go out from there." Helmand was a sideshow; Kandahar was the key. But his capacity to act was limited. Canada was deeply committed to its role as the main player in Kandahar. Not only did the marines want their own battle space, but they went to Helmand with a remarkable condition attached, meaning they were not under McChrystal's command. They would be under the direct command of a marine lieutenant general at CENTCOM, not Kabul. Even if McChrystal had wanted them to move to Kandahar, he could not have ordered it. Marine Corps exceptionalism goes back to their founding legend in the Revolutionary War. The sense they need to look after themselves was strengthened on the beachheads of Guadalcanal, Iwo Jima, and Okinawa, where they felt let down by the army and navy. They are separate, elite—in their minds frankly superior.

McChrystal found the desire for marine autonomy to be "very limiting and frustrating." He could not employ their formidable airpower flexibly across the south, as it was there to support marine operations. "It's the sanctity of the Air-Ground team. And it's stupid; it was stupid in Vietnam and it's stupid now. And it was a real point of contention for me." Gates wrote that agreeing to this command structure was his "biggest mistake in overseeing the wars in Iraq and Afghanistan."[56] It was wasteful of resources, as back-office and support functions were replicated by what was seen by McChrystal's headquarters as a "42nd member of the coalition."[57]

McChrystal may not have been able to decide where troops should go, but he could determine how they could fight. If the population were the prize in counterinsurgency warfare, protecting them should be the first priority of all military decisions. Two weeks after arriving in Kabul, he issued a tactical directive designed to change the way the war was fought. It laid down that airpower and artillery should never be used against Afghan family compounds, except under very restricted circumstances of self-defense, and that mosques should never be entered or attacked. Afghan homes should be entered only with Afghan forces in the lead. There should be more respect shown by military convoys, instead of forcing civilians off the road as they muscled through. To change the mindset, he introduced the idea of "courageous restraint," which meant troops could not open fire if there was any risk of civilian casualties, unless facing imminent threat to their own lives.

McChrystal knew that limiting the capacity to call in air strikes or artillery entailed risks to coalition troops, although there was no change to the principle of self-defense when troops were directly threatened. But more than any commander before or after him, he grasped the damaging impact of civilian casualties on Afghan public opinion. "The Taliban cannot militarily defeat us—but we can defeat ourselves," he wrote in his directive.

He ordered that units should no longer publicize numbers of enemy dead, wanting to take away incentives that made it look as if killing was the "primary goal."[58] Instead, winning depended "on our ability to separate insurgents from the center of gravity—the population." This was driven not only by a moral imperative but to connect people to the state by winning their support. "Gaining and maintaining that support must be our overriding operational imperative."

After failing to get adequate details of one civilian casualty incident, McChrystal let rip at the morning briefing, watched by hundreds of people on screens across the country. "What is it that we don't understand?" he said, pounding the table. "We're going to lose this fucking war if we don't stop killing civilians."[59] To McChrystal, the focus on the people and not the enemy was not a revelation. "You can't win in Afghanistan unless the Afghan people think you should win, it's in their interests. That's not hard."

It turned out that it was hard to get the message down to every platoon. Nine months into his command, he told a virtual town hall meeting of soldiers that on no occasion when a suspect vehicle was shot approaching a checkpoint was a suicide bomber found. "We've shot an amazing number of people and killed a number and, to my knowledge, none has proven to have been a real threat to the force."[60]

☰ GOVERNMENT IN A BOX

The new way of fighting had its toughest test in February 2010—Operation Moshtarak—the biggest battle of McChrystal's time in command. The target was the densely populated farmland west of Lashkar Gah, in the widest irrigated part of Helmand between the river and a big loop in the canal built by the U.S. in the 1950s, an area of about one hundred square miles, with the town of Nad Ali in the south and the small village of Marjah at the center.

Moshtarak was the first operation where McChrystal sought the formal consent of President Karzai. This was the relationship he cultivated above all, seeing the head of a sovereign government as an essential element in the counterinsurgency plan and wanting to build Karzai as the commander in chief in the American model. He called himself "Karzai's general." Now he wanted Karzai to own the war. In their meetings in the Arg, out of respect, he wore his green army service uniform and polished shoes, with a shirt and tie, rather than the combat fatigues and boots he wore the rest of the time. For Karzai, more than the dress uniform, McChrystal's quick acceptance of civilian casualties made the difference. "He would let me know if there was a casualty," Karzai said. "He would immediately call me himself. And he would apologize, and he would say, 'How can I help?'"[61] This had the effect of defusing this most contentious of issues, so instead of emotional accusations, the president would go on TV, say there had been an apology, and move on.

McChrystal encouraged Karzai to travel widely, recognizing his gift for retail politics. A special pod was installed in a C-130 so the president could travel in more comfort.[62] This had the added advantage that in the relative quiet of the pod, McChrystal was able to "frame key issues during uninterrupted flights in a way that hectic palace schedules often prevented."[63]

In seeking Karzai's prior approval for Moshtarak, he sought to move the commander in chief role from appearance to reality. The evening the assault was due to begin, with troops already loading into helicopters, McChrystal's attempt to see the president was initially blocked, as Karzai had a cold. He insisted and met the president in his home—a modest 1970s concrete house in the grounds of the Arg. Karzai was surprised to be consulted, saying it was an unprecedented request. The two leading security ministers, Hanif Atmar and General Abdul Rahim Wardak, were at the meeting, and after briefly seeking their advice, Karzai gave his consent. McChrystal said he would have canceled the operation if approval had been withheld.[64]

The British major general Nick Carter, who had been McChrystal's planning colonel in the tents in Bagram in 2002, commanded Operation Moshtarak. He had taken command of southern Afghanistan in the fall. Carter was an enthusiastic advocate of courageous restraint, although he preferred the term *tactical patience*. "The problem with courageous restraint is it's quite difficult for a soldier to understand what it means." The principle was the same, and however expressed, Carter knew it was hard to grasp on the ground. "What you don't want is them thinking that the brave thing to do is not to fire your weapon, which it may well be, and inadvertently giving first advantage to the insurgent, but it's quite a challenging concept."[65]

In Moshtarak, the plan was to project the *threat* of overwhelming firepower, while using as little as possible. In previous operations of this size, before the new emphasis on reducing civilian casualties, there would have been preparatory salvos of rocket and artillery fire, but not this time. "The rubble the soldiers would have walked through," McChrystal wrote, "would have been the remnants of the bodies, homes and livelihoods of the very people we sought to protect."[66]

No assault was ever better signaled ahead of time through *shuras,* an information campaign, and targeted special operations. The Taliban responded with their own "night letters," dropped in homes to warn of consequences for working with the Americans. Prior warning also meant the Taliban could liberally lace IEDs across the landscape in a lethal welcome to ten thousand American, British, French, and Canadian troops, and five thousand Afghans. When the assault finally began, thousands of troops were dropped from more than sixty helicopters across the region. Others walked in through deep-rutted fields, already green with the first poppy shoots, fording thigh-deep irrigation canals—slow, methodical, dangerous work to dominate the ground, with no prior bombardment to cut a way through.

Moshtarak was designed as the beginning phase of an operation to move east and stabilize Kandahar, but it took a long time and turned into a public relations failure, mainly because it was so oversold at the start. At the start of the offensive, one marine colonel told his troops, "Be prepared for catastrophic success," and reporters were briefed accordingly in Kabul and outside the country.

Less than a month after the fighting started, McChrystal brought Karzai into Marjah to face a *shura* of elders. They did not hold back in the presence of the president. It was fine, they shouted, to clear out the Taliban but not to replace them with the predatory police who had been there before. There were angry denunciations of Abdul Rahman Jan, ARJ, the notorious former police chief, who was at the meeting, whom the elders knew collaborated with the Taliban to protect his poppy fields.[67] Also standing in the shadows, waiting for his chance to return to power, was Sher Mohammad Akhunzada, SMA, the provincial governor Karzai was forced to fire at the insistence of the British.[68] McChrystal knew SMA was corrupt, but he was a skillful political operator and succeeded in shaking McChrystal's hand with a photographer present at the end of the meeting, to try to imply how close they were.[69]

The problem was that in taking Marjah, McChrystal did not have anything better to offer. Since his arrival in Kabul, he had been pushing for better civil-military relations but faced the same cultural divide that had been there from the beginning. A year into the "civilian surge," there was some more capacity, but not enough, and most of those who came were not good enough. There was still not the quick-response military commanders needed, while for their part, civilian officials felt the military had unrealistic expectations.

McChrystal came to regret a phrase he had adopted that behind the marines there would be a "government in a box ready to roll in." One senior aid official said, "It was very clear to us in the embassy that anyone who talked of that did not understand. You can't clear a district, and then roll up with a thing called governance and unwrap it."[70] Without competent officials able to provide services with clear budget lines they could access, it would not work. McChrystal's problem was that USAID were not offering anything better.

After several months of looking, the only choice who could be found for district governor of Marjah was Haji Zahir, who had served time in Germany for stabbing his stepson. Seven other officials, immediately known as the "Magnificent Seven," were supposed to ride into town alongside him and immediately set up government services. At some risk to his own life, the marine brigade commander went to Lashkar Gah to collect them, but they refused to come. A senior State Department official, Marc Chretien, working as an adviser to the marines, personally apologized to the marines for the failure. Haji Zahir did at least go into Marjah, but he had spent so long away from Helmand that he did not speak good Pashto. He did not last long—the first of three district governors for Marjah in the next twelve months. The Magnificent Seven were never heard from again.

Two months after the operation began, the NATO senior civilian in Kabul, Mark Sedwill, came to visit, his helicopter failing to find anywhere other than a field of waving poppies to land in.[71] Sedwill was meeting the provincial governor, Muhammad Gulab Mangal, and the message they heard from people who came for an impromptu *shura* had not changed—the U.S. Marines were fine, but they should not be replaced by Afghan police. In the makeshift district center, still with no functioning administration two months on, young marines patiently took details from farmers lining up to claim damage for property or livestock damaged in the attack. The money for compensation came from the Commander's Emergency Response Program (CERP) fund, which also went to compensate owners of shops in the bazaar for damage by the Taliban and looting by Afghan soldiers in the offensive. Other CERP money went to put loudspeakers on the wall of a mosque to amplify the call to prayer, immediately torn down by the Taliban. As so often, competing visions of development clashed in the field. A cash-for-work scheme to clear clogged canals was soon stopped, as it did not fit the "quick impact" aim of CERP, although the marines who set up the program said it was one of the most effective interventions they made.[72]

This rudimentary halting progress did not offer a better alternative than the Taliban, who did not fight hard to hold on to Marjah, instead hiding their weapons and melting into the population. They still controlled the night and intimidated anyone who worked with the marines, which stalled the growth of new government machinery. With little infrastructure, no substantial towns, and farmland inhabited by illiterate landless tenants, as most landlords lived in Lashkar Gah, there was no "government in a box" that could resolve these problems quickly. Before long, McChrystal was calling the area a "bleeding ulcer."

⬚ . . . AND TRANSFER

In the spring of 2010, the Obama administration went on a charm offensive with Karzai, inviting him on a high-profile visit to Washington to repair relations damaged during long arguments over the 2009 election. Holbrooke had openly maneuvered to get any result other than a second term for Karzai, whose paranoia about the U.S. was further fueled by the suspicion that the former U.S. ambassador Zalmay Khalilzad had considered standing himself. Protracted arguments over the count and the legitimacy of the election further worsened relations. In Helmand, where there had been such a committed effort to secure the safety of voting, the UN calculated that the number of actual voters was below 40,000, but 134,804 votes were recorded, 112,873 of them for Karzai. Even with this scale of apparent manipulation, Karzai was not declared the clear winner, which required more than 50 percent in the first round. After arm-twisting by John Kerry, then chair of the Senate Foreign Relations Committee, Karzai agreed to face a second-round runoff rather than contesting the result. The announcement at a press conference, with Karzai flanked by Kerry and the Kabul head of the UN, Kai Eide, with the ambassadors of the U.S., UK, and France also in the shot, looked like an international stitch-up. Karzai's paranoia-meter went into the red zone when the American deputy head of the UN in Kabul, Peter Galbraith, was fired for campaigning against him.

With Eikenberry's contempt public, McChrystal alone continued to back the Afghan president, sticking to the counterinsurgency requirement to build up the host government, and ultimately because he believed that Karzai was a good man trying to do the right thing in difficult circumstances.[73] Prior approval for military operations was not a rubber-stamp exercise; their meetings would go on for four or five hours as McChrystal went through the military options with Karzai.[74]

In characteristic style, Karzai jeopardized plans for the Washington visit in May 2010 by telling a group of Afghans he might "join the Taliban" if pushed too far by the U.S., but the visit went ahead.[75] He was visibly moved as McChrystal pointed out graves of soldiers he knew who were killed in Afghanistan, buried in Section 60 at Arlington National Cemetery, where the fallen of Afghanistan and Iraq are buried. From there, they went to Walter Reed Army Medical Center, where McChrystal said Karzai was "taken aback by all these young American service members missing limbs, multiple in some cases."

McChrystal said the overall experience challenged Karzai's deeply held view that America was only in Afghanistan for itself. He would often ask, "Why are you really here?" And McChrystal would answer, "Well, it may not be smart, but we're here to help you. If there's an ulterior motive, I don't know it."

Before going back to Kabul, Karzai visited troops about to deploy at Fort Campbell, Kentucky. The scale of the surge meant that for the first time in the war, a whole division, the 101st Airborne, was heading to Afghanistan.[76] Their commander, Major General John F. Campbell, who would later command at ISAF, lined up one thousand soldiers and their families in a hangar for Karzai's visit. Inspired by his experiences at Arlington and Walter Reed, the president made a moving speech, thanking America for its commitment and sacrifice, and then jumped the rope to dive into the crowd, picking up babies and shaking as many hands as he could. Before Karzai climbed back into his helicopter, Campbell handed him a statuette of an eagle, for the Screaming Eagles—the emblem of the 101st. McChrystal counted it a successful visit.

Campbell carried an unusual item in the large document pocket of his combat trousers when he traveled round the mountains and valleys of eastern Afghanistan where he commanded in 2010—a packet of three-by-five cards, each bearing a picture and name of every soldier who died in his command, with some details of the incident, so the sacrifice was not forgotten. By the time his deployment finished a year later, the packet was too big to go in his pocket, and he carried it in a backpack everywhere he went. He would huddle together with soldiers in some remote location and take out the cards and tell them he carried the memories so he would never forget there was a human cost.

He had commanded in Baghdad during some of the toughest fighting in that war and saw the challenges of eastern Afghanistan as "a much more complex set than I faced in Baghdad."[77] He needed to make tough decisions to withdraw troops from places with an emotional hold on the American imagination because of the blood and sweat expended, such as Korengal and the Pech Valley. Many of the remote outposts were hallowed ground, named for soldiers who had died there, such as Restrepo. With withdrawal due to begin a year after they arrived, moving out of remote places in the hills was inevitable. The shape of the troop presence changed to focus on places that could be handed over—"clear, hold, build, and transfer" in the jargon, as transfer to Afghan control was added to the original counterinsurgency trio of tasks.

McChrystal knew the eastern mountains well from his days commanding Special Forces, and early in his time as ISAF commander, he stayed overnight in a remote outpost high up in the mountains in Korengal. He quickly saw that troops had no influence more than twenty feet beyond the wire, and he accepted the recommendation that they should pull back. But the decision brought doubt into his belief in counterinsurgency. How could they secure the population if they could not get out on the ground and interact with them?

> It always kind of bugged me. How are we really going to solve this shortcoming? You want to say that hopefully the Afghan people, or Afghan government and military will be able to do it, but they weren't much better doing that than we were. So, you know, it was always a sense that, yeah, it's the right thing to do, but it makes us wonder if we can ever really accomplish the mission.

The dangers of keeping small numbers of troops in remote locations were emphasized when eight U.S. soldiers died after a fierce Taliban assault on an outpost, COP Keating, at the bottom of a bowl, surrounded by high mountains on the frontier in Nuristan.[78] McChrystal noticed how exposed the site was when he flew over, but it was where the people lived, and that was why it was there. The region had been reinforced at the insistence of Karzai, but there was little contact between the base and the population, according to the army investigation into the attack.[79] For several weeks, there was intelligence that Taliban reinforcements were crossing the border to stage an attack, and there were several probing attacks to test Keating's defenses. As at Wanat, the assault was very well planned, with early precise targeting of mortar defenses. The soldiers of Bravo Troop, 3rd Squadron, 61st Cavalry successfully repelled the attack, causing more than one hundred Taliban casualties in a day of fighting, which included hours when much of the base was overrun and the defenders were penned into a small area. The site had already been slated for closure, and although the defense of Keating was a tactical win, it was a strategic communications victory for the Taliban who shared video of their control of the abandoned base.

When Campbell took over in the east in 2010, there were still more than two hundred outposts. He continued to pull back, not least because he did not have enough civilian advisers to deliver the full spectrum of counterinsurgency operations. Although he knew there was little governance in the mountain villages, he could not solve that just with soldiers. The failure of the civilian surge had a measurable impact on the mission. "We couldn't keep people up there, and put a Band-Aid on it, so we had to look hard at that, how we could sustain that."

The decision had to be based on the overall mission, not on emotional connection with American losses, and the decisions needed to be communicated to soldiers so they understood the value of what they were doing. When troops finally pulled out of the whole Korengal Valley, the codirector of the *Restrepo* movie, Sebastian Junger, wrote that while the pullout was tough for the comrades of men who had died, they knew they had played a role in protecting the key supply routes of the more important Pech Valley. "There is no way to know what would have happened in Kunar Province—or in Afghanistan as a whole—had several hundred local and foreign fighters not been tied up in the Korengal by American forces."[80]

☰ DEPLOY, DEPLOY, DEPLOY

By 2009, U.S. armed forces were in their eighth year of continual conflict and feeling the strain. Units on tough twelve-to fifteen-month tours, fighting all the way, were turning round and going back in with little time for training and recuperation. Obama's quick timetable to get the surge forces into place put the system under more pressure. The intensity of the workload made complex operations like counterinsurgency harder to achieve. Lute, still a serving lieutenant general until 2010, while overseeing the wars for Obama as he had for Bush, had a more acute sense than many in the White House of the reality of life for those in uniform.

> You were probably reintroducing yourself to your kids, getting a divorce, settling a financial crisis. The list on the refrigerator at home was not pretty, for things that you must do, and for six months of that twelve months at home, you were preparing to go back to Iraq. So the stress level here was high and the ability of the Army to adapt was somewhat constricted, impeded by the fact that they were on this treadmill of just deploy, deploy, deploy, and they had no time to go to Leavenworth, read the field manual, absorb what it meant, get it into their training program.[81]

Recruiting standards were dropped to levels not seen since the Vietnam draft. In 2003, at the start of the Iraq war, 94 percent of new recruits had high school diplomas. By 2005, that number had dropped to 71 percent. The proportion of soldiers with what the army called Category IV intelligence went up from just a handful to almost one in twenty recruits. Waivers were granted for felony convictions, and physical fitness standards fell.[82] Among those recruited during this time was an idealistic loner who had been thrown out of training by the Coast Guard after a month and disqualified for further service after examination by a navy psychiatrist. The Iraq surge followed by the Afghan surge had drained the well, and with a signature on a form agreed with his recruiter that he had overcome these issues, he was accepted for the army in 2008. His name was Bowe Bergdahl.

After basic training, Bergdahl was sent to the legendary 1/501—1st Battalion, 501st Airborne Infantry Regiment—who were heading to Afghanistan and short on numbers. He had not been through parachute training at jump school, in normal times obligatory for the 1/501. One night, not long after deploying to eastern Afghanistan in the early summer of 2009, he walked off the base and spent five years in captivity, held by the Haqqani network.

Two months later, again under pressure for the surge, the four thousand soldiers of 5th Brigade, 2nd Infantry Division, were switched at the last minute from a planned deployment to Iraq to go to Kandahar, with no time for specific pre-deployment training. They were equipped with Stryker armored vehicles—the first time the eight-wheeled behemoths had been brought to Afghanistan. Strykers, which carry two crew and nine infantry soldiers, have an eerily similar profile in Afghan villages to the armored personnel carriers used by the Russian forces in their war in the 1980s, whose rusting hulls still litter the Afghan landscape. They had limited utility in a counterinsurgency focused on the people, or in very close country, but their commander, Colonel Harry Tunnell, had not signed up to that project. In his mind, this was unfinished business in a continuum with Iraq where he was badly wounded in the leg in the initial invasion in 2003.[83] In his account of Iraq, he mourned the "political correctness" that dictated the U.S. Army was no longer able to use "oppressive measures" successful in the past. "Military leaders must stay focused on the destruction of the enemy." He saw engagement with civilians as a distraction. "It was counterproductive for a commander to get too immersed in non-combat activity." Heading to Afghanistan, he ordered the motto "Search and Destroy" be painted onto the side of the Strykers—in contradiction with population-centered counterinsurgency.

Tunnell's aggressive posture in training almost led to the brigade not being certified for deployment.[84] He boasted of using more ammunition in training than other units, and to gain the highest marks in combat exercises, he put his senior officers down to command platoons, which meant that the first time some second lieutenants communicated with their troops was in actual combat. He spent almost no CERP aid money and conducted no *shuras,* instead engaging in massive assaults in Arghandab, before pulling out and not holding ground.[85] His soldiers did not patrol on foot, which would have been better both for engaging the population and detecting IEDs, but remained inside Strykers and were often hit. In one incident, where procedure ruled they should have dismounted, seven soldiers and an interpreter were killed when a bomb was remotely detonated as they drove over what an inquiry called a "suspicious chokepoint." He lost twenty-two soldiers during his tour, a high number at that time for a brigade.

In this aggressive environment, some of his soldiers carried out random shootings of Afghan civilians and kept their fingers for trophies. Four were convicted on charges, including murder, although Tunnell personally escaped blame for this. When Major General Nick Carter arrived to command in the south, he immediately took Tunnell's brigade out of Arghandab to patrol the main ring road to assure freedom of movement for the coalition and the Afghan population. Tunnell was furious and began to challenge "virtually every order" given, according to the official inquiry. Carter's American deputy, Brigadier General Ben Hodges, said he should have reined him in. Both he and Carter had "lost confidence in his ability to command."[86]

After leaving Afghanistan, Tunnell became a vocal opponent of courageous restraint. Carter said simply, "Tunnell was unfit for brigade command in the complex environment of Afghanistan, incapable of listening to anybody else."[87]

"THE GOVERNMENT ROBS US, THE TALIBAN BEAT US, AND ISAF BOMBS US"

On January 12, 2010, rioting began in Garmser, the southern desert district in Helmand. It went on into the next day, leading to the burning down of a market area and school and the deaths of between six and eight people. The slight, dark-eyed figure of Carter Malkasian, the Pashto-speaking political officer attached to the marines in Garmser, could often be seen in the street with Afghan leaders, breaking out ringleaders and calming the crowd. But at the same time, the flames of anger were fanned by pro-Taliban mullahs. The spark that lit the flames was a rumor that during a night raid by Special Forces, a knife had been stabbed into a Quran. It later emerged that the Taliban had planted the evidence after the raid. But the rumor was enough.

It was the worst riot during the time the marines held southern Helmand, and caused by a raid that was out of their control. About twice a month, there were raids on suspect houses in their area, with little notice to the marines who had to pick up the pieces in the morning. Mostly they did not provoke a response, although Afghan officials constantly warned about the potential for trouble. Malkasian wrote that the raids were as damaging as anything done by the Taliban.

Pashtuns despised them. A home is sacred. Pashtun men are obliged
to keep out all uninvited guests. Foreigners crashing through doors,
stomping about, and peering in on women had the same effect as
spitting on a man's honor before his whole village. Raids pushed
people towards the Taliban.[88]

The January riots put back the work of the marines by months. They
had engaged in exemplary counterinsurgency practice, particularly under Lieutenant Colonel John McDonough of 2nd Battalion, 2nd Marine
Regiment. Counterinsurgency to McDonough was not a soft option.
When he arrived in November 2009, he raised the tempo of patrolling,
never giving the Taliban a day off. Fifteen posts had been garrisoned by
the previous marine battalion. McDonough doubled that by reducing
the number of marines in a post and on patrols, to be able to increase
the tempo and the reach of his operations. The effort enabled development spending to have some effect, while a successful police recruitment
scheme turned militia fighters into uniformed local police.

The school could be rebuilt at a cost of $150,000, but the riots had
a lasting impact. Enemies of Abdullah Jan, an incorruptible local leader
Malkasian had supported, used the inquiry into the riots to blame him, and
he was removed, with a damaging impact on stability and development.

Every district in the country could tell similar stories about the
helicopters that came at night, counterterrorist fighters from the CIA,
or the special operators of TF-714. The headquarters of TF-714 that
McChrystal had set up in the hangar in Baghdad had now moved to Bagram as Afghanistan took priority. That increased the tempo of the night
raids. And sometimes it was hard to get the truth when things went wrong.

The problem was well known to every ISAF commander and came
up in every review—most memorably identified in the *Ten Wars* report
by Doug Lute at the end of 2008. Attacks on civilians, McChrystal's team
who traveled the country for his 2009 assessment met one group of elders who put it simply. "The Government robs us, the Taliban beat us,
and ISAF bombs us."[89] The problem of the lack of coordination between
special and conventional operations was never solved and was a significant contributory factor in hardening Afghan public opinion against the
international military presence.

On February 12, 2010, five weeks after the Garmser raid, a raid on a compound near Gardez in the east was initially described by ISAF as a success, but with a macabre twist. After a "firefight" with "several insurgents," special operators found the bodies of three women, "tied up, gagged and killed," according to the ISAF press release. The bodies were "hidden" in an adjacent room, "discovered" when American soldiers made their way into the house later in the night. The find was spun as a Taliban honor killing.

This bizarre story quickly unraveled when a reporter for *The Times* of London, Jerome Starkey, visited the site. What he found was that the owner of the house, Muhammad Daoud, was a highly regarded police commander, recently promoted to head of intelligence in his district. The raid was spearheaded by Afghan soldiers speaking what one witness told Starkey was Kandahari-accented Pashto. Understandably, Daoud, who was Tajik, immediately thought they were Taliban. He was one of the first to be shot when he went out to investigate the break-in. One of his brothers was a local prosecutor, another the vice chancellor of the local university. "We are a government family!" the prosecutor, Muhammad Zahir, shouted to try to stop them firing, before he too was shot dead. Seven people died, including two pregnant women. The house was filled with relatives, as they had been celebrating the naming ceremony six days after the birth of a son. Family members began to prepare bodies for burial, which includes binding the head and feet. These were the bodies seen by the American special operators when they came into the house.

The initial ISAF response to Starkey's report was to attempt to discredit him, telling callers he was unreliable, with a background as a tabloid reporter. They put out a press release denying his report, unusually naming him. But their account quickly unraveled, as the full horror of what had happened emerged. Several witnesses told reporters they saw Americans digging bullets out of the women's bodies with knives, and although a subsequent Pentagon investigation did not substantiate this, it quoted an Afghan investigation as saying that "an American bullet was found in the body of one of the dead women."

Vice Admiral Bill McRaven, who had succeeded McChrystal as commander of TF-714, visited the village where Commander Daoud's family were killed, to make amends. He slaughtered a sheep as a traditional offering. "I am the commander of the men who accidentally killed your loved ones," he said. "I came here today to send my condolences to you and to your family and to your friends. I also came today to ask your forgiveness for these terrible tragedies."[90]

It would not be enough to stop night raids happening. McChrystal admitted that the narrow focus of special operators meant they missed the bigger picture. "I can't complain too loudly because for the first part of the war I was a Special Forces guy causing the problems." But he took away the lesson that in future conflicts, the local commander, the "owner" of the battle space, should have total authority over activities in their area of operations. That would lessen the chance of incidents like the Garmser riot. "We always know that to be the right answer. And that's not just true at the theater level, that's also true down on the ground."

If this happened, it would mark a reverse of the trend since 9/11. There were many more nonconventional operators in the field than in previous conflicts. The authority given to the CIA to conduct offensive operations by President Bush marked a watershed in the way America went to war. Special operators and CIA have moved closer together in capacity.[91] As special operations TF-714 has engaged in more intelligence-gathering than previously, so the CIA have developed far more offensive capacity, with counterterrorist fighters available to carry out clandestine operations.

There were several hundred CIA operators in Afghanistan by 2010, along with many off-the-book contractors. The Obama administration had not reversed the policy, and the shadow war continued with more intensity. The CIA supported local allies who were not part of the formal Afghan force structure as Afghanistan became an increasingly dirty war. Afghan militias run by the Afghan National Directorate for Security, the NDS, lived and fought under CIA control across the country. There were five of these operations in the Pashtun south and east, including the Kandahar Strike Force, run by the president's half brother, Ahmed Wali Karzai.[92]

☰ UNDER THE ASH CLOUD

April 16, 2010, was Stan and Annie McChrystal's thirty-third wedding anniversary. They met in Paris for dinner on one of a routine series of European trips to shore up NATO support. When Annie saw *Rolling Stone* correspondent Michael Hastings hanging round Team America, she said,

"Has anybody vetted this guy?" She had read his previous book, unlike any of McChrystal's political advisers and media handlers. Its title, *I Lost My Love in Baghdad,* was one that would not appeal to the male military jock mindset cultivated in Team America. But Annie had picked it up, and she thought Hastings had an agenda to bring people down. In the book, Hastings told the story of his fiancée, Andi Parhamovich, who had followed him to Iraq to work for a pro-democracy program, and was targeted and killed by insurgents. Hastings hated Iraq and Afghanistan, believing no good could come from either war. Only Annie saw the warning signs.

Even without this knowledge, it was surprising that Hastings was given unrestricted access. Reporters, particularly in military settings where there are security issues, routinely accept restrictions where some conversations or events are not reported as a tradeoff for access. But Hastings wrote that there were no ground rules laid down for his access.

Hastings spent far more time with McChrystal in Europe than planned, grounded by the Icelandic volcanic eruption that filled the upper atmosphere with ash for a week. He saw Team America letting their hair down. McChrystal's strictures against alcohol did not travel outside Afghanistan.

The insults he reported were not individually serious. "Did you say: 'Bite Me,'" when Biden was mentioned; "I don't even want to open it," said McChrystal when an email from Holbrooke came in on his Black-Berry, one of the staff responding, "Make sure you don't get any of that on your leg."

It was the cumulative effect that did the damage: "The Boss was pretty disappointed" by his treatment by Obama, Jones was a "clown," Holbrooke "a wounded animal." And there were other off-color comments: "Women don't have rights"; a dinner with a French minister was "fucking gay." Hastings did not drink, but sat and noted and recorded, listening to "the kind of banter I'd heard on the front lines, but not inside headquarters." He continued to wonder why there were no reporting restrictions. "What exactly was I dealing with here?"[93]

In an interview for this book, McChrystal called the article, titled "The Runaway General," an "assassination." He said Hastings clearly had strong feelings about the war and had put spin on them. "Any journalist who wants to blow up a general can do that." When the article appeared online, Hastings was in southern Afghanistan on a military embed and was quickly hustled out of the country for his own safety. At 2:00 a.m., McChrystal was woken to be told what was reported. He knew his military career was over and called Holbrooke and Biden to apologize. Holbrooke was sleeping at the embassy close by and responded with an immediate supportive email, hoping McChrystal's resignation would be rejected, calling him a friend.[94] After consulting his team for an hour, the general went running through the darkness around and around the ISAF compound through the night for the last time.

A PDF of the article was shared across thousands of laptops in Afghanistan overnight. The general response among soldiers and marines in remote forward operating bases was shock that it had been allowed to happen. "What was the public affairs office thinking?" McChrystal appeared at the 0730 meeting and said, "There's an article out there. It's in my lane. I'm dealing with it. Carry on as normal." With some presence of mind, he did a PowerPoint briefing for the ambassadors of the UN Security Council who were in town before boarding a plane to Washington.

While Obama thought McChrystal had been played by the reporter, he did not have much choice when McChrystal arrived in his office to offer his resignation in the briefest of meetings the following day. His instinct was to give McChrystal the benefit of the doubt, but realized he could not. And there were wider issues after the leaks, McChrystal's London speech, and sense of being boxed in during the Afghan review the year before. "In that Rolling Stone article," the president wrote, "I'd heard in him and his aides the same air of impunity that seemed to have taken hold among some in the military's top ranks during the Bush years: a sense that once war began, those who fought it shouldn't be questioned, that politicians should just give them what they ask for and get out of the way."[95]

In the Kabul SAR, as people gathered to watch the news screens, British lieutenant general Nick Parker, McChrystal's deputy, made a rousing speech. "We have just lost a great commander," but they should not lose momentum. "There are people out there putting their lives on the line tonight. We owe it to them. So if you don't have a job to do, bugger off, go to bed and get some sleep. If you've got a job to do, get on and do it."[96] Parker knew the cost of war as well as any. His son Harry lost his legs fighting in Helmand.

Dominic Medley, in his fifth day as the spokesman for the NATO civilian representative in Kabul, said the loss of McChrystal was an easy win for the Taliban strategic communications team. "They must have been scratching their heads and twiddling their thumbs in a cave thinking the general who was thwacking them has just been fired for an interview in a rock music magazine."[97]

Some in Washington made a rearguard attempt to save McChrystal's job, Gates telling the president simply, "I believe if we lose McChrystal, we lose the war."[98] But McChrystal knew his resignation would be accepted. "It hit at a period when there was all this sensitivity about strong military guys pushing the president around, which wasn't true." He denied being part of a "triumvirate" with Gates and Petraeus.

That the military side in the Afghan war were so prominent was partly because the political and diplomatic side were so weak. Division in the UN in Kabul, Holbrooke's maneuvering, the halfhearted, poorly funded, ill-directed civilian surge, Eikenberry's opposition to the war plan and marginalized status—all left McChrystal more exposed than he might have been. Counterinsurgency may have been defined as 80 percent politics. But McChrystal carried more of the political weight than was comfortable and was left high and dry, in an exposed position he felt challenged the ideal relationship between political and military power as defined by Huntington.

> I used to quote Huntington. I used to tell my staff in Afghanistan, particularly as we were writing the assessment and then afterwards, I said, "OK, this is the approach I want you to take. We don't own the car. The President and decisionmakers own the car. We're not even going to decide where it's going; we've been asked to fix the car, so I want to tell them what it takes to fix the car."

He told Lute it was not up to him whether they were in Afghanistan or what they wanted to accomplish. Those were political decisions. "You know what, it's not my call. You tell me if you want to be in Afghanistan, and if you do, what you want to accomplish."

☰ PEAK SURGE

Like General Creighton Abrams, one of the outstanding commanders of the twentieth century, who took over from Westmoreland in Vietnam at the worst time in 1968, McChrystal arrived with a stellar reputation and, like Abrams, wanted to build a strategy centered on protecting the population, which did not have the wholehearted support of Washington. It was said of Abrams that he deserved a "better war" but had only the war he was given.[99] For his part, McChrystal's adoption of population-centered counterinsurgency came after years of under-resourcing the war and faced formidable obstacles—the porous border to Taliban safe havens sheltered by Pakistan, the weakness of the Karzai government, the corruption of the Afghan elite, growing war-weariness in Washington.

And there was another problem—counterinsurgency warfare took a toll on the morale of soldiers on the ground, who thought it meant "they should not shoot even if they are threatened with death," according to Sergeant Israel Arroyo, of Charlie Company, 1st Battalion, 12th Infantry Regiment, in an email to McChrystal. For all the mavericks and odd-balls who ended up handling weapons in Afghanistan during the surge, like Tunnell and Bergdahl, there were tens of thousands of mainstream American soldiers like Arroyo—the backbone of the counterinsurgency effort, leading a nine-person platoon on daily patrols into the vine and marijuana-growing, mud-walled badlands of Arghandab, which Mullah Naqib offered to hand over with no fighting in 2001, and Canadian troops had won at high cost in Operation Medusa in 2006.

Arroyo wrote to McChrystal, asking him to come out on patrol and see what it was like, wanting to share the concerns of his soldiers about courageous restraint. He did not need to add that the general should come without his private security detail. Forty-eight hours later, McChrystal was on a four-hour patrol with Arroyo, being treated as just another soldier. One of those on the patrol, a popular corporal, Mike Ingram, who was soon to be married, was killed soon afterward, bleeding out when it took thirty minutes for a helicopter to arrive after he was hit by an IED. McChrystal went down again and had a hard session with the unit, who did not understand why they could not call in air strikes as they had in Iraq. McChrystal's answer was that it would not be possible to kill their way out of Afghanistan as the Russians had. "Winning hearts and minds in COIN is a cold-blooded thing."

Hastings was at this meeting and wrote a highly negative account of the soldiers' mood. It was the only time McChrystal took him aside to express concern about what he might report, describing what they had seen as a "raw wound." Hastings quoted one soldier as saying that what McChrystal said made sense, but by the time it came down from "Big Army," it became too restrictive.

McChrystal's forced early departure left hanging the most intriguing what-if of the Afghan war. What if he had stayed for another year, been able to carry the war on his terms? Like McKiernan before him, McChrystal was never able to see to fruition plans he had put in place. He had many supporters. State Department official Marc Chretien said, "He did not come with a preconceived idea, he listens and adjusts." Matt Sherman, who worked in various senior advisory roles for four ISAF commanders, said he was an outstanding communicator, good at building huge teams of people who understood what they were doing, "one of the most impressive people I ever worked with." He willed the world to be better than it was, believed in counterinsurgency, believed he could turn the war round, reverse the "creeping fatalistic pessimism."

It was a belief satirized in the movie *War Machine,* starring Brad Pitt as General McMahon (who was based on McChrystal), uncomfortable viewing for Team America. Forced to spend time in Europe by the Icelandic ash cloud, McMahon's team drink too much in the presence of a reporter. There is not a four-star general alive who would not want to be played by Brad Pitt—but not like this. In the movie, McMahon pitches his Afghan war plan in Berlin as McChrystal did and is confronted by a forceful German MP (played by Tilda Swinton) who wonders if his belief in counterinsurgency is delusional. "What I question is your belief in your power to deliver these things that you describe . . . I question your sense of self."

To replace McChrystal, and not to lose momentum, Obama turned to the general most identified in the public mind with counterinsurgency, David Petraeus, in what was at best a sideways career move that he did not seek. It was not his war, and he knew public opinion was moving against it. His friend, the Florida socialite and CENTCOM goodwill ambassador Jill Kelley, told him it was a "failing war." She was lining up donors willing to back a presidential run. Afghanistan was a "shit sandwich."[100]

Petraeus happened to be in the White House for his monthly update with the president as CENTCOM commander the day McChrystal was fired. He was called up to the Oval Office, where there was only one answer to the president's request that he go back into the fight. They talked for forty-five minutes, Obama emphasizing his desire to limit the area of operation and draw down on schedule. There was concern in the White House about Petraeus's political ambition and willingness to accept direction. The president pointedly told his national security staff, "We've agreed to trust each other and to share assessments in private."[101]

Eleven days later, after the swiftest congressional confirmation, Petraeus was on a plane to Kabul. He told Obama he would do one year. Afghanistan presented "what has to be among the most challenging imaginable contexts for a counterinsurgency campaign." While he did not seek it, there was opportunity here that put a gleam in his eye. The timetable laid down by the president meant the first troops would not leave before summer 2011, as Petraeus left. He was to hold a unique military record as the only general to command at the highest level in both of the post-9/11 wars, and as in Iraq, he was arriving at peak surge.

THE BELL CURVE AND THE ANACONDA

*Until you have stood every other night at the back
of a C-17 putting another collection of bodies on an
airplane, and reflected on whether you are to blame for
their death, you haven't really experienced what it's like
to be a commander.*

—General Nick Carter

≡ MALIK D.

General David Petraeus enjoyed an unusually good press. "Brilliant," "tireless," "soldier-scholar," "our very best general,"[1] "widely hailed as the U.S. military's finest strategic mind in a generation,"[2] "the dominant U.S. military figure of our time"[3]—the language lit a trail as bright as a comet. His easy relationship with journalists guaranteed him good press, which he deployed as if a weapon. In his 1987 Ph.D. thesis, he wrote that the "perceptions of reality, more so than objective reality, are crucial to the decisions of statesmen," and after experiencing high command, he had not changed his mind. "Tone is very important ...What generals can do is set tone."[4] For Petraeus, how military actions were *seen* was central to his capacity as a commander.

The image of success in the face of adversity was formed in Iraq in 2003. It was Petraeus who was "prepared to act" in the northern Iraqi city of Mosul in contrast to "the civilian authority in Baghdad," who were still "getting organized." And when he later returned to Iraq after that first glittering tour, the Pentagon was said to be "rushing back one of its most highly regarded generals to help train and equip Iraqi security forces." There were direct comparisons made with Grant in the

Civil War. "There have been situations in our history where American generals were given tough problems to resolve, like Lincoln grabbing U.S. Grant in 1864 ... If anybody can fix this, he can."[5] To some, he was "King David," which he preferred to translate into Arabic—signing emails as "Malik D."[6]

His unplanned move to Kabul in 2010 was widely welcomed, with journalists only worrying how the rest of the world would cope without him. "If Iraq begins to fall apart, and Petraeus is busy in Kabul, who is going to step on?"[7] The "architect of the Iraq war turnaround" was once again coming to help out his country at its hour of need, taking "hands-on leadership of a troubled war effort."[8] There was even a move to give him a fifth star. The last time the U.S. Army had five-star generals was for an elite group toward the end of World War II. A month into his time in Kabul, he began to do media, citing Lawrence's maxim that "the printing press is the greatest weapon in the armory of the modern commander." The first TV reporter in was David Gregory of NBC, who called him "easily America's most famous warrior."[9]

After his Kabul command, his appointment to be director of the CIA was welcomed in the media. "Given Petraeus's extensive experience in a decade of post-9/11 warfare, his new role at the helm of global covert operations is widely seen as a good fit."[10] The only dissenters believed he should have stayed in uniform as chairman of the Joint Chiefs of Staff: taking him out of direct control of the war was like "pulling Ulysses S. Grant away from Richmond to run the Pinkerton Agency."[11] But although a consummate insider, this astute player of the political game fostered an image among sympathetic analysts that he was a subversive, an insurgent,[12] a quality he believed he shared with McChrystal, disrupting and reinventing the army like innovative managers of a corporation.

These two principal military leaders of Obama's Afghan war valued intellectual achievement along with an austere work ethic and rigorous physical fitness. Petraeus's most treasured possession is his Ph.D., and his idea of perfect happiness was "an intellectual gathering in Aspen where you have a morning full of great discussion of weighty issues, a nice lunch, continuing the discussion. You do some work on your laptop back in a hotel room and then you get on a road bike and hammer up the hills of Aspen for two hours, and you come back and stretch out and do some strength work and you shower and go to a delightful dinner and have a glass of wine and talk weighty issues again."

Petraeus was not from a military family. His father, Sixtus, was a Dutch merchant seaman, stranded on the Eastern Seaboard of the U.S. at the outbreak of World War II. His mother, Miriam, was from an old Pilgrim family. He grew up a few miles from West Point and was a cadet there during the cultural convulsions of the Vietnam War, when the superintendent William A. Knowlton likened it to a "stockade surrounded by attacking Indians."[13] Knowlton was appointed in 1970 after his predecessor, Sam Koster, left, tainted by scandal around the massacre at My Lai. Knowlton had been involved in CORDS, the stabilization program that combined civil and military operations in Vietnam, but counterinsurgency was not central on the curriculum at West Point in the 1970s. Petraeus married the superintendent's daughter, Holly, after meeting on a blind date.

In his early years in the army, Petraeus found himself in demand in several influential staff roles, where he learned vital lessons about the relationship between political and military authority. As well as the time he spent with Major General Jack Galvin in the U.S. and Europe, he went to Washington for two years as ADC to the army chief of staff, General Carl Vuono. He told Vuono at the interview that he had been away from the infantry for a long time and would prefer to stay there. Vuono replied, "I wouldn't want you if you really wanted the job. Report in three weeks."[14]

It was when he returned to the infantry in 1991 that Petraeus began to build the legend of a highly competitive leader. Commanding the 3rd Battalion, 187th Infantry Regiment, 101st Airborne, the Rakkasans,[15] he devised a fitness competition he called the "Iron Rakkasan" and challenged anyone in his command to beat his score. None did. Along with demands on physical fitness, he imposed strict discipline, including high-and-tight haircuts and a dress code that insisted on keeping the top button of combat jackets fastened, even in the field. To recover the combat readiness of a battalion just back from the 1991 Gulf War, he introduced small-unit training and live-fire exercises. At the end of his command, the battalion, now renamed the Iron Rakkasans, had more Ranger-qualified soldiers than any in the division, but it came at a price. A memo from a junior officer questioned if "the late hours and weekends away from home were really worth it."[16]

Two serious accidents that might have halted the career of a lesser mortal, being shot in the chest on a training accident during one of the live-fire exercises in 1991[17] and breaking his pelvis on a civilian parachute jump in 2000, could not halt his rise—the legend burnished by the tale that he did fifty push-ups to persuade doctors he was fit to leave the hospital after being shot. He later denied this, claiming, "I never stop at fifty." Shrugging off treatment for prostate cancer in 2009, he did not take any time off work while undergoing more than forty radiation sessions. To test the suitability of a potential biographer, Paula Broadwell, twenty years his junior, and top of her class for athletics at West Point, he carried out a conversation while running from the Pentagon to the Washington Monument, upping the pace to a six-minute mile at the end. Her glowing account described "Petraeus's will" as a "strategic force" of its own, that once "loosed in Kabul" would transform the war.[18]

The announcement by President Obama that Petraeus was to succeed McChrystal was greeted with audible gasps by the headquarters staff watching the big screen in the situational awareness room in ISAF. McChrystal and Petraeus may have been aligned on the war plan, but their leadership styles were known to be very different. While McChrystal sat as one node in a network and encouraged a freewheeling exchange of ideas, particularly from junior officers, Petraeus was remoter, with focused direction from the top of a pyramid. On arrival in Kabul, he ordered there be no surfing the net or reading emails during the morning briefing. "With that, a clicking chorus of more than sixty closing laptops filled the room."[19] Petraeus's will had arrived in Afghanistan.

☰ THE BIG M

Petraeus deliberately cultivated a sense of mystique, a quality his mentor Major General Jack Galvin called "the Big M." "Through your mythology, people create you."[20] To Petraeus, the "aura around a particular leader" was not about ego but about being set apart, the Big M also stood for the mask of command. It was important to Petraeus not to let the mask slip, encouraging belief that he would never give up. Petraeus would have liked a description Holbrooke used of him that he had a "near-mythic persona."[21] The word he used to define his campaigns, in both Iraq and Afghanistan, was *relentless.* The Big M, Galvin said, did not have to be Patton and his pistols, Grant and his cigars. It was about people wanting you to be bigger than you are. "You become part of a legend."[22] And then as a commander, "you try to make it look effortless."

The Big M had to do with the idea of mystique about an individual. In the case of Galvin, someone who was "a true soldier and scholar, and then ultimately statesman, of the highest order." Those were the elements that made up his "Big M," Petraeus said. "And I was also conscious of my Big M." This mantle was confirmed during the surge in Iraq when Galvin, now long retired from the military, wrote him to say, "I hereby bequeath to you status as the Big M." Early in his career, Galvin sent Petraeus a print of *Stampede* by Frederic Remington. The image of the cowboy in control of himself and his horse, surrounded by plunging hooves and horns of panicked cattle in a thunderstorm, informed Petraeus's career in command. "One of my aides called me the world's most competitive human being, and that I thought was OK ... I want the enemy to think that I'm the most competitive human being."

The Big M could overcome adversity, so ramping up the size of the challenge was part of the mystique. In both Afghanistan and Iraq, he said it was "all hard all the time." Putting together what he needed in Afghanistan was like assembling "the pieces of a puzzle," adding, "We didn't get all the places even remotely in place until late 2010." At his confirmation hearing for the Afghan command in the Senate Armed Services Committee, he repeated an image he liked to use, that the command role in the post-9/11 wars was like "building an advanced aircraft while it is in flight, while it is being designed, and while it is being shot at." And in his case, he was moving into the pilot's seat at no notice, after McChrystal's hurried exit. He left with Senator John McCain's endorsement of "one of our finest-ever military leaders" ringing round the chamber.

In Iraq in 2007, there is no doubt that Petraeus changed the course of the war, turning it in the right direction for the first time since the chaos that followed the fall of Saddam. "Petraeus's critical contribution in Iraq was one of leadership," wrote military analyst Tom Ricks. "He got everyone on the same page. Until he arrived, there often seemed to be dozens of wars going on, with every brigade commander trying to figure out the strategic goals of a campaign."[23] It was his good fortune to arrive in both theaters of war, Iraq in 2007 and Afghanistan in 2010, just when counterinsurgency was the policy needed, and crucially for him, when there was a will in Washington to commit more resources to the task. In July 2010, when he arrived in Afghanistan, there were twice as many international troops in theater than when Dave McKiernan was replaced a year before.

It is human nature that all military commanders see their time at the top as being a critical turning point—their focus so absolute on the moment that they could not see it any other way. Petraeus went further, comparing *himself* to great commanders of the past called on to save their nation in seemingly hopeless situations—Grant in the Civil War, Ridgway in Korea, and the British general William Slim in Burma in World War II.[24] He was called on "to retrieve a very desperate situation in Iraq in 2007, and then indeed to halt the Taliban momentum and reverse it in Afghanistan in 2010/2011." His commitment was total, not returning to the U.S. when his father died while he was commanding in Iraq.

This stellar profile did not tell the full story. He had never been in combat until he commanded in Iraq in 2003, and some on his staff felt him too cautious—hesitant to commit troops in a dynamic and fast-moving invasion, and wanting to regroup at the first contact with the enemy.[25] It was not until he reached Mosul that his formidable organizational skills came to the fore, and he negotiated with fractured local administrations to turn around a perilous situation and manage important elements for stabilization such as the wheat harvest. The conclusion to some close to him in this first field command was that he was a brilliant staff officer, but not a war commander.[26]

☰ STAMPEDE

Petraeus took command in Kabul on July 4. In one of his first stand-ups, he put up a slide of the Remington *Stampede* image on the big screen in the SAR. "I use this image to tell you I am comfortable with semi-chaotic situations . . . But we need to do more than hang onto the saddle. We must master our mount and we must flourish in the apparent chaos. I am comfortable with this. It is a privilege to be part of the Kabul stampede—kick on."[27] Unusually for a senior commander by 2010, nine years into the war, he had no previous active experience in Afghanistan and did not much like it. "The terrain is forbidding and the weather is very difficult. The winters in Afghanistan were a grinding experience . . . They will burn anything they can get their hands on to stay warm in the winter, including plastic and other waste, so there's also a terribly noxious atmosphere. It's grey, bone-chillingly cold, and wet . . . It's a tough place for a military campaign." He had first been there at the request of Secretary of Defense Donald Rumsfeld in 2005, who asked him to do a survey of progress on his way back from Iraq. He gave a downbeat assessment, presciently telling Rumsfeld, "The bottom line is that, in my view, Afghanistan is going to be the longest campaign in a long war."

Petraeus was a great advocate of PowerPoint and used slides to harvest knowledge—at one point amassing one thousand slides on the situation in Iraq. His slide deck on Afghanistan in 2005 was titled "Afghanistan Does Not Equal Iraq." He stressed the differences, including relatively developed infrastructure and an educated population in Iraq compared to Afghanistan, desert in Iraq against the mountainous terrain of northern and eastern Afghanistan, and, most importantly, that the leadership of the various Iraqi insurgencies were inside the country, while the Taliban leadership were in Pakistan. "Mullah Omar wouldn't dream of coming into Afghanistan because he knew that if he did he was likely to end up being on the X."

He was clear that Afghanistan would not be "flipped" as Iraq had been. But like the queen in *Hamlet,* in stressing that Afghanistan does not equal Iraq, perhaps Petraeus did "protest too much." Iraq informed his thinking, and when talking about Afghanistan, he often compared the two campaigns. Referring to tribal leaders in Afghanistan, he called them "sheikhs"—an Arab term used in Iraq and not Afghanistan.

In Kabul, he used the same slide he had in Baghdad—called the Anaconda strategy—with the Afghan Taliban and Haqqani network replacing Iraqi Sunni groups at the center of a circle having the life squeezed out of them as if by a snake through twenty-five different lines of effort. He would sometimes say *Iraq* as a slip of the tongue when meaning *Afghanistan*[28] and even made the comparison while talking to President Karzai. An aide advised him not to talk about Iraq so much and said, "It might be a mental exercise for you to try not thinking about Iraq at all." Petraeus said, "I'm working on it."[29] It was not until the arrival of General John W. "Mick" Nicholson in 2016 that international forces in Kabul were led by a commander whose entire post-9/11 combat experience was Afghanistan. Too often, Afghanistan, the other war, under-resourced and misunderstood in Washington, was seen through the prism of Iraq.

Petraeus's Anaconda was designed to portray the whole war on one slide. "In the circle in the center, you have the extremist and insurgent group. In the circle around that, you have all the assets that they need—weapons, money, ideology, command and control, communications, sanctuary, explosives, explosives expertise, fighters, and so forth. Then around that you have all the possible actions that you can take in a comprehensive civil-military campaign to try to squeeze the life out of the insurgency by taking away from them all the different components that are necessary for them to continue to fight."

The twenty-five lines of effort pointing inward were grouped into seven clusters,[30] including several tasks that were not "military" in the traditionally understood sense but were what Petraeus defined as core military tasks for counterinsurgency. The seven clusters were Information Operations; Politics; Intelligence; Services, such as education and justice; International, meaning Pakistan; Kinetic, including counterterrorist special operations as well as conventional operations; and Correction, to manage detainees without worsening the conflict.

During the long debates over the surge for Afghanistan in 2009, he used the Anaconda slide often when commanding at CENTCOM to argue that more troops were needed for this full spectrum of operations. "This was originally constructed to explain to Congress what we later went into depth to explain with the Obama administration review, that counter-terrorism operations are necessary, but not sufficient." He continued to use it in command in 2010, as if Obama had never amended and limited the scope of the operation in the December 2009 terms sheet.

On arrival in Kabul, Petraeus immediately ordered a review of McChrystal's tactical directive, leading to a resumption of night raids as well as a very substantial increase in air strikes, and was arguably the most significant decision he took in his year in command. While he often repeated the mantra "You can't kill or capture your way out of an industrial-strength insurgency," he was clear that offensive operations were an important part of the Anaconda squeeze bearing down on the Taliban, to reverse the momentum of the Taliban and other insurgent groups. "You do have to do lots of killing and capturing of the key irreconcilable leaders, and you have to do it every single night, with some 10 to 15 operations by special mission unit forces in order to increase the tempo of operations."

The surge of forces continued to rise to its peak of almost one hundred thousand U.S. troops in Afghanistan in the later months of 2010, when for the first time, more U.S. troops were in Afghanistan than Iraq. Gates was privately obsessed that it should not go above one hundred thousand, the number deployed by the Soviet Union at the peak of its intervention in the 1980s.[31] With another forty-thousand-plus from allied and partner nations, there was an inevitable increase in the tempo of the war. In October 2010, U.S. forces released 1,043 missiles and bombs from the air, more than in any other month of the Afghan war since the initial invasion, and twice as many as October 2009 under McChrystal's command. The trend continued; the following month, November 2010, recorded the second highest, with 866 weapons dropped from the air. (The average dropped per month between 2009 and 2012 was 375.)[32]

Petraeus knew of the concerns about courageous restraint, amplified by letters to newspapers by the parents of soldiers in the field. In his confirmation hearing for the Afghan post at the Senate Armed Services Committee, he said he was "keenly aware" of the concerns raised by troops on the ground that they were taking unnecessary casualties because of restrictions designed to protect civilians. Not wanting to criticize McChrystal, he chose to explain the problem in terms of its application down the chain of command. "We have to be absolutely certain," he told the senators, "that the implementation of the tactical directive and the rules of engagement are even throughout the force, that there are not leaders at certain levels that are perhaps making this more bureaucratic or more restrictive than necessary."[33]

In his new Tactical Directive, Petraeus took this head-on, with the specific order that "subordinate commanders are not authorized to further restrict this guidance without my approval." Those around him were clear that the gloves were off.[34] While Afghan civilians remained the center of gravity of the campaign and ISAF troops should "redouble . . . efforts to reduce the loss of civilian life," Petraeus removed the effective ban on the use of artillery and airpower, as well as night raids. He secured support for the change from General Jim Mattis, now commanding at CENTCOM, the two architects of modern counterinsurgency agreeing that the doctrine should not tie the hands of tactical commanders who needed to have the capacity to call in support. "We were hobbling ourselves militarily," wrote Mattis, "losing the confidence of our troops in the process."[35]

It was one of the ironies of the change of command that it was McChrystal, whose career until 2009 was defined by special operations, who would lead a counterinsurgency fight, while the godfather of counterinsurgency Petraeus significantly increased counterterrorism operations. Petraeus was a "CT wolf in a CI sheep's clothing," wrote David Ignatius in *The Washington Post*. Far from the doctrinal demand to protect the civilian population as the first priority, "the real action has been 'enemy-centric.'"[36] Petraeus insisted that there was no change. McChrystal's test, judging whether a military action would recruit more insurgents than it removed, was not ignored. Troops in his command needed to constantly ask themselves, "Will this operation take more bad guys off the street than it creates by its conduct?" If the answer in the complex calculus of counterinsurgency was negative, "then you sit under a tree until the thought of the proposed operation passes."

He continued the command model that McKiernan had blocked but McChrystal had adopted, putting Petraeus in strategic authority, "up" and "out," while tactical decisions, "down" and "in," were taken by a three-star underneath him. It suited Petraeus's management style to sit at the apex of the pyramid, with the next layer down staffed by people who were "quietly efficient," according to Holbrooke, "unlike McChrystal's group of cocky and contemptuous cowboys, who thought they were a high priesthood of shadow warriors saving our nation from itself."[37]

The surge of forces allowed Petraeus to employ not only more airpower, he was employing more of everything—more coordination with the civilian side, more intelligence, better management of information, better justice, and anticorruption efforts, aiming to build momentum to leave no space for the Taliban. The tempo of the Afghan campaign was at its highest in late 2010: all the Anaconda arrows pointing inward to squeeze the life out of the insurgency. In counterinsurgency guidance issued at the same time as the new tactical directive in August, he outlined twenty-four separate areas for attention. These included the instruction to "Live among the people. We can't commute to the fight." This became possible to do for the first time, as troops from the U.S. and their allies and partners poured into the country on the front side of the bell curve. Troops were told to walk, take off their sunglasses, work with international and Afghan troops, fight the information war, be first with the truth, help Afghans build governance, confront impunity, identify corrupt officials, use money as ammunition, and win the battle of wits. And finally, troops were ordered to "exercise initiative. In the absence of guidance or orders, figure out what the orders should have been and execute them aggressively." It was an ambitious list.

≣ THE BLEEDING ULCER

There was no doubt of the kinetic nature of the conflict for those fighting in the heat of the Afghan summer in the south, where temperatures rise to 120 degrees. The year 2010 was the bloodiest for U.S. casualties in Afghanistan, with 496 dead, and Petraeus took command in Kabul at the height of fighting that took the lives of 60 Americans in June and 65 in July. Most were in battles for the south. The planned sweep across from Marjah in Helmand eastward toward Kandahar, Operation Moshtarak, that began in February, was bogged down in a landscape laced with IEDs—the campaign called a "bleeding ulcer" by McChrystal. Petraeus knew he could not stop, although the initial momentum had gone.

> Kandahar Province was in a very desperate situation as the surge in Afghanistan materialized. The capital, Kandahar, was seriously threatened, and we had a huge base nearby that was getting hit on a regular basis. The enemy was closing in on the city from a number of different directions, from Uruzgan Province to the north, from Helmand Province to the west, and from two of Kandahar's districts, Zhari and Panjwayi, to the south—two districts which were very important historically, as the districts where Mullah Omar grew up and then where he built the Taliban movement in the beginning.

The Taliban had returned to the dense latticework of orchards and pomegranate fields, divided by irrigation canals on either side of the river, taken at such cost by the Canadian and American force in Operation Medusa in 2006 and where McChrystal had patrolled with Sergeant Arroyo's platoon after they had taken casualties. Parts of the area were virtually unhabitable through multiple improvised explosive devices, with a booby trap in every house, and U.S. forces took a radical decision to destroy thousands of buildings, using bulldozers, high explosives, missiles, and even airpower, now more available under the new Petraeus tactical directive.[38] The operation saved many American lives and limbs, and even though the consequence was that villages in three districts were literally wiped off the map, local officials did not object. Some reporters inevitably reached for the bleak oxymoron from Vietnam, that they had to "destroy villages in order to save them," but independent international and Afghan observers agreed that civilian casualties did not rise significantly, despite the huge increase in the use of airpower and artillery. A group of elders in Zhari District were quoted in the UN annual survey of Afghan civilian casualties saying there were "very, very few civilian casualties. We cannot even give an estimate."[39] U.S. infantry then went into an intensive six-month program to pay compensation and arrange reconstruction. This was the decisive moment in reclaiming Arghandab. The commander in the south at the time, Major General Nick Carter, visited again three years later as the deputy commander of ISAF. The district governor installed after the operation in 2011 was still in place, and he saw families picnicking on a Friday on land once full of IEDs.

☰ ARMING THE MILITIAS

As so often during the long war, support by villagers for international troops was conditional on them being able to provide security. Knowing they would be leaving before long, U.S. troops did deals with local power brokers who were not necessarily connected to the central government. In Kandahar, this meant working with "General" Abdul Raziq Achakzai, a militia leader, who had effective control of the Spin Boldak border post, Afghanistan's southern gateway to Pakistan. There was a simple calculation: "Raziq can beat the Taliban," said U.S. Special Forces lieutenant colonel James Hayes. Raziq was appointed to head the Kandahar police, although U.S. forces knew he was a player in the opium trade, and had a ruthless reputation for not taking prisoners. "The first priority is to beat the Taliban," said Hayes. "Once this is done, we can shift our attention to these illicit actors."[40]

And there was now active promotion of the Afghan Local Police (ALP), drawing on an Afghan tradition of Arbakai, local militias. If villages could be supported to stand up and protect themselves against the

Taliban, then the war would be easier to win. The U.S. tried to stand up local militias on several occasions after 2001, in various iterations, Local Defense Initiative, Auxiliary Police, Public Protection Police, and now the Afghan Local Police. None succeeded in making Afghanistan a safer place. The several attempts might have been an alert that this was a hard thing to do. To Petraeus, the new Afghan Local Police initiative was "arguably the most critical element in our effort to help Afghanistan develop the capacity to help itself."[41] He saw it as essential to provide security as the surge forces drew down.

The creation of local paramilitary forces where necessary was in his counterinsurgency manual, although there was a caution. "If militias are outside the HN [host nation] government's control, they can often be obstacles to ending an insurgency."[42] American willingness to work with informal armed groups, militias, was not shared across the NATO alliance, nor inside the Afghan government itself. They were not the minutemen of American Revolutionary legend but often predatory gangs, infiltrated or easily turned by the Taliban. Human Rights Watch found that the local police were "a government-backed militia that has raped, killed, and robbed."[43] While every Afghan rural home had a weapon, after forty years of uninterrupted warlordism, Afghanistan had seen enough of informal militias. A senior official in the Afghan Ministry of the Interior, Major General Esmatullah Dawlatzai, said the local police were "made for the warlords. They were given uniforms and salaries, but they were the same people, committing the same crimes, with more power."[44]

The hold of warlords on local security nine years into the war was a consequence of the support given to the Northern Alliance forces who had assisted in removing the Taliban from power in 2001. It became clearer every year that acknowledging the legitimacy of these forces rather than marginalizing them at the start was the founding cause of so many of the problems that followed.

The failure to provide alternative security meant that in many places where militias had not been a problem in the past, particularly in the northeast, there was now widespread lawlessness, with armed gangs competing for influence. In 2010, when the Afghan Local Police program was set up, national police reform remained at best a work in progress. Elsewhere, the Afghan security sector was now genuinely improving: the new Afghan National Army was "quickly getting bigger and slowly getting better,"[45] and its Special Forces in particular were able to operate independently and effectively. These more competent Afghan military forces needed police they could trust, not the ill-disciplined ALP.

☰ FLATTENING THE BELL CURVE

Sparring with the Obama administration over the scale and length of the Afghan commitment continued. The White House wanted withdrawal on a timetable, the generals wanted it determined by conditions on the ground. Petraeus said, "When you're in a contest of wills," a clear timetable for withdrawal "shows the enemy that we're not necessarily wholeheartedly into this." But the speed of drawdown was not agreed, and he was aiming to flatten the bell curve into a low hill with a gradual decline on the far side.

Petraeus had one success in moving the end date of transition to 2014—far later than many in the Obama administration, particularly the vice president, wanted. It was two years beyond the 2012 presidential election, which was Obama's ideal end date for boots on the ground in Afghanistan. The date 2014 was never mentioned in U.S. newspapers or mentioned in Senate hearings, but Petraeus successfully lobbied behind the scenes, until it became inevitable, while still needing to keep the surge troops on the ground for as long as possible ahead of 2014.

Mention of 2014 began to be openly discussed toward the end of 2009, even before the Obama announcement that anticipated a far steeper withdrawal. When the UK chief of defence staff, Air Marshal Sir Jock Stirrup, was interviewed in Helmand in November 2009, he said UK forces would "not be ready to leave" before 2014. Stirrup had flown combat missions in the early 1970s in the Dhofar campaign in Oman— one counterinsurgency the UK counted as a success.[46]

Petraeus did not mention 2014 in the Senate Armed Services Committee when he was CENTCOM commander in June 2010—nor when he returned for his hurriedly arranged confirmation hearing for the Kabul post two weeks later. At the time, he was merely pushing the bell curve to the right, without stretching it as late as 2014, ensuring that 2011 was only the start of withdrawal. "It is important to note the president's reminder in recent days that July 2011 will mark the beginning of a process, not the date when the US heads for the exits and turns out the lights."[47] He confirmed in answer to a deliberately helpful question from Senator John McCain that the drawdown date of July 2011 was a political decision; no one in the military was calling for it.

This was just the kind of answer that Obama's staff felt was boxing in the president, reducing his options. When Doug Lute visited Kabul in the fall of 2010 to review progress, he saw a map that had stretched the number of key terrain districts from seventy-two to ninety-six, against the terms sheet issued by the White House at the time of the West Point speech in December. Lute had been opposed to the surge in the first place. Afghanistan, in his view, was "not a good candidate for counterinsurgency." He had wanted to go more slowly the year before, using the marine deployment to Helmand as a pilot. "Let's see how the Marines do in a clear/hold/build/transfer model in Helmand then base numbers going forward on the efficacy of that model."[48] A year later, when he saw Petraeus stretching the terms of the surge—and just six months before the drawdown was due to start—his report to Obama was not favorable. The increase from seventy-two to ninety-six key terrain districts demonstrated that the military had not abided by the terms of the surge, and that "sealed the fate of the surge." The only tool available was to take a tough line on troop numbers. Lute said it was "an awkward, imprecise, not very rational way to do this but limiting the troops was the approach used to constrain the counterinsurgency campaign." The White House was reclaiming the bell curve.

☰ "LEADERS ARE LIKE A VESSEL"

The argument over whether troops left on the timetable or as allowed by conditions on the ground ran on throughout the Obama administration. Delivering continued commitment from NATO involved deft work behind the scenes by Petraeus. Realizing there was a pressing need for more NATO military trainers, Major General Nick Carter, commanding ISAF forces in southern Afghanistan, watched as Petraeus invited influential journalists from troop-contributing nations to visit Kabul ahead of the NATO military committee's visit in the autumn, "so that they arrived, having read about the requirement, with the ground manured for a positive decision."

Media were now front and center of the ISAF operation. Information had a separate line of effort on the slide, which was new since Anaconda first appeared in Iraq. Carter asked Petraeus who he was using for strategic communications, and Petraeus said, "Don't underestimate how much an individual makes this stuff happen for himself. We don't have highly trained staff. People think we have these people, but invariably it's the commander who makes things happen."

President Karzai nearly sabotaged the careful preparations for a key summit in Lisbon to decide NATO troop levels. In an interview for *The Washington Post,* he demanded a big reduction in foreign troops, the opposite of what Petraeus was working so hard for, and sentimentally referred to the days when there was American aid, but no troops. "The Afghans remember with very fond memories, with a lot of love and affection, all the roads and dams that you built in the 1950s and '60s." His main complaint was the increase in night raids under Petraeus. "Terrible. Terrible. A serious cause of the Afghan people's disenchantment with NATO . . . Bursting into homes at night, arresting Afghans, this isn't the business of any foreign troops."[49]

Petraeus was furious, and this was one of three occasions during his command when he threatened to resign unless Karzai apologized. He went to see Ashraf Ghani, then managing the transition to full Afghan military control. He said, "I want you to listen very, very carefully, Ashraf. Your President has put me in an untenable position that means that I cannot remain here. He either clarifies what it is that he said to *The Washington Post . . .* or I head back to Washington and I tell the President that we cannot succeed with him as a partner . . . If he chooses to go down that road it is his absolute right, but he should know that he will do it without me and I'll be on the next plane to Washington and I intend to take the policy with me." There were similar occasions in Iraq, where for Petraeus, a highly disciplined individual with a strong sense of right and wrong, the president of the country where he was serving crossed a line. And he was not without emotion or self-doubt when he took this stand. "This was very, very difficult and you know you go to bed on a night like that and you're not doing a heck of lot of sleeping because this is a pretty big deal. You've said you're going to quit basically on that country."

Karzai backed down and clarified that he wanted U.S. troops to stay. But he found Petraeus difficult to deal with, unwilling to include him in decision-making in the same way McChrystal had, and slow to accept responsibility for civilian casualties. "Petraeus went back to the old ways,"

Karzai said. "He would deny that there were casualties."[50] It did not help that Petraeus described Karzai's government as a "criminal syndicate" in Bob Woodward's book on the first year of the new administration, *Obama's Wars,* which came out two months after Petraeus arrived in Kabul.

The Afghan government believed Petraeus had taken a chilly decision to change the ability of U.S. troops to call in air strikes because of concern by U.S. troops over the rules on courageous restraint. "General Petraeus had to make up his mind to prevent civilian casualties or prevent American casualties," said Karzai's chief of staff, Umer Daudzai. "So he had to make a choice . . . and naturally civilian casualties went up."

There was a mutual lack of understanding between the cerebral ambitious general and the power-broking tribal chief in the Arg. In one curious incident, Petraeus appeared to suggest in an Afghan National Security Council meeting that people had burned their own children to make it look as if they had been hurt in an air strike. Karzai was startled. Daudzai said, "His explanation did not make sense. It was rather more harming the situation than helping."[51] The comments followed an incident where more than fifty people were killed by an air strike in Kunar province in the east. The governor of the province said they were civilians; U.S. officials said they were Taliban.[52] Explaining the reference, the ISAF spokesperson, Admiral Gregory J. Smith, said there were accounts of Afghans disciplining their children by putting their hands in boiling water, and Petraeus was referring to this. It was an unsettling incident.

For his part, Petraeus saw an Afghan president at the end of his tether, who believed the U.S. was "part of the problem rather than part of the solution," and the accumulation of bad news bubbled over the top from time to time. "Leaders are like a vessel and the bad news is poured in at the top and there are holes in the bottom that allow it to drain, but it can only drain so fast." Karzai now had few friends on the American side. He refused to meet the special representative for Afghanistan and Pakistan, Richard Holbrooke, unless Petraeus asked for the meeting and was in the room. And invariably, when the Kabul ambassador Karl Eikenberry came with Petraeus to meet the president, there would come a moment when Karzai would turn to the ambassador and say, "Well, you're the guy that tried to defeat me in the election, tried to force the runoff, that tried to undermine me and get Dr. Abdullah elected."

☰ BAD DAYS AND GOOD DAYS

As a commander, Petraeus knew the cost of war to all sides. He went to many, many ramp ceremonies, and they were physically and mentally wearing. While on a trip to the UK, he spoke personally to the Scottish father of a kidnapped aid worker, Linda Norgrove, killed by a U.S. grenade in a failed rescue attempt. He watched large, angry crowds protesting on the streets of Kabul when a Florida pastor, Terry Jones, threatened to publicly burn a copy of the Quran. To keep fit, he ran half a dozen times round the small base every morning through the mazes of shipping containers that had grown since 9/11 as offices and living quarters, and back to his corner of Florence Village, an enclosed courtyard of shipping containers stacked on top of each other. He had one container for meetings and another for sleeping quarters. Late one night, in May 2011, he slipped out of the container wearing just his running shorts and a T-shirt, crossed the small rose garden, and took the three-minute walk past the volleyball court on the right-hand corner, and the long, low concrete Milano building, with its Thai restaurant and makeshift cinema on the other side of the narrow road. He was ignored by the few soldiers using the free Wi-Fi in the garden that McChrystal had failed to close.

Crossing the small open space surrounded by flagpoles, with its stone memorial to the fallen, Petraeus went up the two shallow steps and pressed the code to open the wooden door of the yellow building. Turning left along the corridor and crossing the large SAR, he went into the smaller control room at the back, where screens filled the walls. The night shift were tracking nine different operations—but not the most important event happening in the region that night. Petraeus told everyone to leave except the most senior officer, and at midnight Kabul time, "Zero Dark Thirty" in Pakistan, which was half an hour ahead, he told the colonel that the raid against Osama bin Laden in Abbottabad was on the ground.

Petraeus had heard that the raid was likely when he was in Washington the week before. And while he did not have any command responsibility for it, as it was directed by the president through the CIA, he would need to respond if things went wrong. The special operators carrying out the raid were Navy SEALs, defined for the night as CIA operatives, "sheep-dipped" in the jargon, a legal fiction to get round the government's prohibition on regular forces entering Pakistan. With no visual feeds coming in, he kept in touch through a secure online chat room and had the confirmation forty minutes later that "Geronimo," the code name for the main target, bin Laden, was dead, after living in secret, close to major Pakistani military bases for almost a decade. Petraeus had flown over Abbottabad just the week before. When analysts went through the treasure trove of documents in the house, they uncovered an order to kill Petraeus, along with President Obama. Petraeus was said to be the "man of the hour . . . and killing him would alter the war's path."[53]

The main cause of the Afghan intervention may have been resolved, but the long war went on. The political justification remained to "stop terrorist attacks on the homeland," but while nation-building was as ill-begotten and lacking in form as ever, there was clearly a political and economic project alongside the military fight, and it was increasingly threatened by corruption, which Petraeus saw as something he needed to confront. His challenge was how to fight corruption without pulling down the frail Afghan state.

THE COUNTERINSURGENCY DILEMMA

Corruption is not just a problem for the system of governance in Afghanistan.

It is the system of governance.

—Dr. Rangin Spanta, Afghan national security adviser, October 2, 2010[1]

☰ STROKING THE FAT

"I am warning you. I will come to your house, and you will disappear." The woman kept up a torrent of threats to customs officers as cellophane bags of white heroin powder emerged one by one from under her dress to be stacked neatly on a desk. Their hiding place strapped to her stomach, back, and thighs would not have passed the most cursory check. She thought her protection strong enough. "Don't you know who I am? I make six men like you disappear in a day. Bring my phone. You must be new." She kept her biggest insult to the end. "I will take off your trousers and put them on your head"—ridiculous sounding, but meant as a humiliation in this repressed society. The head of customs at the airport, General Aminullah Amerkhel, sighed as he showed the video. He had heard it all before. He knew her claims of powerful protection were probably true. After he handed her over to the police, she was released without charge by nightfall. Another futile day on the front line against the corruption that engulfed the country.

Amerkhel filmed everything on a small video camera. Every day, he faced abusive encounters like this. On one of his videos, a man accused as a people trafficker complains with contempt, "You're treating me like a Jew."[2] Amerkhel's customs compound was rebuilt in an international effort to improve airport security and customs revenues. The roof leaked, there was no water in the bathroom, and he stabbed a pencil through the wall to show it was so badly built. "They were supposed to use cement, but this is not cement, just dust," he said. "It is falling apart already." No more than 10 percent of the $1 million contract was actually spent on the building—the rest taken by subcontractors in the chain. "This poor country," he said. "Other countries come to help, and these people just put the money in their pocket and disappear."[3]

Across town in the central park, behind the cinema where the Taliban once made a bonfire of Bollywood films, a former minister, Ramazan Bashardost, set up a tent to hear stories about corruption. It was never empty. People lined up daily to share their stories of lands seized, jobs taken, demands for bribes made. A revenue collector from the northeast said things were worse than when the Taliban were in power. In 1995, when the Taliban took his area, he offered his resignation, but they told him to remain in his post if he were an honest man. After their fall, the warlord who replaced them demanded a cut. When the revenue collector refused, he was fired, losing his house and his car with the job. A Congress report in 2011 found that half of the potential customs revenues of $2 billion were stolen in this way.[4]

From a hidden pocket deep inside folds of tribal robes, another elder brought out ancient title deeds—evidence of what had been taken. The government was still demanding taxes from him although his land had been seized by a thug, who took the opportunity of insecurity after international intervention drove out the Taliban. "Once that man did not even have a donkey to ride," he said. "Now he drives a Land Cruiser." Poetry is held in high regard in Afghanistan, and the elder was respectfully heard as he declaimed a poem about the warlord takeover, including the line that Karzai was "stroking the fat on their backs. But beware. The anger of Afghans will be followed by a storm."[5] The anger in the tent was palpable. They felt let down by international intervention.

Bashardost was an unusual tour guide, stopping on the way south to Ghazni to point out how the ring road, the showcase project of the early years, was crumbling. In Ghazni, he railed about how corruption meant nothing was done properly: a bridge rebuilt with U.S. funding collapsed in a flood, while two bridges built in Soviet times withstood it. The cause of the flood was the breach of a nearby dam—again renovated with international funding since 9/11, but not well enough to withstand winter storms.

There were too few public servants like Amerkheil and Bashardost who stood up against corruption. Stop in any village and you could hear the same story—the government was corrupt, there was no functioning justice, the police were predatory, and international intervention had brought nothing. Time and again when the Taliban were cleared from an area, the first request of civilians would be to ensure the corrupt police did not return. The Afghan countryside was littered with the detritus of good intentions. In one village in Logar Province, three unfinished school buildings stood side by side up a hill. The first was begun by a fund set up to remember some of the 9/11 victims but abandoned for lack of cash, the second abandoned through corruption. The third was a building site for a school funded by the Japanese, who started fresh, as the previous attempts did not fit their exacting earthquake standards.

Corruption had eaten so deeply into the fabric of society by 2010 that extreme depravity could go on as if normal. In the Soviet-built "Four-Hundred-Bed" military hospital, a place where Afghanistan's war wounded should have been tended with all care, American investigators discovered scenes so shocking, a congressional inquiry put out a warning before displaying images. In scenes described as "Auschwitz-like," patients were dying of starvation, with open bowls of blood under untreated wounds and feces on the floor. Operations were done without anesthesia in smoke-filled rooms. Staff stole money that should have gone to buy food. Drugs were sold and replaced by defective alternatives, and more than $150 million was believed stolen.[6] That this was allowed to happen in the best hospital in the country, across the street from the U.S. embassy and largely funded with U.S. money, reveals the extent of the failure of financial oversight. Without fundamental reform of the Afghan state and better management of international spending to ensure it was not fueling corruption, counterinsurgency would always be flawed.

☰ WARLORD PROTECTION RACKET

It took several years before corruption was recognized as a strategic threat to the campaign.[7] It was initially seen as an Afghan issue, part of the fabric of the country and the cost of doing business, to be tolerated and managed by governance projects and tackling narcotics. By 2009, General McChrystal recognized this had the problem the wrong way around. Corruption was *causing* insecurity. In his strategic assessment in September 2009, he saw the "unpunished abuse of power by corrupt officials" as one of two main challenges facing coalition troops, the other being the insurgency itself. If corruption was a cause of insecurity, then the aperture of military responses needed widening, as in Petraeus's Anaconda strategy. Dealing with corruption became a military priority, and that meant looking at the way the military spent money as well as problems in the Afghan state.

Petraeus brought in one of the army's rising stars, Brigadier General H. R. McMaster, to head a new initiative against corruption—Task Force Shafafiyat (meaning "transparency" in both Afghan languages). He rejected the idea that corruption was deeply ingrained in the culture, part of the Afghan social fabric, as "bigotry masquerading as cultural sensitivity."[8] It was not part of the social norm but an aberration caused by the long war. He mapped the relationship between organized crime and politics, and amid a number of high-profile court cases in the U.S., for the first time military contracting came under scrutiny as a cause of corruption. He set up a series of task forces—TF-Spotlight, to find missing equipment, TF-2010 to tighten up contracting, TF-Nexus for organized crime links, working with a vendor-vetting cell at CENTCOM to attempt to prevent funds going to warlords.

Petraeus issued counterinsurgency contracting guidance soon after his arrival in command in 2010 and recalled it quickly. The revision emphasized that it was for the Afghan side to own the problem of corruption. It was necessary to "help" them confront corruption—not for coalition troops to own it themselves.[9] "Make sure the people we work with work for the people," Petraeus wrote, with the specific aim of ensuring money did not empower "malign or corrupt individuals or organizations." It was a hard knot to untie after ten years of looking the other way and signing the checks.

America's fatal embrace with the warlords began with the CIA's payments of $1 billion in the first year of the war when chasing al-Qaeda was the only priority, with no thought of the distorting effect such payments in a fragile economy.[10] The cardboard boxes full of millions of dollars that Gary Schroen's Jawbreaker team used as a coffee table in

2001 were the first ripple in a rolling surf of cash that crashed against the Afghan shore. The warlords revived after containment in the Taliban years, mutated to run private security firms, and were ready to pick up lucrative logistics contracts as more troops came in with the surge. Across the U.S. system, there continued to be a preference for working with contractors rather than through the Afghan state. General Karimi said the state was not trusted to manage the money. "Defence Minister Wardak in my presence talked to many Americans and said, 'Please trust us. We can do it for half of the money you are doing it.'"[11]

It took a report in *The Nation* in November 2009 to sound the alarm about how serious things had become.[12] American tax dollars were literally funding the enemy, paying protection money for passing through land controlled by the Taliban. Around 70 percent of what was needed for a force of 150,000 international troops came overland—fuel mostly from the north, and food, construction supplies, and ammunition mostly from Pakistan. The warlords ran the trucking contracts but needed to pay groups, including the Taliban, for not being attacked.

The Taliban were profiting to a staggering amount, around 10 percent of the $2 billion–a-year contracts, in what a congressional inquiry called a "warlord protection racket."[13] Corruption was an inevitable corollary of a large army that contracted out its needs in an insecure environment with few checks. The bribes fueled the insurgency, worsening insecurity in a negative feedback loop, and if the aim of international intervention were to bolster the Afghan government, Congress found that "U.S. reliance on warlords for supply chain security has the effect of dramatically undermining that objective."

Trucking contracts were a small part of military spending. The military were now heavily involved in road-building, jobs schemes, school-building, and other activities traditionally associated with the civilian side of government. *Most* U.S. reconstruction spending in Afghanistan did not go through State but the Pentagon. The peak year of U.S. military contracting was 2012, at $19 billion, just $1 billion less than Afghan GDP,[14] and there was little coordination between the military and civilian efforts. Commanding in 2012, General John Allen said if there was a joint civil-military development plan, he was not told about it.[15]

Military units had fistfuls of cash to spend through the Commander's Emergency Response Program (CERP). The program had a curious origin in the discovery of $650 million in uncirculated $100 U.S. bills from the Federal Reserve of New York, in boxes stacked in a bricked-up shed in Baghdad in 2003. A further haul of $112 million was found in a nearby dog kennel. President Bush decided that the money belonged to the Iraqi people, and disbursing it became the forerunner of CERP, giving commanders the ability to spend on development and reconstruction.[16] Civil affairs capacity across both the marines and the army was rudimentary at the time, so they were literally making it up as they went along. By the time of the Petraeus–Mattis counterinsurgency doctrine, using "money as ammunition" had become an established idea. The CERP program was run under a scheme called MAAWS, Money as a Weapons System, and it was a response to the desire of commanders for quick impact—delivering development behind military action.

In the right hands, CERP bought at least short-term stabilization gains, but unless linked to Afghan government programs or longer-term internationally funded projects, it was not value for money. Cash-for-work projects or contracts to deliver gravel for military bases had no lasting impact. Built into CERP were "perverse incentives" that led to the "expenditure of millions of dollars with almost no insight or alignment with other U.S. government efforts,"[17] according to a somber analysis by a military investigation under General Joe Dunford, commanding in Afghanistan in 2014. Officers were graded on "the number of CERP projects they could get obligated," said a member of the Commission on Wartime Contracting. "Of course, they got a whole bunch of CERP projects; none of which were completed and most were barely under way when that commander rotated."[18]

Worse, there is evidence that CERP money *destabilized* areas rather than the other way round. As warlords captured the new funding flows, it looked to people in villages as if international troops had sided with them. The large aid flows in quick impact projects tended to increase corruption, lowering confidence in the state and allowing the Taliban to portray international troops as on the side of the warlords—the opposite of the intention of squeezing out the Taliban by connecting citizens to the state.

The idea of "Money as a Weapons System" was enthusiastically promoted by commanders at all levels, who wanted development and jobs to follow offensive operations—clear, hold, *and build*. And the administration were committed to funding it. Michèle Flournoy, undersecretary of defense for policy, called it an "absolutely critical and flexible counterinsurgency tool." But this turned out to be based on a flawed belief.

What people wanted most was fair treatment, justice, security, and an end to predatory policing, not schools and hospitals. "Paktia has lots of problems, but lack of clinics, schools and roads are not the problem," an elder in the mountains of the east told researcher Andrew Wilder. If the police and courts were corrupt, Taliban justice looked attractive. Aid fueled that corruption, and Wilder was told that in the villages that more aid would make that worse, not better. "If you increase the amount of money it will also be useless because the government will simply steal more."[19] Warlords became astute players of the system. They knew the drawdown would begin in 2011. The bonanza would come to an end; they made money while they could.

☰ MORE IS LESS[20]

The corrupting potential of international aid cut deep in Afghan villages. In a country with a profound sense of right and wrong and duty to society, getting something for nothing struck people as foolish. So while understandably demanding what they could get, they thought donors to be fools. Democracy brought corruption, so it quickly became a tainted idea, associated with immoral behavior, such as wearing jeans and drinking wine. One elder told Wilder, "Now we have democracy. People do whatever they want—loot, steal, and only think about themselves." Ultimately, education, mobility, and development might open up different opportunities, but for now, conservative, traditional values were a rational defense against insecurity. The money came in grants, not loans, and associated social reform programs encountered a clash of culture between Western donors who value individual liberty, and people in Afghan villages governed by collective duty, where concepts like liberty and women's rights literally have no meaning.

In functioning Pashtun society, duty and responsibility feed both ways through widening concentric circles of family, clan, tribe—with the nation as a remote wider circle. Individuals have no place outside this web of mutual responsibility, but are given respect inside, as duty flows up and down through patronage and service. The network was under attack from a Taliban campaign of murdering prominent elders in the south and west. A British diplomat in Helmand in 2009 said, "We are trying to work with the tribal grain, but it's very coarsened."[21] That meant that there was little resilience, as the amount of aid money in the system lubricated new patronage networks, run by warlords who in their turn sidelined traditional elders, while co-opting patronage networks. To secure a senior police or regional government appointment cost upward of $100,000 in big provinces, with the money flowing upward to elites with roots in the 1980s mujahideen parties, whose corruption and banditry in the 1990s had provoked the rise of the Taliban in the first place.[22]

This represented a profound dilemma for the counterinsurgency doctrine. The plan was to connect citizens to the state, but if the state were corrupt, then the doctrine had a fatal flaw. It was Vietnam redux—massive military effort squandered by a failed administration, with the difference being that in Vietnam, America was propping up a post-colonialist state; in Afghanistan, the state was an American creation. ISAF commanders were exposed by their proximity to warlords, appearing in public with people the public knew were thieves.

McChrystal heard this problem in his first week in command in 2009, visiting a remote village in the east where he was told, "The number one complaint from Afghans is that the Afghan government doesn't deliver on promises."[23]

The international community had too few people with the political capacity to navigate these treacherous waters. Just as American officials failed a test of realpolitik in 2001, not recognizing the weakness of the warlords, so they later failed to recognize how the aid was worsening insecurity by empowering warlords. However adept the international project in Afghanistan may have been at democratic process, such as elections and *jirgas,* it failed the test of Afghan politics in the raw, lacking strategy and will both to limit the power of the warlords and successfully encourage civil society institutions who could grow non-warlord political parties.

The Taliban's first military operation in 1994, when they had fewer than a hundred men and a handful of weapons, was against corruption and banditry. They opened the road between Kandahar and the border, taking down illegal roadblocks.[24] When roadblocks returned, under the eye of international soldiers, it was an easy propaganda win for the

Taliban, as was the corruption of the police and justice system. An Afghan political activist explained the process. "In any country there are 4 percent thugs and 1 percent extremists. Foreigners did not understand this and gave money to the thugs [warlords]." Supporting the Taliban was a logical defense mechanism in a system where international troops looked as if they were on the side of the warlords as they condoned corruption. "The 95 percent were patient for a while, but eventually, we had to align with the extremists [the Taliban] to throw out the thugs [the warlords]."[25]

☰ THE SECOND JUGGERNAUT

At the same time as the military were flooding Afghanistan with cash, USAID also hugely increased its spending.[26] William Byrd, the former World Bank economist, now at the U.S. Institute of Peace, saw this second wave of cash as more damaging than the first off-budget "aid juggernaut" he identified in the early years. With the bonfire of corruption consuming Afghan hopes, more cash was just fuel on the fire. It further delayed the day when Afghan elites were accountable to their people for the money they spent. "What's the political strategy of relying on warlords, how does that move forward if you really want democracy?" asked Byrd. "It's all short-term fixes."[27]

Most funding was still off budget, spent outside the state, against what was now internationally agreed best practice—that aid was better spent building state capacity than replacing it. Donor nations, including the U.S., signed up to the Paris Declaration on aid effectiveness back in 2005, agreeing that putting aid on budget was the best way to go forward because it connected people to the state. At an Afghan conference in London in January 2010, Hillary Clinton committed to put most cash on budget. But it was hard for the U.S. administration to get out of the habit. Looked at from Washington, the Afghan government was hardly a safe receptacle for hard-earned tax dollars, so grants and contracts delivered off budget continued.

Holbrooke insisted on running all USAID decisions on Afghanistan through what he called his "shitty office," where he ran the AfPak program in a cramped, stuffy, first-floor corner of the State Department, overlooking an inner courtyard, next to the cafeteria.[28] He was a restless vortex of energy, and would arrive in Kabul sending a bow wave crashing ahead of him that left nervous staffers bobbing in his wake. It did not deliver better scrutiny of projects—in fact, the opposite.

As spending grew, the need to shovel cash out the door became more urgent. U.S. civilian contracting, still with too few officials managing large sums of money, little inspection, and short timelines, brought its own perverse incentives. Quantity mattered more than quality, and since it took as much effort and time to deliver a large contract as a small one, there was a tendency to contract out functions to other companies, who would subcontract and subcontract down the line, with each layer taking a slice of the cash, until there was little left for the contract itself. Across Afghanistan, there were signs outside schools saying, "Gift of the American people," but behind the signs, children were being taught in substandard buildings or even just tents. An aid official described the pressure on Afghan contractors.

> He can get second-rate materials because no one will check the work (or he can likely pay off inspectors). He will hire family to do the work. He, and every other contractor, is graded not on quality but on how many schools he builds . . . So, even for honest contractors, the incentives are for expensive, shoddy, uncoordinated, quickly built schools. And that is often what we got.[29]

Those who became adept at spending international money for their own purposes did not only come in dark-windowed pickups surrounded by gunmen but wore Western suits and spoke good English. They had undue influence among the thousands of international staff now in Kabul to manage aid projects. These were the peak years for expatriate life in Kabul, with a dozen places to eat and drink highly priced alcohol, sourced from the back doors of compliant embassies who shipped it in by the pallet-load, in the "diplomatic bag." It was highly priced because of the bribes needed to serve it in a Muslim country. There were Chinese-owned late-night drinking clubs, a couple of French restaurants, and a Croatian restaurant, staffed by fierce Croatian women who took no nonsense from overmuscled boozed-up security guards on a night off.

The longest-running foreign-owned bar and guesthouse was opened by an English romantic, Peter Jouvenal, soon after the fall of the Taliban in 2001, in a house once occupied by Osama bin Laden. Moving to a more central location a couple of years later, he shipped out the interior of an old English pub, with table mats showing hunting scenes, and had china made with a crest showing the face of the fictitious rogue Flashman, antihero of a series of novels set in Britain's nineteenth-century wars. Jouvenal called it Gandamack Lodge, after the location in eastern Afghanistan of the final defeat of an entire British division in the winter of 1841/42. The restaurant and garden of the Gandamack were the location where much business was done by spies, soldiers, journalists, and aid workers among the birdcages, rugs, antique Afghan muskets, swords, and tribal-made *jezails* that lined the walls.

Occasionally, if they could give a good reason, and get security, which meant two armored SUVs with discreetly armed guards, USAID and other embassy officials would be allowed out for the evening to a residence or the Gandamack, but it was hard to escape the demands of security officials with low appetite for risk. They were generally restricted to life hunched over computers behind the high walls of the embassy compound. They might as well have been in Foggy Bottom.

Peaking at close to one thousand people in 2010, the civilian surge never delivered the numbers or quality of people anticipated by Obama the year before. Only around three hundred people made it outside Kabul, and many did not last in the austere surroundings of rural Afghanistan, although it was what they had signed up for. Between 2009 and 2010, of the civilians assigned to Helmand, 40 percent did not last six months.[30] Marc Chretien, the senior civilian representative with the U.S. Marines in Helmand, watched one woman arrive out of the cloud of dust of a helicopter landing, wearing a business suit, with good suitcases. He asked her if she had development experience, and she said, "Yes, I do, with the UN, in Manhattan." He said, "You need to go to Kabul." She said, "This is my assignment." A week later, the marine commander told him, "She's complaining about the size of her hooch, how big her little refrigerator is. She lives better than I do or any of my Marines."[31] Chretien had her transferred to Kabul.

Holbrooke harbored a career-long appreciation of the value of agricultural projects from his first overseas posting in 1972 working in villages in Vietnam, and when he took on the AfPak portfolio, he doubled spending on agriculture. There is no doubt that some of the agricultural experts made a difference, especially those with genuine farm experience. A California apple farmer spent three years in Ghazni improving orchards; cotton experts revived antique ginning plants and made another attempt to encourage Helmandis to grow cotton. Also in Helmand, there was a model agricultural research institute, Bolan Farms, which pioneered new ways of growing crops and showed them off to farmers, handing out seeds as they did so—hundreds of millions of dollars of seeds. In 2010, the enormous sum of $250 million was sent to a few districts in the southern provinces of Helmand and Kandahar. Rajiv Chandrasekaran of *The Washington Post* calculated that every resident of Nawa, one remote, poor Helmand district, received $400, higher than the annual per capita income.[32] But it took more than the best of intentions. Holbrooke reminded staffers that when in Vietnam, he stuck on his office wall a Charlie Brown strip then just out that would become a classic. After losing yet another baseball game, Charlie declares, "How can we lose when we're so sincere?"[33]

The economy was stacked against success, however good the advisers were. An Afghan poultry expert, Dr. Ihsanullah, studied the best practice in the Netherlands and set up an innovative chicken project in Helmand. He would sell day-old chicks to farmers, buy local corn, fortify it, and return it as chicken feed. Even with a USAID grant for his incubation plant and price subsidies, the farmers could not compete with low-price chickens crossing the border from Iran and Pakistan. International financial institutions demanded open borders and free trade, missing the experience of so many countries that had made real strides from poverty to wealth, like Korea and Taiwan, who had managed trade, supported agriculture, and subsidized exports—essential stepping-stones on the way to prosperity.[34]

Similarly, the cotton could not find a market. In 2012, watching cotton arriving at a gin in Helmand, I asked farmers what they would plant the next year. Without hesitation, they chorused, *"Koknar, koknar"* ("Poppies"). And it was easy to see why. A wide concrete apron next to the gin was stacked as far as the eye could see with piles of unsold cotton bales. It was too hard to compete with imports of cotton from Pakistan.

Southern Afghanistan had plentiful water, and winter sunshine meant they could double-crop some fruits and vegetables, growing all year round. But without refrigeration, and better support for international trade, the agricultural sector would find it hard to recover the global trade it had before the decades of war began without more systemic support, and a decade of thoughtful interventions to provide alternative livelihoods to growing opium poppies was wasted.

In Garmser, southern Helmand, the dirt-poor gateway to the Pakistan desert, the huge sum of $21.5 million was spent from 2009 to 2011 across military and nonmilitary aid projects. The political officer Carter Malkasian wrote that there were not enough conditions attached to the spending. "Too often locals were happy to take the projects and do nothing in return." That much money was overkill. "As of early 2011, most of the projects had provided a short-term boost rather than long-term economic growth."[35]

The pity was that beyond the tsunami of cash for military contracting and troubled southern provinces, much had changed for the better. There was a real improvement in revenue raised in Afghanistan. Technical support for key ministries, in particular the Finance Ministry, meant the government could effectively handle more cash, as after years of mentoring they had developed the technical capacity to account for spending, "absorb" it in the jargon. This progress was more marked than in comparably sized economies in Africa. The World Bank found that Afghanistan had developed a "sound tax collection and administration system."[36] But it warned, "The overriding lesson of the last 10 years is that too many actors and projects chasing too many short-term stabilization—rather than development—goals leads to poor service delivery and an institutional environment that supports quick fixes over longer-term capacity development."[37]

☰ BAGS OF CASH

Ahmed Wali Karzai, the half brother of the president, a mournful-faced man, heavier set but with the same trimmed beard as his more famous relative, sat in a crisply ironed white *shalwar kameez* and reminisced about how Kandahar was a long way from Chicago, where he had run a restaurant near Wrigley Field. The American diplomat was not taken in. "He appears not to understand the level of our knowledge of his activities," he wrote in a cable, and "demonstrated that he will dissemble when it suits his needs."[38] AWK, as he was known, was suspected of involvement in drug-dealing and other criminal activities. The president always demanded to see proof when diplomats complained. No court will ever test the evidence. AWK was shot by his own bodyguard in 2011.

There was another problem in confronting him. He was a CIA asset who recruited fighters for the Kandahar Strike Force, an irregular military unit, operating out of the former home of the Taliban leader Mullah Omar, alongside the CIA, who had occupied the compound since 2001.[39] They had carried out a number of attacks that caused concern, including the death of a Kandahar police chief.[40] The counterinsurgency dilemma was defined with precision by Eikenberry after one encounter in October 2009. "The meeting with AWK highlights one of our major challenges in Afghanistan: how to fight corruption and connect the people to their government, when the key government officials are themselves corrupt."[41]

Under constant international pressure to clean up the government, Karzai set up an oversight body as early as 2004. His first appointee as head of the body, Azizullah Lodin, used it to pursue personal vendettas. The second, a childhood friend of the president, Ezatullah Wasifi, had spent more than three years in jail in Nevada for selling heroin. After donor pressure, Karzai simply abolished the organization rather than cleaning it up.[42] The same cycle was repeated several times, as internationally funded bodies delivered little effective oversight, and by 2010, Karzai was willing to be even more defiant. He openly admitted receiving carrier bags full of cash from Iran after it was revealed in *The New York Times*. "They do give us bags of money—yes, yes, it is done."[43] It was a pointed reminder that the president had other international friends at a time when he was in a bitter argument with General Petraeus over control of Afghan private security companies who provided guards for Western organizations in Kabul. Karzai said the contractors killed civilians. He blamed the U.S. government, who he said "send the money for killing here."[44]

Karzai had already tested the limits of international authority in 2010 by ordering the release of an official in the National Security Council, Muhammad Zia Salehi, arrested on corruption charges a month after Petraeus arrived in Kabul. Salehi was caught in a phone tap demanding a bribe of $20,000 to buy a Toyota for his son, in return for blocking an investigation into the New Ansari currency exchange company.

The bribe was small beer compared to the huge sums involved in the investigation of New Ansari, suspected of involvement in money laundering, including the movement of tens of millions of dollars stolen from Kabul Bank. Set up with $1 billion to develop credit for new business, the bank was run as a giant Ponzi scheme, whose directors handed out money with no conditions attached, much of which went to buy houses on Palm Jumeirah, a new luxury island in Dubai. Arresting Salehi was one thread in attempting to recover the cash from the Kabul Bank sinkhole by a new anticorruption unit set up with FBI support, the Major Crimes Task Force.

The bank's founder, Sherkhan Farnood, was a colorful character—a world-class poker player who gambled with the Afghan economy. Investigators got lucky when he fell out with Khalilullah Ferozi, his former driver and bodyguard whom he had appointed chief executive, and decided to talk.[45] When the fraud was discovered, the bank was handling salaries for Afghan security forces and civil servants, as well as other crucial government services, and its collapse could bring down the state. But the capital had gone—in a failing airline, property in Dubai, and into thin air in bribes and $100,000 credit cards. Farnood told the whole story, implicating the vice president and the brother of the president, as well as many other prominent Afghans in scams that included setting up fake companies to siphon money out of the bank.

Karzai opposed the investigation all the way, proud of how he had ordered the release of Salehi at the beginning. "Yes, absolutely, I intervened," he said. "Not only I intervened, but I intervened very, very strongly."[46] He demoted two prosecutors involved in the case against Salehi and forbade the UK from continuing to pay top-up salaries for anticorruption investigators, so their salaries dropped from $800 to $200.[47] When Kabul Bank charges were finally brought in 2013, he ensured some bank regulators who had tried to stop the rot also appeared in the dock, and they were jailed for negligence. It turned out that Salehi was Karzai's main conduit to the Taliban.

These were murky waters. There were no public protests from the international community to Karzai's intervention in the Salehi case, and the reason soon became clear.[48] He was on the CIA payroll, and the U.S. were beginning to discover limits to what could be done against corruption in 2010, if they were not willing to restructure the state. As the Special Inspector General for Afghanistan Reconstruction (SIGAR) put it, "The Afghan government was so deeply enmeshed in corrupt and criminal networks that dismantling them would mean dismantling major pillars of support for the government itself."[49]

The international intervention had done a deal with the devil that was hard to unravel. As U.S. Marines stabilized northern Helmand in 2010, they insisted the police chief of Musa Qala, Commander Koka, be fired. He was believed to be taking $20,000 a day in taxes on opium. Security immediately became worse, so he was reinstated. Just at the time when the military force was at its largest, peaking at 150,000, the limits on action to combat corruption exposed frailty at the heart of the counterinsurgency.

Congress, who were paying the bills, were asking increasingly tough questions about corruption, voting to suspend aid flows until there were improvements. Senator Lindsey Graham said, "Karzai needs to be told that how you handle Kabul Bank depends greatly on what kind of support you're going to get in the future."[50] But heading for the exit, the administration began to accept that corruption would not be resolved. In his White House statement in the summer of 2011 announcing the surge drawdown, Obama said, "We won't try to make Afghanistan a perfect place."

The White House coordinator for the war, Doug Lute, always a surge skeptic, said he never thought they would be able to end corruption, so the counterinsurgency was flawed from the start. "I didn't believe that we had a capable partner there. Corruption was endemic, capacity for governance was so limited, and the balance between the center and the periphery politically was so skewed, that counterinsurgency wasn't going to work."

☰ FRAGILE AND REVERSIBLE

Before he left Afghanistan in July 2011, Petraeus wanted to do more to ensure the surge would deliver its full potential, and troops would not be pulled out until Afghanistan could fight on its own. But just as Obama felt boxed in by generals pushing for more troops in 2009, so he felt himself "gamed" in March 2011 after Petraeus told a NATO meeting that transition to Afghan forces should "commence" at the end of 2014.[51] For the president, 2014 was to be the end date of transition.

In a marathon session of more than three hours in front of the Senate Armed Services Committee two weeks later, Petraeus continued to push for a sustained commitment. Leaving immediately would damage

Afghanistan, since the plan was working but was not finished, so needed more time. "While the security progress achieved over the past year is significant, it is also fragile and reversible."[52] He had first used the phrase in Iraq and now deployed it for Afghanistan to persuade politicians to continue supporting a cause that ten years after the fall of the Taliban was being seen with skeptical eyes. He was aware of other political pressures on the president—"congressional politics, national politics, strain on the force, budget deficits, coalition politics, you name it." Obama wanted the surge over by the 2012 election. But Petraeus had seen the surge deliver success in stabilizing parts of Afghanistan for the first time for many years, including Helmand and Kandahar, and knew those gains were "reversible."

Before the NSC met to decide the date of the end of the surge, Gates made his twelfth and last trip to Afghanistan as secretary of defense, including an emotional journey to visit marines holding Sangin in the Helmand River valley. The 3rd Battalion, 5th Marine Regiment, lost 25 killed and 184 wounded during their deployment, the highest loss for any marine unit during the Afghan war. One of the dead marines, Robert Kelly, was the son of Gates's military assistant, Lieutenant General John Kelly, who spent some time in private with his son's comrades. They gave him a photograph of Robert taken shortly before he fell, signed by the marines in his platoon. There was discussion of pulling the 3rd Battalion out early, as they had suffered such grievous losses. But commanders in the field strongly opposed the idea, and Gates supported them. The marines were "proud they had succeeded" in stabilizing Sangin, "where so many others had failed."[53]

That is why Gates came down on the side of those, led by Petraeus, who wanted surge troops to stay longer; American armed forces needed the chance to finish the job. He agreed with Petraeus that "the pieces were coming together" and that Washington analysts were missing signs of progress on the ground. As always, the CIA analysis was less rosy than what was reported by commanders in the field. He told Obama that the picture was much better than sometimes depicted on the news. The surge had delivered results, and "the closer you get to the front, the more optimistic things are." Sangin was the main insurgent route into the capital of Helmand, Lashkar Gah, and it was a sign of progress that this district was to be in the first tranche to transition to full Afghan control in 2011.

General John Allen, preparing to take over the Kabul command from Petraeus in July, was deeply concerned about a timetable-driven drawdown. "We would have troops actually leaving the theater before the full surge got on the ground." He was facing a double transition, to repurpose ISAF from combat to advising, and to stand up more Afghan independent capacity. To him, the end of the surge should be decided on whether the task was done—"an end state not an end date."

The decisive meeting to decide future troop levels was June 21, 2011, less than a month before Petraeus left Afghanistan. Obama opened the meeting with a decision to pull out ten thousand troops the following month, and twenty-three thousand in July 2012, saying, "You are welcome to try to change my mind." This was more troops out, more quickly than Petraeus had advised. Clinton said she would support Gates's date of late September, although she and "the entire State Department team preferred December."[54] Biden had been campaigning for months for an earlier drawdown and was a strong counterweight in the room. The president's only compromise to his commanders in the field, and secretaries of defense and state, was to push the 2012 date a few months to the "end of the summer." He asked each person in the room if they would support the decision.

Petraeus reminded him that his confirmation hearing to be director of the CIA was later that week, and he would be asked to provide his recommendation, which he was required to do. He told Obama he intended to say that the timetable was "more aggressive" than he would have preferred. He added that he would also say, "I fully support the decision of the Commander-in-Chief (the President) and will do everything humanly possible to implement the decision." But he was not changing his recommendation. Petraeus could almost "feel the oxygen being sucked out of the room." His rationale was solid. There had been no change in the facts on the ground in Afghanistan during the week since he made his recommendation, and that was the basis for him noting that his recommendation was unchanged.

In his confirmation hearing to be CIA director, Petraeus was asked if this was a resigning issue, and his answer was clear: "Our troopers don't get to quit. And I don't think that commanders should contemplate that . . . this is not about me, it's not about an individual commander, it's not about a reputation. This is about our country."[55]

Obama was refocusing his presidency in drawing down troops to bring the war to what he called "a responsible end." Eighteen months after launching the civilian surge alongside the troop surge—the most ambitious, if flawed, civil-military cooperation since the CORDS program in Vietnam—the president was turning his attention inward. "America, it is time to focus on nation building here at home."[56] The enormous cost of the war in blood and treasure would be reduced, and not a moment too soon for public opinion. In 2009, when the surge began, Pew Research were tracking 40 percent against keeping troops in Afghanistan. By the summer of 2011, as Allen took over command, this had tipped above 50 percent for the first time.

Decision-making on the end date of the surge was reminiscent of earlier arguments, if higher octane because of Petraeus's high public profile. The president set a mission—in this case, transition to Afghan control; military commanders made recommendations based on what they needed to achieve success, and the president, suspicious he was being manipulated, approved a smaller force for a shorter period of time than the commanders thought they needed to do the task he had set.

The impending departure of troops had its own destabilizing effect. On the ground in Helmand, Carter Malkasian saw the effect of the president's 2011 announcement. Villagers held *shuras* to decide what to do, believing that police officers would desert and the Taliban would return. Two elders traveled fifteen miles to tell him they had heard the speech. "Without the Marines the situation will go backwards," they said. "The people have great fear . . . Because of the announcement, the Taliban's morale has risen, the government's morale has fallen."[57]

Until then, there had been a steady trickle of ex-Taliban laying down their weapons and coming over to the government side. That stopped overnight. Malkasian had successfully used local militias as a stopgap, cycling members through training to build a uniformed police force as fast as possible, handing over the war to competent Afghan forces. Between September 2009 and 2012, the number of U.S. Marines went down from 1,000 to 150, while the number of Afghan soldiers increased from 200 to 1,200, and the police went from 50 to 300. But only two years later, after the withdrawal of the marines, the district was in the hands of the Taliban.

Malkasian now saw it was a vain hope that "the impending U.S.

drawdown would spur cooperation, rallying Garmser's leaders together against the common Taliban threat."[58] As Petraeus said, "fragile" progress was indeed "reversible."

☰ I'M NOT SURE I KNOW HIM

Dave Petraeus had not wanted to go to Afghanistan; it was thrust on him at the end of his military career. He admitted that when he arrived in Kabul, he did not have the knowledge he had of Iraq, although he had written reports on the conflict and visited many times as commander of CENTCOM.[59] He left Kabul knowing he had not made the decisive change he wanted—delivered a turning point, "flipped" the country. Violence was up, and while there was clear progress against the Taliban in Kandahar and Helmand, they were growing in strength, particularly in the ring of provinces around Kabul itself. Petraeus's will alone was not enough to turn the war in America's favor. While he liked to quote Lawrence, Petraeus exerted far tighter central control than Lawrence, who saw himself as an adviser, a partner in another man's war. Lawrence would never have talked of his role in fighting counterinsurgency warfare as "guiding a sometimes frightened and unthinking herd of cattle to its destination," Petraeus's favored *Stampede* image.

Petraeus spent his life thinking, reading, and writing about counterinsurgency operations, from his first encounter, fresh out of West Point, with French troops who had served in Indochina, through his distinguished rise to the top. But when it came to it, his take on his year in Kabul was clear. "I don't think you can characterize what we did in Afghanistan as *truly* being a fully-resourced counterinsurgency campaign—though, to be fair, the Obama Administration *did* very significantly increase the levels of forces and other resources. We just about got the inputs right from late 2010 through the summer of 2011, but then the drawdown began and it became increasingly difficult to continue to push the Taliban and other groups back in order to maintain the space and time needed to develop the Afghan Security Forces and essential institutions."

On the same March day that Petraeus was trying to win continued political support for the war at the Senate Armed Services Committee, making the case to keep more troops in Afghanistan for longer, nine Afghan boys were killed while collecting firewood in the eastern province of Kunar by a strike from Apache helicopters. A lone survivor, Hemad Khan, came down through the snow to his village, bleeding from shrapnel wounds, to raise the alarm. An inquiry carried out by the commander of 101st Airborne, Major General John F. Campbell (who would later himself command ISAF in Kabul), found that the Apaches were responding to two rocket attacks on a U.S. base in the Pech Valley.[60] In the face of an outcry, Petraeus issued a rare public apology for civilian casualties, immediately rebuffed by Karzai. A week after the attack, U.S. forces finally pulled out of the Pech Valley.

On July 4, 2011, Petraeus served his seventh Independence Day since 9/11 in a combat zone. He handed over to General John Allen two weeks later. The speculation that he was planning a political career had followed him into the field in Kabul. A Fox News correspondent, who came ostensibly to interview him, offered him his owner Rupert Murdoch's support if he ran. And at a dinner in New York, a Republican booster said, "I'll contribute a billion dollars if you'll just run for president." Petraeus told him, "You've never even asked me what my views are. So let me tell you I am a thoughtful internationalist, that's probably okay, a fiscal Conservative, probably okay and a social inclusive, not okay and you'll be torn apart by the base." He was approached by Democratic boosters too, but he told them the same thing—that he stopped voting when he became a two-star and was not going to change his mind now. Rumors of his political ambition affected his dealings with the Obama White House, particularly when he was in the long discussions over the surge in 2009. "Some of them felt that I had presidential ambitions which I went to great lengths to assure them I did not have."

Any thoughts he might have had of a political career were cut down by the revelation of an affair with his biographer, Paula Broadwell, subsequent conviction for mishandling classified materials connected with giving her access to his emails, and swift exit from his new job as CIA director. In his first public speech after the affair on November 11, 2012, the sea captain's son spoke of "slipping his moorings," promising to return to the values he held before.[61] After so many years in the limelight, America's best-known modern general remained something of an enigma, even to many close to him. The counterinsurgency expert David Kilcullen said, "I worked with him. But I am not sure I know him."[62] Perhaps that was the way Dave Petraeus wanted it—behind the mask of command.

PHASE FOUR
2011-2014

DRAWDOWN

PIVOT POINT

*Let's pray for God to rescue us from these two
demons . . . There are two demons in our country now
[meaning the U.S. and the Taliban].*

—President Hamid Karzai, March 17, 2012

☰ THE FAR SIDE OF THE SURGE

"History," said President Karzai, "is a witness to how Afghanistan deals
with occupiers." The occupiers he was talking about were the international coalition in Afghanistan. His remarks betrayed the best hopes of
the international intervention. Standing shaded by tall plane trees and
larches in the large garden area of the Arg for a press conference on a fine
May day in 2011, the president added to a growing catalog of complaints.
He demanded an end to night raids; an end to all U.S. military operations if not partnered by Afghan troops; an end to foreign-owned private
security companies; and the closure of provincial reconstruction teams,
the joint military and development bases across the country, which he
called "a parallel state."

As Karzai's list of grievances grew longer, he was barely on speaking
terms with General David Petraeus. In his last year in uniform, the most
celebrated American commander of the modern age fought a relentless campaign, using the surge troops to their full potential, which put
pressure on the Taliban but increased civilian casualties.[1] Petraeus took a
more transactional approach to the president than had McChrystal.[2] The
Afghan president's renewed demand to end all air strikes in 2011 followed an attack in Now Zad in Helmand Province, where a U.S. Marine
patrol called in a strike in a firefight that took the life of a marine. When

265

the smoke cleared, more than twelve civilians, including several children, were dead in the house the Taliban had been firing from.

When Petraeus's successor, General John Allen, took command in July, his task of building a better relationship with the Afghan president was made easier, as there was a change of ambassador at the same time. Out went Karl Eikenberry, who had been on borrowed time since his contempt for Karzai became public knowledge. He had lost the confidence of Clinton a year earlier and was moved only when what Gates called the "protective umbrella" of the White House was removed. In came Ryan Crocker, persuaded to return to the field despite health concerns.

When Crocker was ambassador to Iraq in 2008, Allen had been deputy commander during the Sunni Awakening in Anbar and instrumental in delivering the province tribe by tribe. There were eighty-eight tribes, and Allen came to know their sheikhs, each color coded for loyalty on a map on the wall of his situation room—charting progress as the map of the large, sparsely populated desert turned gradually, piece by piece, to green. The turning point came when one of the key leaders, Sheikh Abdul Sattar Abu Risha, was approached by some of the original Sunni insurgents, asking for his support to attack U.S. forces. He told them that if they harmed one coalition soldier, the tribes would turn on them. Allen said, "We had a very tight relationship, and they were like brothers to me in so many ways." His understanding came from the British explorer and later colonial official Gertrude Bell, who traveled in the region in the first two decades of the twentieth century and mapped the tribes, working part of the time during and after World War I with T. E. Lawrence. Allen made the reading of her books and letters compulsory for his officers in Iraq. But he realized early in his time in Kabul not to make comparisons between the two countries. He found Afghanistan vastly more complex. "About the third time I said, as the commander in Afghanistan, I want to do this because this had been successful in Iraq, I suddenly realized I've got to expunge that word from my vocabulary. If I'm going to offer my views on how to do something it can't be explained as a result of my experience in Iraq."

On arrival in Kabul in 2011, Crocker arranged for Allen to walk with him down the aisle of a large tent at the embassy erected for his swearing in, so the assembled Afghan and international guests could see that the diplomatic and military missions were marching in step. Crocker had known Karzai since the first winter of the war, when he was the first ambassador after the fall of the Taliban, and Allen listened as the two reminisced about the days when they met in that room in the Arg, the windows shot out, with torn furniture to sit on, and only a primitive stove to keep out the harsh cold of a Kabul winter. Allen's political adviser Marc Chretien said, "Allen understands one-on-one relationships better than anyone else I know."[3] In the hard negotiations with the Afghan president in the months to come, he would stay in the room, however much the provocation, and keep going at times when Crocker would lose his patience.[4] Other times, when Karzai complained about the conduct of American troops, it would be Crocker who put a restraining arm onto Allen.[5] Their professional bond was a valuable partnership.

Allen is tall and imposing with a high-and-tight Marine Corps haircut and the posture and bearing of a general from central casting, able to fill a room with expansive arm movements and a big, warm Virginian baritone voice. He has a curiously latex face, with features that are not well defined, and while highly disciplined and focused, emotions are never far below the surface. He set a ferocious pace in Afghanistan, working until one o'clock in the morning, up again at five, day after day. But he was not a remote figure. Once, when commandant at Annapolis, he rappelled down a rope from the ceiling into a full mess hall, with camouflage war paint on his face, yelling, "Go, navy! Beat army!" before the annual army-navy game, one of the most enduring rivalries in sports.[6]

Allen embodied the best of American warrior virtue and was never in doubt of a career in the military, inspired by a childhood fictional hero, John Carter, who had a "sense of overpowering fascination" toward Mars, the planet and the god of war. Carter is transported to Mars from a post–Civil War skirmish with Apaches, and the books tell of his adventures there, rescuing women and slaying villains. His first encounter with a Martian might be from the counterinsurgency manual. "Placing my hand over my heart I bowed low to the Martian and explained to him that while I did not understand his language, his actions spoke to the peace and friendship that at the present moment were most dear to my heart."[7]

Less publicly demonstrative than his predecessors, Petraeus and McChrystal, Allen was out on the ground as much as they were, consoling and encouraging, going on patrol to steady troops after bad incidents, and attending the sad ritual of the ramp ceremony more often than bearable. The month after he arrived was the worst for U.S. casualties in the war, with seventy fatalities, thirty-eight of them in one helicopter crash, brought down when the Taliban got lucky and hit the tail rotor of a CH-47 Chinook with a rocket-propelled grenade. The dead included seventeen Navy SEALs from Team 6 that killed Osama bin Laden, although none of those on the bin Laden mission died in the crash. During a six-week period that summer, the Taliban also attacked a couple of governors' compounds, killed the mayor of Kandahar, and hit the British Council in Kabul, burning it to the ground. Twelve security guards, eight of them Afghan, were killed, but the civilian staff remarkably all survived, locked into a safe room that endured the shooting, explosions, and fire.

The first marine to command the international coalition in Afghanistan, Allen took over on the far side of the surge—with more than eight hundred bases to close, and U.S. troops leaving Afghanistan more quickly than he believed was in the best interests of his mission of securing the country. "I had to get the Afghan army ready to take over operations a year earlier than we had anticipated." His undergraduate training was in operations analysis, and he would need higher math skills to manage the complex matrix of delivering combat effect, while drawing down the surge and moving the mission from fighting to advising. He had given the president his best military advice; now he had to fight the war he was given. Chretien said Allen was "haunted" by the withdrawal timetable. "It was the biggest albatross round his neck." To Chretien, announcing the end date of the surge was "like playing poker, raising, while saying you're going to fold next round."

President Obama's decision, setting the end of summer 2012 for the date the last surge troops should leave, had some in the NSC reaching for an almanac for the date of the autumn equinox. Obama wanted Afghans to shoulder more responsibility. "We will not police its streets or patrol its mountains indefinitely. That is the responsibility of the Afghan government, which must step up its ability to protect its people."[8] Allen's British deputy, Lieutenant General Nick Carter, on his third deployment to the country, said the challenge was to get "the machine to recognize that it's time that the Afghans really did lead." It required extraordinary leadership to understand there was "huge wisdom in not doing things."[9]

As a reminder of the urgency of the mission to deliver better Afghan forces to take on the war for themselves, on his first day in Kabul, Allen signed the move order to send ten thousand surge troops home. An hour later, he called together his most senior staff round the large, polished wooden table in the cramped setting of the Herat room at ISAF HQ to reexamine the war from the ground up. They included Germans, Italians, and British as well as Americans—an alliance Allen valued above all. To him, the *strategic* center of gravity, which he defined as "the thing which if it was attacked or it came apart would bring about the failure of the campaign," was the fifty-nation coalition of countries under his command. "If the coalition fragmented or began to disintegrate, the campaign would come apart, there's just no question about it." Protecting the population, the center of gravity in the counterinsurgency years and in particular for McChrystal in 2009, was now defined as the "*objective* of the campaign." Allen's *operational* center of gravity was the Afghan army. Getting it up to strength meant that the ISAF coalition needed to be reshaped from war fighting to being "principally an advisory force."

So was it still a counterinsurgency? If there was any doubt of the way the wind was blowing, it was dispelled six months into Allen's command, January 5, 2012, the date America formally closed the era of COIN. "U.S. forces will no longer be sized to conduct large-scale, prolonged stability operations," declared the new defense strategic guidance.[10] Counterinsurgency was demoted to the "lessons learned" corner of military doctrine. Allen believed the Afghan campaign was in many ways "more of a counterinsurgency" than before, but one now led by the Afghans themselves. Building them up for the task in the limited time he had left faced a new and complex threat from inside the Afghan army itself.

☰ GREEN ON BLUE

Kevin O'Rourke was a New York City firefighter who assisted in recovery efforts at Ground Zero. The event would define his life. He was a founding member of HEART 9/11, set up by first responders in the wake of the attacks on America to assist in disaster areas, and he volunteered when they assisted in relief operations in New Orleans after Hurricane Katrina, and in Haiti after the 2010 earthquake. And he answered the call for advisers to serve in Iraq and Afghanistan. In 2012, he died in a remote outpost in rural Afghanistan, shot by the very Afghan soldiers he had gone to help. Sergeant First Class Daniel T. Metcalfe from the

173rd Airborne Brigade Combat Team was shot in the same incident at a routine checkpoint—his death marking a grim milestone, the two thousandth member of the American armed forces to die in the war in Afghanistan. Metcalfe joined the army just months before 9/11 and, like O'Rourke, had served multiple tours of Iraq and Afghanistan—heroes killed in a cowardly attack.

Exactly what happened at the Sisay outpost in Wardak Province on September 29, 2012, was never fully explained. There is no doubt that Metcalfe was shot dead first, and another American soldier wounded, by Din Muhammad,[11] the sergeant commanding the Afghan platoon. Swift answering fire by U.S. soldiers downed the rogue Afghan sergeant but provoked further Afghan firing and, amid confusion, led to a general exchange of fire, including the use of hand grenades. It took some time for a U.S. second lieutenant to stop the mayhem. When the firing died down, O'Rourke had fallen, and two other Americans were wounded. The Afghan toll was four dead and two wounded. The Americans and Afghans knew each other, although not well; the 173rd Airborne had arrived in the area just two months previously.

Allen immediately flew to Wardak to try to understand the corrosive effect of what were known as "green-on-blue" attacks (where green were local allied forces and blue were friendly troops).[12] He went on a foot patrol with the remnants of the platoon who were in shock. Metcalfe, twenty-nine years old, had been a father figure to the unit, and Allen could see his death really hit them. "Their souls had been wounded . . . they felt alone, they felt betrayed, they were angry as hell."

Until 2011, there were only a handful of such attacks a year, each one an individual tragedy, but they did not threaten the mission. Now as the surge troops were heading home, there was a spike, with a chilling effect on operations far beyond the raw numbers. Allen knew that it would be hard to recover the training mission if trust broke down to the point where ISAF and Afghan troops fought each other at unit level. The attacks represented an existential threat to the campaign to train and mentor Afghan forces.

The green-on-blue attack that had the most impact caused the deaths of five French soldiers in January 2012; twelve others were wounded, shot by an Afghan soldier as they finished a workout session on a shared base in Kapisa in eastern Afghanistan. The shooting came just weeks after two French legionnaires were killed in a similar incident. The French defense minister, Gérard Longuet, immediately flew to Kabul. All French military operations in Afghanistan were suspended, and just days later, the decision was made to end the French military mission. The timing of the attack could not have been worse. President Nicolas Sarkozy was facing an imminent election where the challenger, François Hollande, was campaigning to bring the troops home. Sarkozy made an emotional speech saying the shootings left him with no option but to pull out a year earlier than planned.

Allen's biggest fear was a domino effect, where other nations followed France and pulled out early. It was election year in the United States too, where the Afghan war was increasingly unpopular, and voices were growing for an early withdrawal. Secretary of Defense Leon Panetta hinted after the French announcement that U.S. troops could "step back" from combat operations in 2013, a year earlier than the current schedule.[13] Allen knew that any lack of resolve could damage the mission. Michael Clarke, the head of the London-based think tank the Royal United Services Institute, likened the effect to a false start in a hundred-meter race. "If the Americans are now flinching in their block there will be two or three actors who get off to a flier. The suspicion that America is going to pull out early will create a self-fulfilling prophecy and there will be a rush to the exit."[14]

When the attack on French troops in Kapisa happened, Allen was in Germany after a meeting of NATO defence chiefs in Brussels. As always when in Europe, this most coalition-centered commander visited other capitals to weave them into continued support for the mission. Allen's Gulfstream took him on to France, where the first thing he saw on arrival was a front-page story in *The Washington Post* highlighting a report from inside ISAF that the U.S. training mission was doomed to fail because the troops were culturally incompatible. The report was a "Red Team" inquiry, a way of thinking outside the box, instigated during Petraeus's command the previous year, when green-on-blue attacks began to become a concern. The author, Jeffrey Bordin, concluded that personal clashes and "strong dislike, even contempt" were leading to a "crisis of trust" where green-on-blue attacks were an inevitability. Bordin characterized the opinions of Afghans and Americans in a colorful list. "One group generally sees the other as a bunch of violent, reckless, intrusive, arrogant, self-serving, profane, infidel bullies hiding behind high technology; and the other group generally views the former as a bunch of cowardly, incompetent, obtuse, thieving, complacent, lazy, pot-smoking, treacherous and murderous radicals."[15] Allen was deeply concerned that the publication of the report would feed into a growing view in the U.S. that this was mission impossible—that cultural incompatibility meant the task of training and advising, the operational center of gravity of his campaign, was fatally flawed. If Bordin was right, he said, "we would never be able to work together. Any strategy that relies upon an advisory presence is a failed strategy because there's just no compatibility."

Shortly afterward, the North Atlantic Council, the ambassadors of NATO countries, met in Brussels. Fifty countries, including non-NATO partners, were represented in the room round the long oval table. Allen could see it would be a tough meeting when the French ambassador spoke forcefully about how the Kapisa attack fulfilled "in the French mind the futility of the campaign." The French operation was code-named Task Force La Fayette—a name with powerful resonance in America since the days of the Revolutionary War. Allen did not want any other countries following La Fayette out of theater. While the ambassador was speaking, white name cards round the room popped up one after another, signaling that people wanted to speak, and Allen sensed he was in for a rough ride. But the mood changed when the Australian ambassador, Brendan Nelson, sitting opposite the French ambassador across the wide, oval space, spoke next. "And he said this remarkable thing. He said, 'Look, nobody's suffered more casualties from green-on-blue than Australia has, and we have two options here, one is to cut and run and the other is to double down, and Australia is going to double down.'" To Allen's relief, the intervention ended the conversation. "The French still pulled their operators out but not another country did."

With the coalition steadied, and no one following France to an early exit, Allen quickly needed to find a solution to the rising toll of green-on-blue attacks, which exploded after the French decision as the Taliban had a tried and tested route to fracturing the coalition. There is no evidence that green on blue was a tactic originally devised by the Taliban, but intercepted Taliban chatter revealed that once they understood the effect, particularly on coalition cohesion, they moved to attempt to insert infiltrators into Afghan army ranks and assist disaffected soldiers. If the contagion spread, it would wreck the mission.

August and September 2012 were the worst months of the war for green-on-blue attacks. On the evening of August 10, three U.S. Marine special operators were killed while exercising in the gym in Garmser District in Helmand. The marines, Staff Sergeant Scott Dickinson, Corporal Richard Rivera, and Lance Corporal Gregory Buckley, were in a shared base with Afghan police they were training. The killer, Aynoddin, was aged seventeen and looked younger. He was wearing civilian clothes and shot the marines with an AK-47 assault rifle he'd picked up from an unguarded room. He then walked out to say to police officers before they disarmed him, "I just did jihad. Don't you want to do jihad, too? If not, I will kill you." Aynoddin could come and go from the base with ease. He was a "tea boy" for the district police chief, who allegedly kept him for sex—a common practice in southern Afghanistan that international troops had failed to stamp out.[16]

Allen arrived in Garmser later that night, and stood in the dark in a circle of silent bearded special operators just back from patrol, comrades of those killed. "I was trying to explain to them that this moment is one where we can lose our motivation or we can double down with our discipline and still win." But Allen was beginning to doubt himself as the attacks piled up. He would say to the press that the troops were well trained and well led, and he was sure they would remain focused on the mission, but attacks like this one, or the one that took the lives of Metcalfe and O'Rourke, made him question his own public reassurances. After every incident, he would stride up and down mess halls and tents, rallying young troops. "After about two or three of those I thought to myself, hell, I don't know whether I'm right or not, I'm just assuming that I am." Perhaps green on blue really would harm the morale and effectiveness of ISAF troops. He needed to find out what was going on.

As the withdrawal rolled on, ISAF troops became more vulnerable. The marines killed in Garmser in August were in one of just three bases left in the district, down from sixty at the peak.[17] "Our troops and Afghan troops absolutely in the field eat together," said the British brigadier in charge of transition to Afghan control, Richard Cripwell. "There are unquestionably some very close relationships all over the country between

ISAF forces of all nationalities and the Afghans."[18] This closeness made the attacks more lethal than normal combat. The ratio of wounded to dead in combat is around 12 to 1; with green-on-blue attacks, it was 1.5 to 1, causing nearly a quarter of coalition deaths in 2012. Attacks during missions outside the wire were rare. Most were carried out inside compounds when ISAF troops were relaxed and not wearing body armor.

New analysis of the motivation of the attackers came from a psychiatrist, Marc Sageman, brought to Kabul in September 2012, the month after the worst spike—twelve attacks in August. Most of his previous career was in the CIA, including time working with the Afghan mujahideen during the war against Soviet occupation in the 1980s.

Sageman disagreed with Bordin, and his report carried more weight since he interviewed surviving green-on-blue shooters in jail, not troops on the ground as the Red Team report by Bordin had done. Bordin recorded incidents of personal humiliation and cultural incompatibility, but that did not explain motivation for attacks. Sageman showed that the actual attackers were mostly strangers; none was reacting to a personal slight. Most significantly Sageman believed that 75 percent of the attackers had some link with the Taliban—a conclusion that faced considerable pushback. The view inside ISAF until Sageman arrived was far closer to the "cultural incompatibility" argument put by Bordin, which concluded that the Taliban were not responsible for the upsurge in attacks. Bordin's research had fitted an easily understandable narrative, that Americans and Afghans did not like each other and never would. If Sageman was right, though, it meant there could be a solution, since preventing Taliban infiltration "was easier than trying to teach your soldiers to be good Afghans."[19]

Sageman found that fellow soldiers would often know an individual was planning an attack. But one obvious answer, better intelligence inside Afghan ranks, was blocked by security ministers. The interior minister, Bismillah Khan, and the defence minister, General Abdul Rahim Wardak, had both commanded mujahideen forces in the 1980s war against Soviet occupation and remembered the excesses of the Soviet-backed KHAD secret police. They did not want KHAD's successors spying on their soldiers and police to save the lives of Americans. It was only when Afghan soldiers too became the subject of insider attacks that they agreed to the plan. Allen was in a meeting at the Ministry of Interior when he saw the change. Interior Minister Khan was called away from the room and returned with the news that ten Afghan police had been shot dead by a fellow police officer at a checkpoint in Farah Province in the southwest of the country—a "green-on-green" attack. Khan and Wardak were now more receptive to putting spies into the ranks.

As well as better intelligence, responses included armed "guardian angels" always present when Afghan and coalition forces were together, better monitoring of recruits, and discharge of some soldiers. Allen ordered all U.S. troops to carry a loaded weapon at all times.

The measures finally turned the tide on the problem. But the new security regime changed advising and mentoring; trust was never as complete again as when gifted linguists like John Darin Loftis had worked as an adviser in the Ministry of Interior, a valuable asset, as he conversed easily in both Afghan languages. He was shot at his desk with colleague Robert Marchanti in February 2012, a month after the killing of the five French soldiers. The attacker escaped and was never identified. Allen arrived while the bodies were still lying in pools of blood and knelt to pray.[20] After that incident, scarce security assets that could have been better deployed pointing outward had to point inward to protect advisers on the core mission. And even with tighter security and better intelligence, some attackers still got through. As late as 2014, Major General Harold Greene was shot by a soldier inside the officers' training academy at Qargha, west of Kabul, the most senior American officer to die on active service since the Vietnam War.

☰ METEOR STRIKES

Abdul Basir, the soldier who opened fire on French soldiers dressed in T-shirts and shorts as they finished a workout, told Sageman that he carried out the attacks because he was outraged by a video of U.S. Marines urinating on Taliban corpses. He did not see the video, which Allen quickly ordered to be taken down from the internet wherever it could be found, but he had a dream that international troops were in Afghanistan for the purpose of defiling Islam, and that inspired him to turn against the French soldiers. Another green-on-blue attacker in January told Sageman that he too was inspired to act by the report of the video. A month later, waves of anti-American rioting raged across the country after U.S. soldiers were discovered burning copies of the Quran at the country's biggest military detention facility, Parwan, inside Bagram Air Base. Almost five hundred Qurans, and more than one thousand other religious texts, were taken from the prison library after interpreters said they contained handwritten extremist messages. Acting only on the word of the interpreters, and against rising warnings from other Afghan soldiers, boxes of books were hauled to the burn pit. After many had been thrown into the flames, other Afghans gathered and called colleagues to rescue the books. The Americans withdrew "frightened by the growing, angry crowd." A later inquiry showed that the markings in the margins of the books were mostly names and addresses, not extremist messages. But the damage was done. There were several deaths in street riots as Afghan police fought to regain control.

Sageman connected a spike of green-on-blue attacks to the burning, among them a bizarre attack on the Camp Bastion airstrip at the giant joint ISAF/Afghan base[21] in Helmand. An Afghan interpreter grabbed a vehicle and drove at a group of dignitaries waiting for the arrival of Secretary of Defense Panetta. He narrowly missed them before driving into a ditch and setting light to himself. Sageman saw these attacks not as cultural incompatibility but a clear causal link between what Allen called "meteor strikes" and the decisions of young soldiers to turn on their ISAF mentors.

Meteor strikes were events that came unpredictably out of the blue and absorbed a huge amount of time and effort to limit damage. The year 2012 brought a shower of them. In March, U.S. staff sergeant Robert Bales walked off his base in Panjwayi in Kandahar and killed seventeen civilians in their homes. In September, there were nationwide protests over the production of a movie titled *Innocence of Muslims,* a crudely made low-budget production, lasting just fourteen minutes on YouTube, described by one prominent film critic as a "bigoted piece of poison calculated to inflame the Muslim world."[22] Both the film and the Bales attack led to clusters of green-on-blue attacks. Afghan forces were supportive. When Allen visited Marjah in Helmand while violent protests following the Quran burning were at their peak, Afghan troops told their U.S. marine partners to stay in the base. They said, "Let us patrol outside the wire for a couple of days; we have this for you."[23]

The meteor strikes further strained relations with Karzai, who said after meeting survivors of the village shot up by Bales that he was "at the end of the rope." He publicly questioned the American account that only Bales was involved. "This behavior cannot be tolerated. It is past, past, past the time." Speaking after Friday prayers in the mosque in the garden in the Arg, he said that American forces and the Taliban were "two demons" ravaging the country. As so often during the long war, at times of high tension when anti-American feelings ran high, the Afghan president did little to calm public anger.

≡ SNAKE CHARMERS AT NIGHT

Karzai liked Allen personally, calling him to express condolences when Allen's mother died, although Allen had not told anyone in the Afghan administration that he was returning to Virginia to bury her. His wife of thirty-five years, Kathy, both of whose parents had died the year before, nursed Allen's mother at the end, not disclosing the extent of the threat until she died so as not to distract him from his mission. It was a typically selfless gesture from a family committed to public service. After the funeral, he was in a restaurant with Kathy and their two daughters in his favorite place in the world, the Shenandoah Valley, when he got a call from the Arg to say Karzai wanted to speak to him. "So I'm in the parking lot, it's just surreal," he said, "talking to the president of Afghanistan, who is gripped with emotion saying words to the effect that our mothers are so precious to us."[24]

But whatever the personal warmth, for Karzai, "relations with America had gone totally to nil."[25] Actions now mattered more than personalities, in particular to reduce civilian casualties from ISAF strikes and to end night raids. Allen recognized that he needed to walk the Afghan president back from ordering a total ban on the use of U.S. airpower, which he was close to ordering. He issued a new tactical directive, significantly tightening the occasions when there could be the use of air strikes or artillery and ordering more thorough investigation on the ground of allegations of civilian casualties. Researchers investigating civilian casualties had more access to higher levels of the ISAF command than before. They said they found soldiers concerned not just for "what they *could* legally do in a given situation, but what they *should* do."[26]

This most methodical of commanders established that the number of times it was necessary to engage air strikes or artillery on a building to accomplish a mission without knowing who was inside was so small, that he could tighten the rules without damaging operational effect. "It was quite controversial, I got some pushback from below and from above on that issue." Apart from the propaganda value for the Taliban of air strikes on civilian targets, Allen felt the human cost. "We had wiped out, sometimes, entire families, not one person left alive. And I tell you that really, for me, was so tragic I can't even begin to describe it."

The new rules changed the burden of proof on the part of troops who wanted to call in an air strike. They now needed to presume that every Afghan was a civilian, and all buildings were civilian unless proved otherwise. The rules were tightened still further in June 2012 after eighteen civilians, including seven women, five girls, and a baby, were killed in an attack where the target was a gathering of Taliban commanders in Logar Province.[27] Allen now ordered that there should be no air attacks on civilian buildings, unless in extreme circumstances, and then only if sanctioned by senior commanders. Allen would take the phone calls from special operators who had tracked a target into a building. "My question was always, who's in there? Do you know that person is in there, yes or no? 'Yes, I know he's in there.' Who else is in there? 'I don't know.' All right, do you have heel to toe, unblinking, full motion of that structure? 'Yessir, I do.' Okay, so he'll probably have to leave eventually. Since we don't know if somebody's in there or not, don't strike that structure because you don't know who's in there." Allen made the bold claim at the time that the changes meant civilian casualties caused by air strikes would "plummet immediately,"[28] and so it proved.[29]

Another tactical directive tightened rules on night raids, which had gone up significantly with Petraeus's relentless "killing and capturing" of the enemy, with fifteen operations a night. Allen recognized that this had become the most pressing issue for the Afghan president, not least because among those killed by mistake at the height of the campaign in March 2011 was Yar Muhammad Karzai, a relative of the president, shot when U.S. Special Forces arrived at night in the family ancestral village of Karz, near Kandahar.[30]

Not only did special operators conducting the raids sometimes have faulty intelligence, they were entering homes where every male occupant had a weapon as a matter of course. In May, they killed a fifteen-year-old boy sleeping in a field in Nangarhar Province, mistaking the hunting shotgun he had next to him for a more offensive weapon. A baby died in the same attack, which came just three days after a twelve-year-old girl died nearby in a raid on a house owned by a member of the Afghan police.[31] The Nangarhar raids provoked angry street demonstrations, causing the police to open fire, killing another young boy.

The number of night operations reduced considerably after Allen took command, to less than half. But he was keen not to lose the capacity altogether, since "the Haqqanis are operating twenty-four hours a day."[32] With superior night vision and communications, U.S. Special Forces had a significant advantage at night, and night raids had a measurable effect: in 83 percent of cases arrests were made, either of the target or a known associate, and shots were fired in less than one in ten operations.[33] A tribal elder in Helmand Province, who welcomed them as a key factor in better security, used a graphic image in an interview for *The New York Times,* that the Taliban were like snakes and night raids were snake charmers.[34] Allen told a Senate committee that in 9,200 night operations, the number killed and injured was just twenty-seven. "That would argue for the power of night operations preserving life and reducing civilian casualties in all other kinds of operations."[35] But what was not measurable was the alienation and loss of support caused by the continuing sound of drones and the threat of boots through the door at night.

Allen's two new tactical directives on air strikes and night raids at the end of 2011 came just after a Loya Jirga where Karzai sought support from his nation to impose conditions on U.S. troops if they were to be allowed to remain after the end of combat operations in 2014. After several exhausting rounds of talks with Karzai and his anti-American national security adviser, Rangin Spanta, Allen tightened the rules further, agreeing that in the future, Afghan forces would always take the lead in night operations. In practice, Americans still played a significant role in planning and execution. "It all adds up to U.S. boots on the ground," said a CBS report, "if not inside the house."[36] But the deal was a step on the road to Afghan sovereignty that Karzai was now on. Another step that would take hours of negotiations, and not be fully resolved in Allen's time, was the management of detainees.

☰ TORTURE OR RELEASE

Karzai had been demanding full control of detention centers since 2005 without success. His opening gambit ahead of talks in January 2012 was to insist that all detainees should be handed over to Afghan authorities in a month. The main location at issue was the Parwan Detention Facility at Bagram, where more than three thousand prisoners were housed. It was designed as a state-of-the-art facility, replacing earlier makeshift prisons like the CIA's notorious "Salt Pit," set up in an abandoned brick factory near Kabul, where prisoners died in brutal interrogations in the freewheeling early years of Bush's war on terror, when there were few checks. A senior CIA officer said just being in the Salt Pit was an enhanced interrogation technique. Detainees were "kept in complete darkness and constantly shackled in isolated cells with loud noise or music and only a bucket to use for human waste," according to a Senate Intelligence Committee report.[37] One inmate is known to have died of the extreme cold. Detainees were routinely stripped naked, bound with Mylar tape, and beaten while being dragged by a rope along a corridor. The Salt Pit was closed with other CIA black sites in an executive order by President Obama in January 2009. Detainees had died at the Parwan Detention Facility too, but by 2011, Allen believed that the abuse had ended.

Allen's concern in handing over detainees to full Afghan control was that they would be tortured in the Afghan system—risks highlighted in October 2011, when the UN mission in Kabul reported the results of a nationwide investigation. Around half of the men they interviewed in the custody of the Afghan security service, the NDS, said they had been tortured.

> Detainees described experiencing torture in the form of suspension (being hung by the wrists from chains or other devices attached to the wall, ceiling, iron bars or other fixtures for lengthy periods) and beatings, especially with rubber hoses, electric cables or wires or wooden sticks and most frequently on the soles of the feet. Electric shock, twisting and wrenching of detainees' genitals, stress positions including forced standing, removal of toenails and threatened sexual abuse were among other forms of torture that detainees reported.[38]

Allen immediately ordered that no more detainees should be sent to the worst of the Afghan facilities, including one in the center of Kabul. Since General McChrystal had first put the detainee issue at the forefront of military concerns in Afghanistan, there was another concern with that of torture in Afghan jails—that detainees would be released. American troops did not want to risk their lives taking dangerous men off the battlefield, only to find them quickly back in circulation.[39]

After months of tough negotiations, in March 2012, the U.S. agreed to hand over the Parwan Detention Facility six months later. At the time of the deal there were 3,100 detainees in the large hangar-like buildings of the jail. The twin U.S. concerns—that detainees be tortured or too easily released—led to more being kept in American-run facilities during 2012, against the plans for phased handover to Afghan control. And by the fall, there were a further 600 detainees at Parwan. They included foreigners—Pakistanis captured fighting with the Taliban, and some brought by the CIA from other countries like Yemen and Egypt, and kept in the same suspended legal status as those at Guantanamo. It became inevitable during the year that part of the Parwan facility, and many hundreds of detainees, would be kept under American control for longer than Karzai wanted.

☰ RENDEZVOUS AT MIDNIGHT

The deals in Kabul on detainees, air strikes, and night raids in March 2012 came ahead of the signing of a new strategic partnership governing future relations between Afghanistan and the United States. Hard as it was to negotiate, the partnership agreement that emerged was more symbolic than substantive, with fine words on an enduring relationship, but no detail on payments, numbers of bases or America's military commitments. At the beginning of May, a year to the day since the death of Osama bin Laden, President Obama made a brief midnight visit to Afghanistan to sign the deal. Pausing at Bagram Air Base for a speech and selfies with troops, he took a helicopter ride to the Arg. After the briefest of meetings for a signature, Obama moved on, leaving Karzai bruised in his wake. Obama's swift midnight turnaround committed the worst of insults for the Afghan president. "He didn't even take a cup of tea with us."

The White House had invited Karzai to America for the signing, but he refused, wanting the deal on Afghan soil. "I wanted to have a good ceremony . . . to have Afghan leaders, to have all the Afghan traditions and dress."[40] In his mind, this would have presented the deal to the Afghan people in a better way. But Obama's security detail refused to admit tribal elders without full security checks. Since the head of the government's peace council, Burhanuddin Rabbani, had been killed after being embraced by a man with a suicide bomb in his turban, they were not taking any chances. As a compromise, Allen arranged for the elders to watch on a TV feed from just outside the Arg, while the signing was held with the minimum of ceremony.

The mercurial Afghan president now had few friends in the U.S. administration. The White House deliberately kept the signing low-key in an election year when Obama did not want to remind voters of an enduring relationship with Afghanistan. Even where America's interests coincided with those of Afghanistan, such as in stopping fighters coming across the border from Pakistan, it was hard to coordinate policy.

The problem was that Karzai swung around like a weather vane. In an interview with a Pakistani TV channel, he said his government would support Pakistan if it came under attack by the U.S.[41] Allen had to fire a senior officer in his command, Major General Peter Fuller, for criticizing Karzai. "You've got to be kidding me," Fuller said. "I'm sorry, we just gave you $11.6 billion and now you're telling me, 'I don't really care?'"[42]

To Allen, Karzai would say, "You're fighting the war in the wrong place. You're fighting the war in the homes of the Afghans, you ought to be fighting the war in Pakistan." The wrong enemy in the wrong country. It was the same formulation used by Holbrooke. America's two fundamental security interests over Pakistan had not changed: to keep Pakistan's nuclear arsenal in secure hands, and end global jihad coming from the region. By 2012, in the years since the money taps were turned on again after 9/11 when the military dictator Pervez Musharraf signed up to President Bush's war on terror, the U.S. had given the country $15 billion in military aid.[43] But there was a new willingness expressed by senior voices in Washington to stand firmer against Pakistani threats and call out their clear duplicity. The Obama administration was becoming less willing to sign a blank check.

⌐ PAKISTAN'S INSURANCE POLICY

Allen worked at his relationship with General Ashfaq Kayani. Several attacks on Kabul, tracked to the Haqqani network, were stopped after direct appeals to the Pakistani army chief. But the assault on Kabul continued. September 13, 2011, Allen's headquarters and the adjoining embassy complex came under sustained attack for several hours from fighters who had found their way into a multistory building under construction that overlooked the site.

The administration had had enough. Ten days after the embassy attack, the outgoing chairman of the Joint Chiefs, Admiral Mike Mullen, in his last press conference, went further than any senior U.S. official before in naming this for what it was. "The Haqqani network," he said, were a "veritable arm" of the ISI. He had evidence for their complicity in several recent attacks, and they were just one of the extremist groups operating with "impunity" from Pakistani soil.[44] The Pakistani state's response, as so often, came in the language of a mobster demanding protection money. The foreign minister, Hina Rabbani Khar, said any threats by Mullen to change the relationship could harm the U.S. "If they are choosing to do so, it will be at their own cost."[45] Kayani saw the Haqqani network as Pakistan's insurance policy for influence in Afghanistan when U.S. troops left.[46]

Despite the growing war of words, Allen continued to keep contact with Pakistan at several levels. He did not meet the civilian government, whom he saw as irrelevant. But at the local level, there were coordination mechanisms along the border, and above that, his senior commanders had regular contact with their opposite numbers in Pakistan. He maintained links with Kayani and in November was taken aside by him at a map table in Peshawar military headquarters while planning joint operations along the border. Kayani took an envelope out of his pocket and showed Allen a letter he had written to Mullen after the killing of bin Laden. Kayani warned Mullen that if anything like that happened again, he may not be able to restrain Pakistan's forces from doing something violent in response. Taking the letter back, he said to Allen, "If something bad ever really happens, you and I need to be careful what we say publicly so that we can, at some point, recover the relationship."

Allen stayed overnight and was woken to be told that U.S. forces were involved in a major fight on the border with Pakistani troops. Allen said his troops never crossed over, although it was not clearly marked, and the actual border is disputed. In places, there is a gap as wide as eleven kilometers between the original Durand Line, marking the boundary in 1893 between British India and Afghanistan, the Soviet-imposed border, the modern Afghan border, and the line recognized by Pakistan.

He needed to leave Pakistan fast. As he drove to the airport, he had updates of the Pakistani dead. By the time he arrived at the plane, the figure had climbed to twenty-seven as he pieced together the story. American Special Forces had been on a night operation on the ground in Afghanistan close to the border region, and every time they came out of cover on high ground, they took heavy fire from two Pakistani posts on the other side. It was a dark night, and the special operators could only be identified through infrared strobes on their helmets. The Pakistani soldiers who opened fire must have been watching with night vision goggles. The American response was a show of force by Apache attack helicopters, F-15 fighters, and even low passes by a B-1 bomber. But the firing continued. Finally, an AC-130 was brought in. Allen knew the devastating effect that would have had. When he called Kayani, the Pakistani general was shaken and said, "You realize what you've done. You've taken away any white space that I had to have a relationship with you and with ISAF and the war in Afghanistan." Allen reminded him of their conversation over the letter to Mullen, and both agreed they had to be careful about what they said publicly so they did not burn their relationship.

Pakistan closed the border for eight months and ordered the closure of a secret U.S. drone base in Baluchistan in the southwest of Pakistan, where flights had anyway been restricted since the killing of bin Laden. The border closure added to the cost and complexity of withdrawal, and it would take months of hard bargaining to reopen, which happened only after an apology from Clinton for the attack. Some months later, through a trusted intermediary, Allen sent a message to Kayani to say that he had kept his end of the bargain and not said anything publicly against him. In response, Kayani called to rebuild the contact.

But having the channel of communication did not stop the attacks. On Fridays in the summer, young Kabulis head out to the guesthouses and kebab shops lining the large Qargha lake west of Kabul with friends or family—renting small, plastic pedaled boats with duck or swan heads to go out on the water. Traditional musicians play in small cafés set on the forested hillsides above the lake. It is hardly a den of vice, but this is just the kind of activity that threatens the Taliban's view of the world. On June 22, 2012, a minivan pulled up outside the Spozhmai hotel by the lake late at night, and a group alighted, dressed head to toe in the powder-blue coverall burkas worn by some Afghan women. Throwing off the burkas, seven insurgents, wearing suicide vests, shot their way into the hotel. They demanded to know where the alcohol and prostitutes were. In vain, hotel guests and staff denied any such activities and were shot as the fighters said they must be there. A young boy who survived said he had a gun pointed to his head, with the gunmen insisting he show them the alcohol. At ISAF headquarters, Allen listened to the communications with the gunmen as they took hostages and settled in for a siege that went on for more than twelve hours through the next day. The instructions were coming from Miramshah in Pakistan, admonishing the raiders to come off full auto in their AK-47s and go to single shot, so they could conserve ammunition to kill more of the guests at the hotel. Afghan Special Forces saved the lives of more than forty guests when they stormed the hotel, but twenty died. In September 2012, after pressure from Allen, the Haqqani network was designated a terrorist organization by the U.S.

Allen discovered by chance that he had one secret weapon for relations with Pakistan, his British deputy, Lieutenant General Adrian Bradshaw. On one occasion when Allen could not make a routine meeting with Kayani, Bradshaw went instead, and the tall upper-class Englishman, whom Allen called "a consummate gentleman," had a good effect, to the point that Pakistani officers were saying Bradshaw should always go. Drawing on the shared history of Britain and Pakistan, and connections through the Commonwealth, Bradshaw was able to have conversations no longer available to Allen because of the breakdown in trust. On another occasion, Allen planned to send his most senior French officer. The Pakistanis, with quite a different relationship with the French, said, "You might want to rethink that."

☰ MEASURING THE UNIVERSE

Allen was the most educated of the ISAF commanders, with four degrees. "For the first time since Obama became President," reported *The Washington Post,* "White House aides have ceased complaining about the military command in Kabul."[47] After two ISAF commanders were fired and the high-wire act of Petraeus, Allen's cool analytical style suited the temperament of the president. Walking out of a lunch in the White House, the president put an arm around Allen and said, "John Allen is

my man."[48] It did not mean there was any letup in the imposed dead-
lines for withdrawal, but it did give Allen some breathing space in how
he delivered it. In one National Security Council meeting, there was a
lot of advice being offered around the table in Washington to Allen on
a video link from Kabul, but the president cut it off. "This is between
the Commander-in-Chief and the commander on the ground," he said.
"Leave him alone. Let him get the mission done."

The Taliban could read the plan as bases were closed down. "The
enemy sees what's happening," Allen said to his fellow marine, General
Jim Mattis, commanding CENTCOM. "He's trying to fix me in place
and create a lot of casualties." Mattis took his request for significant
extra combat power to the White House—three thousand troops—a
reinforced paratrooper task force in the north, and a reinforced marine
task force in the south. The president said, "So long as you don't break
your ceiling, and you don't keep them for a longer period than about
a month, you can have them." Allen used the extra combat capacity "to
fight like hell for a month to buy me the white space to close down a
whole series of bases."

As the surge troops left, a continued commitment from NATO allies,
Allen's strategic center of gravity, became more essential. May 2012 at a
summit in Chicago, America secured the support of other NATO nations to stay with the mission beyond the end of combat operations in
2014. The new operation would focus on building Afghan forces with a
price tag of $4.1 billion annually—a "mythical budget plan," according to
the analyst Anthony Cordesman, "based on a cost model that never seems
to have serious review."[49] It was not the only figure now being questioned.

The military were good at counting inputs—people, ammunition,
fuel, food, and so on. But in the highly complex environment of Afghanistan, a robust and meaningful method of measuring progress was
elusive. The metrics the public could see, as opinion shifted decisively
against continuing in Afghanistan, were the cost in lives and limbs and
the enormous payouts to what was increasingly seen as a lost cause. It
was harder to measure outcomes—stabilized villages, better education
opportunities, access to justice, confidence in the future, and better Afghan forces. In his first speech on Afghanistan in March 2009, Obama
had set the tone, talking of the need to "set clear metrics to measure
progress and hold ourselves accountable."[50]

By 2013, there were serious doubts as to whether such metrics existed. Cordesman called out "largely dishonest claims of progress."[51] He criticized nonmilitary metrics too. "The State Department has never issued a meaningful report on its role in the war," while the UN had done "no useful reporting on economic development and aid."

The twice-yearly Afghan data reports to Congress, called the 1230 reports,[52] began to censor inconvenient statistics, removing maps that showed reverses in security and other failures; "shades of the follies in Vietnam," according to Cordesman—where statistics showing progress were mocked for missing obvious ground realities that showed the opposite.[53] And where progress was claimed, such as an increase in economic growth, the real reason—better rainfall, so better agricultural income— was not mentioned in the report.

The principal indicator of the campaign counted "enemy-initiated attacks." As recently as March 2011, 90 percent of these had involved ISAF. If the figures can be believed, September 2012 was the real crossover point of the war, when more enemy-initiated attacks involved Afghan forces than international troops. But the value of the indicator was coming under increasing question. The 1230 report to Congress said counting enemy-initiated attacks was "not particularly useful in evaluating progress against the insurgency." A successful offensive by coalition and Afghan troops would inevitably provoke many enemy-initiated attacks, but meanwhile, the insurgency could be expanding its influence and strength in ways including "kidnappings, intimidation tactics and assassinations," not counted in the same way.

With combat troops going home and advisory capacity far more thinly spread, Allen also had far less knowledge of what was going on. "The ground was shifting under our feet, our assessment process had to change as well." He had lost the granular knowledge at a local level that 150,000 troops had brought previously. "As we became smaller we didn't have that kind of statistical clarity and we had to both measure something different and measure it in a different way, and that was the challenge that I put to my analysts." His solution was to move from quantitative to qualitative analysis—judgments by individual advisers rather than raw numbers. He knew the limitations of the assessment process, since "it's not possible to measure a war." In February 2013, his last month in command, ISAF suspended public reporting of a number of indicators, admitting that claims of progress had been a "clerical error." A reduction highlighted in January had officials declaring a "decrease in violence can be attributed to progress made in beating back the Taliban."[54] But when the figures were reexamined, there turned out to be no change in this key indicator, as information sent by Afghan forces had not been inputted into the database.

Already some units had streamlined the assessment process. The 10th Mountain Division had a hard fight in 2010/11 to finally stabilize Panjwayi and Arghandab in Kandahar and reduce the capacity of the Taliban to threaten Helmand, and during it, they revolutionized the way they recorded progress. When they arrived, the system recorded 240 different metrics—in order to build the all-important scale of unstable to stable areas, going from red, through orange, yellow, to green, with white as unknown. Commanders inevitably wanted to move every district toward green during their tour, a preoccupation known as "shade-shifting."[55] The counterinsurgency expert David Kilcullen wrote that too often the U.S. tried to "measure the universe—attempting to analyze everything and accomplishing little."[56] To make more sense of actual progress, 10th Mountain built more multidimensional models than a simple color scale, cutting the number of metrics down from 240 to just 11, with 18 indicators to measure as inputs.[57] This cut assessment down from six weeks to a matter of days, making it a far more valuable tool.

Progress in Kandahar was matched in neighboring Helmand. The surge since 2010 had made a significant difference. I was able to travel widely to report on development initiatives in 2011, going into areas previously in Taliban hands. U.S. Marines had fought hard to retake the populated zone, running like a spine down the center of the province, where the canal system allowed farming on a wide strip of land on either side of the Helmand River. This included Marjah, now finally coming under control after a false start with the non–Magnificent Seven, and the failed government in a box. The foreman of a road gang, employed to build a new road to better connect the capital with the countryside, told me that until the previous year, he had been the local Taliban commander. He deserted in the winter, after too many of his friends died, and hanging round the bazaar, he picked up the job to build the road. It was a perfect metaphor for the positive feedback loop that was the aim of the operation—improve security, fracture the Taliban, build local economic opportunities (both through employing the road builders and the improved commerce the road would bring), all to connect people to the state by standing up local government and justice, and reduce the chances for the Taliban to recruit to damage security. This picture was hard to capture in the traditional indicators used to measure progress.

Had the surge troops stayed alongside Afghan troops for just one more year, Allen believes the Taliban would have had their backs to the wall. "Another year of that beating probably would have driven them to the peace table, and probably to peace talks." Cordesman agreed that the withdrawal decision was "tailored largely to meet political timing in an effort to rush to the exits."[58]

≡ THIS IS VICTORY

There was one more meteor strike before Allen finished in Afghanistan, and it was personal to him. When he was deputy commander at CENTCOM, Allen and his wife, Kathy, had socialized with the woman appointed by Petraeus as a "goodwill ambassador" at CENTCOM, Jill Kelley, in her Florida home, including spending Christmas with her and her husband, Scott. Kelley knew a number of generals and, in her words, created a role to "cement relations between our military brass and the foreign leaders who came to Tampa to visit with them."[59] But Allen's emails from Kabul to Kelley were trawled by the FBI after she was stalked and threatened online by Petraeus's lover, Paula Broadwell.

The idea of Allen having an affair is absurd to anyone who knows him well. He was a "Southern monk," according to his political adviser Chretien, deeply devoted to Kathy and valuing traditional virtues of loyalty above all. "The Petraeus train-wreck was so big," said Chretien, "that the locomotive landed on our track." The supermarket tabloids had a field day, and the story proved an unnecessary distraction for the last months in command for the longest-serving ISAF commander of the combat era.

Allen had an emotional connection to Afghanistan. Leaving was "like leaving family behind to an uncertain future."[60] He asked a nearby school to send a girl and boy from the senior year to sit in the front row at his handover to his marine comrade and friend General Joe Dunford. The young people were symbols of the future America and the coalition were building—"Afghan forces defending Afghan people, and enabling the government of this country to serve its citizens. This is victory, this is what winning looks like, and we should not shrink from using these words."[61] But as he departed the base in a Black Hawk for the last time, he knew it was victory at a high cost in coalition and Afghan lives. Afghan independent capacity "would have happened far more easily with far fewer casualties amongst the Afghans if we'd had one more year to get them ready." Soon after leaving the command, he wrote a personal letter to Karzai, warning of the dangers of corruption. The Taliban were an "annoyance" compared to the threat of corruption, he wrote. "The existential threat to the long-term viability of Afghanistan is corruption."[62]

Allen was offered one of the best plums on the tree—the Supreme Allied Commander Europe—the job created for Eisenhower after the end of World War II. It was a job made for him, given his deep understanding of the value of the NATO alliance. Quickly cleared of any suggestion of impropriety in the Kelley scandal, the job was his. But citing Kathy's health and the long periods away from home he had already spent in Iraq and Afghanistan, he chose to retire. He soon found himself in demand as an adviser to the Obama administration and was the president's special envoy on the Islamic State crisis in Syria and Iraq. Later as president of the Brookings Institution, he had challenge coins made, of the sort given out by generals when they "coin" people in a handshake—the first head of the think tank to do so.

The month he left Afghanistan, there was one metric he could be proud of. Civilian casualties fell for the first time since the UN started collecting figures in 2009, and a large part of the cut was a reduction in people killed by air strikes.[63] Kabul never left him. He has a persistent cough he puts down to two winters in that air, and he sleeps only a few hours a night, blaming that on the pressure of the command responsibility.

TRIPLE TRANSITION

It's less about what you do than why you do it.
—General Joseph F. Dunford Jr.

≡ BACK TO BASICS

Joseph F. Dunford Jr. grew up in the shadow of one of the oldest military sites in the U.S., the pentagon-shaped seventeenth-century Fort Independence, commanding the entrance to Boston Harbor. Three uncles fought in World War II. His father, Joseph F. Dunford Sr., joined the marines as soon as he was old enough in 1948, and spent his twentieth birthday as one of the "Chosin Few," who fought their way out of the frozen Chosin Reservoir against eleven Chinese divisions in the Korean War. Joe Dunford Sr. went on to serve in the Boston Police.

Joe Dunford Jr. joined the marines after Vietnam—a war that took the lives of twenty-five men from the tight-knit Irish Catholic communities of South Boston where he grew up, traditional recruiting ground for the marines.

To encourage recruitment to rebuild the Marine Corps amid widespread drug abuse and lack of discipline, officers were offered commissions for just two years, and Dunford took the opportunity to resign two years in. Vietnam was tearing America apart at the time he was recruited, and the reality of military life did not live up to the idealistic picture in his mind. His commanding officer, Colonel Joseph Hoar, a fellow Bostonian, failed to talk him out of it, but his gunnery sergeant succeeded. As a first lieutenant, Dunford was in charge of about 150 marines, and when he called his senior NCOs together to tell them he was leaving, the sergeant said, "Well, that's great, Lieutenant. What about the rest of us?" So he stayed for his men, because like all good officers, he had built a team and could not leave the men he loved.

Thirty-three years later, now a four-star general, he once again requested to leave, but this time to retire, from his post as assistant commandant of the Marine Corps. When the chairman of the Joint Chiefs, General Marty Dempsey, asked him to consider commanding in Afghanistan instead, he did not even tell his wife, Ellyn. He thought there would be a few people in the frame, and he had never served there. "I knew there was a lot of people who felt like, you had to have been in Afghanistan for a significant period of time to command there, and so I didn't think much about it." There was already a marine commanding in Kabul, making it less likely that another would get the post. It was only after he saw President Obama, who said, "I think we're going to be seeing more of each other," that he told Ellyn he might be going.

Dunford had commanded the 5th Marine Regiment when they were first over the line into Iraq in 2003, the day before the rest of the invasion force, and his troops painted the name "Fighting Joe" onto their vehicles. The 5th Marines had a storied history going back to the Battle of Belleau Wood in World War I, which earned them the right to wear the fourragère, the braided cord marking the award of France's highest military honor, the Croix de Guerre, to the entire regiment.[1] Promoted to brigadier general in the field in Iraq, Dunford looked set for high command positions when he skipped the rank of major general on the way up, going straight from one to three stars as a lieutenant general in 2008.

Joe Dunford is a tall, well-built, square-headed man, "the damn epitome of a Marine leader," in the words of a former sergeant major of the corps.[2] He has a warm manner and intent gaze and is a people person, remembering the birthdays of staff and names of camera crews who interview him. His greatest extravagance is the black Jeep Sahara he drives; he does not consider himself an intellectual, seeing this as an overrated virtue, and has little interest in the political maneuvering of Washington. But he knows the military lane better than anyone and knows how to stay in it. "My job was to provide military advice; my job wasn't to advocate." This attracted Obama, who replaced one cool, clear-thinking, no-dramas marine with another, when time came for General John Allen to retire. Dunford would do eleven days fewer than the nineteen months of Allen's time in command in Kabul.

Dunford saw the campaign through a clear counterterrorist lens as the overarching structure that contained all military effort—a view that could be muddied by the several audiences for any message. In NATO nations in Canada and Europe, there was more attention paid to governance and development, and in Afghanistan, more concern about the growth of their own forces. "I had fifty nations in a coalition when I arrived, and we had the Afghans we had to work with, and this thing had to be characterized as something that was being done to address all those interests." It meant mixed messages were heard in the U.S. when the counterterrorist bell should have been rung more soundly. "We weren't singularly focused with the American people on counterterrorism."

Counterterrorism was America's "enduring objective" in Afghanistan—Dunford saw development and governance as subsets of that strategic requirement. Preventing Afghanistan from once again becoming the launchpad for attacks on the homeland needed a "place to do counterterrorism operations from," and that needed a legitimate partner in the Afghan government who would share intelligence, and effective Afghan security forces. "So we're helping Afghan governance develop, we're helping with development, we're helping develop the Afghan forces." All these efforts were "enabling capacity for counterterrorism."

Like generals before him in many conflicts, he wished that political leaders at home spoke "more forcefully about the need for us to continue the mission in Afghanistan. We had people dying, so presumably everybody agreed that we needed to be there." By now, though, that was no longer true. A poll in the summer of 2013 showed just 28 percent of Americans supported the war—a steep decline of 11 percentage points since the spring. Afghanistan was yesterday's war, eclipsed for attention in the media and in Washington by the unraveling horror of Syria. Dunford's focus on the counterterrorist mission suited Obama's desire to put Afghanistan into proportion alongside other challenges. He would ask, "Why can't you conduct operations in Afghanistan like we do in Somalia, with a relatively low U.S. footprint?"[3]

Five years into his presidency, Obama had become a confident, if reluctant, war leader. Dunford found he gave clear guidance and listened to discussion, with a well-defined appreciation of the ownership of risk. Risk management is of course an important skill for military commanders at all levels. The Kabul commander's task was to give the best advice to inform the president, who owned the risk to the mission. Those discussions became more critical as troops were reduced.

The decision to cut U.S. troops to thirty-four thousand by the end of 2013 had already been taken when Dunford succeeded Allen in March 2013—and they were set to reduce further. Obama was relaxed about the precise numbers during 2014, allowing Dunford twenty thousand for the Afghan election and its aftermath. Dunford said, "He really did give me the latitude on the timeline so that we could conduct the campaign and conduct the retrograde simultaneously and still provide the requisite level of support to the Afghans." There were long discussions about what level to keep when the combat operation "ended" on December 31. The president wanted as few as possible.

But events elsewhere added to nervousness about what would happen if there were a total withdrawal of troops in Afghanistan. The collapse of authority in Iraq following the withdrawal of all U.S. troops in 2011, and the terrifying emergence of the Islamic State group, led to heightened political noise around the Afghan discussions. And then there was the violent mess of Libya—which had been showcased back in 2011 by Obama as the sort of intervention he preferred, with no U.S. ground troops, and was now the poster child for the failure of the policy, revealing why halfhearted intervention does not work.

Against this backdrop, Senator John McCain, with his usual showmanship, said he was "disappointed" that Dunford, in his first hearing after taking up command in April 2013, could not tell the Senate Armed Services Committee how many troops he believed should stay after 2014. McCain saw this as sending a signal to terrorists worldwide. "They see us withdrawing every place in the world . . . And they know which way the wind is blowing." McCain wanted more troops to stay for longer. Dunford answered that he had not at that time made a recommendation, which to McCain was "a tragic and terrible mistake for which we may pay a very heavy price."[4]

The discussions went on through the summer—with four options of fifteen thousand, ten thousand, five thousand, and the lowest option of two thousand that many around the president favored, led as always by Vice President Joe Biden—minimal counterterrorism forces, embassy-level security, and no more. Dunford told Obama that the last two options, with forces below ten thousand, put the mission under too great a risk. "My perspective was that if we were going to be below ten thousand, we ought to think about getting out completely." It would be hard to deliver either an effective U.S.-led counterterrorism campaign or support for Afghan operations. "The probability of success would be so low that the risk of putting people on the ground during that period of time would not be worth it."

There was also a question of how long the troops should remain. In the grand language of international summits, the NATO agreement in Chicago in 2012 that set a new course for Afghanistan talked of a "decade of transformation" for Afghanistan. Dunford preferred to talk about a "decade of opportunity." But there was no agreement over how long into that decade there would be international troops in the country, beyond the "end of combat" in 2014. In a BBC interview in June 2013, with a new take on "fragile but reversible," Dunford moved the target to 2018. "At this point we have made significant progress, but we are not yet at the point where it is completely sustainable," he said. "That's why we need to start now, especially with the Afghan security forces, to talk about 2018 not 2014."[5] The comments were a surprise to NATO allies, but it was a classic Dunford pitch—clear, sending a political message without making waves in Washington or demanding a surge, just more time to do the job.

The comment was based on a pragmatic assessment of Afghan capacity. While Afghan forces were now improving—after many false starts over the years—there were still glaring gaps in key areas, such as logistics and maintenance, and Afghan airpower was negligible. Some of this was basic stuff. The landscape was littered with Ford Rangers and Humvees, supplied to the Afghan forces, that had gone into ditches or broken down for lack of maintenance. Sorting this required better Afghan leadership, which would take time to develop. But like Allen before him, Dunford found himself doing what he could to stand up Afghan forces with less time than he wanted as the drawdown went on.

≡ UNFINISHED BUSINESS

The challenges faced by Afghanistan were daunting amid a triple transition. Not only were international forces reducing substantially and changing their mission to one of "train, advise, and assist," but there was a significant cut in international aid and a political change as Karzai would complete two terms in 2014. Managing security around the prolonged dispute over the election result would be the main security preoccupation through 2014. But the aid cut too was a significant security challenge, as it dramatically worsened poverty. Much of the economy was kept artificially afloat by foreign support and collapsed as the money was withdrawn.

The chart showing the country's economic growth was like that of a very sick patient, with massive swings—sometimes up to 13 percent annually and averaging 9 percent. In 2014, growth fell to 1.5 percent, not keeping up with the massive pressures from an increased population, with a bulging youth demographic.[6] Income per head fell to less than $600 a year. The end of big spending was like a balloon bursting, letting the economy crash to the ground. Both at the beginning and now near the end of the intervention in Afghanistan, development spending had unforeseen negative consequences.

To communicate to his troops, Dunford did not issue lengthy tactical directives. Instead, he put five clear phrases on a five-by-eight card, which could be slipped into the side pocket of combat trousers. The card was entitled "What Winning Looks Like," and the first of the five lines was the most important—about security transition to Afghan control. Then there was prevention of safe havens for al-Qaeda, a credible Afghan election, a constructive relationship between the Afghan and Pakistani military forces, and the "reposturing" of ISAF for training and the small residual counterterrorism combat force that would remain. There was no reference to the Taliban, and apart from the prevention of al-Qaeda safe havens, there was no mention of combat. Twenty-two months ahead of the timetabled end of combat operations, Dunford was sending a message that things would be different.

Transition to Afghan forces, *Inteqal*, had been in hand since 2011, as district by district, province by province, Afghan troops took the lead for security in their own country. Dunford's temperament was not to try to invent the wheel but to communicate the transition process to his forces in doctrinal language they understood from basic training about supported and supporting forces. "I didn't need a new buzzword because everybody, really even in a NATO context, understands this idea of supported/supporting."[7] It meant the Afghan forces, now responsible for the security outcome of the provinces under their control, were supported by ISAF troops. "The key point," for Dunford, "was that the Afghans were responsible for the outcome."

This did not affect the continuing U.S. counterterrorism fight, now mostly in the hands of small detachments of Special Forces. On February 25, two weeks after Dunford took command, the governor of Wardak Province, Abdul Majid Khogyani, made the one-hour drive north to Kabul to complain to the Afghan National Security Council about the conduct of a U.S. Special Forces unit that had taken over a base from conventional troops in 2012. The governor brought reports of dozens of tribal elders who said they had been unfairly arrested and beaten, and specific allegations about nine missing men whose neighbors said had disappeared after being interrogated by U.S. Special Forces.[8] Karzai immediately issued a strong public statement, claiming U.S. troops were responsible for the torture and murder of the nine men. For some months, he had been demanding the Special Forces leave Wardak complaining "What does Afghan control mean if these operations go on." Nerkh District, where the mistreatment is said to have taken place, had only recently transitioned to Afghan control. Soon after Dunford took over command, there was a large, angry demonstration outside parliament demanding justice for the events in Wardak.

The main north-south route linking Kabul to Kandahar goes through Wardak, but once off the road, it feels much farther from the capital than just the one-hour drive, remote from modern civilization and vulnerable to exploitation by the Taliban. The dense valleys and apple orchards have for many years been a launchpad for attacks on Kabul. That made it an obvious focus of U.S. operations. Only one man, an Afghan interpreter, was convicted for the killings in Nerkh District in the winter of 2012. And while the official inquiry findings have never been made public, investigative reporter Matthieu Aikins uncovered shocking material suggesting a U.S. Green Beret unit went rogue after a popular NCO was shot and wounded. They are alleged to have rounded up Afghan farmers at random, killing some in the fields and torturing and killing others back at their base. The Green Berets knew there was political pressure against their operations. One thanked their Afghan interpreters, including the one ultimately convicted, in a Facebook post. "We fucked up the bad guys so bad nonstop for 7+ months that they did everything they could to get us out of Wardak Province."[9] Aikins reported that after

Karzai succeeded in getting the Special Forces pulled out at the end of March, villagers found ten bodies in separate shallow graves, wrapped in U.S. body bags. Most were unrecognizable, but one of the missing men was positively identified,[10] and through pieces of clothing, others too were given names.

By the time Dunford was facing Karzai on the Wardak issue two weeks into his Kabul command, the president had already made another move against air strikes, banning his forces from calling for air support in populated areas. Dunford agreed to withdraw the Special Forces from Wardak.

No relationship mattered more than with President Karzai. Dunford donned a marine dress uniform every time he went to the Arg—a shirt, necktie, and green jacket with a high belt, pressed trousers, and polished shoes, not combat boots and khakis. The first time he went in, Karzai said, "I haven't seen this uniform. What is this uniform?" Dunford answered that he was treating Karzai "in terms of professional courtesy exactly the same way that I treated my own president." He would change into the uniform for every trip to the Arg, sometimes more than once in a day. "I wanted him to know that I respected him; I wanted him to know that I understood Afghan sovereignty."

Karzai's tone had not changed. Sometimes he would take thirty minutes at the beginning of a meeting to complain about America's failings. Dunford would soak it up, looking for the shared space in the Venn diagram where would be common ground for dialogue. "I do believe that during a very difficult time, we were successful. If you step back at ten thousand feet, the relationship with President Karzai was effective enough for us to continue to move forward." But the meetings were not conducted from a height; they were punishing face-to-face encounters in what Dunford saw as an "eighty-twenty" relationship, where he had to go 80 percent of the way all the time. Jim Cunningham was U.S. ambassador for the whole of Dunford's command, having served as deputy for a year previously. He had a similar low-key approach as Dunford, patient and determined, allowing his deep frustration to come out just once, a week before he left in 2014, following another intemperate speech by Karzai. Cunningham told the media the Afghan president was "ungracious" and that he "dishonored America's war dead."[11]

Dunford and Cunningham were working through the complexities of the bilateral security agreement (BSA) that would determine the status of U.S. forces in Afghanistan after the end of combat in 2014. Without it, all troops would have to leave, and failure to agree sat like a boulder in the way of progress in any other areas. The BSA was the substance of the future relationship, building on the principle agreed in the partnership deal—the one signed at midnight in Kabul ahead of the Chicago NATO summit in May 2012. What the American negotiators did not know was that Karzai had already made up his mind never to sign the BSA—a decision founded in his misunderstanding of the scope of the 2012 partnership agreement.

Three weeks after the partnership deal was signed, Pakistan began their seasonal routine harassment across the border, lobbing artillery rounds at random into Afghan villages. It is remarkable that this goes on with no international opposition; every year, it kills and injures people living in the remote mountainous region. America's failure to stop it fed into Karzai's sense that their agenda was really at one with Pakistan's ISI intelligence agency. In 2012, this was confirmed in his mind. The partnership agreement did not commit America to defend Afghanistan from attack, but Karzai interpreted it as a mutual security pact, and demanded that the U.S. forces act to stop the shelling. That was the first stage toward his decision not to sign the BSA.

In what turned out to be Karzai's last trip to Washington as president, despite red-carpet treatment across the city and an honor guard at the Pentagon, it was while meeting Obama that Karzai finally made up his mind not to sign the deal. It seemed to him that as well as requesting the right for future U.S. bases, Obama was suggesting that he allow Pakistan more influence in Afghanistan. Karzai replied, "I give you bases, and I give Pakistan my sovereignty. What's in it for us?"[12]

Karzai did not make his decision public until a Loya Jirga ten months later, which he called to consult the Afghan people. If they agreed he should sign, this would have been the perfect cover for him. He knew the gibes made by the Taliban that he was just another Shah Shuja, the "puppet" king put on the Afghan throne by British troops in 1838.[13] Dunford sat impassively in his dress uniform with Cunningham in the front row of the diplomatic corps in the Loya Jirga tent as Karzai laid out the benefits for Afghanistan of the BSA in a speech that, for 95 percent of the time, was positive. But in his closing words, based on his distorted view of the partnership agreement and memories of Obama's demands on his last trip to Washington, he said he would not sign, sticking to this even though the Loya Jirga agreed that he should.

While the assembled tribal elders were proud Afghans, wanting foreign forces out, there was a deep nervousness, especially in Afghan cities, that the withdrawal would lead to the return of warlords and civil war, as had followed the Russian withdrawal twenty years before. Karzai's failure to listen to the Loya Jirga was one of the events that gave Dunford a sleepless night. But he would still try to understand Karzai, telling his team, "Look, this guy has been the president of Afghanistan for twelve years, a country at war. The pressure on him has to be enormous." As long as he "retained operational flexibility," he could deal with the moods of the Afghan president.

☰ PROPAGANDA OF THE DEED

A large, thin-skinned modern hall, like a delivery warehouse, was the setting for a piece of political theater in Afghanistan in June 2013—the formal handover of sovereignty of the last provinces to Afghan control. From now on, the ISAF coalition would formally be the "supporting" force right across the country, as the war was supposed to be led by a sovereign nation, who could call on the coalition for air strikes and medical evacuation. Dunford remembered his first visit to Afghanistan, when the marines went to Helmand in 2008. It was "at best an Afghan face on a Marine capability." There were ten international troops to every Afghan soldier. By 2013, the ratio was three to one the other way.

The practical effect of the final handover was not great—involving a handful of districts, mainly along the eastern frontier, and in Kandahar. But the symbolic impact of a new nation emerging was profound, marked by the modern building, the rows of smart Afghan troops, and the black, red, and green of the Afghan flag now in pride of place ahead of the U.S. and NATO banners. A giant digitally printed image of Afghan soldiers filled the backdrop of the hall as Karzai's helicopter arrived to herald the playing of the Afghan national anthem by a military band who marched stiffly in, stamping their feet in the approved Afghan drill, wearing ill-fitting, bright red uniforms, and playing energetically, if tunelessly. It was an Afghan event to mark an important moment in the reinvention of the Afghan nation.

But in a stunning piece of political theater of their own, the Taliban rained on the parade. Out of the blue that morning, Al Jazeera TV went live to a Taliban press conference from Doha, Qatar, announcing the opening of a political office. Given that the Taliban had deliberately kept out of the limelight since they fell from power in 2001—apart from occasional hard-to-get secret interviews by Western reporters, often with spokespeople concealing their identities—the livestreamed event was a revelation. The Taliban broke every condition they had made to the Qatari government to be allowed to open an office. They flew a Taliban flag, and the building had a brass plate outside proclaiming this the government of the "Islamic Emirate of Afghanistan."[14] Karzai was furious—inevitably the first question from the press at the transition event was about the Taliban, not his historic regaining of sovereignty.[15]

Dunford was deeply disappointed. "We had spent the previous five months working up to that day, with messaging, optics, implementation, all designed to give us momentum into the summer and into continued transition, and in one fell swoop, we lost what I thought was a critical opportunity. So, candidly, that was one of the darkest times for me in the campaign."

Dunford had a keen interest in the perception of the campaign and the value of communications, seeing much of the Taliban's activity as deliberately designed to manage the news agenda. In particular, they exploited the narrative of "abandonment"—that international forces would quickly leave. "Every December," Dunford said, "we were dealing with a Y2K situation." The Taliban would promote their inevitable victory, as ISAF looked as if it would "go off the cliff at the end of the year." A concerted series of attacks on Western civilian targets in Afghanistan in early 2014 were part of this process. They were designed to raise uncertainty in Western capitals as Afghanistan moved toward the election to replace Karzai. "The high-profile attacks were in reinforcement of that overall narrative," as the attention shifted from taking ground to delivering results from the "psychological effect" of killing Westerners. In early 2014, more international civilians died than ISAF soldiers in Afghanistan.

The first attack of the series was the worst, when twenty-one people, including foreign development workers and elite Afghans, died in an attack on a Lebanese-owned restaurant. The Taverna du Liban was a popular meeting place, with chintz curtains and fake wood paneling, where beer and wine was served discreetly when available. It was close to the British embassy compound, had armed security, and was crowded as always on a Thursday evening, the end of the working week in Kabul. One Taliban suicide bomber detonated his vest at the entrance, and two others entered the restaurant, killing everybody inside. Two of the diners had armed security guards with them, but both were killed, and the restaurant burned to the ground. Apart from two local staff who climbed out through the roof, no one survived. The attack closed down nightlife for Westerners in Kabul for good. Even the longest-open, the Gandamack Lodge, closed its doors.

The attacks went on. In March, a Swedish journalist, Nils Horner, was shot and killed while walking in a street nearby in broad daylight. Horner had come to Kabul to cover the presidential election. A week later, March 20, Afghan New Year's Eve, five international election monitors were among those killed in an audacious attack on the Serena Hotel, the fourth time it had been targeted. The city's only modern five-star, it was already statistically the most dangerous place to stay and the only place in Kabul where any foreign journalists had died since 2001, but because of high gates and intense body searches, security experts mistakenly advised companies they should send their staff there. Four teenage Taliban recruits with tiny pistols in their socks evaded the tight security, entering at a busy time as people came for a New Year's dinner. A popular Kabul journalist, Sardar Ahmad, his wife, and two of their children were among the dead.

The attacks continued through the summer, on guesthouses and offices where foreigners lived and worked. There was even an attack on a provincial office of the International Committee of the Red Cross—the most neutral humanitarian organization, who had good links with the Taliban, one of the very few organizations to stay in Afghanistan throughout the civil war and Taliban years in the 1990s. This attack crossed a line, but it was one that the Taliban, or particularly the allied Haqqani network—the group backed by Pakistan—were prepared to cross.

☰ CIVILIAN CASUALTIES AGAIN

As well as Taliban psychological operations, there was another narrative running against the international community, promoted by Karzai. Friction over civilian casualties began early in Dunford's period in command when he denied that international forces had caused the deaths of at least seventeen women and children in a remote part of Kunar Province close to the Pakistan border. He did not have the same problems that the earliest ISAF commanders had, of not being sighted on some U.S. elements carrying out offensive operations. "I was never surprised by U.S. military operations in Afghanistan." He would discuss operations that might involve civilians with special operations commanders involved. "I'd get a detailed brief on the operation and have an opportunity to either modify the operation or cancel the operation if I thought it was high risk." In the Kunar incident, there had been a fierce firefight. Dunford insisted that any civilian deaths were not caused by air strikes,[16] but the Afghan government disagreed, paying compensation to the victims, and the UN took the government side, finding the deaths were caused by "shockwaves from the aerial bombardment."

Dunford is a Catholic, attending mass at the church in the Italian embassy in Kabul every Sunday during his command, and driven by a moral obligation not to cause the loss of innocent lives. He would frequently tell his team, "When we go to war, we've got to bring our values with us." There were wider reasons, though, why civilian casualties should be avoided, particularly at this stage of the war. As a supporting force of a sovereign power, he knew there was a risk of Karzai limiting the flexibility they needed. "We needed to conduct operations in a way that satisfied the Afghan leadership." There was also the danger of civilian casualties provoking green-on-blue attacks. Dunford saw every potential tactical action through this framework of its strategic risk to the overall mission, frequently telling both American and other coalition forces, "If we're taking risk to achieve a tactical end, we're probably not in the right place."

Karzai highlighted pictures of the dead children in Kunar and would raise the issue of civilian casualties as loudly as he could publicly and privately, telling *The Washington Post* that he was "forced to yell," because he "did not get attention behind closed doors."[17] Dunford tried to put himself in his shoes. "Rightfully, I think, as the president of Afghanistan, he was focused on that."

But while Karzai had an understandable concern for the loss of Afghan lives at the hands of international troops, he moved into a world where he would believe anything of them. He was now keeping a list of terrorist attacks where he thought the U.S. was colluding with the attackers to worsen instability and weaken him, including the Taverna attack.[18] His office, led by his strongly anti-American chief spokesman, Aimal Faizi, began to exaggerate claims against international troops using fake material. Ten days after the Taverna attack, the Arg issued a dossier to reporters, including a video, purporting to show the aftermath of an air strike in Parwan, near Kabul, by U.S. forces, said to have killed fourteen civilians. The dossier contained a video of anguished faces at a funeral, pictures of damaged houses and dead bodies—one a graphic image of a woman missing her face, which Karzai highlighted in an angry meeting with Dunford. Reporters quickly uncovered inconsistencies in the dossier. One image was from a funeral in 2009, another showed two bodies in a burial shroud, previously often used in Pakistan on anti-American websites. Even the governor of Parwan dismissed Karzai's dossier, saying that anyone who said large numbers of civilians were killed in the incident must be a "supporter of the Taliban."[19]

☰ "THIS IS HOW WARS END"

Inevitably in this atmosphere, the U.S. looked to the next government, to be elected in April. But that government took time to emerge. As if in a portent of the storms to come, April 5, 2014, election day, the skies opened with heavy rain that burst through Kabul's storm drains, filling the streets with water. It did not stop queues of people forming from early morning to cast their vote; democracy, however flawed, was popular. Karzai had successfully opposed reforms that would have built a transparent register of voters, and despite measures that included inking the forefinger of people who had voted, corruption was widespread. There had been three issues of polling cards in the post-Taliban era, the cards were easy to fake, and any card could be used in any polling station, so some polling stations inevitably ran out of ballot papers. But there was a vigorous campaign with mass rallies and TV debates.

There was little policy difference between the candidates, who were divided instead on ethnic and tribal lines. Historical resistance to the creation of political parties in Afghanistan goes back to wariness of the divisiveness and cruelty of the Communist years, as well as the corruption of the mujahideen, and this has not been challenged by any post-Taliban politician.[20] Karzai's unwillingness to anoint a successor meant that eleven candidates, including his brother and several other Pashtuns, were in the race. With no clear front-runner, the election was always likely to go to a second round, where the contest would be between the last Pashtun standing, and Abdullah Abdullah, running in his second election for the influential Tajik minority—the standard-bearer for the slain Ahmed Shah Massoud.

In the event, it was Ashraf Ghani who came through the Pashtun pack. Brought up in Kabul, he spent most of his life in the U.S. as an academic and then with the World Bank. He was one of a group of reformist ministers who gathered around the first Karzai government in 2002, but within two years, he had resigned and traveled the world as an adviser to failed states, writing a manual, *Fixed Failed States*, with Clare Lockhart, a British lawyer who spent some years in Afghanistan working in development. He first ran for president in 2009, receiving a derisory number of votes in a two-horse race between Karzai and Abdullah. Ghani had a higher public profile in 2014, as he had spent the previous two years running the *Inteqal*—transition—process, going district to district to re-establish Afghan sovereignty as international troops handed it over.

The second round of the election was set for June 10, but Obama was not going to wait for the Afghan election process to deliver a final result before moving forward with his own plans to cut troops. America did not have a strong negotiating hand to try to get a signature on the BSA allowing them to stay, since the threat for not signing was that troops would leave, which was what the negotiating partner, Karzai, wanted. American public opinion too was weary of the long war. In February 2014, Secretary of Defense Chuck Hagel was planning for the "zero option"—all troops out by the end of the year—a "prudent step" since there was no movement on signing the BSA,[21] although both Ghani and Abdullah said they would sign if they took power. Dunford did not see the zero option as a bluff. "I think it was very much on the table if we couldn't get an acceptable agreement."

In the last week of May, Obama announced his decision on the future of American involvement. He began a series of carefully choreographed Afghan events with a Memorial Day weekend visit to Bagram Air Base. Karzai snubbed him, saying he would not go to the air base but would meet the president only "in Afghan tradition in Kabul." But the Afghan president was not the audience for a visit designed to tell the American people that the long war would end. To loud cheers from troops gathered in a hangar, Obama said, "For many of you, this will be your last tour in Afghanistan."

Back in Washington, the president set a quicker departure date than Dunford had wanted for the post–combat phase, halving troops to five thousand during 2015 and drawing all troops out, to "embassy level" cover by the end of 2016. This was taken to mean around two thousand. The announcement was made in a businesslike statement in the Rose Garden, so he could focus on a wider foreign agenda in a major set piece speech to cadets at West Point the following day. "This is how wars end in the twenty-first century," he said in a classic Obama performance—elegiac, hopeful, idealistic—and as it turned out, wishful thinking. He wanted to "turn the page" on the period of America's military involvement in Afghanistan and Iraq, but another phrase in the speech that "it's harder to end wars than to begin them" was more prophetic. Karzai will have been happy to hear him say Americans would "no longer patrol Afghan cities or towns, mountains or valleys." But even that turned out not to be true, as the counterterrorist struggle went on and troops would stay in Afghanistan well beyond Obama's end date of 2016.

☰ PRISONER RELEASES

Early on a cold February morning in 2014, sixty-five men walked along the half-mile-long grilled corridor to exit Bagram Air Base dressed in identical white *shalwar kameez* pajamas, black waistcoats, and round white hats. The long corridor, with tight turnstiles a man could just squeeze through at each end, were a security feature to survey Afghans coming in and out of the base. At the far end, there was a narrow slit between blast walls, and the men, Taliban suspects, released from the Parwan detention center on the base, were out on an Afghan street. They were released by Karzai rather than being put on trial, against American advice, once he finally secured full control of the jail. To Karzai, Parwan was a Taliban factory, a place where innocent Afghans "learned to hate." He had already released more than five hundred detainees—this last tranche was the hard core. Negotiations over Parwan had taken days of Dunford's time, and he saw that it had a "symbolic value" to the Afghan leadership. "That was a physical manifestation of sovereignty." Dunford's communications team put out a list of the evidence against the men, calling the release "a major step backward" in developing the rule of law in Afghanistan. The suspects were connected to the deaths of dozens of ISAF troops, and the evidence against them included fingerprints on bomb-making equipment, incriminating literature, and positive tests for explosives residue.

Waiting for the men as they were released into the cold February dawn, his woolly hat low over his brow, was the squat figure of Mahfouz Zubaide, pretending to be a taxi driver. He had a four-wheel drive and small Toyota saloon car, and he filled the cars with as many of those who were released as he could, offering a ride to Kabul. Once inside the cars, Mahfouz, who was a BBC producer, lent them his phone to call families and offered them breakfast. I was waiting in a restaurant next to the Kabul River, with piles of kebabs and bread, taking the chance to interview the ex-detainees before they disappeared back into Afghanistan. They all proclaimed their innocence. One, Nurullah, was a commander said to have ordered an attack that killed one U.S. soldier and injured four others. He had dark eyes and a watchful air. He claimed he was working as a plasterer when arrested. The former detainees said they had been tortured and held in solitary confinement and that some of those held were children, while others were very old.[22]

While Karzai's clearing of the cells was seen by the American military as a threat to security, they too were releasing some dangerous men without due process. The last wing of the jail held foreign detainees, and in an effort to avoid another Guantánamo, where men taken on the battlefield could not be released or tried, several were released. They included Latif Mehsud, a leading figure in the TTP, the Pakistani Taliban, who had been picked up a year previously in highly contentious circumstances. When arrested, he was being driven from the Pakistani border to Kabul by the NDS, the Afghan security service. He had come to discuss peace terms with Karzai. The TTP are a relatively new phenomenon, mainly operating against the Pakistani state, but also hitting American targets through links with al-Qaeda and the Taliban. The leader Hakeemullah Mehsud, killed in a drone strike in November 2013, was believed to have been responsible for the failed Times Square bomb plot in 2010.

The arrest of Latif Mehsud was one of the few occasions when Dunford saw Karzai in a real rage. He was being prevented from running his own operations, including potential peace tracks; it made a mockery of American claims that he was now sovereign. And rather than handing Mehsud over to Karzai as they emptied the jail, he was given to

Pakistan. At the same time, America was running its own negotiations with the Taliban, with no reference to Karzai. A week after Obama's choreographed visit to Afghanistan announcing, "This is how wars end," Sergeant Bowe Bergdahl, the only American military captive in the long war, walked free. Karzai volubly complained that he had not been consulted and claimed the release of the Guantánamo Five, high-value Taliban prisoners in exchange, was against international law.[23]

The Taliban put out a video of the release: a Black Hawk circles the site before landing, wary of Taliban fighters carrying rocket-propelled-grenade launchers on the slopes around; Bergdahl, beardless and shaven-headed, sits blinking in unaccustomed light in the back of a four-wheel drive, dressed in a white *shalwar kameez,* with an Afghan scarf on his shoulders; the helicopter lands, and he walks forward, helped by two Taliban fighters carrying a white flag; three special operators come out of the helicopter and approach; they put out left hands when the Taliban want to shake hands, keeping their right arms ready to shoot at all times; one walks forward with Bergdahl to the helicopter, while the other walks backward, watching all the time; they pat Bergdahl down twice, once when they meet the Taliban for the handover, and more thoroughly before boarding the helicopter, deliberately dropping a small bag he is carrying before they take off in case it carried a bomb. Twice in the video, a caption flashes up across the screen in black letters: *Don'come back to afghanistan.* The Black Hawk is on the ground for less than a minute. Questions about it have not stopped since.

The immediate response from the chain of command was relief that America had honored its promise never to leave anyone behind. But there was ambivalence about the five-for-one exchange. A jubilant statement put out in the name of the Taliban leader Mullah Omar, calling it a great victory, strengthened the hand of Republicans who thought the price paid too high.

☰ COMBAT FIT

General Joe Dunford was the only American ISAF commander to go on to another four-star command in uniform, succeeding General James Amos as commandant of the Marine Corps who retired in 2014.[24] Just four months before the "end of combat operations" in Kabul, he handed over the command to General John Campbell—whose Afghan experience went back to Kandahar in 2002. Once back in the Corps, Dunford completed the Marine Corps Combat Fitness Test at age fifty-nine, which includes pushing a thirty-pound ammunition can overhead for several repetitions, and carrying another marine through obstacles for seventy-five yards. A year later, he was appointed chairman of the Joint Chiefs of Staff, with Obama praising his "unvarnished military advice" from Afghanistan. His first National Security Council meeting as chairman was on Afghanistan, and his intimate knowledge meant it would not be forgotten as other security concerns took more attention from the administration. As chairman, Dunford unveiled a memorial to the Battle of Chosin Reservoir. His father, Joe Dunford Sr., was in pride of place at the front of the audience with his surviving shipmates from the battle.

In early 2013, soon after arriving in Kabul, Dunford had written his judgment of the situation. "The Afghan forces were capable of securing the majority of the Afghan population, were capable of securing the elections and were capable with some enabling support of providing security to Afghanistan." But even if this upbeat take was right, Dunford thought troops needed to remain until at least 2018, to give Afghan forces support at the right level, not the two years allowed by Obama after 2014. In any event, the president's hope of finishing America's military involvement in Afghanistan by the end of his term would not be realized. Toward the end as at the beginning of the long war, there was no clear sense of the long-term view. And beyond the transactional prisoner swap, there was still no route to talk to the Taliban or agreement in Washington that there should be a negotiated end to the war.

December 3, 2001. Hamid Karzai with Special Forces Unit ODA 574. Jason Amerine is on the right of Karzai in light-colored combat fatigues and a boonie hat. Jefferson Davis (*standing right*) and Dan Petithory (*kneeling front right*) were killed by an American bomb two days later.

December 6, 2001. Defense Secretary Donald Rumsfeld rejected the Taliban surrender deal negotiated by Karzai.

"Make damned sure they're wearing turbans," the instruction of the Islamabad CIA Chief Robert Grenier, backing the warlord Gul Agha Sherzai to be reinstalled as Governor of Kandahar in 2001.

December 14, 2001. Journalists outnumbered international troops at the battle of Tora Bora. Local forces under Hazrat Ali, interviewed here, were used instead of the 4,500 marines who were available, commanded by Major General Jim Mattis. Osama bin Laden escaped. Peter Jouvenal (*standing left*) went on to found the longest-running guest house in Kabul, Gandamack Lodge.

May 6, 2002. Five months after the battle, Canadian troops exhume al-Qaeda graves to extract DNA for identification.

September 9, 2004. Shaded by an army camouflage tent, U.S. Ambassador Zalmay Khalilzad at the ground-breaking ceremony for a new road from Kabul to Kandahar, which became known as "the most expensive road in the world."

June 9, 2008. General David McKiernan talking to marines in Helmand.

February 4, 2007. Change of command ceremony in Kabul. President Hamid Karzai sits between incoming American general Dan McNeill (*left*) and outgoing British general David Richards (*right*).

January 10, 2009. Incoming vice president Joe Biden, meeting the Afghan president, on the evening of the "dinner to remember."

January 2, 2010. General Stanley McChrystal talking with Karzai in a public meeting in Helmand before the Marjah offensive.

March 14, 2010. McChrystal was an enthusiastic whiteboard user to explain "insurgent math," which holds that "for every innocent person you kill, you create ten new enemies."

July 9, 2010. General David Petraeus in Kandahar with the British major general, Nick Carter (*right*).

July 12, 2011. Petraeus working out in Kabul. "I want the enemy to think that I'm the most competitive human being."

August 4, 2011. General John Allen talking to elders in Marjah, Helmand.

June 12, 2013. The author interviewing General Joe Dunford for the BBC in Kunduz.

March 30, 2016. General John Campbell handing over command to his West Point classmate General Mick Nicholson.

June 16, 2018. Afghan minister of the interior Wais Barmak talking to Taliban fighters on the street in Kabul during a three-day ceasefire for the Eid holiday.

Mural on a blast wall in Kabul by ArtLords showing the handshake on the Doha deal on February 29, 2020, between U.S. negotiator Zalmay Khalilzad and Taliban negotiator Abdul Ghani Baradar. (The eyes are part of an anticorruption drive.)

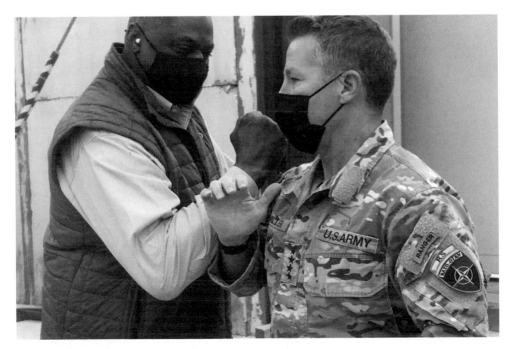

March 21, 2021. General Scott Miller greeting defense secretary Lloyd Austin in Kabul as a new administration grapples with the challenges of the long war. (Two weeks earlier Miller had become the longest-serving commander of U.S. and NATO forces in Afghanistan.)

Afghanistan has changed since the Taliban, with a vibrant music scene, and singers like Aryana Sayeed. But for the country's battered security forces, the long war has not ended.

TALKING TO THE TALIBAN—I

Success often starts with crazy ideas and comes in
unexpected bursts. And failure can happen regardless of
your best efforts.[1]
—Norwegian peace negotiator Alf Arne Ramslien

≡ FIVE FOR ONE

Sunday, May 31, 2014, was a bright, clear early summer's day in Washington, D.C. Bowe Bergdahl's parents, Bob and Jani, were in town for the annual Rolling Thunder demonstration, when black-clad bikers take over the Mall in a show of solidarity for soldiers who never came back from Vietnam and have no known grave—keeping a flame alive in the face of what they see as a long-term government conspiracy of silence. During the five years Bergdahl had been held, the bikers had taken up his cause. Bob and Jani were called in their hotel by Special Operations Command, who put the president on the line. "We got him," he said simply.[2]

A few hours later, they were embraced in a Rose Garden appearance, the president putting his eloquent shine onto the moment, calling the release a "reminder of America's unwavering commitment to leave no man or woman in uniform behind on the battlefield." A series of communications missteps that day would reduce the political space for deals to be done with the Taliban in the future. Details of the five-for-one prisoner exchange were tweeted by a *Washington Post* reporter seven minutes ahead of the first White House statement on Bergdahl's release. But the White House statement made no reference to the exchange or that five Taliban prisoners were now on their way to freedom in

Doha.[3] It made it look as if the administration had something to hide. In the Rose Garden appearance, Bob Bergdahl, wearing a beard he had grown to appeal to the Taliban, spoke three words in Pashto, which he had learned to try to communicate to the kidnappers, and the briefest Muslim prayer in Arabic in what was otherwise a personal and moving expression of gratitude to the rescuers. He said no more than a blessing and "I am your father," but this became the headline of the day.

When National Security Adviser Susan Rice, ahead of any investigation, said that Bergdahl had served with "honor and distinction," she compounded the sense of a White House that badly misjudged the public mood. Congress had passed a law to prevent any further releases from Guantánamo Bay without their approval, and Republican disapproval of the exchange was intense. Rumors were circulating of discontent at a Republican fundraiser some months before when Bob Bergdahl offered prayers for the families of those holding his son.

After five years in captivity, Bergdahl thought he had valuable intelligence information to share, but faced court-martial as a deserter. It would be impossible for him to get a fair hearing, as he had already been found guilty in the court of public opinion, on the evidence of a Taliban disinformation campaign claiming he had gone over to their side, complaints (never substantiated) that soldiers had died looking for him, and his father's demeanor—judged un-American. Donald Trump, campaigning for president, called him a "dirty rotten traitor" and said he should be shot, offering to drop him out of a helicopter over Afghanistan himself.

The reality seen by those who met Bergdahl had no traction in this atmosphere. His first debriefer after his arrest, Terrence Russell, told the reporter Sean Langan that Bergdahl resisted arrest from the beginning and was tortured for escaping twice. "It's absolutely crazy that anybody would consider him to be a traitor, when in captivity he was an honorable soldier."[4] After the second escape attempt, he spent three years in a cage, which his captors would pack up and reassemble every time they moved. The cage was suspended from the floor, and the bars cut into his feet. "I ended up having permanent nerve damage," Bergdahl told Langan, who had himself been kidnapped by the Haqqani network, and held for twelve weeks. "After the first winter in the cage," said Bergdahl, "I lost the feeling in my feet."[5] The release of Bergdahl did not lead to a wider negotiation with the Taliban. Even by 2014, it was not universally recognized across the U.S. administration that the war might end only with a peace settlement.

☰ "MISSION ACCOMPLISHED"

It took the U.S. a long time to realize they would need to talk to the Taliban. "Mission accomplished," the Bush boast, was a significant policy error at the beginning of the war. The Taliban were out of power but not destroyed and could not be wished away by the U.S. president declaring, "The Taliban no longer exists in Afghanistan." The illusion lingered in Washington that there was a military solution that could be prosecuted to the end without talks. Unmatched physical power was deceptive, bringing an unquestioned sense that America could prevail, that against the historical trend, this would be the guerrilla war where the more powerful conventional force could win.

Even discussion of negotiation was seen as weakness—a distraction from the business of war. Before the end of the first year of Bergdahl's long ordeal, a handwritten letter arrived at a U.S. base in eastern Afghanistan, brought by an intermediary trusted by both sides, purporting to come from Mullah Sangeen Zadran, the leader of the gang known to be holding Bergdahl. He requested talks in flawed English, saying, "I have something with me from the Americans." The response from the U.S. side was a letter back in Pashto, threatening to kill him and all his men if they did not surrender, and soon afterward, a bomb was dropped on the intermediary to close the channel down permanently.[6]

The pattern of not negotiating was set at the beginning of the long war when opportunities to pursue a settlement were ignored as America believed military victory was enough. After the Taliban were ousted from Kabul in November 2001, it was some weeks before they were defeated in the south. In the fast-moving events in December that included the international conference in Bonn, where Hamid Karzai was appointed as interim Afghan leader on the day he was nearly killed by a misdirected American bomb, he also met senior Taliban figures who said they wanted to hand over Kandahar peacefully.[7] In retrospect, it looks like a missed opportunity for a cheap peace deal—they would lay down their weapons and withdraw from further conflict in return for immunity from prosecution, and the freedom to return home. The Taliban group who met Karzai included Khairullah Khairkhwa, later one of the Guantánamo Five released in exchange for Bergdahl.

In the summer of 2002, after twenty-three years of war, the big tent of the supposedly all-Afghan Loya Jirga should have been big enough to include some Taliban delegates. Many of those who came to power then with international support had more blood on their hands than the Taliban but had not harbored al-Qaeda, so had a free pass. The former Taliban foreign minister Wakil Ahmed Muttawakil failed to persuade American diplomats in Kabul to engage in peace talks. Instead of heading a negotiating team, Muttawakil spent eighteen months in the Parwan detention center at Bagram.

The difference, of course, between the former warlords who the U.S. empowered after 9/11 and those they opposed was that the Taliban harbored America's enemies. "We will make no distinction," said President Bush, "between those who planned these acts and those who harbor them."[8] But in favoring the likes of Gul Agha Sherzai in Kandahar, America destabilized the south of Afghanistan. The aim of Bush's war on terror was to stop further terrorist attacks. But the narrow policy focus on hunting down the Taliban and al-Qaeda targeted the symptoms; it did not cure the disease. "Entire tribes were systematically targeted and denounced as Taliban members, leading to their arrest," wrote Felix Kuehn and Alex Strick van Linschoten, analysts who lived in Kandahar at the time.[9] The CIA's active promotion of southern warlords created the very conditions the Taliban needed. "Individuals and communities who saw themselves marginalized," wrote Kuehn and Strick van Linschoten, "reached out to the Taliban leadership that was regrouping across the border from Kandahar, in Quetta, Pakistan."[10]

☰ RED LINES

In 2009, the Riedel report was influential on the Obama administration's initial policy that continued the Bush stance of not talking to the Taliban. "Mullah Omar and the Taliban's hard core that have aligned themselves with al Qaeda are not reconcilable," wrote Bruce Riedel. "We cannot make a deal that includes them."[11] But Richard Holbrooke, who had been the architect of the Dayton peace deal that ended the Bosnian war, thought otherwise, and during the year, others in the administration began to share his view that there might need to be a political track of negotiations along with the military one. Holbrooke brought Barnett "Barney" Rubin into his office—a veteran of Afghan affairs, and a strong advocate for a peace track, talking to the Taliban. He had been an adviser on the Obama campaign in 2008 until told to resign by Riedel, who told him public advocacy of talking to the Taliban was "poison."

Riedel's view that the Taliban leadership were tied to al-Qaeda and irreconcilable defined policy for the first eighteen months of the Obama administration.[12] Rubin drafted a proposal for a peace track to be considered during the long discussions on Afghan policy through the fall of 2009. When it came to a crucial White House meeting on October 13, 2009, to decide the way forward, Secretary of State Hillary Clinton did not mention the proposal.[13] She was preparing her run for the presidency and did not want to appear weak on the Taliban. Rubin wrote, "Obama and Clinton each wanted the other to take the political risk of opposing the military option."[14]

But the idea of a peace process was gaining traction. In early 2010, shortly after President Obama's surge announcement of thirty thousand extra troops requested by General McChrystal, Doug Lute met Holbrooke, Rubin, and one or two select intelligence officials to chart a way forward. Lute had become convinced that the counterinsurgency strategy would not work because of the corruption of the Afghan government, the weakness of Afghan armed forces, and Pakistan's safe haven policy. While he was wary of Holbrooke's special representative role, which raised inevitable questions of hierarchy between them, the two shared skepticism about counterinsurgency. Early in his career, Holbrooke had written the section on "pacification" in Vietnam in the McNamara review, which became notorious when published in *The Washington Post* as the Pentagon Papers. Holbrooke told Rubin over dinner one night, "Though the government had changed the names of the programs since Vietnam, one thing had not changed: they still didn't work."[15]

Lute was looking for a plan B, to be deployed if the Taliban were not defeated by military force. He was helped by an intelligence assessment for the fall 2009 review of Afghan policy, which led to the surge. That assessment concluded for the first time that the Taliban and al-Qaeda were not joined at the hip.

Remarkably, it was not until that review that the question was asked. Lute said, "Our intelligence community is based on not making policy recommendations. So you have to be careful about the question you ask them." Internally, the intelligence assessment had developed since the early days after 9/11 when there was a U.S. disinformation campaign designed to prove close relations between bin Laden and Mullah Omar. The two were said to go fishing together, and Omar had apparently married bin Laden's daughter. None of it was true. Omar was wary of his troublesome guest. He even went to his ancestral village in Maiwand and took a fourth wife (the maximum allowed) to prevent bin Laden offering his daughter when it was suggested.[16] The Taliban leader issued a ruling that any fatwa issued by bin Laden was "null and void."[17] After 9/11, their relationship became more complicated. They were allies against the international coalition and bound by Pashtun hospitality rules. They led distinct organizations, but for nine years, it was enough that the Taliban refused to abandon al-Qaeda, for the U.S. conviction that the two were closely allied never to be questioned.

Failure in the early years to build channels of communication with the Taliban had consequences as the mood changed toward talks. The deaths of seven CIA operatives at Camp Chapman, a remote base close to the Pakistan border, in December 2009, showed the risks. They were killed by a suicide bomber they thought they had turned. And as well as tragedy, there was farce. In 2010, a Baluchi shopkeeper persuaded British MI6 agents that he was the Taliban deputy commander Mullah Akhtar Mansour. He was even flown from Pakistan to Kabul in a NATO plane, but was called out when an Afghan who knew the real Mansour was brought into the process, and the fake Mansour promptly disappeared, but not before pocketing tens of thousands of dollars.

As the wind changed toward a more nuanced approach, Lute expanded his small group exploring peace talks to include the CIA and DOD, setting up an interagency "conflict resolution cell." Their first task was to lift a Bush-era prohibition on talking to the Taliban, which involved taking around twenty-five Taliban figures off the list of people facing U.S. sanctions. Then there were the red lines, the preconditions the Taliban would have to accept before there were talks—renouncing violence, severing links with al-Qaeda, and agreeing to the constitution. These were the same obstacles routinely imposed by those in power against insurgents ahead of peace talks. They were tantamount to a demand to surrender and were a clear obstacle to progress toward talks. Privately, Lute's group were now able to explore a talks process, finessing the red lines from preconditions into desirable end states. One of

Holbrooke's senior advisers, Jarrett Blanc, called it a "Jesuitical debate between the difference between setting a precondition and describing your minimum end state."[18]

While the U.S. had invested little in cultivating political contacts with the Taliban, some European nations had done far more. Some NATO allies, in particular the UK, Germany, and Norway, were pragmatic, knowing there was no clear victory to be won on the battlefield; all the military could do was shape the space for a negotiated peace. This had led to mistrust in the coalition, adding to the American sense that their allies were not really in the fight.

After his release from Guantánamo, the Taliban's former ambassador to Pakistan, Mullah Zaeef, lived openly in Kabul and was a potential intermediary as he retained close links with the organization. He came to the UK, where as well as meeting government officials, he went deer stalking in Scotland. It was an unofficial sidebar to the main visit, but the best kind of confidence-building. His eyes lit up when he was handed a rifle, and he shot two deer. He returned to Kabul carrying a bolt of Stewart tartan.[19] Norway, a traditional peacemaking nation, without any of the baggage of the U.S. or former European imperial powers, came closest to the Taliban. Their intermediary, Alf Arne Ramslien, claimed he even met Mullah Omar among a group of Taliban leaders in a secret location he believes was near Karachi in southern Pakistan.[20]

On one occasion, the Norwegian negotiators hosted emissaries from both the Afghan government and the Taliban in the same Oslo hotel, but the Taliban side pulled out ahead of the planned meeting. Norway's initiatives did not bear fruit at the time, although "success often starts with crazy ideas and comes in unexpected bursts" in peace negotiations, Ramslien told *The New York Times*. "And failure can happen regardless of your best efforts."[21]

Ramslien and his colleagues showed considerable courage, in particular going to the frontier region of Pakistan, where Western hostages were being held, and where *The Wall Street Journal* correspondent Daniel Pearl was murdered in 2002 while meeting Taliban contacts. The Norwegian embassy in Islamabad received a crudely worded threat, sent by Taliban members who did not approve of the process. "We will attack with chemical weapons and destroy all Norwegians."[22]

Norway encountered another block of granite in the middle of the

road toward peace talks—Pakistan. The Islamabad government continued to ride two horses, holding on to the need to use the Taliban to
have influence in Afghanistan, while supporting America's war. When
Norway and the UN began to put out feelers to bring a senior Taliban
leader, Mullah Baradar, to Kabul for talks with the government, Pakistan
arrested him.

In Afghanistan, General McChrystal was on-message as the policy
shifted, building consensus for negotiations among the troops in his
command in 2010. "We were visiting the Special Forces HQ in Bagram,
so he's among the guys he knows best," said his senior civilian adviser,
Matt Sherman. "And his whole thing was like going, 'Hey guys, you and
I have been killing these guys for years. And if I am open to talking with
them, then so should you. We all have killed them and they've killed us.
And if I can do this, you can do this.'"

But just as the Obama administration was feeling its way toward peace
talks, McChrystal was replaced by the American commander most convinced of the possibility of military force to prevail. General Petraeus's
Anaconda strategy was not about squeezing the Taliban to the negotiating table. It was about squeezing them, period. "You have to kill, capture
or turn the bad guys."[23] While Petraeus talked about "reintegration and
reconciliation," this was bottom up, not an attempt to engage with the
whole movement. What if the Taliban would not be turned or fractured?
There was no space in his policy for Lute's plan B.

In August 2010, a month after taking command in Kabul, Petraeus
told Holbrooke that it was too early to negotiate. "He wants to do it
only when the time is right, which he says will be next year," Holbrooke
recorded in his diary. "Frankly, I just don't believe him."[24] Holbrooke
was not against the need to put significant military pressure on the Taliban as long as the clear aim was to persuade them they needed to talk.
He derided "well-intentioned but misguided members of the European
and American left," who opposed an increase in troop numbers. "The
chances of success of any reintegration or reconciliation policy will be
significantly increased by battlefield success."[25] But he wanted a clear negotiation route laid out. In December 2010, Holbrooke wrote a memo
titled "How Does This Thing End?" characterizing Petraeus as believing
it would show "weakness" to engage with the leadership of the Taliban.

"David does not foresee, and so far opposes, any real discussion with the leadership of the Taliban."[26]

☰ A HAMBURGER IN HARRY'S

If it came to talks, Holbrooke always presumed he would be the lead negotiator. Since his first work in villages in Vietnam in 1963, he saw diplomacy as best built from the ground. He showed courage going into Sarajevo under fire before constructing the Dayton peace deal that ended the Bosnian conflict in 1995, and in 1999, he sat with guerrillas while engaging in negotiations in Kosovo, crossing a Serbian front line to do so.[27] But he had made too many enemies in the administration. Clinton knew she could never persuade the White House to make him the lead on as delicate a subject as talking to the Taliban. There had been attempts to oust him from his job in early 2010, and Obama had left him behind in Washington when he went to see Karzai in Afghanistan.[28] Holbrooke was not the person to do a deal involving an Afghan president who could hardly be in the same room as him after Holbrooke's heavy-handed moves against him in the 2009 election.

Lining up the variable geometry of peace talks remained elusive. The Afghan government would talk only inside Afghanistan, in particular to reduce the influence of Pakistan. The Taliban as an organization would not talk to the Afghan government, which they saw as illegitimate, a "puppet" of the "invaders." And they would talk to the "invaders" only to secure the release of prisoners and discuss the withdrawal of foreign troops, a consistent approach they held in peace talks over the next ten years.[29]

When the Taliban re-formed in 2003—united now with the Haqqani network—they had a political council, military council, and administrative council. They appointed shadow governors and military commanders for every province in the country, with a clear hierarchy under Mullah Omar.[30] A coherent movement, with a political plan, they were now seeking international recognition and a political office to enable them to operate outside the region.

Karzai had held informal talks with a number of current Taliban commanders by phone, and occasionally in person. As America began to explore the contours of a peace process in 2010, he called a peace Loya

Jirga in Kabul, preparing his own nation for dialogue, calling the Taliban "brothers," and setting up a High Peace Council. The *jirga* faced a rocket attack—and a furious Karzai forced the resignations of two able ministers in the security sector in response. The High Peace Council was not as positive a step as it sounds. The first head, Burhanuddin Rabbani, was hardly a neutral bystander. He was the leader of the Jamiat-e Islami, the Tajik northern force who were the Taliban's main military opponent.

While on the beach in the South of France, Rubin was called by an old Saudi contact, who requested to meet in Dubai. When they met, he said the mainstream Taliban, the so-called Quetta Shura, under the leadership of Mullah Omar, wanted talks. They had appointed an intermediary, Tayyib Agha, in his thirties, one of Omar's closest advisers when in government and related to him by marriage. He spoke good English and was in the group who attempted to surrender Kandahar peacefully to Karzai in November 2001. When Pakistan heard about the initiative, they closed it down, persuading Saudi Arabia not to allow Agha to visit.[31]

Agha had also reached out to Germany through an Afghan exile living in Europe, who contacted the BND, German intelligence, in late 2009. After a face-to-face meeting with Agha in Doha in the spring of 2010, Germany brought in America. Before they agreed to meet, Lute's team wanted proof that Agha spoke for the leadership, and Rubin suggested some tests. First, the U.S. asked for proof of life of Bowe Bergdahl, the soldier kidnapped when he walked off his base in June 2009. That was significant, as it would show that Agha had a link with the Haqqani network, allied to the Taliban. The second test was a statement of support for "our brothers in Somalia," to be inserted into the annual Eid statement by the Taliban leader, Mullah Omar, in September 2010. Agha passed both tests.

In November 2010, Holbrooke's deputy, Frank Ruggiero, went to Munich, where a safe house in a nondescript Munich suburb was prepared for the first face-to-face talks. A German executive jet was waiting on the tarmac at Doha to bring Agha when there was a last-minute hitch. The German AfPak envoy, Michael Steiner, called Lute to say, "The deal is off."

"What do you mean, the deal's off?" Lute replied.

"Agha won't get on the plane because he's afraid that when it lands he will be in Cuba."

He feared he would suffer the fate of so many potential intermediaries in the past and end up in Guantánamo. Lute walked upstairs to the Oval Office, got in to see Obama, who gave his personal assurance for Agha's safety, putting his own credibility on the line.

Agha, who trimmed his hair and beard, unlike many Taliban, arrived in Western clothes, changing into traditional *shalwar kameez* for the first sessions of talks over two days.[32] Holbrooke's one instruction was to open the door to a process, make sure there was a second meeting, listen to what he had to say. But Agha felt there was an impatience on the other side to move too fast.[33] There was a mismatch of expectations. The Taliban had a limited agenda to secure prisoner releases and open a public political office to give them an address. The U.S. side wanted a swap for Bergdahl and to build a series of confidence-building measures toward a wider peace process. There was also a cultural difference—Afghan meetings can take a long time to get to the point.

Rubin was heading to Kabul the day Ruggiero came back from Munich, so they met for a debrief at Harry's Tap Room in Dulles International Airport. Holbrooke was so keen to hear what had happened that he made the trip out to the airport and heard the full account while Ruggiero devoured a burger. Eleven days later, just before Christmas 2010, Holbrooke died, collapsing with a ruptured aorta, on the seventh floor at Foggy Bottom, while actually in the secretary of state's office that he never occupied as his own.

▤ TOUGH CHOICES

Two months after Holbrooke's death, at a memorial speech in his name at the Asia Society in New York, Clinton made an important readjustment of America's position on peace talks that Holbrooke had wanted. She accepted in public what Holbrooke and Lute had been using as a working assumption in private. The three red lines—renouncing violence, severing links with al-Qaeda, and agreeing to the constitution—were pushed down the track. No longer preconditions, instead they were to be "necessary outcomes."[34] She called the move toward negotiations a "diplomatic surge," to go with the military and civilian surges.

The new AfPak envoy, Marc Grossman, was more methodical and process-driven than his mercurial predecessor. Gone were Holbrooke's creative pyrotechnics; in their place a steady series of meetings between

Ruggiero and Agha, around seven in all. The U.S. was not negotiating a peace deal. It was a clear policy of the Obama administration that the final settlement needed to be between the Taliban and the government, "Afghan-owned and Afghan-led." What was being constructed was a series of confidence-building measures—lifting of sanctions on Taliban individuals, the release of five Taliban leaders from Guantánamo, and the recognition of a Taliban office in Doha. In return, the Taliban would sever their links with international terrorism, release Bergdahl, and commit to talks with the Afghan government.

The talks faced opposition from hard-liners in the Taliban, as well as the U.S., who would move to block negotiations if they became public. Resentment in the Afghan government at being excluded led to the talks being revealed. On May 25, 2011, Afghan officials leaked the name of Tayyib Agha and the detail of German involvement in the U.S.-led process to the German magazine *Der Spiegel*. The government in Pakistan were already upset about the raid to kill Osama bin Laden earlier in the month, and Clinton immediately flew to Islamabad to lower the tension and persuade them they had not been cut out.[35] The Taliban leadership had kept the talks secret from their fighters but now needed to confirm they were talking to the U.S., justifying it as a way of securing the release of the Guantánamo Five.

After a gap, the talks resumed again in August. Agha brought a letter purporting to come from Mullah Omar for Obama. He called on the U.S. president to make "tough choices" on reconciliation and to work to end the war.[36]

In September, it was America's turn to downgrade their involvement in the talks, after a daylong Haqqani assault on the U.S. embassy. Skeptics threw out anchors to slow things down. Blanc saw that as an inconsistent response. He was in the embassy when it was under attack and said it was "extremely unpleasant," but that did not mean they should stop the talks. "If the Taliban weren't capable of threatening US interests then we wouldn't bother to talk to them." Blanc prevailed, they returned to the table, and by December, Clinton was confident that they would be able to announce the opening of the Taliban Doha office at an Afghan conference in Bonn on the tenth anniversary of the first Bonn conference. But Karzai had other ideas. He had been kept informed by Grossman and Blanc every step of the way, but now he told Clinton he never knew what had been going on. He pulled the rug from under the talks, demanding they should end unless the Afghan government was represented. Since the whole process was designed to promote an Afghan lead, they could hardly go on. In March 2012, the Taliban closed the process down for good in response to the shooting spree by Staff Sergeant Robert Bales in the south, who murdered sixteen Afghan civilians in their homes.

☰ THE OFFICE

The year 2012 was wasted for those who wanted a negotiated settlement. But toward the end of the year, Qatar suggested a different approach, a new way of choreographing the sequence of events with the same goal of direct talks between the Taliban and Afghan government. If they could secure a statement from the Taliban severing their links with international terrorism, then the Taliban could open their office, and that would be used as the venue for talks on the prisoner exchange and then direct talks with the Afghan government. Karzai was due to come to Washington in early January 2013 for what would turn out to be his last visit as president. During the trip, Blanc met the Afghan foreign minister, Zalmay Rassoul, and the national security adviser, Rangin Spanta, in Blair House and succeeded in getting their agreement to restart talks. He flew directly to Doha to engage the Qatari government as mediators.

This time around, there were no direct talks with the Taliban, as Qatar brokered the deal, securing what Blanc called a "more or less acceptable" statement from the Taliban distancing themselves from al-Qaeda along the way. The subsequent opening of the office with a fanfare, live on Al Jazeera, and all the trappings of a government-in-exile, with the devastating effect in Kabul witnessed by General Joe Dunford, was not what Qatar expected.

The flag and sign calling this the office of the "Islamic Emirate of Afghanistan" directly challenged the sovereignty of the Karzai government. The U.S. knew this was not acceptable. Even a nondescript office was a lot for the Afghan government to swallow. The U.S. had pulled out their negotiating team, but Rubin was in Doha. He had been working for four years to bring the U.S. and the Taliban this far and did not want to lose the talks process over a nameplate. The official embassy vehicles were all out of commission, so he persuaded an American diplomat to drive him to the Taliban office in his own car. When they arrived, Rubin marched up to the Qatari police and insisted they call someone to take down the nameplate and flag, meanwhile calling everyone he could on his mobile. He refused to leave for forty-five minutes, until someone came out of the building and unscrewed the nameplate. He took a picture with his phone to send to the U.S. embassy in Kabul and to TOLO TV, to make sure the Afghan government would see it.

☰ AMERINE DIVERSION

By 2013, there were other attempts to secure the release of Bergdahl. Lieutenant General John Campbell, who would take over from Dunford as ISAF commander in August 2014, knew the inside track on efforts to find the missing soldier from his previous role as commanding general of the 101st Airborne in eastern Afghanistan. He also knew there was good intelligence showing Bergdahl was taken across the Pakistan border within three days of being captured.[37] In early 2013, as the army G-3, deputy chief of staff for operations and plans, Campbell was in a position to order a fresh look. He asked Lieutenant Colonel Jason Amerine to see what he could do. Amerine was the commander of the Green Beret unit hit while supporting Hamid Karzai in his attempt to rally southern tribes against the Taliban after 9/11. He was an all-American hero who had been featured in a video game for an army recruiting campaign.

By 2013, twelve years into the long war, there were a lot of contractors running around Afghanistan and the frontier region of Afghanistan funded by different programs, with contacts who could be mined. Through them, Amerine believed that rather than the five-for-one deal, the Taliban would be prepared to release Bergdahl and other Western hostages in exchange for Haji Bashir Noorzai. He was a Kandahar tribal leader lured to the U.S. under false pretenses and imprisoned on drug charges in 2005—along with lurid headlines that he was Afghanistan's Pablo Escobar. One of the richest landlords in Kandahar and leader of one of the most powerful and numerous tribes, Noorzai was a key backer of the Taliban from their emergence in 1994, seeing them as a Pashtun uprising against chaos. For him and other business leaders and power brokers in the south, the new movement provided a measure of stability to allow trade and commerce and stop the violence and banditry of the civil war years in the early 1990s.

Noorzai had also assisted the U.S. after the Soviet war, when he tracked down and returned Stinger surface-to-air missiles supplied to the mujahideen. And in 2002, after the Taliban collapse, he handed over fifteen truckloads of weapons, including antiaircraft guns, to U.S. forces. At the same time as this record of cooperation, there is little doubt that poppies and marijuana were grown in his fields, and he profited substantially from them. In 2004, he was lured to the U.S. by two Americans, "Mike" and "Brian," who identified themselves as officials from the Pentagon and FBI.[38] They told him they wanted to talk about terrorist financing and promised him safe passage to and from the U.S., but it was a sting. Soon after his arrival in New York, he was arrested by officials from the DEA and subsequently sentenced to life for drug trafficking.

Securing the release of a felon facing a life sentence was a complex maneuver, and Amerine faced skepticism across the administration. He had not done the exhaustive checks required to prove his contacts could deliver. He said the system never gave his plan a chance. "I didn't think it would be very difficult to negotiate his release, but we had a bureaucracy that was incapable of doing it."[39] In February 2014, his team had a meeting with the Taliban canceled with no explanation.

He went to Republican congressman Duncan Hunter, since he wanted to report the obstruction he had faced, believed illegal ransom payments had been paid for an attempt to release Bergdahl that failed. He found himself facing a criminal investigation for contacting Hunter over the failures in the efforts to release Bergdahl. Citing whistleblower protection, he fought off the charges and was cleared, and forced a DOD investigation into whether a ransom was paid, which would be illegal "if their effort constituted material support to terrorism."[40] The DOD Office of Inspector General's report did not substantiate the ransom claim but did find that the administration conveyed "misleading and obfuscatory" information about the case, so it was hard to reach a definitive verdict.[41] Jason Amerine retired with honor and received a Legion of Merit medal.

☰ THE DEAL

Toward the end of 2013, the Qataris came back to Blanc with a new suggestion: Why not just do the prisoner exchange as a single confidence-building measure, with the hope of building something out of it toward other talks? He put together a small team, and they requested a new proof-of-life video, which horrified those who saw it. Bergdahl's condition had deteriorated markedly, spurring efforts to get him out. Since this deal did not involve a wider Afghan peace process but just a prisoner exchange between the Taliban and the U.S., Blanc did not inform the Afghan government. And he kept the loop of people in the U.S. system who knew very small to prevent the process being sabotaged once again by leaks. The guarantor for the deal was the Qatar government, not the Taliban. The U.S. needed assurance that the Guantánamo Five would not immediately go back to the battlefield but would be monitored in Qatar.

In late May 2014, Blanc was in Qatar for what felt like another routine visit to negotiate the terms, when everything began to fall in place quickly. He stayed to close the deal. The last sticking point was that Qatar did not have a plane capable of the round trip to Guantánamo, and the Taliban did not want to fly in an American plane. As a compromise, Qatari government prosecutors were sent to Guantánamo to accompany the five back on an American C-17.

Then Blanc had the anxious wait for Bergdahl to be taken to the agreed pickup point. "That movement period was going to be one of the most dangerous for Bergdahl. We were always afraid that one of his guards was going to be unhappy with the order." All the moving parts fitted into place as designed. The Guantánamo Five were waiting next to the tarmac. Less than half an hour after the news came that Bergdahl was safely in the Black Hawk, they were on their way to Qatar.

The moment of maximum opportunity to move on to a more comprehensive negotiation could not be grasped because the political stars were not aligned. Blanc returned to Washington hopeful that he could build something. He now had a definitive answer to the question he was always asked by skeptics—"How can you be sure the Doha group is authoritative?" But the Republican backlash against Obama for the prisoner swap blocked further negotiations, while the Taliban were cruising on empty, with no fuel for more talks. Their leader, Mullah Omar, was dead, although that would not be revealed for another year, and there were no instructions for the next stage of negotiations.

On balance, the deal was a good one for the Taliban. They had recovered five senior leaders and now had a known address in Doha even if it lacked a nameplate and a flag. But they were not rushing to open talks with Kabul, where the political elite were tearing chunks out of each other in a fierce dispute over the presidential election result that consumed the whole of 2014. Blanc concluded, "I just think it's one of the many tragedies of the American adventure in Afghanistan that at this moment when we should have been able to get something going, the politics of all three parties fell apart."

PHASE FIVE
2015-2021

ENDGAME

AFGHANISTAN'S WAR

*Combat and war and transition, as you know, it's a
very complex thing.*

For me, it's not black and white.[1]

—General John F. Campbell

≣ WHO DO I TRUST?

In a large, red-draped meeting room upstairs in the Arg, the heavy, over-
stuffed chairs with gilded arms looked gloomy as ever. Three weeks after
Ashraf Ghani's inauguration in September 2014, he was meeting the
foreign media for the first time as president. A caricaturist for *The New
York Times,* in Kabul to sketch the first democratic handover in the history of Afghanistan, grumbled a little about the cheap ballpoint issued
by security, who had overzealously confiscated all writing equipment.
He settled into one of the gilt-armed chairs and turned out some pretty
good likenesses of the president.

We were a small group. I had one more year as the BBC correspondent, the last expatriate in a role that had been consistently staffed since
the Russian war in the 1980s—the world had wearied of Afghanistan.
Other news organizations were the same, cutting down staff. When the
call came from the Arg, most of the few remaining resident foreign press
were out of town, taking the first break possible after reporting the endless negotiations over creating a national unity government in the disputed election of 2014.

Ashraf Ghani is tall, lean, balding, with a close-trimmed beard, ready
smile, and quick mind. He eats little after an operation for stomach cancer. He has an academic mindset, working eighteen-hour days, proud of

absorbing large amounts of information. In that first briefing, he spoke of his influences and ambitions in government. He said he had learned from President Johnson, praising his capacity to build coalitions, in contrast to Eisenhower, who failed to cope with the fluid demands of political life. He was inspired by the ability of FDR to build a social consensus, as well as Lincoln's political wisdom. In twentieth-century history, he saw plenty of negative examples of what not to do, but South Korea and Singapore were two models he admired. He cited post-Franco Spain in 1975, Chile in the 1990s, and more obscurely, Finland in 1921, as other models. He was a new breed of Afghan politician—with no baggage from the Soviet war or the civil war before the fall of the Taliban, returning after 9/11 on a one-way ticket. He abandoned American citizenship to run for office, and when he won in 2014, he brought new hope to a country weary of war and the politics of the warlords. He had spent time in the World Bank, and he literally wrote the manual for the challenges he now faced, *Fixing Failed States.*

The ideas flew in an uninterrupted stream as he talked in theoretical terms about the way software companies live on the edge of chaos to make change. He wanted to learn from that to combat the Taliban and other networks of insurgents. Since they were inherently unstable, there was no point in using tactics developed in stable systems against them. This echoed the ideas of McChrystal, during his time commanding Special Forces in the region.

But the difference was in turning words into action. In contrast to the restless disruptive innovation of McChrystal's command, Ghani did not have the machinery available to put his plans into practice. Three weeks into the administration, he did not have the basics in place. There was, for example, no press officer for the president. This absence cut him off from the Afghan people and his international backers. Reporters faced a simple problem. Who did we call? I put the question to him at the end of the briefing. He said testily, "David, who do I trust? I don't want someone to defame me," as if there was literally no one in the country he could put confidence in.

One of his first decisions in government was to agree to the hanging of six men, five of them for a vicious gang rape of women returning from a picnic. There was widespread public demand for the executions but international disquiet over a trial that lasted less than a day. Ghani visited the notorious Pul-e-Charkhi jail, where the hangings took place, and the experience put reform of justice at the top of his priority list. He asked if I thought organizing a press office more important than sorting out the mess of Pul-e-Charkhi. It was an odd response—comparing two quite different functions. Without a media capability, the new president was making his job far harder. Smartphones are now widely held across Afghanistan, and Facebook is a universal tool of communication, alongside an impressive array of feisty and independent newspapers and TV and radio stations—one of the few real success stories of the post-Taliban period. Failing to harness the opportunities available felt like an unforced error, an own goal.

Ghani's staff found it hard to work the levers of power. With no precedent for a nonviolent democratic handover in Afghanistan, there were no transition documents and little clarity over which jobs were political appointments. He was saddled against his will in a national unity government with the other leading election candidate, Abdullah Abdullah, as the "CEO"—a post that does not exist in the Afghan constitution. The compromise was forced on him by Secretary of State John Kerry in a dozen visits to Afghanistan over the summer to broker a dispute over the 2014 election.

The lack of media capacity meant that quite important reform announcements, such as the recovery of much of the stolen money from the collapsed Kabul Bank, drifted out with no impact. Who did he trust? This was Ghani's Achilles' heel, reducing his opportunity to make the changes he could see were necessary to reform Afghanistan.

☰ DEAL WITH THE DEVIL

One of Ghani's early decisions was to make all provincial governors acting positions, with the aim of methodically confirming them one by one. This fatally weakened their power to act, to arbitrate in disputes, and to appoint new staff. The governor of the restive eastern province of Nangarhar, Mullah Attaullah Ludin, was a popular reformer, but found his power undermined when his post became "acting." Nangarhar Province took in the caves of Tora Bora, as well as the vital lifeline to Pakistan and the world through the Khyber Pass. Ludin was courageously acting against corruption and warlordism and had bulldozed illegal buildings in the provincial capital, Jalalabad, to settle a land dispute. This muscular approach against corruption required authority. He complained to Ghani, "I don't have the capacity and the power to implement reforms that I am expected to by the people." A deputation of worried elders from the province came to plead Ludin's case, but Ghani was unmoved. Shorn of power by his acting status, the governor resigned, and a reformist successor left less than a year later for the same reason. Two years later, Nangarhar was one of the places where the Islamic State group first seized a foothold in Afghanistan.

Politics is the art of the possible, securing consent, winning arguments, and often deciding between the least worst of two bad options—as Bismarck put it, "the art of the second best." Ashraf Ghani was not accustomed to the second best. Growing up, he was keen on individual sports—running, swimming, not team games. He may have had a theoretical understanding of the guile of LBJ and the wisdom of Lincoln, but lacked the political support to build an administration for a nation riven by decades of war.

There was no doubting Ghani's political ambition. In the summer of 2006, he ran to be UN secretary-general, but his candidacy got nowhere; Ban Ki-moon was elected unanimously by the General Assembly. In 2009, his first run for the Afghan presidency, he won around 2 percent of the votes cast, in a poll marked by low turnout and violence. Because of his long residency in the U.S. and fluency in English, his chances then were overestimated by some foreign media, and by Richard Holbrooke, in a colossal error of judgment that put the final nail into the coffin of his relationship with President Karzai. Ghani did not even finish third—that place going to the gutsy anticorruption campaigner Ramazan Bashardost, who had launched his campaign from the tent in the park in Kabul. Bashardost had no rich backers and fought for every vote, campaigning village to village across the country in a battered Toyota Corolla with no security.

Ghani was written off by the old warlords, now so firmly entrenched back in power. To them, he was as derided as one of the "doctors without borders," highly educated returnees with no war record—not really Afghans.** What turned him into a more credible candidate in 2014 was

---

** This is a play on words of the English translation of the medical charity Médicins sans Frontières.

his appointment by President Karzai as the main civilian representative in the transition of provinces from NATO to Afghan military control after 2012. Ghani went from city to city, making speeches and contacts, building the potential for a better run in 2014, but not constructing a political party or movement in the Western sense. He never saw the need for that. To make certain of votes from the north, where Pashtuns are in a minority, he did a deal with the devil, giving the most prominent northern warlord, General Abdul Rashid Dostum, the leading vice-presidential slot on his ticket,[2] a move that severely questioned Ghani's reformist credentials.

Dostum had a checkered history, beginning as a private soldier in the Soviet-backed Afghan army, and rising to command them in the north, transforming the force quickly when Soviet forces withdrew in 1989 into a personal militia—fiercely loyal to him and his Junbish political movement. This force changed sides often during the civil war years and was as responsible as any for the destruction of Kabul before the arrival of the Taliban. They were feared and known out of their hearing as the *kilim-jans,* literally "carpet men," since when they came they rolled up everything in the house and took it away. Dostum had a ruthless reputation for crushing opponents under tank tracks. I spent some time with him shortly before the Taliban took the north in 1997, to film a profile, and he arranged an inspection of his praetorian guard, lined up in front of armored personnel carriers, before leaping onto the APCs and racing toward some open ground to play *buzkashi,* the fierce wild contest between men on horses for control of the carcass of a calf. Dostum himself mounted a giant horse and spent some time in the mêlée of younger riders, crashing into each other in the dust.

He had a weakness for very expensive Scotch whisky and by 2014 was a bloated caricature of his former warrior self. Before the campaign, Ghani went north to negotiate terms with Dostum. Ghani settled in a room in a large, soulless hotel in Shebargan, calling up Dostum and other local warlords one by one. After one meeting, Dostum came down into the lobby, slumped into a chair, and said, "He just doesn't listen."[3] In his 2009 campaign, Ghani had called Dostum a "known killer."[4] But now he was convinced Dostum had "tired" of war, saying in a BBC interview, "National reconciliation is our key goal. We must avoid the politics of refusal."[5]

Without any real role as vice president, Dostum continued his warlord ways, competing for influence across the north of the country, sometimes violently. Three years after the election, he fled to Turkey, facing investigation for the alleged brutal torture and kidnapping of a political opponent, Ahmad Ishchi, at his central Kabul home. Ishchi, the former governor of Jowzjan Province, said he was sodomized with the barrel of an assault rifle, and Dostum threatened to rape him himself.[6] For the next year, until he was able to return still theoretically with the post of vice president, Dostum held court in Turkey with others disaffected by Ghani's rule, including some ministers from Ghani's government, revealing the depth of failure of the national unity government project.

The ploy of allying with this rogue secured the election for Ghani, but it empowered a man who would become a dangerous force at the heart of the administration. Ghani's government had a troubled start—uneasily sharing power with his rival in the election and with an unstable and violent warlord as his vice president.

☰ IN EXTREMIS

General John F. "JC" Campbell, who took over from General Dunford in August, put his packet of three-by-five cards on his office desk in Kabul, each bearing the name and personal details of those who had died under his command in Afghanistan. He had served there twice before, in Kandahar in the winter of 2002, as more troops were sent in the realization that the war might not be over soon, and commanding the 101st Airborne in the east in 2010 at the height of the surge, the only division-strength deployment in the long war. He also had long experience commanding in Iraq—an illustrious career that nearly did not happen.

Campbell initially wanted to follow his master sergeant father, Ernie Campbell, into the air force, attracted by post-Vietnam air force training academy incentives in the mid-1970s, including a Corvette sports car. But salt tablets he was taking as a high school soccer player in California put up his blood pressure, and he failed the medical. Off the tablets, he reapplied to a number of military colleges and was accepted to West Point, not enjoying it much at the start. He said, "I wasn't sure I wanted to go in the army, but what I did know is they paid for my education." He thought he would do the minimum commitment, a five-year commission. He stayed for nearly thirty-seven years.

In command in Kabul, he had just a few weeks with President Karzai before the change of administration. Ghani's arrival pressed reset on the relationship. He had raised his family in the U.S. and spoke appreciatively of American and international support for Afghanistan. "Every time he talked," Campbell said, "he talked about the sacrifice that the coalition, all the forces made." Karzai retired to a compound adjacent to the Arg, "not in government but still a big factor we had to deal with." He could be a problem or an asset.

Campbell knew the value of good personal relations and saw President Ghani almost every day, including visiting his home late into the night, giving him detailed written reports of a length and density Karzai would not have read. Like Dunford, Campbell would wear dress uniform for the meetings, respecting the office and the man who held it. He established secure phone lines so he could speak directly to Ghani and Abdullah, and a new building was put up for the Afghan National Security Council with American money, its glass and marble slabs shimmering incongruously against the thick stone outer wall of the Arg complex, close to the grand main gate originally built for an elephant procession. Inside was a room with VTC connections to all the Afghan corps commands. Campbell's prominence in TV coverage of the meetings led Afghan media to call him the "real Afghan defence minister."

Afghan ownership of their own war was a work in progress. The final NATO summit for the International Security Assistance Force (ISAF), in Newport, Wales, in September 2014 revealed the shaky foundations of the security they had built. The soldier sent to carry the Afghan flag in a parade claimed asylum as soon as he arrived in Britain and disappeared. As overnight replacement, Colonel Zia Karimi, General Sher Muhammad Karimi's son, then on an advanced officer training course in the UK, was woken and bundled into a cab, arriving just in time to head the parade.

On December 28, 2014, in a low-key ceremony on a cold basketball court inside the Kabul military base, Campbell rolled up one flag and unfurled another. ISAF, born at the post-Taliban Bonn conference thirteen long years before, was no more. The new flag, in green, had the letters RS written in white, for Resolute Support, with "Train, Advise, and Assist" written in Dari round the bottom. NATO's combat mission ended, not with the defeat of the enemy but on the timetable.

Campbell knew the next phase would not be as tidy as rolling up a flag.

"Fighting a war based on a number, a headcount, you know, boots on the ground, was very, very difficult as opposed to having a plan, a strategy and then following that plan or strategy." Just as the long war began in 2001 with a lack of clarity over command and control and the object of the mission, so at the end there was improvisation by troops on the ground to deliver effect, without real understanding by those who sent them.

About a third of the 9,800 U.S. troops under Campbell's command were engaged in counterterrorism missions against the Taliban leadership and the remnants of al-Qaeda, with Operation Enduring Freedom now rebadged as Freedom's Sentinel, but he could see that the distinction between this and the more limited authority to use lethal force only in self-defense for the majority of his troops on the train, advise, and assist mission of Resolute Support was not always clear. An ISAF spokesperson used an image like a Russian doll to explain the relations. "Think of it as a big box marked RS and inside that you have a small box marked Freedom's Sentinel but inside that box you have two smaller boxes marked Resolute Support and another one marked counterterrorism."[7] Putting the NATO mission inside the Freedom's Sentinel box unnerved allies who were remaining for a strictly noncombat mission. They had signed up to train Afghan troops, not fight alongside them. The continued presence of more than forty nations, half in NATO, was a vital element in the post-ISAF campaign plan. Italians in the west, Germans in the north, and Turks at the Kabul airport were essential pillars of the international operation. But they were not there on a combat mission.

During the months before the "end" of combat, there were several meetings in the White House over when troops would be able to use lethal force in the future. Campbell wanted rules clear enough for the "private or sergeant on the frontline, where he's faced to make a split second decision whether he shoots or doesn't shoot civilian, friend, foe." He pushed back against the instinct of Obama's advisers for a checklist or the need to refer all decisions upward, telling them, "Don't give me fifteen things I've got to have to check, check, check, check."

Discussions centered round the words *in extremis.* Beyond the right of self-defense in the case of imminent threats, Campbell wanted the ability to act when pressure was "in extremis." When a White House counsel objected, as this stretched the self-defense rules, Obama intervened. "Hey, let me give you a steer here. If we have folks in harm's way, we're going to protect them." Turning to Campbell, he said, "John, that's good enough for me. I'm going to authorize you for that use of force."[8]

Campbell's legal adviser, navy captain Pat McCarthy, was instrumental in expanding the ability to operate against long-range threats like truck bombs, where there was actionable intelligence. And after many weeks of argument, he successfully made one further crucial change—U.S. troops would be able to defend Afghan troops too "in extremis." The thought of being in an advisory capacity with Afghan forces but not being able to bring in close air support if they were in danger was an uncomfortable one for Campbell. "I knew from the very beginning that if the Afghans didn't have some sort of capability, their own air force or airpower, it would be a very long hard haul." McCarthy saw some in the White House as unrealistic about the situation faced by troops on the ground. "It was almost as if they thought somehow, we would keep 9,800 folks there, we'd train the Afghans and we could do it with clean, white, lily-white gloves."

The immediate impact of the "end" of combat operations was dramatic. In January and February 2015, the U.S. dropped seventy munitions from the air, less than half the total for the same months the year before and a tenth of what was dropped in January and February 2011 at the peak of the surge. As the Taliban inevitably probed the capacity of Afghan forces, not taking a winter pause, Campbell was assisted in his desire for a more robust response by the new Afghan president. That the transformation in the relationship was more than symbolic became clear when Ghani lifted Karzai's restriction on Afghan forces calling in U.S. air strikes. By October 2015, more munitions were dropped than in the same month in 2013, during the "combat" years.

Campbell denied media reporting that he was going beyond what was allowed. "I understand my authorities and what I have to do with Afghanistan's forces and my forces." The decision to use lethal force was solely American. Officers from allied nations were in the command center, watching images from drones, when decisions were taken to use munitions, but they were not in the chain of command. It led to what McCarthy called "some spirited conversations."

☰ ATTRITION

In the early months of 2015, General Karimi had one last major task to fulfill for his country. As head of the Afghan army, he visited the five

corps commands to formally mark the moment this became Afghanistan's war. NATO had held moving transition ceremonies before the
"end of combat operations" the year before to hand over the war to
Afghanistan. The events in 2015 were all-Afghan affairs. The old warrior had the unmatched record of serving at a senior level under every
Afghan administration for fifty years—through a coup, a revolution, two
assassinations of leaders, an invasion, an unstable foreign-backed government, a civil war, and even the Taliban for a short time, before fleeing just
once, and returning soon after 9/11 to rise to the top as chief of army
staff. He might have finished this extraordinary career as defence minister when Ghani appointed him to his first cabinet. But as if to prove
they were more corrupt than any in the last decades of disruption and
war, the elites in parliament, detached by stolen wealth from the reality
of the poverty of their country, refused to endorse the appointment of
this great public servant. He would not pay the bribes needed to secure
his post.

Standing in front of thousands of troops on parade with armored
vehicles and helicopters, observed by viewing stands full of watchful
elders, the tall, barrel-chested general told them that while grateful for
ISAF's support, this was now their fight. "It is for us to defend our
homeland, to fight alone for Afghanistan." At the end of the speech, the
massed ranks responded with a deep-throated triple roar of *"JOUAND,
JOUAND, JOUAND"*—literally "Life, Life, Life"—the Afghan army
battle cry. There was no doubting the public demonstration of morale,
but this was an army that was losing lives at a rate that would be unsus-
tainable for any modern Western country. As Afghan forces took on the
war for themselves, their casualties rose to a post-2001 peak in 2014,
the last year of formal NATO combat operations, and then continued
to rise. There were 5,523 deaths in the first six months of 2016, and although the losses were rarely reported in the Afghan media, everybody
knew what was going on.

Internal flights from Helmand or Kandahar would be delayed for
military coffins to be loaded in after the civilian baggage. At the Four-
Hundred-Bed military hospital in Kabul, the morgue was filled to overflowing, and a sad line of taxis and cars waited to tie a coffin to the roof
to be driven home for burial. Many relatives would take off the Afghan
flag, given to honor their dead, and leave it behind. With widespread

Taliban influence in rural areas, identification as a military family could be a death sentence.

The attrition rate meant that at the time America was spending most on building Afghan forces, the Afghan army was actually declining. To try to fill the gaps, they raised the maximum age of enlistment from thirty-five to forty. About one-third of the force was taken out every year by death, discharge, or desertion. Although new recruits were going through training as fast as possible, the army was 25,000 short of its target of 195,000. And in many places, the ranks were thinner than the figures suggested, as "ghost soldiers" were entered into the register, their wages taken by senior officers. Attempts to introduce electronic direct payments had been blocked for years by corruption and institutional inertia. This turnover made it very difficult to build advanced warrior skills or promote good NCOs. As the congressional watchdog SIGAR put it, "Such high attrition increasingly created a military with little to no training."[9]

Low morale because of the pressures of the war led to an increase in insider attacks—green on green—which took the lives of more than 250 Afghan soldiers in the first eighteen months after the end of NATO combat operations.[10] This meant the army's leaders could not trust their own troops. At the parade in Helmand where General Karimi spoke so passionately about Afghan pride, the recovery of sovereignty, and the need to protect the homeland, armed soldiers from Special Forces units stood at every ten yards in a line facing the troops to protect the elders and the senior officers from the risk of attack.

☰ TEN-FEET-TALL TALIBAN

While the new model Afghan army was now being tested as never before, America was heading for the exit. In terms of the surge bell curve, the American mission was now leveling out. The only remaining question was the thickness of the rim of the bell. Campbell liked to talk of a "glide path" out,[11] but it had a clear end, that landing point of "embassy level" military cover set for the end of 2016. At both ends of the surge, the strict timelines and troop numbers set by President Obama left little room to maneuver. When pressed to criticize the president for setting a firm deadline by Senator John McCain, Campbell dodged the question, quoting General Dunford, who said, "he hoped that there'd be more ambiguity here."[12] The outgoing Kabul ambassador, James Cunningham, was blunter. "The timeline is probably too short and the rate of with-drawal is too steep."[13]

On his appointment, Obama told Campbell not to hide bad news and to remember the context. When he was asking for resources for Afghan-istan, the president had "the whole world to worry about." Campbell told him, "Mr. President. I got it." The first White House meeting to discuss post-2016 troop levels, in April 2015, did not go well for him. The deadline of "embassy level" troops would then be only a year away. Deputy National Security Adviser Denis McDonough said they should "re-imagine" the conflict in Afghanistan, implying they should allow the Taliban to take over part of the country, which Campbell did not see as a helpful way forward. Vice President Joe Biden continued his push to end the campaign, and Defense Secretary Ash Carter, only recently appointed, did not back Campbell's aim to keep a larger presence for longer.

The case for a continuing presence was made in a series of papers put together by the head of Campbell's advisory group, Cliff Trout. He put five options on the table, with assessments of the risks attached to each. They ranged from 1,200 troops at embassy level, up to 8,500, which would keep a headquarters in Kabul, with troops in Bagram, Kandahar, and two bases in the east. This presumed that Italy would keep troops in the west, Germany in the north, and Turkey at the Kabul airport. Trout said that rather than asking for an increase for more offensive capacity, the plan was to build the case from the bottom up, defining "a pathway of how we can reduce the force presence for the United States over the long term."[14] The memory of McChrystal's battles for more troops in 2009 were fresh. Campbell knew that if they went in demanding a large increase, they would get nowhere. "That was a non-starter and would fall on deaf ears, and it would be like crying wolf."

There were several ghosts in the room during the deliberations—from the British garrison in Kabul left with too little support and slaughtered in the winter of 1841, through the staircase on the roof in Saigon, and the 2012 incident in Benghazi, when Ambassador Chris Stevens and three other Americans were killed when the consulate was overrun. Na-tional Security Adviser Susan Rice was blamed for what looked like a cover-up of the Benghazi incident. The implication of the lowest of Campbell's five options, with the clear risks to troops at "embassy level," was uncomfortable for her. "It becomes very difficult," said McCarthy, "especially for someone like Susan Rice, who's already had Benghazi hung around her neck, to ignore the commander in the field who says if you do that, that will be high risk to mission and force."

The way Campbell brought Carter round when he came to Kabul in the spring was to point out that the reductions to 1,200 troops, the "embassy level" option, would not provide any regional counterterrorist capacity. That got Carter's attention. The U.S. would lose the opportunity to use Afghanistan as a launchpad for attacks, which might be needed when facing instability in nuclear-armed Pakistan.

After his two terms, Obama wanted to be able to say he had closed down Bush's other war. But he recognized the counterterrorism imperative, and Campbell continued to press his case, believing Afghanistan deserved it. "They wanted our help. They wanted to get rid of the Taliban. They wanted to have a democratic and peaceful and secure, stable Afghanistan. We had a government that wanted to work with us, I felt we needed to give that a chance."

Obama's change of course was announced in a low-key event in the Roosevelt Room in the White House in October 2015. The president was flanked by Biden and Carter, and the chairman of the Joint Chiefs, General Joe Dunford, two weeks into his new post. Still setting himself against "endless war," Obama conceded that 5,500 troops would remain beyond the end of 2016. He was persuaded that some troops should remain but did not take the maximum option of 8,500. One further base in the east would close, leaving less oversight of the Pakistan border. Close to the end as at the beginning of the long war, successive administrations continued to frame the Afghan project narrowly. Just chasing terrorists at the beginning rather than focusing on the environment that created them was one reason why the war took so long. The mantra that this was not a nation-building project remained intact.

Campbell returned from Washington after the announcement and laid into Afghan forces for their failure to manage the situation for themselves. At a meeting of the Afghan National Security Council, he said, "The Taliban are not Ten Feet tall." He said, "The blame game must stop now . . . If I hear one more policeman complain about the army or vice versa, I will pull my advisers immediately."[15] In a transcript of the meeting obtained by *The Washington Post,* the Afghan army chief of staff,

General Qadam Shah Shahim, admitted that recruitment could not keep up with deaths and desertions. The Afghan army were in danger of losing Helmand Province. The CEO, Dr. Abdullah, admitted, "We have not met the people's expectations."

Helmand Province had totemic status. Much British and American blood was spilled in taking it. In the meeting, the head of the NDS intelligence service, Rahmatullah Nabil, said that for the Taliban to have retaken much of the province was their "biggest recruiting tool." But with 40 percent of Afghan armored Humvees in Helmand out of action because of poor servicing, troops were stuck at vulnerable checkpoints—sitting ducks for the Taliban. Campbell tried to rally his Afghan partners, saying the U.S. was as guilty as they were of "just putting our finger in the dike in Helmand." He offered increased U.S. support, but reclaiming ground was the responsibility of Afghan forces. "You have much more equipment than they do. You're better trained."

Less than a year after General Karimi had addressed the gathering of elders and Afghan soldiers in the former U.S. and UK bases at Camp Leatherneck/Bastion, to mark the handover of Helmand to full Afghan control, the area surrounding the huge desert base was effectively under Taliban control, particularly at night. Campbell sent U.S. troops back into "the same camp within a camp because it got so bad in there."

☰ KUNDUZ HOSPITAL

On October 3, 2015, Campbell touched down at Joint Base Andrews ahead of the final National Security Council meeting on Obama's troop decision, to be told of one of the worst mistakes of the war. While he was in the air, an AC-130 had attacked a hospital run by the French agency Médecins sans Frontières (MSF) in Kunduz in the northeast, killing forty-two people. There were running battles for the town for most of 2015—with the Taliban twice holding the center—the first time they had taken a provincial capital since 2001. U.S. special operators, who had arrived to shore up local forces four days before, had to turn back retreating soldiers at gunpoint at the airport. Their plane was nearly overwhelmed in what they said was like "the scene from the Saigon embassy."[16] After securing the airport, they turned to the city, mostly in the hands of the Taliban. The hospital was in the area under their control. There is no doubt that some Taliban fighters were among the patients, but they respected the neutrality of the hospital; they were not using it as a base.

The night of the attack was clear, and the hospital was one of the only buildings in town with lights on, as it had a generator. Two MSF flags had been placed on the roof that day, as well as their flag flying at the gate. The hospital was overflowing with patients from the fighting, who spilled into corridors. One hundred MSF staff were sleeping in the basement, taking refuge from the fighting in the city. An internal MSF inquiry found that "those who were awake after 10:00 p.m. report having noticed how calm the night was in comparison to the intense fighting of the previous days."[17] Guilhem Molinie, the head of MSF in Afghanistan, had written to a contact in the Third Special Forces Group, the U.S. unit deployed to Kunduz after the fall of the city, to confirm the hospital's neutral status, and sent the GPS coordinates to a dozen Afghan and international entities in the country. But this was not enough. The AC-130 is a huge, slow-moving airplane, stable enough for cannons, a Gatling gun that will fire 350 rounds in twelve seconds, and a 105 mm howitzer, and it devastated the hospital complex during several runs, lasting more than an hour.[18]

From the moment of the first shots, MSF contacted anyone they could, from Resolute Support headquarters in Kabul to the political adviser of the chairman of the Joint Chiefs, but they could not make it stop. At 2:59, forty minutes into the attack, MSF received a text from RS saying, "I'll do my best, praying for you all."[19] The shooting did not stop for another twenty minutes. Amid scenes of horror, an MSF doctor died on an office desk, turned into a makeshift operating table, as colleagues tried in vain to save his life.

In Washington, Campbell initially stated that U.S. troops were under threat when the air strike was called in, the information he was given.[20] Initial media attempts to uncover what happened were confused by Afghan government statements that there were Taliban in the hospital. In a brief news conference at the Pentagon a few days later, Campbell changed his account to say that Afghan forces near the hospital were under fire and called in the strike. His style was to allow command decisions to be taken at the right level, not approving every action. "I didn't keep everything to myself. I would make sure that my commanders on the ground had the ability to make some tough calls as well."

Six weeks later, back in Kabul, Campbell announced the results of an investigation he had ordered, headed by someone outside his command, and including a special operator and an AC-130 pilot. Their report showed a catalog of errors. The aircrew had not followed the rules of engagement, since the strike was called without eyes on the target and was unnecessary for force protection. Calling in an air strike of this sort against a Taliban target was an offensive operation, not then authorized for U.S. forces.

The investigation found that the aircraft had initially taken off to support Afghan troops who were under pressure, but its mission changed to target an Afghan NDS building in the hands of the Taliban. The coordinates the crew were given took them to an empty field because of a technical malfunction, so they attacked the "closest, largest building," the well-lit hospital. Worse, through computer failure, the crew had lost the ability to send or receive information.[21] The TF-714 command at Bagram were looking at the building that was the planned target, and inexplicably, the control room at Resolute Support in Kabul were looking at another building. When they began to receive desperate messages from MSF to stop the attack, they sent a Predator drone to circle round, and it saw the attack on the hospital a long way from the target, but they took no action to stop the onslaught of fire. Calling it a "perfect storm" of errors, Campbell recommended that several people be relieved from their positions, but was overruled by Special Operations Command, who took no disciplinary action.

≡ NOT THE LAST FOUR-STAR

Campbell was called the last four-star in a CBS *60 Minutes* film by Lara Logan. She reported that one troubling factor in the conflict remained unchanged since she interviewed him in the east in 2010—Pakistan's continued backing for the Taliban. Like so many commanders before him, Campbell had tried to influence the relationship with Pakistan so the Taliban could no longer have the safe haven they had enjoyed. He talked weekly to the army chief Raheel Sharif and visited when he could. Pakistan claimed it was doing what it could to prevent insurgents from crossing. In 2014, the Pakistan Army launched a big offensive across the frontier region against insurgents, whose actions now threatened to destabilize the Pakistani state. They pushed back thousands of

Afghan refugees, many of whom had lived in Pakistan since the 1980s, and they began to fence the frontier, causing clashes with Afghan troops as the boundary line was disputed. But there were still big questions over whether Pakistan had also acted against the Haqqani network. Sharif flew Campbell over the Haqqani heartland, Miramshah. The town was deserted after the offensive, but they did not land. Campbell flew over a madrassah known to be under Haqqani control, wondering if they had "let the senior Haqqani network leave before they actually went in."

There was one authority to use military force he did not succeed in winning, and that was to go after the Taliban leadership. It was frustrating that the Taliban were on the offensive, but he could not respond in the same way. "That's why the whole Pakistan issue was such a big thing."

He would not be the "last four-star." On March 2, 2016, Campbell handed over command to his West Point classmate, General John W. "Mick" Nicholson Jr., who would command until September 2018.

Campbell retired from Afghanistan. Of all the U.S. commanders, only Joe Dunford went on to another military role. The post was so exposed, and the close contact with senior politicians over contentious issues always rebounded on Kabul. Campbell's frank advice to keep more troop in Afghanistan for longer, against the wishes of the administration, cost him a promotion.[22] He reflected that the administration's focus on troop numbers sometimes obscured the need to see the bigger picture of where U.S. long-term interests lay. "Where we failed as a government was seeing how Afghanistan could play a constructive role in the national security interest of the wider region." In a retirement ceremony with full honors, reviewing an old guard fife-and-drum parade in their Continental army uniforms, the army chief of staff, Mark Milley, called "JC" Campbell the "most respected four-star among us today."

ENDURING COMMITMENT

By 2017, the Afghan war effort seemed like a plane crashing on autopilot.[1]

—H. R. McMaster

☰ THE FAMILY BUSINESS

If General John W. "Mick" Nicholson Jr. had not been moving house on 9/11, he would have been at his desk in the Pentagon, one hundred feet from the nose of the plane that hit the building. His office was destroyed. "For me and for many of us it's personal," he said.[2]

Few Americans in uniform have spent as much time in Afghanistan since 9/11 as he had. In 2006, he was in the mountains of the east, commanding a brigade, where he introduced counterinsurgency principles ahead of the general change in doctrine. In 2008, he became deputy commander of ISAF forces in the south when the marines arrived in Helmand. In 2009, he headed the Pakistan-Afghanistan coordination cell in the office of the chairman of the Joint Chiefs of Staff, when Richard Holbrooke was hyphenating the two countries in his diplomatic role. In 2010, Nicholson returned to Kabul as deputy commanding general of U.S. forces and deputy chief of staff for ISAF. This long engagement in Afghanistan was followed by command of the storied 82nd Airborne Division; Nicholson was the first out of the plane over France when the division joined celebrations to mark the seventieth anniversary of D-day in 2014.

He developed close links with partners in India, and in Delhi visited the simple slab of stone marking the grave of the other General John Nicholson, who died fighting the 1857 Indian uprising against British colonial rule. The modern General Nicholson's background and experience were described as "unique" for the role of Kabul commander by Senator Mark Kirk at his confirmation hearing on January 28, 2016.

Nicholson called the military the "family business."[3] Three cousins and his daughter, Caroline, were serving. His father, John W. "Jack" Nicholson Sr., and his uncle Jim Nicholson fought in Vietnam, both served in the Department of Veterans Affairs, and Jim was the Republican Party national chairman through the 2000 election, which saw George W. Bush into the White House.

American public opinion may have believed Afghanistan a lost war, but not those most closely involved. "We do need to think about an enduring commitment to the Afghans," Nicholson said in his Senate confirmation hearing. His view, that America needed to stay the course, repeated in press conferences and in a further hearing at the Senate a year later, was shared by an influential group of thirteen former generals and diplomats who had served in Afghanistan. Led by John Allen, they wrote an open letter to President Obama arguing that troop levels should be kept at around 10,000 rather than cutting to 5,500 as he wanted by the end of his term. The group included all the generals appointed to command in Afghanistan by President Obama, apart from the two still serving—Nicholson and General Joe Dunford, who had become chairman of the Joint Chiefs of Staff in October 2015.[4]

Since the end of 2014, when the combat mission ended on the timetable, support for Afghan forces was designed to be at only the most senior level, in the six corps headquarters round the country. Pulling advisers out from further down had a damaging effect—in particular on unglamorous but essential areas like maintenance and logistics. Campbell began to stretch the envelope of support below the corps level when he sent troops back to Helmand. They took the units in the Afghan 215th Corps out one by one, completely refitting them with U.S. support before sending them back into the fight. The decision stretched his manpower capacity as well as his authorities, the rules that governed use of force. He needed to provide troops "out of hide" since he was given no new forces.

In July 2016, when he had seen Nicholson's first review, Obama made the announcement he had avoided so far. Far from the war ending, there would be an expansion of the mission, with "tailored support" for Afghan forces at a lower level. For the first time since 2014, conventional U.S. troops would be in the field with Afghan forces who were fighting the Taliban. And other NATO nations also agreed to equip "expeditionary advisory packages" to advise below the corps level.

General Joe Dunford, chairman of the Joint Chiefs of Staff since October 2015, said the change meant that the U.S. and its allies would have the right number of troops, working at the right level, providing advice "where it matters to advance the campaign." There were risks in putting more troops in harm's way, judged worth it for the overall counterterrorist objective. Until then, among Afghan forces, there was "a perception, even if it wasn't always a reality," said Dunford, "that we were holding back support."

The group of former generals and ambassadors wrote a second open letter ahead of the 2016 election, this time to the next president, calling for an "enduring partnership" with Afghanistan and troop levels to be maintained. "We should prepare and posture ourselves for what could be a generation-long struggle against extremism, with Afghanistan a key part of that struggle."[5] After the lengthy, cerebral debates in the National Security Council in the Obama years, there was a very different atmosphere in dealing with Afghanistan with the arrival in the White House of a very different leader in President Donald J. Trump.

☰ PLAN FOR VICTORY

The new president trusted his instincts over his advisers, and his instincts were to quit Afghanistan. It was a "loser war" he said in an infamous encounter in "the Tank," the secure meeting room in the Pentagon in July 2017. Surrounded by the flags of the most powerful military in the world, broken along one wall by *The Peacemakers,* a painting that depicted President Abraham Lincoln and his chiefs of staff in 1865, the president railed at their successors. "You're a bunch of dopes and babies," he is reported to have shouted to the assembled generals. "You're all losers."[6] The meeting had been called to find a way forward in Afghanistan and ranged more widely into U.S. global interests, angering the president, who wanted to withdraw from most of them. Trump said of Nicholson, who was not in the room, "I don't think he knows how to win." Dunford tried to explain the strategy of reducing the footprint while training Afghan forces, but was cut off with the words, "We don't win wars anymore." The tirade by a president who had dodged the Vietnam draft on questionable medical grounds challenged the most fundamental compact of those in uniform, that they obeyed the commander in chief. Only Secretary of State Rex Tillerson spoke up to defend the generals. "Mr. President, you're totally wrong. None of that is true." After the meeting, Tillerson was overheard calling the president a "moron."

Those trying to keep a coherent Afghan strategy together were already concerned about the president's open contempt for NATO. Reliance on NATO allies to cover the whole of Afghanistan was proportionally greater as the American presence reduced. Troops from Germany, Italy, the UK and Turkey were the largest contingents alongside American troops in Afghanistan. But during the 2016 election campaign, Trump had mused, "It's possible we're going to have to let NATO go," calling it a Cold War relic.[7] His first visit as president to NATO's gleaming new Brussels headquarters in May was disastrous. He gave no reassurance of America's continued resolve, instead calling on NATO countries to "pay up," saying, "Most of these nations owe massive amounts of money from past years."[8] This clearly misunderstood the nature of the alliance, which does not require members to pay dues but commit to spending 2 percent of GDP on their own defense. Other leaders laughed publicly, enraging the thin-skinned American president.

But only a month after the tirade in the Tank, Trump delivered a speech on Afghanistan that ticked all the boxes his generals wanted. The "grown-ups" in his White House, in particular the national security adviser, H. R. McMaster, and Defense Secretary Jim Mattis, both of whom had served in Afghanistan, had turned round the president's declared instinct for withdrawal. In a rerun of the conversations in 2009—the first year of the Obama presidency, which resulted in the surge—a new president who wanted to pull out of a war not of his making was persuaded to give it one more heave. Mattis made changes to the speech after the first draft from the White House adviser and speechwriter Stephen Miller came straight from the "America First" Trump playbook. Miller's draft lacked any reference to the role of allies and talked of "waging war on Afghanistan," not on terrorism.[9] Mattis put his speechwriter Guy Snodgrass onto it, telling him, "America first doesn't mean America alone."

On August 21, 2017, at 9:00 p.m., in front of his cabinet and an audience of troops at the historic Fort Myer, Arlington, Virginia, President Trump stood up to reset the Afghan campaign. The Snodgrass rewrite retained much of Miller's language, calling terrorists "nothing but thugs, and criminals, and predators, and—that's right—losers." Trump said there were "big and intricate problems" in the region, but "I'm a problem solver." He said the "American people are weary of war without victory," and he "shared their frustration." Things would change. "We are not nation-building again. We are killing terrorists."

Beyond the bombast, in the meat of the speech, Trump detailed the threats that had made him change his mind about pulling out—twenty-one foreign terrorist organizations in the region, the unresolved India-Pakistan nuclear standoff, and the language now came from Mattis, not Miller. "We will work with allies and partners to protect our shared interests." The war was not about a victory on the battlefield but building conditions for peace talks. "Military power alone will not bring peace to Afghanistan or stop the terrorist threat arising in that country. But strategically applied force aims to create the conditions for a political process to achieve a lasting peace."

Breitbart news agency, opponents of the war and backers of Trump's America First stance, reported contemptuously that the speech was a sign of "the swamp getting to him." Other reporting of the speech said the strategy had gone back to CT-plus, Vice President Joe Biden's plan rejected during the McChrystal review in 2009. But it was more than that. Mattis and Dunford were patiently constructing the enduring commitment to Afghanistan they wanted. Nobody knew if peace talks would happen. Meanwhile, "America will continue its support for the Afghan government and the Afghan military as they confront the Taliban in the field." Dunford saw the campaign as "an insurance policy" for the U.S., that he thought affordable in the medium term.[10]

The most important change in the speech, which Trump called a "plan for victory," gave Nicholson expanded authority to go on the offensive against terrorist and criminal networks across Afghanistan. "Micromanagement from Washington, D.C.," the president said, "does not win battles." Even before the speech, in the early summer of 2017, he had given Mattis the right to determine troop levels. Now he went further. "Retribution will be fast and powerful, as we lift restrictions and expand authorities in the field." To Dunford, the change meant that "the Afghans saw that they were getting all the support that General Nicholson could possibly provide."

The tight head count on uniformed troops led Nicholson to improvise, maximizing the number in frontline roles, while bringing in contractors behind them. This had the effect of significantly increasing costs, and reducing long-term capability, as troops who might have come to Afghanistan in maintenance roles were left behind. Nicholson liked to quote the example of a combat aviation brigade from the 1st Infantry Division, Fort Riley, Kansas. Pilots came to Afghanistan with their helicopters, but ground staff were left behind to keep the number of uniformed troops at the set level. "This contract for maintenance runs into the tens of millions of dollars," he said. "The soldiers who were trained to be mechanics are sitting back at Fort Riley, not having the opportunity to do their job. So this has a direct impact on Army readiness."[11]

"War is a contest of wills," Nicholson said. "Since 2011, we have announced we were leaving, and we were steadily drawing down our forces all the way until last December"—that is, until the end of the Obama presidency. He said that the new policy sent a different signal to the Taliban: "We will stay, and we will only leave based on the conditions being right."[12] The long, anguished debates over troop numbers were over. That was no longer the only metric that mattered. For the first time, the Afghan campaign was genuinely based on conditions, not on a timetable. By the spring of 2018, there were more than fourteen thousand U.S. troops in Afghanistan, 50 percent up on the figure at the beginning of the Trump presidency. They were not there to win the war as in the heady days of the surge but to set conditions for peace talks. Defense Secretary Jim Mattis thought the change in policy sent a clear message to the Taliban. "You will not win a battlefield victory—we may not win one, but neither will you—so at some point, we have to come to the negotiating table and find a way to bring this to an end."[13]

Another factor that made the continued presence of U.S. troops inevitable was the emergence of Islamic State in Afghanistan. President Ghani said that with the rise of Islamic State, "the situation has changed, the context has changed."[14] He talked up the threat, wanting to internationalize Afghanistan's plight to keep international troops in his country in the face of what he called a fifth wave of terrorism, "Terrorism 5.0." And al-Qaeda had not gone away. The chance discovery of a huge al-Qaeda training camp that took several days to destroy, in the trackless wastes of the southern Kandahar desert, was cited as another reason not to abandon Afghanistan.[15]

☰ BLACK FLAGS IN THE LAND OF KHORASAN

The first appearance of Islamic State in the region was a statement by a disaffected member of the Pakistani Taliban, Hafiz Saeed Khan, on January 11, 2015, in a video shot in the frontier region of Pakistan, in front of the IS black flag. There is little evidence that the early leaders of what became known as Islamic State–Khorasan, IS-K, were in contact with the headquarters of the "Caliphate" in Iraq. They were freelancing, changing the white flag of the Taliban for the black flag of IS to try to recruit fighters to the more violent cause. Within months, they formally joined the global movement, celebrating by beheading a police officer in Nangarhar in eastern Afghanistan.

The black flag and use of the term *Khorasan* were powerful lures for young men drawn to extreme violence in the name of religion. There is an Islamic prophecy that before the end times, the Mahdi, the returning messiah, will appear bearing black flags in the "Land of Khorasan," an old name for the region including western Afghanistan, a strip of Central Asia to the north, and the eastern part of modern Iran. Another story credits the black flag to Abu Muslim al-Khurasani, an eighth-century warrior famous for rising up against corrupt Arab Muslim rulers and founding a dynasty in the Khorasan region.[16]

A year after the emergence of IS-K, in a conflict where symbols matter, they staked their claim to be the main international jihadi opposition to the West, moving into the former al-Qaeda cave complex at Tora Bora. As the capacity to operate in Iraq and Syria reduced, Afghanistan's importance to the organization grew. When Khan, the first leader, was killed in a drone strike, Nicholson tracked intelligence showing consultation over the succession with the headquarters of IS in Iraq. "There is a degree of command and control provided from the parent organization to the satellite."[17] By 2018, the Center for Strategic and International Studies were reporting that Afghanistan was the "top destination for foreign terrorist fighters in the region, as well as fighters leaving battlefields in the Levant."[18]

American focus on killing leaders was relentless. In the first three months of 2016, up to 80 percent of U.S. air strikes in Afghanistan were against IS targets, mostly in Nangarhar. But they were still far less intense than against IS in Syria and Iraq. David Petraeus, one of the signatories of the two open letters, cowrote an op-ed in *The Wall Street Journal* calling for U.S. troops to once again go on the offensive against the Taliban in the field. "We need to take the gloves off."[19] He wrote that the U.S. was failing to use its asymmetric advantage.

Nicholson changed that. The number of bombs and missiles dropped from the air in 2017 was five times the number in 2015, the first year of the "post-combat" operation. And they almost doubled again the following year—to 7,362, or 20 a day—the highest annual total of the war, far higher than when there were 150,000 troops in 2010, and Petraeus was "killing and capturing" every night. Nicholson hit other records, dropping 24 precision guided missiles from a B-52 on one raid, the largest number to date to be released from the Cold War–era bomber.[20] In April 2017, he made the first use of the largest nonnuclear bomb in the U.S. arsenal, a GBU-43/B Massive Ordnance Air Blast—more commonly known as the "Mother of All Bombs."

The MOAB exploded by design in the air over a large complex of caves in Nangarhar where IS-K fighters were dug in, sending a shock wave down into cave entrances across a wide area, and there was no doubt of its tactical effect. At the time, I had recently started a one-year contract to advise President Ghani's office on strategic communications, and witnessed the unusual sight of tribal elders from Nangarhar appearing in the Arg with a white horse—a gift to the president as a great war leader. But IS-K would not be defeated by a single devastating attack, and their radio station claimed a propaganda victory, since the dropping of the huge bomb proved their jihadi status. The message was "skillfully tailored for young radicals," wrote the analyst Borhan Osman, "since for them American hostility is a stamp of a group's credibility."[21] Nicholson had no reservations. "This was the right weapon against the right target. The enemy had created bunkers, tunnels, and extensive minefields, and this weapon was used to reduce those obstacles so we could continue our offensive."[22]

IS continued to spread to several districts in northern Afghanistan, picking up commanders and fighters disaffected by the Taliban or other jihadi groups. And pressure on them continued, with an attack every day of the year against al-Qaeda or IS-K sites. By the end of the year, Nicholson claimed to have reduced the Islamic State footprint, but they were not defeated.

▤ THE BATTLE FOR KABUL

On May 30, 2017, I had just arrived for work in the Arg, when I felt what I first thought was an earthquake as the air in the building moved. I heard it an instant later—the largest suicide bomb yet to be detonated in the center of Kabul. Explosives had been packed into a sewage truck— smart cover since it would have been waved more quickly through checkpoints who wanted it out of the way. The truck came very close to the secure zone, leaving a huge crater in the roundabout where it was detonated when stopped at the last major checkpoint. It lifted a line of blast walls into the air, devastated the German embassy, and damaged the Iranian embassy. But as always, the main casualties were Afghan civilians. The bomb was detonated at 9:00 a.m., and the streets were full of people on their way to work and children going to school. The damage covered a wide area, destroying the headquarters of 1TV, the Roshan mobile phone company, and a quixotic Kabul landmark, the office of the World Philosophical Mathematical Research Center. Around 150 people were killed. The blast was close to the offices of the CEO, Abdullah Abdullah, and former president Hamid Karzai, and broke windows across a wide area, including in the Arg compound. It set off a week of events when order seemed close to spiraling out of control.

It's easy to look at Kabul as a permanent war zone from outside, but I have been there at some point in every year since the mid-1990s, and the intensity of the violence from 2016 to 2018 was of a different order, and had a more damaging effect on morale, than anything since the worst days of the pre-Taliban civil war. There were attacks on government buildings across the center of the city, parliament, the Four-Hundred-Bed hospital, and a siege at the American University. Suicide bombs were often followed by gun battles in complex attacks that sometimes took hours to quell. Attackers went room to room at the Intercontinental Hotel, killing guests, after accomplices who had smuggled weapons inside created a diversion to allow them through checkpoints. There were several attacks on Shia mosques, including one when many of the casualties jumped from high windows as the building was ablaze, and once again, the city held its breath hoping there would not be revenge attacks, sparking Sunni/Shia conflict.

Many of the attacks, including the sewage truck bomb, were traced to the Haqqani network. But Islamic State attacks were now frequent in the capital. An ambulance was detonated in a crowded street, killing ninety-five people. In another IS attack, a suicide bomb blast was followed by a second, targeting journalists who had gathered to report the incident. The second bomber was carrying a TV camera packed with explosives. Nine journalists were among the twenty-five killed in the double bombing. In this atmosphere, security forces became jittery. The private guards of one of Abdullah's deputies, Muhammad Muhaqiq, opened fire on a passing wedding procession when they thought they were coming under attack, killing the bride.

Public anger at the government's failure to quell the violence spilled over after the sewage truck attack, and demonstrators marched toward the Arg, to be faced by police firing live rounds. Several were shot dead, including the ringleader, who turned out to be the son of the deputy speaker of the senate, the Meshrano Jirga. This put a harsh political spin on the events that followed. A number of senior figures, including Abdullah, were at the dead protestor's funeral when it was targeted by a suicide bomber. Fifteen people died, and many others were injured.[23] Protestors set up camp in the center of town, pitching tents across the road, paralyzing the center of Kabul, and demanding the government should resign. It would be several days before they could be cleared.

On the day of the sewage truck bomb, Nicholson visited the bomb site, shook hands with relief workers, and talked to journalists at the scene. The president remained hunkered down, made a long statement broadcast too late at night, and visited a hospital for security forces injured in the attack, but did not take Afghan press with him. The government media machine did not advise him to do more. They put up senior generals from both the police and army side to talk at a press conference daily in the days after the attack in an attempt to rebuild public confidence, but the opportunity for the president to reconnect to the people was lost.

☰ "WHO DO I TRUST?" REDUX

Although personally a gifted communicator, the president did not have the strategic communication tools to wield the power of his office to do the vital task of building confidence in the nation. This left a vacuum, and the response of many Afghan citizens was to fall back on a short-term view of the future, damaging the capacity of the economy to grow. In states experiencing conflict, instead of Adam Smith's hidden hand of the market creating wealth and encouraging equilibrium, self-interest at times when confidence is low undermines economic opportunity, com-pounding millions of short-term decisions to create a general air of de-spair and hopelessness. Instead of building and investing in permanence, people keep assets as liquid as possible, expecting things to get worse.

The price of flour is about as good an indicator of confidence there is in Afghanistan. In the wholesale market, a large warehouse in a maze of streets near the river, the market manager sits cross-legged, Buddha-like, in a box mounted above eye level, completely coated with white flour on his face and turban and clothes, like a street performer, as he watches over sacks of flour coming and going on the shoulders of porters below him. He knows when fear is growing of the Taliban's return, as the price goes up. People buy in bulk, wanting a sack to be able to put on the back of a donkey and run. But when confident of the future, they buy smaller amounts from market stalls, so the price goes down.

Changing the narrative to build hope and confidence is the work of strategic communications. In countries confident of the future, families make different decisions from those they would make if they thought things would get worse. And every decision feeds into a virtuous cycle—the opposite of the negative cycle that creates and feeds on short-termism. During my time advising in his office, when President Ghani did a good open press conference, exuding confidence, the impact was immediate. After one, a newspaper that had been critical of his administration did an editorial asking, "Where has this president been hiding all this time?" But such appearances were too rare, as strategic communications was never given the attention it deserved.

The week after I arrived to work as an adviser, there was an auda-cious Taliban attack on the main army headquarters of the 209th Corps in the north of the country. In hijacked Afghan army vehicles, wearing stolen army uniforms, the attackers were waved through several check-points inside the base to reach the mosque and adjacent dining hall. It was the time of Friday prayers, and few soldiers in that part of the base were armed. The government never admitted how many were killed, and while there were few publicity wins in such a catastrophe—the crisis management was an object lesson in what not to do. Every daily news cycle was dominated by stories that did the government damage. At no point was there an attempt to regain the media initiative.

From the beginning, the government went into a defensive crouch, refusing to share information, particularly on the number of casualties. Ghani went up the following day to see the site of the carnage, taking only his own media team, and not meeting local journalists or saying anything on camera—doing nothing to rebuild confidence. This was an open goal for an outspoken northern opponent, Atta Muhammad Nur, the governor of Balkh Province where the attack happened, to criticize the president. The next day, the main headline was about the Defence Ministry spokesman accusing a reporter of not being "Afghan" for asking reasonable questions about the disaster. The spokesman, General Dawlat Waziri, an amiable relic from the Communist-trained army of the 1980s, was loved by soldiers. In his daily briefings, he would willfully make up material about how government forces were "sweeping forward on many fronts" and the Taliban's defeat was inevitable.

As the government continued to deny casualties on a mass scale in the attack on the 209th Corps HQ, the best-financed of the new news channels, TOLO TV, sent crews into every province, filming lines of coffins, and did their own count of the dead, coming to 135. The final toll was probably higher. Continued government silence looked like a cover-up.

Ghani's public relations problem had been obvious since the beginning of his presidency. The natural instinct of many round the president was to produce a Soviet-style diet of dull announcements of meetings, no proactive messaging, little meaningful social media, and few appearances. Ghani, like Karzai before him, did more interviews with foreign than Afghan media.

When I arrived as an adviser in 2017, the sixth head of communications, Schah-Zaman Maiwandi, had just been appointed. He was one of the new generation of foreign-educated technocrats brought in by Ghani in an attempt to shake up the system. Many were good linguists, cycling through different languages from meeting to meeting. Maiwandi was ahead of most, speaking his mother tongue, Pashto, as well as German, English, and the main Afghan government language, Dari, all to a high level. Wanting to work with Ghani in the 2014 campaign, he found out when he would be traveling and arranged to be on the same flight. He was employed in the departure lounge. Three years on, he had his reward—with the *tashkil,* staff total, of 250, that went with the communications office, and daily meetings with the president. As his adviser, I settled into the corner of a traditional carved wooden Afghan seat in his office on the day I arrived and did not leave that spot. Maiwandi had brought a precious asset with him—a German coffee machine. I had access to better ground coffee than was available locally, and the individual bags had to be taken away to be scanned and kept overnight by Arg security when I brought them in, before being delivered ceremonially to Maiwandi's office. He was a capable reformer, with an ambition to create a functional media operation, but it was an uphill struggle.

☰ THE OLD GOVERNMENT DIGS IN

Changing the way Afghanistan did business was complex after thirteen years, when President Karzai empowered a corrupt new elite under the ever-present shadow of the old warlords, who were hard to shift. Ghani's instinct was to include this group, while building up a new governing class. His aim was to be able to build a more enduring system, while squeezing the corruption and patronage capacity of the old system to limit its power. He knew that the ambitions of the reformist 1920s king Amanullah, whose desk he worked at, were cut short by a revolution started in conservative rural Afghanistan, and he wanted to keep the country with him as reforms took hold.

Ghani's big tent even included one former warlord who had been allied with the Taliban for many years. In 2017, he concluded the only peace deal with any former insurgent group until then, when Gulbuddin Hekmatyar, who had been fighting for forty years, came down from the mountains. Hekmatyar had allied with the Taliban against the U.S. intervention after 2001 but was successfully brought in with a promise of being treated respectfully. More than that, he was given a red-carpet welcome at the Arg. There was enormous interest in the homecoming. A screen grab of Hekmatyar at the event sitting next to Sayyaf, another 1980s warlord, that I tweeted, with no other comment than that it was extraordinary to see them sitting side by side in a democratic country, had many retweets and comments.

At the same time, Ghani aimed to squeeze the warlords out of real power. Later in the year, Ghani fired one of his biggest opponents, Atta Muhammad Nur, as governor of Balkh. He was one of the old mujahideen leaders stood up by Gary Schroen's Jawbreaker team in 2001. Nur had a series of daily rolling news conferences to protest his treatment, but while he remained a significant influence, he did not regain the post as governor.

Ghani was saddled with the U.S.-brokered power-sharing deal that gave Abdullah half of the government posts, but that was not the obstruction to the second half of his strategy to reform leadership—putting younger technocrats into key roles. Instead, the opposition to this came mostly from inside his administration. The appointment of his first chief of staff, Abdul Salam Rahimi, an uncharismatic figure with little international profile, weakened his ability to build the government he wanted.

Rahimi fought off an attempt by the president to move Daud Noorzai, one of the most talented of the new reformers, into the heart of government. Brought up in Germany and trained by Deutsche Bank, Noorzai had made enough money to return to his ancestral homeland and work to rebuild it. He is a direct descendant of Mahmud Tarzi, the foreign minister in the 1920s, whose daughter, Soraya, married the reformist King Amanullah. Like many of the Afghan-origin Europeans, Canadians, and Americans now with Ghani after spending most of their lives abroad, his family reclaimed lands and were recognized as tribal leaders in the tough southern province of Kandahar; his father sat in the Afghan senate. The German Afghans, mostly from Hamburg, were closely related across generations—Maiwandi's cousin Nisar Barakzai became the president's private secretary.

After the 2014 election, Noorzai set up what was called the Administrative Office of the President in a large, rented house in the center of town—a test bed of a new kind of government of the sort Ghani wanted. It was like no office seen in Afghanistan before: large, open-plan rooms with big islands of shared desks and modern computers. Noorzai had a ready answer to the many foreign diplomats who asked how the government could afford it. "The office was not expensive," he said. "The cost breaks down to 85% people and 15% kit. We had the desks made locally to my design, and 15% of even a small sum buys a lot of very good computers if you don't steal it"—such a simple explanation as to why corruption is the worst affliction.

Noorzai's bright young staff were inputting government data on procurement, spending of budgets across key ministries, and land registration—until then, there was no centralized knowledge of Afghan land ownership. Young men and women sat together at the desks, the men all in dark suits. Like some other modern offices in Kabul, Noorzai insisted on a strict dress code for men.[24] He smoked incessantly— particularly in a breakout room upstairs, the nerve center of the new reformers, constantly full of arguments and plans. He saw them as a new disruptive force, facing both inertia and actual opposition from what he called "old government."

One of the more surreal days in my year in the Arg came when Ghani attempted to take significant functions from Rahimi and give Noorzai a bigger role at the heart of government. Negotiations over dividing responsibility took place on the day of a major funeral in the Arg for the president's uncle Akmal Ghani Ahmadzai. In scenes as from *The Sopranos,* men in dark suits, white shirts, and somber ties came and went between Noorzai and Rahimi, carrying sheaves of documents, carving up the government. Noorzai had an office in one of the most beautiful buildings in the whole complex, the Harem Serai, built for the many wives of King Habibullah at the beginning of the twentieth century, set in a garden courtyard with giant ancient plane trees and a vine-covered walkway along one side. On another side was an ornate meeting room, dominated by a shallow indoor ornamental pool with goldfish, and a bar along one wall left over from the more tolerant 1920s, now of course shuttered.

Amid giant computer screens incongruously set up among the faded furniture and tapestries of the former royal harem, Noorzai's team sat huddled together, with the president's cousin Ajmal Ghani at the center of them. It was his father who was to be buried with full state honors. Ajmal was close to Noorzai and paid a price, with vicious internet attacks claiming he was a CIA spy. He said to me, "Watch out, they will say you are MI6." The strategic communications operation was collateral damage in the carve-up. Rahimi held on to it, and Maiwandi was replaced by a nonentity whose only qualification was loyalty to Rahimi, and defaulted to the old ways.[25] He was Ghani's seventh head of communications in less than three years.

The argument was a waste of time and human capacity, squandering scarce resources, while in the world outside this squabble in the Arg, patronage and corruption had captured much of the power, and the Taliban were as threatening as ever. Within weeks, Rahimi had sidelined Noorzai altogether, who had to bide his time for a couple of years before masterminding part of Ghani's reelection campaign in 2019 and coming back in a cabinet-level role as head of the national electricity grid—an influential job in a country where electric supply was not universal.

☰ HELMAND GROUNDHOG DAY

Some of the most radical reforms of the Afghan armed forces happened during Nicholson's two years and seven months in command. When he arrived, there were more generals in Afghanistan than the U.S., where the army is three times the size. "We don't even know how many generals [there are]," said John Sopko, the special inspector general for Afghanistan reconstruction. There were one thousand generals on the books, but there were suspected to be more. "It's pretty pathetic, and here we are, 15 years into this."[26] The generals, many of them Soviet-era holdovers, drew full salaries, and many lived in government property but had little responsibility. Nicholson devised a scheme to retire most of them on very generous terms to open promotion opportunities all the way down and transform the fighting capacity of conventional forces.

Afghan Special Forces had doubled in size since 2015 and were now the best in the region, capable of complex operations on their own, but they were becoming worn out fighting conventional battles, always sent in first, as they were so much more competent than the regular army that lagged behind. It was not until the end of 2016 that biometric ID cards were universal for soldiers, and salaries could then not be paid without them. But it was hard to change the way things were done. In 2020, SIGAR reported that 50–70 percent of police positions in the most contested southern provinces, including Kandahar and Helmand, were still filled by "ghost police."[27]

Corruption and lack of good leadership cost lives. Police commanders still needed to buy their posts, so they needed to recoup the cost. In early 2016, a member of the district council in Helmand, Haji Ahmad, described the impact of corruption to The New York Times. "There's 24 hours of fighting going on and at night the commander runs out of ammo. So he goes to his district commander and says, 'We need ammo,' and the commander says, 'Well, give me money so I can give you ammo.' And he doesn't have any money, so the Taliban overrun the checkpoint and nine policemen are killed. That's what happens."[28]

In April 2017, the marines returned to Helmand, raising the same flag they had lowered when they left at the end of 2014. Half of those who came back had been there before, disheartened to have to support Afghan troops again to fight over the same ground they had previously taken at some cost. The Afghan military failure made their return inevitable. "It feels like Groundhog Day," said Staff Sergeant Robin Spotts on his third deployment to Helmand.[29]

But some of the places where they had fought before were now effectively abandoned to the Taliban. Afghan troops were no longer trying to hold remote areas. All districts in the country were now categorized into three groups, as places where they would *hold, fight,* or *disrupt.* Areas they would *hold* included all major towns and other strategic locations. Other locations they would *fight* to retain, and some only *disrupt* where the Taliban presented opportunities. While the Taliban controlled a third of the country by some estimates, Nicholson pointed out that they ran only sparsely populated districts. He assessed that in terms of the population, the Taliban controlled only 10 percent, the government controlled 70 percent, and they were fighting over the rest. The hold/fight/disrupt division was an attempt to move Afghan forces away from their modus operandi of sitting in fixed positions and move them to more flexible maneuver warfare. But it meant withdrawing from large areas and was an acceptance of a significant Taliban presence—at variance with the strategy adopted by General Stanley McChrystal eight years before, who wanted to ensure that he "owned the villages."

TOUGH NEIGHBORHOOD

On January 1, 2018, Trump signaled his priority for the new year in his first tweet, which read in full, "The United States has foolishly given Pakistan more than 33 billion dollars in aid over the last 15 years, and they have given us nothing but lies & deceit, thinking of our leaders as fools. They give safe haven to the terrorists we hunt in Afghanistan, with little help. No more!"

The president was stating clearly what many in the administration, and in particular in the military, had been saying for years. But Pakistan's perceived fragility and the capacity of its nuclear arsenal to fall into the wrong hands had generally caused the U.S. to pull back to a more cautious policy. Tillerson had already put Pakistan on notice in the fall of 2017, adding it to its watch list for religious freedom, and threatening to withhold aid after Hafiz Saeed, the founder of one of the most powerful terrorist groups in the region, Lashkar-e-Taiba, was released from house arrest. Saeed had a $10 million U.S. bounty on his head, but they could not touch him in Pakistan. After the president's January tweet, there was a freeze on military aid payments, then running at $1.3 billion a year. The new hard line was backed by Pakistan's former ambassador in Washington, now settled in the U.S., Husain Haqqani. "The United States would be acting as a friend," he wrote, "helping Pakistan realize through tough measures that the gravest threat to its future comes from religious extremism it is fostering in its effort to compete with India."[30]

Nicholson had long experience dealing with Pakistan as commander of U.S. forces on the frontier early in the war and while heading the Pakistan-Afghanistan desk in the office of the Joint Chiefs of Staff. He tried to work with Pakistan, saying the country needed to be dealt with "through a holistic review."[31] Terrorism crossed the frontier, so the U.S. needed a strategy to deal with that. The twenty-one terrorist organizations in the region live among "300 million people in Pakistan and Afghanistan, many of whom don't have education, job opportunities, hope. So this provides fertile ground for these groups to recruit from."[32] One of the effects of the major military operation that Pakistani forces had begun in 2014 to recover the frontier region was to push militants over the frontier into Afghanistan, so there needed to be close military and political links. There were times when the two sides cooperated, as when U.S. special operators rescued Ali Haider Gilani, the son of the former Pakistani prime minister, being held by al-Qaeda, and killed the Pakistani Taliban leader Umar Khalifa, who had carried out the Peshawar school attack in 2014 killing 130 children of Pakistani soldiers.

Nicholson's desire for better regional relations was shared by Ghani, who sought to reposition Afghanistan as the key link between Central and South Asia, turning its geographical isolation from a liability into an asset. He often quoted the poet Muhammad Iqbal, who talked of Afghanistan as the "heart of Asia." In early 2018, Kabul hosted the military leaders of Pakistan and five Central Asian republics, bordering

Afghanistan to the north. Afghan officials handed the Pakistani delegation what was described as "undeniable" evidence that the series of deadly attacks in Kabul had been planned in Pakistan. Pakistan's chief of army staff, General Qamar Javed Bajwa, delivered the usual denials, claiming, against the evidence, that Pakistan had eliminated all terrorist sanctuaries from its soil.[33] Faltering talks continued for some time over a new joint security pact between Afghanistan and Pakistan, but nothing changed.

In what Nicholson called a "tough neighborhood," Russia also continued to play a disruptive role.[34] It was payback for the defeat of Soviet forces by U.S.-backed mujahideen in the 1980s and an opportunity to pick at an open wound as the long war went on. The success of President Putin's campaigns of *dezinformatsiya* have become well known. In Afghanistan, they successfully planted the absurd idea that the U.S. was arming and financing Islamic State forces. There was a story—never properly sourced, so hard to deny—of white helicopters landing at night in the north of the country to drop the weapons. It was picked up in public by the Russian foreign minister Sergey Lavrov, who talked about "flights of unmarked helicopters." He conjured a vision of thousands of IS fighters massing on the southern borders of Central Asia, "and it is not difficult to get to Russia." The story "grossly exaggerated" the number of IS fighters, according to Nicholson.

Russia was using the story to justify its support for the Taliban, against the worse threat of Islamic State. "This narrative is used as a justification for the Russians to legitimize the actions of the Taliban," said Nicholson. They clearly "provide some degree of support to the Taliban."[35] He had credible evidence of Russian support to the Taliban beyond the disinformation campaign, when Afghan elders handed over weapons taken from the Taliban that investigators tracked to Russia.

☰ MUTUALLY HURTING STALEMATE

Analysts who watch peace processes like to say the one essential precondition is a "mutually hurting stalemate," where both sides know they cannot win on the battlefield and both are still under military pressure. While keeping up that military pressure, Nicholson was more focused on the possibility of a peace deal to end the long war than any commander before him. The "number one metric," he said, was how reconciliation was going, and said in 2018, "There's tremendous potential to advance the reconciliation dialogue."[36]

As early as 2016, General Dunford called the conflict a "stalemate."[37] There was no doubt that the government was hurting. Attrition rates in the Afghan army, through both death and desertion, meant recruitment only just kept up with demand. Figures were not publicized, but at the beginning of 2019, Ghani said forty-five thousand Afghan troops and police had died since his presidency began in 2014.[38]

There was pressure on the Taliban too that led more of them to want to negotiate. Research of every violent death by the BBC over the month of August in 2019 revealed that 50 percent of those who died across the country were Taliban.[39] After an attack on the southwestern city of Farah was repulsed, fifty Taliban fighters, including some key leaders, were tracked by the marines to a house in Musa Qala in Helmand, destroyed with a HIMARS rocket. "So where does this leave us at the end of that action?" Nicholson said. "Afghan forces in control of Farah, and many of the enemy leaders who led the attack are now being pulled out of the rubble in Musa Qala."[40]

The Obama administration had accepted the Afghan government's desire to lead on talks—they should be "Afghan-owned and Afghan-led." That meant the negotiations should be between the Afghan government and the Taliban, with the U.S. and other international actors facilitating the process, but not directly talking to the Taliban about the future shape of Afghanistan. Another issue was over the location of talks. The Afghan government did not want to go to Doha or Norway, both places that had been mentioned as possible venues, but hold talks in Afghanistan. The geometry of peace was hard to align, as the Taliban, for their part, did not recognize the Afghan government and would not talk to them in Afghanistan or anywhere else, so there was no progress. But they were under sustained military pressure, increasing the influence of those in their ranks who thought it was time to talk.

TALKING TO THE TALIBAN—II

It is not the duty of America to draft laws and suggest systems for other countries.
—Taliban open letter to the American people, 2018

☰ "OUR LIFE IS UGLY"

On March 26, 2018, hundreds of people had gathered to watch a wrestling match between Helmand and a visiting squad from neighboring Farah Province. It's a big Afghan sport, and the stadium was full. Elsewhere in the sports universe, Afghanistan's cricket team had just qualified for the World Cup for the first time, after beating Ireland, and people were in good spirits. At sunset, as the last wrestler was downed in the dust, a suicide bomber drove his car at an upmarket SUV leaving the stadium. Perhaps he thought it contained a government official. In fact, the car was driven by Haji Mauladad, a popular local figure, who had brought the team from Farah and was leaving to arrange a celebration meal for the wrestlers. He was among fifteen people killed; many others were injured. Mauladad's children were seen screaming in his car as it burst into flames, but only one could be saved.

The incident had an impact beyond any other attack, sparking an extraordinary protest. "These were sportsmen, they had nothing to do with politics. There were a lot of children there," said BBC reporter Auliya Atrafi, who was in the stadium with members of his family. He said the protest that followed was caused by an "accumulation of violence." The sight of the screaming children in the back of the burning SUV "was horrific even by Helmand standards."[1]

A group of local people began with a simple sit-in and hunger strike in a tent. "The only aim of the sit-in is to stop fighting from both sides," said one of the organizers, Iqbal Khyber. "The Taliban should not send bombers and the government should not drop bombs on them."[2] They took only water for several weeks, some were hospitalized. Qais Hashemi said as a drip was inserted to keep him alive, "If they save my life today, tomorrow I will die in a suicide attack."[3]

They then took a new approach, setting off to the northern Helmand town of Musa Qala, a Taliban stronghold, walking defiantly through some of the most dangerous territory in the country. From there, they headed to Kabul. Just nine men when they started, they gathered people and support along the way, striking a chord everywhere. The violence had gone on too long for no good reason anyone could see. They blamed the corrupt governing elite as much as the Taliban. The Kabul-born, U.S.-educated *New York Times* correspondent Mujib Mashal chronicled their progress, as they walked through the fierce heat of the Afghan summer not eating or drinking in daylight hours during the fasting month of Ramadan.

> Among them is a high school student who went home to complete his final exams before rejoining the others; a poet who still carries in his chest one of the four bullets he was shot with; a bodybuilding champion who abandoned his gym and has lost 20 pounds of muscle on the journey. They are day laborers, farmers, retired army officers, a polio victim on crutches, a mechanic who was robbed of his sight by war.[4]

A shopkeeper, Muhammad Anwar, took a bus from the western city of Herat to join them. "I told my wife I am going to join my friends," he told Mashal. The marchers walked in single file along the edge of the highway, staying in mosques and depending on well-wishers to wash their clothes and give them food. Their message was simple: "Our life is ugly," one man would call through a megaphone, the marchers responding, "It is war. It is war."

The Taliban did not touch them, although they moved them on from one village just as they were sitting to eat, saying an offensive was about to start. They did not want to be blamed if the peace marchers were hurt. Once in Kabul, the marchers staged sit-down protests outside a number of embassies and delivered a letter stained with the blood of one of the marchers to the UN and to the Pakistan embassy.

☰ DEATH IN THE DESERT

There had been evidence for some time that the Taliban too were weary of war. They were taking heavy casualties, particularly in continued offensives, against provincial capitals, that were always repulsed. Some Taliban commanders interviewed for the British defense think tank, the Royal United Services Institute, were concerned at the deterioration of the movement. One said, "There are thousands who think that the war has nothing to offer but destruction and the slaughter of Afghans, but they keep this [close to] their heart."[5] The tight security around the relatively few foreign soldiers now in the country meant the Taliban were no longer killing "infidels" but fellow Afghans. Some of those interviewed said they would be willing to sever all links with al-Qaeda and even allow a limited U.S. military presence to continue in Afghanistan.

President Ghani had been trying to start an "Afghan-owned, Afghan-led" peace process since he took office in September 2014. Pakistan, though, wanted to exert continued influence, and under pressure from the U.S. and China, Ghani agreed to cross his red line that insisted talks should be in Afghanistan. On July 7, 2015, the Afghan deputy foreign minister, Hekmat Karzai, nephew of the former president, sat down for the first face-to-face talks between an Afghan government delegation and the Taliban. The talks took place in the Murree hills, close to the Pakistani capital, Islamabad, with American, Chinese, and Pakistani observers.

A number of senior Taliban leaders opposed the initiative, and their demands for assurance from the leader of the movement, Mullah Omar, forced out a secret. The founding leader of the Taliban had died of tuberculosis two years previously, and Mullah Akhtar Mansour had assumed leadership, issuing statements in the name of the *Amir ul-mu'minin,* "commander of all the faithful," as if Mullah Omar were still alive. The peace process was put on hold in a power struggle for control of the Taliban after the announcement of his death, including gun battles in Helmand between rival factions.

Mullah Mansour emerged from the fighting as leader, a more worldly and more public figure than the reclusive Mullah Omar. As aviation minister in the Taliban government in the 1990s, he was familiar with international business. In early 2016, Afghan government officials met Pakistani officials, again with the U.S. and China in the room to draw a new road map for peace. The same day, a Canadian hostage, Colin Rutherford, who had been held for five years, was released.[6] Mansour put out a statement saying the release was due to the Taliban's "humanitarian sympathy."

In Doha, the international peacemaking group Pugwash held "Track II" talks—meetings bringing together the Taliban with leading Afghan figures, including those in government but not present in an official capacity. There were women in some of the meetings, who said they had good discussions with the Taliban. One said they and the Taliban ate together and were surprised by how much they had in common.[7]

Although the Taliban political office had not been recognized since the debacle over the opening in 2013, it remained intact, and with the consent of the U.S., Doha remained the place where they could meet visitors.[8] Expectations grew that the talks in Pakistan, halted after the announcement of the death of Omar in July 2015, could start again. But the Taliban were taking a harder line than in 2015, insisting this time on preconditions before entering a talks process—complete withdrawal of foreign forces from Afghanistan, official recognition of their Doha office, removal of Taliban leaders from the UN blacklist, release of prisoners— and the process foundered.[9]

The new Taliban were different from the group who emerged in Kandahar twenty years earlier to counter the banditry of the mujahideen warlords. The older generation, now comfortable in Doha, were more urbane and more willing to talk to outsiders than previously. They had a competent professional media policy, increasingly putting out material in English to communicate beyond Afghanistan. The commanders on the ground were a new generation, more ruthless than their predecessors, confident in their military capacity, and with more of a sense of their role in international jihad than the inward-looking nationalists of the 1990s. They were also far more involved in criminal networks through their control of much of the opium industry.

On May 21, 2016, Mansour was killed by an American drone strike on his taxi as it crossed the enormous expanse of desert in the Pakistani province of Baluchistan, south of Afghanistan. His mobile phone signal had been tracked from the Iranian border. The attack crossed a political line.

Up to then, drone strikes across the border had been limited to the "Tribal Areas" of the northwest frontier, governed differently from the rest of Pakistan. Mansour, though, was killed in a mainstream Pakistani province.

It will never be known whether Mansour would have been a peacemaker. Barney Rubin, the former senior adviser to Richard Holbrooke, a skeptic of the military effort, wrote sharply, "The Taliban do not seem to have interpreted the assassination of their leader as an outstretched hand for peace."[10] General Nicholson had no such reservations. It led to "leadership and financial disruption" in the Taliban, and he counted it a "policy success." President Obama, who signed off the raid, said Mansour's death eliminated "one roadblock to peace."[11]

Evidence was pieced together by *New York Times* correspondent Carlotta Gall that made a persuasive case for Pakistan's complicity in Mansour's death.[12] They shared vital intelligence about his movement. He had made the trip from Iran across the southern desert before, but unusually this time, there were some three hundred Pakistani troops at the border, where he was detained for two hours. A Taliban commander told Gall that Mansour called his brother in the six hours after he left the border before he was hit, telling him to look after his children, talking of his own death. She reported that he had been trying to distance the movement from Pakistan, seeking more Iranian support.

In the same way as the Pakistani intelligence service, the ISI, arrested Mullah Baradar in 2010 when he was seeking peace talks outside the country, so they may have given the U.S. the information they needed to kill Mansour, fearing he might make a peace deal. The Kandahar police chief, General Abdul Raziq, said Pakistani Frontier Corps soldiers were on the scene within minutes and must have been tailing Mansour's taxi. They had brought reporters with them and conveniently showed them Mansour's passport in a fake name, as if discovered at the scene, suspiciously undamaged for being retrieved from the fireball that had destroyed the vehicle and two bodies.[13] The new Taliban leader, Mullah Haibatullah Akhunzada, was an uncharismatic hard-line ideologue with no military experience. There was little progress toward a peace deal during 2017.

☰ EID TRUCE

On June 18, 2018, the Helmand peace marchers finally arrived in Kabul, footsore and burned by the sun after their epic journey, on the last day of the four-day Eid holiday ending the Ramadan month of fasting. It was an Eid like no other, as an unprecedented cease-fire during the holiday allowed the country to glimpse a different future. Bearded fighters, wearing the voluminous black turbans that mark the Taliban, came into the center of towns up and down Afghanistan. Social media was full of images of Taliban fighters embracing police officers, eating ice cream, and in one remarkable encounter, shaking hands with Wais Barmak, the minister of interior, who stopped his vehicle in the middle of a group of Taliban fighters in Kabul.

The cease-fire came about after months of a kind of megaphone diplomacy as all sides stated their positions publicly. It began on February 14, with a 2,700-word open letter in English from the Taliban "to the American people." The letter spoke in lurid terms about the "felonious act" of the American "war-mongering government" in invading Afghanistan, saying they had failed in all their war aims. After several pages of this, there was an olive branch. The Taliban appealed directly for peace talks. "Our preference is to solve the Afghan issue through peaceful dialogue." It was clear though that the geometry of peace talks was still not aligned.

In a conference in Kabul to build international consensus for peace, President Ghani tried to break the deadlock with a series of unconditional offers to the Taliban. He offered recognition as a political party, an end to sanctions, lifting of the UN travel ban and the issue of passports to Taliban leaders, release of prisoners, and most crucially, a cease-fire. "We are making this offer without preconditions in order to lead to a peace agreement." As is the Afghan custom at international conferences, his speech was trilingual, in both Afghan languages and English. The meat of this speech was in Pashto, the language of the Taliban. It was directed at them.

The Taliban's public response to the Ghani offer was contempt, calling it a demand to surrender. Ghani had not mentioned foreign troops, and the Taliban would need to recognize the existing Afghan government to enter negotiations.[14] They still saw themselves as the "Islamic Emirate of Afghanistan" and did not recognize the legitimacy of the Islamic Republic led by Ghani. In an emirate, authority is divinely ordained, not derived from the consent of the people as in a democratic republic. This would be one of the most contentious obstacles to talks.

At the beginning of June, Ghani went further. It was then that he put out the idea of an unconditional Eid cease-fire. The Taliban's answer came two days later in a WhatsApp message to journalists. They would suspend fighting, but only for the first three days of Eid, and only with government forces; they would continue to target "foreign occupiers."

The truce was the first pause for breath and sign of hope for many years, and in a heady atmosphere, Ghani wanted to keep the momentum toward peace. After meeting the Helmand peace marchers, he offered to extend the cease-fire, unnerving Afghan military commanders, who watched Taliban fighters move into new positions and they could do nothing to stop them. Many Taliban had handed in their weapons at police stations before going into town during the truce, but many had not, and there were reports that they were using the opportunity to build up weapons stores close to vulnerable locations. Amrullah Saleh, a prominent hard-liner against the Taliban, who became vice president in 2019, tweeted that "the anti-Taliban constituency . . . feel betrayed, confused & sold out." Ghani's offer of a truce extension was not reciprocated, and fighting soon began again. The peace marchers kept going, now heading north toward Mazar-e-Sharif.

In the summer, the Taliban put intense pressure on the strategically important town of Ghazni—halfway between Kabul and Kandahar. It took four days of hard fighting to recover. The war was taking a toll on the government. The highly experienced national security adviser Hanif Atmar resigned soon afterward, along with the head of the intelligence service, the NDS, Muhammad Masoom Stanekzai. Both had been reformers with Ghani since the early days of post-Taliban Afghanistan. And Farkhunda Naderi, a former MP Ghani brought into his team to liaise with the UN, also resigned, as she found herself constantly sidelined in meetings and faced problems getting her team paid. Atmar was replaced as national security adviser by a reformer, Hamdullah Mohib, as Ghani's options narrowed and he brought his most loyal followers into key roles.

In August, Ghani again put out his hand to the Taliban, making an offer of a pause in hostilities for the second Eid holiday, again unconditional, and was willing to extend it for three months. But Taliban leaders were wary—concerned about the battle readiness of their fighters if they once again came into cities. Fighters had been instructed to stay at their posts for the cease-fire, not stream into the cities for selfies and ice cream. Mullah Omar's son Muhammad Yaqoob was recorded saying fighters had "totally disobeyed the terms of the ceasefire."[15]

Across the country, there were reports of Taliban fighters not going back to the fight after the first cease-fire. They had seen they were not the decadent Western places they had been told. "I went to the city and the mosques were full of people," one fighter, Muhammadullah, told *The Guardian*. "I did not notice anything against the Islamic rules. After the sweet three days of peace, going back to bloodshed looks strange. How can you even compare peace with war?"[16] Taliban commanders would not take the risk again. They reverted to their consistent position that they wanted a peace deal with the "occupiers," not their "puppet government." But the relentless U.S. bombing since Trump had allowed it in 2017 was having its effect.

☰ GENERATIONAL CONFLICT

On September 2, 2018, General Mick Nicholson handed over to General Austin Scott Miller. In a low-key ceremony in bright sunshine, under the larch trees in front of the yellow building, in the country where he had spent so much of his life, Nicholson said, "It's time for this war to end." He appealed to the Taliban to stop listening to Pakistan and instead to listen to "the voices of your own people who are encouraging you to peace."[17]

Miller's whole career had been as a special operator. He was wounded twice—when ground commander in the Black Hawk Down firefight in Mogadishu in 1993, and in Fallujah in Iraq. At the time of his promotion to the Kabul command in 2018, he had been the commander of Joint Special Operations Command for two years. Inevitably, he had spent a lot of time in Afghanistan, where he was one of the first special operators on the ground in 2001. His son, Lieutenant Austin Miller Jr., four months out of West Point, was at his confirmation hearing in the Senate. Acknowledging "this young guy sitting behind me," Miller called the Afghan conflict "generational." He said, "I never anticipated that his cohort would be in a position to deploy as I sat there in 2001."

Senator Elizabeth Warren mocked the number of senior generals and administration officials who had come to the Senate Armed Services Committee hailing "turning points" in the Afghan conflict. "We've supposedly turned the corner so many times that it seems now we're going in circles." She called the war an "impossible task." Miller did not offer a turning point, nor did he "guarantee a timeline or end date."

The flexibility afforded by the Trump administration meant the military presence in Afghanistan was now based on conditions, not an arbitrary timeline. Critics like Warren were concerned that it meant the U.S. was now "heading further down a path that does not have success at the end." It was still not clear what success looked like.

The chairman of the Joint Chiefs of Staff, General Joe Dunford, was instrumental in the appointment, describing himself as a "very big Scott Miller fan." Dunford called Miller to see if he was interested before putting him forward. "I think Scott Miller is one of the most professionally mature, thoughtful individuals that we have in uniform," he said. "His nuanced approach to developing relationships with the Afghans, his understanding of how to balance issues such as civilian casualties with prosecuting the mission, I think was tailor-made for a really complex environment that we found ourselves in in Afghanistan." When Dunford commanded in Kabul, Miller was for a year the commander of the Special Operations Command for Afghanistan, who had a role in training local forces. Dunford watched Miller create a "deep partnership with the Afghans."

In 2009, working with Lieutenant General Stanley McChrystal in the Pentagon, Miller had developed the AfPak Hands program, where officers were taken out of their mainstream careers for five years, trained in Dari, Pashtu, or Urdu, and sent on multiple tours to the region. McChrystal had been the only commander who had really cared for the program. The Hands had found themselves shunted into jobs in Afghanistan that did not call on their specialist skills. When it started, Miller envisaged that those on it would be people likely to progress to senior command positions. But it did not work. Hands found they were losing promotions, and the quality of recruits went down, as genuine volunteers were replaced by many who were "voluntold." Ten years after creating the program, Miller saw it wound up under his command. "The institutional bureaucracy of the military promotion system does not support the survival of programs like the [AfPak] Hands," said retired navy captain James Muir, who ran it in Afghanistan in its early years.[18]

⩉ THE ROCK IN THE POND

Trump paid little attention to Afghanistan. He allowed the Afghanistan/Pakistan special representative role, originally founded for Holbrooke, to wither, and never met Nicholson. But three days after Nicholson left, September 5, 2018, with just the kind of disruptive flourish that marked his presidency, he threw a rock in the pond, appointing the evergreen Afghan envoy Zalmay Khalilzad to negotiate a peace deal with the Taliban. Khalilzad had a limited mandate—to bring the troops home with honor. Instructing his new envoy to talk to the Taliban about U.S. withdrawal, without the consent of the Afghan government, President Trump tore up the received wisdom of the "geometry" of peace talks, not the Afghan government talking to the Taliban, but a separate U.S. deal with the Taliban. And all the time Khalilzad was operating under what Rubin called "the Tweet of Damocles," the likelihood of an abrupt withdrawal of U.S. forces being announced by tweet by the restless occupant of the White House.[19]

Khalilzad planned first to negotiate the withdrawal of U.S. troops in return for the Taliban agreeing to sever links with al-Qaeda and allow safe passage for the pullout, followed by a cease-fire and negotiations between the Taliban and the Afghan administration. The Taliban were skeptical, holding preliminary meetings with Khalilzad in Dubai to see if he could really deliver a withdrawal of U.S. troops, before they would agree to engage in talks in Doha. According to Taliban sources, Khalilzad made assurances in those early meetings that he could secure the release of the Kandahar landowner Haji Bashir Noorzai, in jail in the U.S. for drug-running.[20] This was just one of the plates that Khalilzad kept spinning as he moved tirelessly from capital to capital, keeping a lot of ideas up in the air, all the time with the Tweet of Damocles hanging over his head.

Khalilzad worked to build as wide a consensus as he could for a peace deal, traveling frequently to Afghanistan's neighbors, as well as European capitals, between nine rounds of talks with the Taliban. The process left the Kabul government out in the cold. The Afghan president had known the American envoy, since they were just two years apart in the same Kabul school in the 1960s and '70s. When Khalilzad first came to Kabul to report in his new role, there were no niceties. Without even offering tea or a seat, Ghani looked at Khalilzad and said, "Well?" waiting for a report. One observer said he had the manner of a headmaster with an errant student.

In March 2019, Ghani's frustrations came out into the open. On a visit to the U.S., the Afghan national security adviser, Hamdullah Mohib, publicly accused Khalilzad of wanting to set up a transition government in Kabul and setting himself up as a "Viceroy"—a loaded term in South Asia from the days of the British Empire. The comments were not just behind closed doors but in a TV interview with CBS News[21] and background meetings with think tanks. The response was icy. "Attacks on Ambassador Khalilzad are seen as attacks on the State Department, and only serve to hinder the bilateral relationship and the peace process."[22] The U.S. cut off contact with Mohib for several months. Mohib's wife, Lael, is American, and he had served in Washington as ambassador, so his temporary banishment came as a personal blow as well as a significant rift in the relationship with Afghanistan's most important ally.

Further humiliation for Ghani came in a series of meetings between Khalilzad in 2019 in Moscow and Beijing. In previous years Russia had brought together Taliban representatives with a broad cross section of the Afghan elite—including former President Karzai, and the old warlords, the 1980s mujahideen leaders. To Ghani, it looked like a deliberate Russian attempt to confuse and disrupt the process, and he would not send government representatives. Until 2019 the U.S. ignored the Russian negotiations, but in agreements with Russia and China, Khalilzad agreed that all would work together for peace in Afghanistan, engaging a wider representation of Afghans than just the government. The deal signed in Beijing in July pushed for talks between the "Taliban, Afghan government, and other Afghans."[23] As president, Ghani thought he represented all Afghans and saw this as another snub. He felt his leadership usurped, especially when it became clear that Khalilzad was offering the Taliban an interim government to replace him ahead of peace talks. The Khalilzad process was a long way from being Afghan-owned and Afghan-led.

The U.S. was also courting Pakistan's support. Given Pakistan's continuing support for the Taliban, this was seen in Kabul as further provocation. President Trump sent a letter to Pakistan's new prime minister, Imran Khan, requesting Islamabad's assistance in facilitating U.S. talks with the Taliban. In March 2019, General Joe Votel, the outgoing commander of the U.S. Central Command, told Congress, "We've seen Pakistan play a more helpful role in helping to bring Taliban representatives into negotiations."[24] Pakistan was invited to the Beijing summit in July, a move that further angered the Kabul government.

But Ghani's government did not take the available opportunities. Early in the process, Khalilzad requested that Kabul nominate a negotiating team to be ready for the second phase, recommending it should be broadly representative. The peace process may not have been sequenced as Ghani wanted it, but he could have engaged more constructively from the start. Instead, he appointed his low-profile chief of staff, Abdul Salam Rahimi, as minister for peace—whom I had previously watched blocking reformers as he played petty palace politics. His first attempt at an "inclusive" negotiating team was greeted with derision on Afghan social media and quickly abandoned. The incapacity of the government side to put forward a credible team reached farcical levels when a list of 250 names went to Doha—leading the Taliban spokesperson, Zabiullah Mujahid, to tweet that the "Afghan elite are treating the peace talks like a wedding at Kabul's Intercontinental Hotel."

By September 2019, Khalilzad believed he had a deal ready to sign with the Taliban, principally concerning the withdrawal of U.S. and other international troops. But just as Trump had kicked off the process with a disruptive tactic the year before, so he abruptly tweeted the cancellation of a summit meeting at Camp David, even before it was public knowledge. His stated reason was the death of an American soldier in Afghanistan, so he could not sign a peace deal with his killers. But it emerged that he had invited President Ghani to the summit, perhaps hoping to broker a settlement, trusting in his wizardry in the "art of the deal." When the Taliban heard this, they pulled out, as they did not want face-to-face talks with the Afghan government, leaving him with no option but to cancel. The Afghan presidential election had been postponed twice already in 2019 in the uncertainty over the peace deal, but went ahead in September, putting the peace process on hold.

ELECTION AND AFTER

The United States has rarely accomplished long-term goals after any conflict without an extended American military presence to ensure proper results from the peace.
—U.S. Army historian Dr. Conrad C. Crane[1]

☰ THE GERMANZAIS

September 28, 2019. Election day in Kabul. Haris Helmand made break-fast like the boxer he is—a box of eggs, chopped peppers and tomatoes, and a whole packet of sliced cheese, all thrown into a pan. "There is no-where I would rather be," he said. "I am so excited to be here." A large, well-built man, he is a worryingly good shot, talking while splitting a ballpoint mounted on a block at the bottom of the garden some thirty yards away with an air-rifle slug. A banker as well as a boxer, he was one of a small group of Afghan-origin Germans who took leave from senior jobs to put something back into the country they left as children, when Daud Noorzai, the reformer who had been forced out of the government two years before, called them to oil the wheels of Ashraf Ghani's election campaign. Among the hundreds of young volunteers in the campaign headquarters, they were known as the "Germanzais," a new Afghan tribe.

The contours of their lives had been shaped by Afghanistan's long wars. Helmand's family left their ancestral home in Lashkar Gah, Helmand, in 1985, when the area was under relentless attack from Soviet forces. His father, a wealthy landowner, stashed money on staging points along the route east to Pakistan and took sixteen members of his family on a perilous journey. They had to slip across the border evading checks, walking alone, carrying nothing. They spent a year not far from Quetta, while his father secured fake passports for $50,000 each. Helmand was struck by the austere religious practice demanded of the boys his age in school in the Pakistan desert; ten years later, they would be the Taliban. The family ended up in Germany after a circuitous route flying from Karachi via Singapore, Bangkok, and Kuala Lumpur. Ripping up their fake passports on the last leg of the flight, they arrived to seek asylum.

Traditional Afghans do not have a last name in the Western sense, and this family were named after their province for immigration papers. Many of those around the president had similar stories and were named for where they came from—Helmand, Maiwandi, and Mirwais Farahi, the director of international relations for the Ghani administration—a refugee nation returning home. Navigating the cultural tides of their lives was complex; the Germanzais were treated as Afghans in Germany, although they had lived there for forty years, and were seen as Germans on this brief return to serve in Afghanistan. They had successful jobs in German businesses, so lived a Western lifestyle, but most married into the Afghan community in Germany, holding to tradition.

The Afghan presidential election, originally scheduled for March 2019, then July, could finally be held in September, close to the last time there could be nationwide voting without disruption by winter snow. The delays were partly caused by uncertainty over Zalmay Khalilzad's peace track, which proposed putting elections on hold while the country was governed by an interim administration during peace talks. The president's cousin Ajmal Ghani accused Khalilzad of a "pathetic attempt to sell the republic,"[2] by allowing every prominent Afghan to think they would lead the interim government. "Zal did such a great job for Karzai," he said. "Zal has misled the Americans, misled our neighbors, when he guaranteed to them that there would be no election."

The delay stalled the campaign of one of Ghani's strongest rivals, his former national security adviser Hanif Atmar, who emerged in the spring of 2019 as the effective leader of the opposition, marshaling support from other presidential candidates to push for an election on the timetable that year. Despite his background as a Communist, losing a leg fighting on the Soviet side against the mujahideen in the worst battle of the war at Jalalabad in 1989, Atmar constructed an election platform that included the main mujahideen factions. Afghanistan's politics without parties ensured there was no effective democratic counterweight to the power brokers of the 1980s and 1990s, so these deals still needed to be done. But Atmar's platform proved too broad to hold together, facing the well-resourced campaigns of Ghani and Abdullah Abdullah, through the year of delayed elections, and he withdrew from the race.

Tribal heritage and wartime experience remained more important than any policy differences between candidates. When advising in Ashraf Ghani's office in 2017, I wrote a paper reminding his staff of the success of Emmanuel Macron in putting together a party from nowhere that succeeded both in parliamentary and presidential elections in France. With an Afghan parliamentary election then coming up in 2018 and the presidential poll a year later, perhaps this could be a model. If Ghani ran a recognizable slate of candidates for parliament, that could be the springboard, providing a machine for the presidential poll. But opposition to political parties in Afghanistan runs deep, and the proposal had no traction. The reform-minded Daud Noorzai did try to run one hundred candidates in the parliamentary election who would be acknowledged as a Ghani bloc, but he quickly pulled out when it became clear that the election was more mired in corruption even than previous polls.

As incumbent, the 2019 election was Ghani's to lose. In a traditional society, people asked why he needed to be replaced if he had not died, and voted accordingly. But he was vulnerable to attack. The rumor grew that his was a Pashtun-centric administration. A popular insult was that you had to be "LLE" to get on in the Arg—from the Pashtun provinces of Laghman or Logar and speak English. It was never true; even among senior staff, there was a balance of tribal identities. But the Arg were not proactive at combating falsehoods and telling their own story.

There was some progress. In 2019, Afghanistan paid 60 percent of the $140 million cost of their own election, the first fought on a new biometric register. A version of this technology was available in 2001 and used to register returning refugees. But President Karzai wanted to keep control of the voting register and had opposed the retention of the database of more than a million identities collected by UN refugee agencies. Continued opposition to a reformed register meant that in elections up until 2018, any one of three polling cards issued since 2001 could be used in any polling station in the country—a license for fraud.

After every election, international donors said, "Never again," and every time it came to the crunch, they shelved their reservations, held their noses, and paid up.

Once Karzai had left office in 2014, it became possible to bring in a register with biometric data. There were tortuous negotiations over what information would be on the identity card. For many citizens of Afghanistan, and in particular Tajiks and Hazaras, the word *Afghan* means "Pashtun," and they insisted that if they be called Afghans, they wanted their own tribal identity recorded on the card as well. The risk in measuring tribal identity was that it would reveal the actual proportions of each community in a country where there had not been a census since the 1970s.[3]

To vote in 2019, as well as these new biometric cards, people also needed a specific stamp, which for the first time had to be registered at a particular polling station. The complexity of this novel technology meant that on election day, many voters found they were not registered. That most patriotic and loyal of Afghans, the former army chief General Sher Muhammad Karimi, led fifteen members of his family to the polling station in his south Kabul neighborhood, and they found they were not on the list, despite having all the right documents, with relevant stamps.

≡ STRAIN ON #ENDURINGPARTNERSHIP

Another factor in the low turnout were questions over who the U.S. were supporting. For the first time, Ashraf Ghani did not have an American blank check. The openly stated resentment of his administration at their exclusion from Zalmay Khalilzad's peace efforts had an impact. A month before the election, the president announced the early release from jail on health grounds of Khalilullah Ferozi, the chief executive of Kabul Bank, and one of the few people arrested for the loss of most of the $900 million deposited in the bank. Ghani angrily denied that he ordered the release in return for donations to fight the election, but the Kabul ambassador, John Bass, tweeted that the decision "called into question the government's commitment to combating corruption and making best use of donors' support." Bass pointed to a further widespread failure to pursue "those accused of corruption."

In the ten days before the election, there were three more direct American attacks on the government's competence over procurement, an area

Ghani had made his direct responsibility. On September 18, Bass raised questions over why the National Procurement Authority had stopped buying fuel for the power station that supplied nearly all Kabul electricity. And the following day, Secretary of State Mike Pompeo blocked $160 million in aid, a move he connected directly to the election process just over a week away.[4] The U.S. would still spend $100 million of the aid in question—but off budget through contractors, not through the state. The decision felt like a kick in the teeth to a president whose professional life inside and outside Afghanistan was spent arguing for the merits of on-budget development support. A further $60 million of U.S. aid was withheld from the National Procurement Authority.

The head of the National Procurement Authority, a mild bookish engineer, Elham Omar Hotaki, requested the U.S. embassy identify the $100 million in question. In his mind, there was no secret about this; Ghani himself had flagged up problems with the southern power contracts, but there were not $100 million in pending payments. They could not have hidden anything, as the U.S. congressional watchdog, SIGAR, had a seat at the commission overseeing procurement. Afghans concluded that Pompeo was looking for anything he could find to weaken Ghani.

Two days before the election, Ghani called USAID "one of the most ineffective donor agencies" in a TV interview, adding that not more than ten cents in every dollar committed to Afghanistan actually reached the intended beneficiaries. Bass immediately took to Twitter, expressing disappointment that Ghani "overlooked the excellent work of @USAID and the details of our #enduringpartnership to improve the lives of Afghans."

In a country where honor and respect really mattered, this spat felt serious, with strong echoes of the machinations of the U.S. and UK embassies against the reelection of President Karzai in 2009. Rumors spread on Afghan social media. If America were not backing Ghani, who were they backing?

Two-thirds of the Afghan population now had a mobile phone subscription, a revolution with liberating potential—particularly giving women in remote areas a window on the world. Watching material on smartphones in some homes in Afghanistan is a bit like the early days of television in the West, collective viewing on small screens. The eighteen presidential candidates had mixed success in social media. The various

Ghani sites had many more followers than others, while one former Communist in the race, Hakim Torsan, had just twenty-five followers on Twitter, and his Facebook site was taken down by hackers. Inevitably, there were fake accounts—with many more attacking Ashraf Ghani than his main challenger, Abdullah Abdullah. And there were poorly faked images, crudely doctored images of Ghani and Abdullah alongside women, not as sophisticated as the deepfakes challenging Western democracies.[5] There was little evidence of Russian or other foreign tampering of the election through bots. With "regional and international actors who want to intervene in our election with money and guns," said Samira Sayed-Rahman, the head of Ghani's social media campaign, "I would prefer bots over that."[6]

☰ WARLORDS

One of the most prominent of the 1980s warlords, Gulbuddin Hekmatyar, was a candidate in the election. This was progress; in previous polls, several old warlords stood. He had no social media presence, as his violent Islamist history contravened Facebook policies, and sites were immediately taken down. Hekmatyar's Hezb-e Islami faction were responsible for the murder of thousands of liberal opponents in refugee camps in Pakistan in the 1980s, the targeted murder of several journalists, and the promotion of severe restrictions on the rights of women well before the Taliban came on the scene, as well as fighting for sixteen years against international forces after 9/11. He was hugely wealthy as a result of the lavish U.S. and Saudi funding of the mujahideen in the 1980s, when the most fundamentalist Islamist groups were the best rewarded, and when he made peace in 2017, he came down from the hills with his militias intact.[7] Racing around Kabul fully armed during his election campaign, they reminded people of the dark days of the early 1990s when Hekmatyar rocketed the city indiscriminately in bitter fighting with other mujahideen factions, before the Taliban arrived with their ruthless version of law and order.

Hekmatyar proved he had not changed when, in one election TV debate, he was asked by the hugely popular Pashtun singing star Naghma if she would be able to sing in Kabul's soccer stadium under his rule, as she had just done at the Afghan Premier League final. Hekmatyar answered, "Women will enjoy more rights than men under my leadership." But it was quickly clear that his view of rights was not as widely understood. "First, let's allow an Islamic government to be established. Then you will not ask for a concert at the Ghazi Stadium. Rather, you will ask permission to go to the battlefield"—an answer ridiculed on social media. A new generation of Afghan women did not want to have to ask permission to do anything, and Hekmatyar stood no chance of winning. But that he stood at all showed how deeply entrenched were the values of Afghanistan nearly two decades into the long war.

In that debate on TOLO TV, Hekmatyar faced Abdullah with an empty chair between them. Ghani chose instead to do a one-on-one interview at the same time on another channel, Ariana TV, a decision that either looked presidential or frightened, and was seen as such in social media posts on both sides. The Arg media machine was at last in professional hands under its new head, Sediq Sediqqi, a highly experienced and well-connected operator. So the general output was far better than previously, but Sediqqi was a government appointee, not a Ghani loyalist, and stood back over campaign decisions.

☰ ELECTION STREET

There were three separate Ghani campaigns. The president's closest team, the national security adviser, Hamdullah Mohib, and a political adviser, Fazel Fazly, decided his media appearances. A former minister, Daud Sultanzoy, ran a conventional top-down operation with press conferences.[††] The third team, led by Daud Noorzai and the president's cousin Ajmal Ghani, set up in a short street in central Kabul they renamed "Election Street" for the campaign, and were responsible for getting most votes out. Renting a couple of houses on one side of the street, and with volunteers working in a speculatively built empty hotel on the other side, managed by the Germanzais, Noorzai persuaded the few other occupied houses to allow him to seal off the street with blast walls and put up big tents, holding back-to-back rallies for thousands of people as he gathered support to reelect the president.

Unlike previous Afghan elections, there were few large rallies. A week before polling, twenty-six people were killed when a suicide bomber

---

†† Sultanzoy's wife, Zohra Yusuf Daud, was crowned Miss Afghanistan in 1972, the only year there was a competition. She went on to become a prominent advocate for Afghan women's rights.

rode a motorbike into a security checkpoint at a Ghani rally in Charikar, north of Kabul. The same day, twenty-two people were killed in another bomb outside the U.S. embassy. That drove the campaign mostly onto social media. The Mohib-Fazly team made a long, dreamy video profile of Ghani as a man who came from nowhere, full of shots from helicopter swoops along misty valleys. In contrast, Noorzai's team posted a more contemporary video of a pair of rappers with a patriotic riff about modern women, the army, and youth, and finishing with a rap version of the national anthem. It was shot with lots of drone footage, on clear, bright days, mostly around the gleaming Darul Aman Palace, that had stood as a giant ruin and reminder of war in the west of the city until its restoration in Ghani's administration. The chorus, "Ghani Baba—King Asti," went viral.

Using data gathered during the months up to polling, the Ghani campaign targeted up to eight thousand voters a day by phone ahead of election day, while tens of thousands more came through Election Street. The bottom-up approach was repeated nationwide, with small events working through Afghan influence networks, rather than the top-down patronage approach of previous campaigns. On election day itself, hundreds of volunteers were given lists to get out the vote in the improvised call center in the underground garage of the hotel, while in a conference room upstairs, tables of people worked individual provinces, including retired military officers, prepared to respond if there were security issues. Young people with smartphones sat next to war veterans with brick phones, and each played their role. There was a floor of hotel rooms higher up given over to influential backers, including a notorious warlord with a self-appointed role "protecting" Kabul.

In the event, the Taliban failed to disrupt the polls in a significant way. But a look at incidents reported in Kabul showed the risks people took while voting. Some rural areas were even more threatened. (PD: Police District. IED: improvised explosive device.)

08:20hrs, PD 11. Abdul Qadir Bidil High School Area. IED detonated near a polling station. No casualties reported at this time.

09:00hrs, PD 7. Chilesaton area. IED explosion. No casualties reported.

09:00hrs, Bagrami District, near police station. IED detonated
against police vehicle. One police officer injured.

09:20hrs, PD 12. Arzan Qaimat Area, Hussain Khil High School,
Explosion near polling station. No casualties.

09:20hrs, PD 8. Abdurrahman Pazwak high school, IED explosion
inside polling station. 2 civilians injured.

09:35hrs, PD 19. Two mortars launched from Koh Safi which
impacted in open area in PD 19 area. No casualties reported.

09:50hrs, Bagrami District, Puli Bagrami area, roadside IED
explosion, no casualties reported.

10:00hrs, PD 7. Takhnikom area. Report of explosion on polling
site.

10:20hrs, PD 12. IED Explosion reported in Bot Khak area

11:15hrs, PD 12. Ibrahim Khalilullah high school. Second explosion.
Polling station closed.

Ghani voted in a school inside the wide security zone around the
presidential compound, making a short, gracious speech thanking the
Americans and others for helping with the election. The group around
him included his new vice presidential candidate, the former head of the
NDS intelligence service, Amrullah Saleh, who replaced Abdul Rashid
Dostum on the ticket. Saleh was a Tajik with a mujahideen record, who
worked closely with the CIA after 9/11. He was vehemently opposed to
Pakistan and to peace talks with the Taliban.

Across town shortly before Ghani finished at his polling station, Abdullah appeared at the same time, forcing live TV channels to choose, and
most chose a split screen; bad timing for Abdullah, who was downplayed,
despite wearing the smartest powder-blue, double-breasted suit. In Election Street at the end of the day, Noorzai arranged simple street-food
deliveries, and there was live drums and musicians as young Ghani volunteers, delirious with fatigue, whirled around in the traditional Afghan
dance, the *attan*.

In the end, for all the hard work, of the fifteen million Afghans of

voting age, only nine million were on the register, and fewer than two
million valid votes were counted.[8] There were many reasons for the low
turnout—people were disillusioned by the American imposition of a
national unity government in 2014. What was the point of voting if it
did not deliver a result? And clearly, the complex registration and voting procedures did not work well. The biometric system set a high bar
for votes to be counted valid. All the staff on the Independent Election
Commission, who ran the process, were replaced after the corruption of
the parliamentary election in 2018. This high turnover lost institutional
memory, and the new staff needed to learn how to run an election. So it
was year one for the eighteenth time, not just for rotating international
staff in Kabul but also for Afghan institutions.

≡ PARALLEL CEREMONIES

It took five months, until February 18, 2020, before the votes were
counted. Ghani was declared victor on the slimmest of margins—50.64
percent. With his total of less than a million votes, there were inevitable
questions over his legitimacy. This took the shine off what was actually
an unprecedented success. Karzai had never achieved the 50 percent
necessary to avoid a second round. Abdullah disputed his 39.52 percent
vote share, and armed gangs roamed the streets, declaring him the victor.
He appointed two governors in provinces in the north, in a direct challenge to Ghani's authority, and a number of other leading politicians
supported him.

Meanwhile in Doha, Zalmay Khalilzad had taken up where he left
off when the Camp David summit was abruptly canceled in September.
With the election result declared, he had a deal ready to go. All it needed
was a one-week pause in hostilities to confirm the Taliban's goodwill—
not a formal cease-fire but what was called a "reduction in violence."

Against the febrile political backdrop, with rumors of a coup, the reduction in violence had a very different atmosphere to the 2018 Eid
truce. The Taliban did not stream into cities but stayed at their posts,
warily eyeing their government opponents. The overwhelming sense
from reporters who visited the quiet front lines was of a war that had
run its course—men and weapons worn out. "This war is just destroying
everything," said the army commander in Helmand, Lieutenant General
Wali Muhammad Ahmadzai. "We are tired, and the Taliban is tired."[9]

Out on the ground in Marjah, the district that was supposed to have been secured with a government in a box back in 2010 under General Stanley McChrystal, *Washington Post* reporter Susannah George found police relieved to be able to venture from their posts without being shot. Curious Taliban visited one post, and the police invited them in, saying they had a chicken for lunch. But the Taliban said they were under orders not to go any further. Farmers between the front lines said things had improved when the Taliban returned in strength to Marjah in 2015. Now it was time for it to end. "Tell the foreigners, just sign the agreement," said Abdulbaqi Atrafi. "Because if they don't, we are ready to fight for 25 more years."[10]

With no major outbreaks of fighting for a week, the way was clear for a grand signing ceremony in a convention center in the Doha Sheraton—witnessed by two lines of Taliban negotiators sitting impassively at the back of the hall and afterward agreeing to selfies with visitors and delegates. They had gotten what they wanted—a commitment for foreign forces to leave a lifting of sanctions against the Taliban, and a phased release of five thousand of their prisoners from government jails. Throughout the agreement, they were referred to as the "Islamic Emirate" as they wanted to be, even if in couched in the most convoluted twenty-two-word conditional description—"the Islamic Emirate of Afghanistan which is not recognized by the United States as a state and is known as the Taliban." Moreover, there was no mention of the Ghani administration as the government of Afghanistan, nor as a future negotiating partner. The Taliban agreed only to negotiations with "Afghan sides" and to release one thousand prisoners "of the other side."

In a parallel ceremony in Kabul at the same time, Ghani's grievances scorched off the first page of the agreement he signed with Secretary of Defense Mark Esper that outlined the terms of the U.S./Taliban deal. Ghani insisted on a twenty-eight-word description clarifying his legal status—"the Islamic Republic of Afghanistan, a member of the United Nations and recognized by the United States and the international community as a sovereign state under international law." The NATO secretary-general was a witness in Kabul, but this was an American-Afghan deal; other coalition troops would withdraw on a timetable set in Washington.

Understandably, Ghani was not going to be bounced into releasing prisoners without further guarantees, and from the next day, the ambitious timetable set in Doha of talks beginning in March began to slip. But the clock was ticking in Washington. Patience for the Ghani government was in short supply. Secretary of State Mike Pompeo had been twisting Ghani's arm once again to accept a national unity government, giving Abdullah half the posts.

On March 9, with no deal agreed, and with opposition from his closest Western allies, Ghani went ahead with his second inauguration. The talks to try to broker a compromise with Abdullah went on all night, pushing the event from 9:00 a.m., through 11:00, finally taking place at 3:00 in the afternoon. The setting was the beautiful inner garden of the Arg, the Harem Serai, the scene the week before of the signing of the deal with the U.S. The event developed along characteristically Afghan lines—formal, but with haphazard improvisation. Interruptions by individuals leaping to their feet and shouting a chant or lines of poetry are welcomed and respected at such gatherings. Groups of men, wearing the distinctive northern Afghan rolled woolen hat, the *pakhool,* climbed up into the lower branches of giant plane trees for a better view. There were blocks of dignitaries—ministers, MPs, senators, the supreme court judges who would administer the oath, in black robes with gold trim, and at the back, the orange hats of a representative group of street cleaners. At the front were some 1980s warlords, but more attended a parallel event close by where, in what felt like a very dangerous moment, Abdullah too was inaugurated as president by his supporters.

There is a military saying that the "enemy has a vote," and that day, it was exercised by the firing of four rockets from the back of a car close to the events while Ghani was speaking. One fell inside the Arg compound, although no one was injured. The sound of the explosions crashed across the small garden area, full of people with only one narrow exit, causing momentary panic. But these people had heard many explosions before and did not run away. Security guards tried to hustle out Zalmay Khalilzad and General Miller, sitting in the front of the diplomatic section, but they stayed as Ghani remained on the podium. Pushing off his security guards, Ghani opened his jacket and pointed to his white shirt, saying, "This is not body armor. This is just a shirt. This body is ready to be sacrificed for the Afghan people." Standing firm may have given him some political breathing space. Immediately, there were thousands of pictures on social media of people opening their jackets, with #belikeghani.[11]

In further negotiations after the parallel inaugurations, Ghani was forced to accept Abdullah as a partner again, giving him 50 percent of the posts in government. But this time, it was not a national unity government. Instead, Abdullah was given the role of supervising the peace process. Like everything in the world in 2020, movement forward on this was affected by COVID-19, but the prisoners were released, and the Afghan government finally put together a credible, representative, tightly focused group of negotiators, led by the former minister Muhammad Masoom Stanekzai—the best-qualified person for the job. Time was not on their side. American patience, on both sides of the aisle, was running out.

☰ STANDING ALONE?

The Arg has been the seat of Afghan power for 140 years and has seen foreign supporters come and go. Unable to bring Afghanistan into the British Empire after two wars in the nineteenth century, Britain gave subsidies of both cash and guns to the amir who built the Arg, Abdur Rahman, to keep him on their side against Russian intervention in British India. In 1893, they cut the weapons supply, restoring it only when he agreed to the Durand Line, the contested border with what later became Pakistan. After a third war with Britain in 1919, the subsidies stopped, and King Amanullah's need to raise taxes in the 1920s was one of the reasons for his downfall in a revolution against his reforms. Germany, Italy, and France began long relationships with the country then.

In the early days of the Cold War, the Afghan defence minister Daoud Khan went to Washington and failed in his request for military support. The alternative, he told them, was for him to seek it from Moscow. But Afghanistan was not a concern for the U.S., who had decided their regional ally was Pakistan. So from 1954 onward, Afghan troops went to the Soviet Union for training, and their forces were armed with Soviet weapons. Not supporting Afghanistan had consequences for long-term U.S. interests. When Daoud Khan replaced his cousin as the king in a coup in 1973, it set the stage for the gathering storm that would lead to his death in a more violent coup and closer Soviet involvement, culminating in the Christmas invasion in 1979.[12]

The U.S. then backed the mujahideen in their ten-year campaign against the invasion until Soviet troops pulled out, and that aid continued for a further three years to help the mujahideen combat the Afghan government the Soviet Union had left behind. When the aid from both sides dried up with the collapse of the Soviet Union in 1992, Afghanistan entered nine years of darkness, civil war between the mujahideen, and then rule by the Taliban.

Afghans fear a return to 1992 if the military support and other aid dries up. Some of those voting in September 2019 were not even born on 9/11 and owe their lives and education to the American-led intervention, but after all the blood and treasure expended, their fragile democracy still depends on international support.

The warlords responsible for the civil war in 1992 have not gone away. When in August 2020 Ghani finally announced the reconciliation council who would oversee the peace process with the Taliban, most of the names were those warlords. At some point, they need to be retired with honor to make way for a new generation. Ghani wanted them in the tent, while standing up his more reformist administration, with the aim of ultimately replacing the old guard. Five years on that reformist agenda was still a work in progress, now also challenged by new corrupt elites who did not draw their power from the time of the mujahideen.

American military intervention in Afghanistan after 9/11 was inevitable after a grievous wound on the homeland. But twenty years on, more than three thousand American and other international lives lost, many, many more Afghan casualties, and $1 trillion spent, no one could argue that the policy was managed well.

At the start, President Bush held two contradictory views that ran on parallel tracks. One was the idea of a quick strike against the Taliban and al-Qaeda leaders, the second his more whimsical sense of America spreading the fruits of democracy. Bush directly invoked the postwar reconstruction of Germany. "We did not leave behind occupying armies; we left constitutions and parliaments." He forgot the painstaking preparations made in the years before 1945 for the postwar phase. In Afghanistan after 2001, there was a rush to a constitution and elections. In contrast, post-1945 German institutions were rebuilt from the bottom up, with local and regional institutions prioritized over national elections. "Throughout history this has been the best approach to building states," according to army historian Dr. Conrad C. Crane. There were also far more forces available in postwar Germany than in Afghanistan, and a willingness to stay the course. "The United States," Crane wrote, "has rarely accomplished long-term goals after any conflict without an extended American military presence to ensure proper results from the peace."[13]

Were the mistakes all at the beginning? There is no doubt that the light-footprint approach did not bring all the capacity the U.S. had at its disposal to leave a stable country. The lack of military power on the ground let even the main prey, Osama bin Laden, escape, and sowed the seeds for a long bitter harvest of war. American (and wider international) unwillingness to properly prepare for complex interventions like Afghanistan, the wars they mostly fight, meant that the Afghan war was improvised from the start. After the Afghan experience, and with the bloodbaths of Libya and Iraq along the way, there will be no appetite for the foreseeable future for military intervention. One prominent political adviser, who spent many years in Afghanistan, told me in early 2020 with crystal clarity, in a bar near the State Department in D.C., "Anyone who argues for nation-building in this town now is mad." But there are already a number of small interventions underway, Mali and Somalia most prominently. Not harvesting the lessons of a twenty-year campaign would be a dangerous act of amnesia, dishonoring the sacrifice of those who died.

The key lessons are to understand the context of the country itself, coordinate development with military force from the beginning, and put in enough troops to stabilize the situation—alongside forces configured to manage policing, customs collection, border controls, power, water, and the other basic necessities of a state. And successful intervention takes time. The veteran nation-builder Jim Dobbins divides people involved in intervention into three groups.

> First are the regional experts, those who understand how the society in conflict currently operates. This group often finds it hard to envisage substantial change and is consequently pessimistic about the degree of reform that may be possible. The second category is made up of experienced nation-builders. These individuals may know little of the society in question but do understand the process by which its transformation is to be attempted. These individuals are likely to advise that fundamental reforms are possible, but time

consuming and expensive to effectuate. The last group is composed
of those who know little of the society in question or of the na-
tionbuilding process. People in this third category are most prone to
believe that change can be achieved quickly and easily. It is also the
members of this last category who are normally in charge.[14]

Joe Biden, the fourth president to be faced with the dilemma of Afghanistan, entered the White House with more knowledge than his predecessors, from his years on the Senate Foreign Relations Committee,
and as vice president when he was the strongest opponent of increased
troops in the Obama administration. During the 2020 campaign he ruffled feathers in Kabul by questioning whether Afghanistan could survive
as a unified state. "There's no possibility to unite that country, no possibility at all of making it a whole country."[15]

His leading foreign advisers, in particular Secretary of State Antony
Blinken and National Security Adviser Jake Sullivan, were steeped in the
debates during the Obama years, when they had been in Biden's vice-
presidential office. Blinken kept Khalilzad in post in January 2020, and
had sight of the secret annexes to the peace deal that Khalilzad had agreed
with the Taliban. The administration faced a strong lobby to keep the
troops in Afghanistan for longer. Less than two weeks after the inauguration, the former chairman of the Joint Chiefs of Staff, and Afghan commander, General Joe Dunford, in a Congress-mandated review of policy,
argued that the final troop withdrawal date should be based on conditions
on the ground, not an arbitrary timetable.[16] Pulling troops out before the
country was stable risked Afghanistan once again turning into a haven for
global terrorists.

Biden had heard the same argument in 2009 and was not persuaded
by it then or in 2021. And now he was in a position to act decisively. On
April 13, speaking from the Treaty Room of the White House, where
President Bush had announced the start of the campaign on October 7
2001, he signalled the end of the long war. All troops would be out by
September, the twentieth anniversary of 9/11. Keeping troops in Afghanistan until the country was stable meant they could be there for
ever. "We cannot continue the cycle of extending or expanding our
military presence in Afghanistan, hoping to create ideal conditions for
the withdrawal, and expecting a different result."

The decision was greeted with dismay in Afghanistan. The Taliban had not negotiated in good faith since securing the release of thousands of their fighters from Afghan jails in 2020. Talks with the Afghan government side in Doha had made no progress. Instead of negotiating, since the beginning of 2021 they had engaged in a campaign of intimidation against journalists, women's rights campaigners, and others working for a new country—killing dozens of people in targeted assassinations. A prominent women's group, Equality for Peace and Democracy, said that Afghans were "being deserted at a time when violence is at an all-time high." The international troop presence may have been small, but provided them reassurance.

The timetabled exit was also opposed by many in the military, and earned a rare note of public dissent from the head of Britain's armed forces, General Sir Nick Carter, who said it was "not a decision we had hoped for." There were many more troops from other NATO countries than America on the ground in Afghanistan, and on the principle of "in together, out together," when this book went to press the plan was they would all leave by September.

Could it have been different? What if the Bush administration had not gone to war in Iraq? Afghanistan was always second best, the other war, an "economy of force" operation. "In Afghanistan we do what we can, in Iraq we do what we must," said the chairman of the Joint Chiefs of Staff, Admiral Mike Mullen, in 2007. And there were other counterfactuals. What if Abdul Haq had survived, the other leader who might have come in rather than Karzai as the first president?[17] What if Karzai's deal with the Taliban in December 2001 had been pursued, or the Taliban leaders who continued to approach the U.S. through 2002 had been listened to, rather than imprisoned? What if ISAF troops had garrisoned Kabul more quickly ahead of Fahim's Northern Alliance forces in 2001, and then been reinforced across the country with a large enough force of troops trained for the task? What if aid had followed Afghan direction from the start, building infrastructure and human capacity, not a parallel system? What if General Dave McKiernan had the troops he wanted when he asked for them in 2008? What if the ash cloud had not delayed General Stanley McChrystal in Europe in 2010 and he had done another year? Might counterinsurgency in his hands have been really different from what General Dave Petraeus adopted, could it have delivered the effect it promised? What if all CIA and SOF activities were fully coordinated so that night raids did not destabilize other operations, and their local militias were brought under more conventional (and accountable) command?

What if General John Allen had been able to keep his surge troops for longer, out on a gentler glide path, rather than on President Obama's calendar in 2011? Allen saw a mismatch between what he was being asked to do and what he was being given for the task. "Our military objectives, that we had created as a direct result of the political objectives in the campaign plan, did not envisage their accomplishment based on a timetable." And after the campaign morphed from combat into train, advise, and support in 2014, what if General John "JC" Campbell had retained more offensive capability in air operations from the beginning? Would that have stalled the Taliban? What if Pakistan had not shared the coordinates of Mullah Mansour's car traveling across the Baluch desert with the Americans in 2016? Would he have been willing to make peace earlier?

Twenty years after the U.S. sent troops to Afghanistan for its longest war, the giant plane trees planted by Amir Abdur Rahman in the 1880s shed their leaves for another fall in the Harem Serai, the inner garden in the Arg—the venue of the signing of the U.S./Afghan deal in 2020 and Ghani's contested inauguration just nine days later. When I worked there, the only trace I could find of Taliban occupation were the heads of deer crudely scratched-out on the nineteenth-century tiles on the narrow gateway into the garden, victims of their mad opposition to images of human or animal form. The legacy of the Taliban in the minds and lives of Afghan people may last far longer. That depends on the capacity of the representatives of the frail, new democratic Afghanistan, squeezed by the Taliban, the old warlords, and a new corrupt elite as they stand up for a fair settlement in a peace process, and create a country where all can live without fear and with equality before the law. They will need support for some time yet.

ACKNOWLEDGMENTS

I have been fortunate in my traveling companions in Afghanistan. The wise and courtly Rahimullah Yusufzai, who won the trust of the Taliban and unlocked exclusive access for the BBC to the front line of their advance into Kabul in 1996, when I was with camera operator Fred Scott, and video editor Vladimir Lozinski. Najibullah Razaq, who, among many other acts of wizardry, negotiated my safe passage across front lines in Helmand for an interview with Taliban senior leaders in 2007. Vaughan Smith, who hitched rides on helicopters and walked with me through the Hindu Kush during the initial U.S. invasion in 2001, and a few months later we survived being stoned by a large mob in Helmand while reporting the return of poppy growing after the fall of the Taliban. Mahfouz Zubaide, whose constant resourcefulness is the heart of the BBC operation in Kabul, and who, with camera operator and editor Malik Mudasir Hassan, made my two years based in Afghanistan, 2013 to 2015, such a pleasure. And Robert Adams, who joined me on a shared quest to visit the Buddhas at Bamiyan in the winter of 2000. We had gone to shoot a story about a famine, which included haunting images of starving people living in caves carved in the hillside 1,500 years ago for monks. Once we had completed that we spent a day taking pictures of the remarkable vast stone Buddhas and the remnants of once beautiful cave paintings in the niches behind. We knew they were threatened by al-Qaeda and just a few months later they were no more.

And there were many other producers and videojournalists whose ideas, pictures, and perceptions added to the kaleidoscope of images, impressions, and ideas that have informed my writing and understanding of Afghanistan, and so contributed to *The Long War,* along with archive research and new interviews: Auliya Atrafi, Shoaib Sharifi, Bilal Sarwary, Massud Popalzai, Jafar Hand, Waheed Massoud, Aleem Agha, Ismael Saadat, Amir Shah, Duncan Stone, John Boon, Daud Qarizadeh, Paul Mongey Sanjay Ganguly, Andrew "Sarge" Herbert, Adam "Moose" Campbell, Bhasker Solanki, Rachel Thompson, Philip Palmer; and BBC reporting colleagues, among them William Reeve, Alastair Leithead, Martin Patience, Quentin Sommerville, Harun Najafizada, Lyse Doucet, and Hugh Sykes. Many Afghan journalists, other than those I worked closely with in the BBC, shared valuable insights into their country, in particular Danish Karokhel, Sharif Hassanyar, Lotfullah Najafizada, Javed Hamim Kakar, Massoud Hossaini, and Abdullah Khenjani (later a government minister).

During the year that I worked as an adviser in the Afghan president's office, 2017 to 2018, I was fortunate in having a good friend, Dominic Medley, in Kabul at the same time. I had already begun research and interviews for the book and I have been able to draw on Dominic's encyclopedic knowledge of the international intervention, learned in long years as a strategic communications expert on both the military and civilian sides in ISAF and the UN in Kabul. Dominic played a significant role in developing the free media in Afghanistan after 2001, one of the few real success stories of the last twenty years, and founded the now-defunct *Afghan Scene* magazine in the heady early days when there was a hope that tourism would follow the fall of the Taliban. He was justly honored with a medal by the British government for his contribution. I also benefited from the friendship of a real expert in strategic communications, Brett Boudreau, who was in Kabul at the same time as my 2017 role. Brett's account of the NATO strategic communications effort in the combat years—*We Have Met the Enemy and He Is Us*—was invaluable source material.

The Long War began as a project to conduct in-depth interviews with the commanders in Kabul covering just the eight years of the most intense combat from 2006 to 2014, and I am grateful for them spending time to share their experience. (Where quotations from the ISAF commanders are not footnoted, they come from those interviews.) The focus of the idea changed to cover the whole narrative of the long war when it became clear that there was no way to understand the challenges of the "surge" years without examining the background and context that led to this becoming America's longest war, or the long, slow drawdown of troops. The scope also broadened to include analysis of the development and diplomatic strands of policy, as well as the defense challenge—the "three Ds."

I had specialized in international development reporting for the BBC, and this gave me the background to look at the intersection between the "three Ds" and the tensions between the different communities. I write in the introduction about their different calendars, with military officers impatient for quick spending after taking ground, frustrated by development officials who know that lasting change will take far longer. I have been involved in all these worlds. At the peak of the combat years I learned much about the dynamics when I was one of a small group of civilian experts on Afghanistan who lectured every incoming British army brigade during their preparation for a tour, and I led on an in-career training course for British diplomats on policy in South Asia and Afghanistan. I have also worked as a strategic communications adviser on U.S.-funded programs in Kabul since 2015. I am grateful to Bill Byrd for looking over some of the material on development with the professional eye of an ex–World Bank economist with Afghan expertise.

Sources for *The Long War* include news accounts, online research, books and interviews, as well as my own notes from visits to Afghanistan every year since the early 1990s. Some of the most revealing books have come out only in the last few years, as CIA officers consider that enough time has elapsed to be able to give their account, which can now be tested against other evidence. It is striking how much open-source material there is online, including leaks of confidential military memos, blogs by military and development officials, academic research, and large volumes of official data. But it is also striking how many of the URLs, including from official sources, soon become unusable. The internet is a fleeting friend for modern historians—catch it now before it is gone. In checking endnotes for *The Long War,* links that worked only a year ago are no longer alive. This is an ongoing challenge for writers and archivists. Parchment survives for one thousand years; much key open-source Afghan data has gone in a couple of years.

The primary source material is interviews, conducted either when I was reporting in the field or specifically for the book. Among other interviews, I would like particularly to thank General Sir Nick Carter for taking time out of his role as the chief of the UK Defence Staff to talk about his significant experience in Afghanistan, beginning as a colonel in a tent in early 2002, up to his role as the deputy commander of ISAF, taking in several important command positions along the way. I am grateful for the time of a number of analysts and military and development officials who shared their perceptions of the long dilemmas of Afghan policy for this book. Some I have agreed not to name, but others include Ambassador Ronald E. Neumann, Francesc Vendrell, Scott Guggenheim, Jeff Eggers, Doug Lute, Barney Rubin, Jarrett Blanc, Chris Kolenda, Carter Malkasian, Matt Sherman, Pat McCarthy, Cliff Trout, and Andrew Steinfeld. I spent a memorable day with Marc Chretien at his cider barn in the Virginia countryside talking about Afghanistan and visiting Civil War graves in a nearby churchyard with him on the way back to Washington. It was in early March 2020, and I had to cut the trip short and flee back across the Atlantic as COVID-19 began to close things down. Just over a week later I was in Kabul as a guest at the second inauguration of President Ghani, taking the opportunity on a brief trip to interview Hanif Atmar, then out of office but appointed Afghan foreign minister shortly afterward. That was to be the last face-to-face contact before I went onto Zoom with the rest of the globe in order to complete the interviews.

I had by then done a number of interviews with key Afghan players, and I am very grateful for their time, notably among them former president Hamid Karzai, owner of TOLO TV Saad Mohseni, former interior ministers Umer Daudzai and Wais Barmak, former deputy foreign minister Jawed Ludin, and former governor of Nuristan Tamim Nuristani. And I spoke at length to that great Afghan public servant, the former head of the army General Sher Muhammad Karimi, who is currently working on a Pashto translation of this text. I should also highlight among many others, a few people who have been influential in informing my understanding of Afghanistan, including Lynne O'Donnell, Jolyon Leslie, Kate Clark, Abdul Waheed Wafa, and Haseeb Humayoon.

Reporters from other news organizations are friends and traveling companions as much as they compete for stories, particularly in foreign news, and I have benefited from their insights, shared particularly in the memorable years when the Gandamack Lodge in Kabul provided shelter and a bar, the ideal location for rest and recuperation. It was founded by freelance camera operator Peter Jouvenal, who has been traveling in Afghanistan since the early days of the Russian war in the 1980s, sometimes with me (I tell his story in my book *Frontline*). Peter led the BBC news crew who were the first into Kabul when it fell in 2001, and he soon put down his camera to find a location for the Gandamack.

In *The Long War* I have tried to describe the Afghanistan that is being constructed by the post-2001 generation, whether educated in Afghanistan or abroad, and how different this is to clichéd perceptions of the country seen from outside. I have learned a lot from the new reformers. Along with the journalists, figures in the government and civil society sector have a new vision for the country—people like Sadat Naderi, Nadir Naim, Daud Noorzai, Schah-Zaman Maiwandi, Farkhunda Naderi, Mirwais Farahi, Timor Sharan, Nargis Nehan, Adela Raz, Mariam Wardak, Nisar Barakzai, Hamid Khan, Samira Sayed-Rahman, and Omaid Sharifi, whose brilliant Artlords project has brought color to the gray-lined blast walls of Kabul with inventive political stencils. The 1980s warlords still hold disproportionate power, but the traditional society they stand for no longer has consent. The change that has come may be lasting if it is cherished. Women's rights are not an irrelevant Western obsession; opinion polls show that women's participation in the peace process is a popular demand across the country. Meetings between women's groups and conservative religious leaders have come out with remarkably progressive agendas for women's employment, education, and married rights.

The Long War is not a first-person account. It is a step back to deliver a historical narrative, and take a view of what the American war was (/is) about, and how it was (/is) conducted. I have tried to credit other accounts as comprehensively as possible where I have drawn on them. "I" am not much in the book, except where essential to tell the story. Where there are incidents recounted that are not footnoted, that is often because I witnessed them as a reporter, but I have not written myself into the account in the book.

For clarity, Afghan names have been standardized to the usual American first and last name format, although this is not the way they are always used in Afghanistan, where many people have only one name. The reason for the odd double name of the leading politician, Abdullah Abdullah, was that when he first encountered Western journalists in the

1980s and said he was called just "Abdullah," they insisted he needed something else. So he said "Okay, then I am Abdullah Abdullah." There is also usually no standard spelling of names, which are transliterations of Arabic script, so I have tried to take an informed view. As an example of the challenge, the name of a police chief, Aminullah Amerkhel, whose fight against corruption is told in chapter 10, can be spelt in the following ways, according to the excellent research resource www.afghan-bios .info—Amarkhel, Amerkheil, Amerkhail, Amarkhail, Amerkhil, Amar Khil, Amar Khail.

My agent, Charlie Viney, has been a great support during the journey toward the publication of *The Long War*, and many thanks also to lawyer Rupert Grey. Marc Resnick has had a clear guiding hand as editor, and his team at St. Martin's Press, in particular Lily Cronig, have provided timely support.

First and last thanks go to Jean Seaton, my first reader, and the best partner for life a writer could have.

PICTURE CREDITS

Lance Cpl. Richard P. Sanglap-Heramis: John Allen.
First Lieutenant Brian Tuthill: Stanley McChrystal and Hamid Karzai.

Dedication extract from *The Art of War,* Sun Tzu; edited by James Clavell; Dell; 1983.

BIBLIOGRAPHY

Ahmad, Jamil. *The Wandering Falcon*. New York: Riverhead Books, 2011.

Allen, Charles. *Soldier Sahibs: The Daring Adventurers Who Tamed India's Northwest Frontier*. London: John Murray Press, 2000.

Alter, Jonathan. *The Promise: President Obama, Year One*. New York: Simon & Schuster, 2011.

Berntsen, Gary. *Jawbreaker: The Attack on Bin Laden and Al-Qaeda: A Personal Account by the CIA's Key Field Commander*. New York: Crown Publishers, 2005.

Bergen, Peter. *The Longest War: The Enduring Conflict between America and Al-Qaeda*. New York: Simon & Schuster, 2011.

———. *Manhunt: The Ten-Year Search for Bin Laden from 9/11 to Abbotobad*. New York: Crown Publishers, 2012.

Birtle, Andrew J. *U.S. Army Counterinsurgency Operations Doctrine 1860–1941*. Fort Lesley J. McNair, Washington, D.C.: U.S. Army Center of Military History, 1998.

Bishop, Patrick. *3 Para*. New York: HarperPress, 2007.

Blehm, Eric. *The Only Thing Worth Dying For: How Eleven Green Berets Fought for a New Afghanistan*. New York: HarperCollins, 2010.

Bolger, Daniel, S. *Why We Lost: A General's Inside Account of the Iraq and Afghanistan Wars*. New York: Eamon Dolan/Mariner Books, 2015.

Boot, Max. *The Savage Wars of Peace: Small Wars and the Rise of American Power*. New York: Basic Books, 2002.

Boudreau, Brett. *We Have Met the Enemy and He Is Us*. Latvia: NATO StratCom Centre of Excellence, 2016.

Burroughs, Edgar Rice. *A Princess of Mars*. Chicago, IL: A. C. McClurg & Company, 1917; reissued 1968.

Bush, George W. *Decision Points*. London: Virgin Books, 2010.

Chandrasekaran, Rajiv. *Little America: The War Within the War for Afghanistan*. Bloomsbury, 2012.

Chayes, Sarah. *Punishment of Virtue: Inside Afghanistan After the Taliban*. London: Portobello Books, 2007.

Chayes, Sarah. *Thieves of State: Why Corruption Threatens Global Security*. New York:
W.W. Norton, 2016.

Churchill, Winston S. *The Story of the Malakand Field Force*. London: Longman, 1898.

Churchwell, Sarah. *Behold America: A History of America First and the American Dream*.
London: Bloomsbury Publishing, 2019.

Clinton, Hillary Rodham. *Hard Choices: A Memoir*. New York: Simon & Schuster, 2014.

Coll, Steve; *Directorate S: The C.I.A. and America's Secret Wars in Afghanistan and Pakistan,
2001–2016*. New York: Penguin, 2018.

Collier, Paul, and Augustin Kwasi Fosu, eds. *Economic Policy in Post-Conflict Societies*.
London: Palgrave Macmillan, 2005.

Crile, George. *Charlie Wilson's War: The Extraordinary Story of the Largest Covert Operation in History*. London: Atlantic Books, 2003.

Cunliffe, Marcus. *Soldiers and Civilians: The Martial Spirit in America, 1775–1865*.
Boston, MA: Little, Brown, 1968.

Dam, Bette. *A Man and a Motorcycle: How Hamid Karzai Came to Power*. Netherlands:
Ipso Facto Publishers, 2014.

Dobbins, James F. *After the Taliban: Nation-Building in Afghanistan*. Nebraska: Potomac
Books, 2008.

———. *America's Role in Nation-Building: From Germany to Iraq*. Santa Monica, CA:
RAND, 2003.

Dobbins, James, Seth G. Jones, Keith Crane, and Beth Cole DeGrasse. *The Beginner's
Guide to Nation-Building*. Santa Monica, CA: RAND, 2008.

Donati, Jessica. *Eagle Down: The Last Special Forces Fighting the Forever War*. New York:
PublicAffairs, 2021.

Doyle, Michael W., ed. *Liberal Peace: Selected Essays*. London: Routledge, 2012.

Edelstein, David. *Occupational Hazards: Success and Failure in Military Occupation*. Ithaca,
NY: Cornell University Press, 2008.

Eide, Kai. *Power Struggle Over Afghanistan*. New York: Skyhorse Publishing, 2012.

Fairweather, Jack. *The Good War: Why We Couldn't Win the War or the Peace in Afghanistan*. London: Jonathan Cape, 2014.

Farrell, Theo. *Unwinnable: Britain's War in Afghanistan, 2001–2014*. London: Bodley
Head, 2017.

Farwell, Matt, and Michael Ames. *American Cipher: One Soldier's Nightmare in the
Afghanistan War*. London: Wildfire, 2019.

Felbab-Brown, Vanda. *Aspiration and Ambivalence: Strategies and Realities of Counterinsurgency and State Building in Afghanistan*. Washington, D.C.: Brookings Institution, 2013.

Fergusson, James. *Taliban: The Inside Story of the World's Fiercest Guerrilla Fighters*.
London: Bantam Press, 2010.

Fergusson, James. *A Million Bullets: The Real Story of the British Army in Afghanistan*. London: Transworld Publishers, 2008.

Filkins, Dexter. *The Forever War*. New York: Vintage Books, 2009.

Franks, Tommy. *American Soldier*. New York: Harper Collins, 2009.

Gall, Carlotta. *The Wrong Enemy: America in Afghanistan 2001–2014*. Boston, MA: Houghton Mifflin, 2014.

Gall, Sandy. *War Against the Taliban: Why It All Went Wrong in Afghanistan*. London: Bloomsbury Publishing, 2012.

Galula, David. *Counterinsurgency Warfare: Theory and Practice*. Santa Monica, CA: RAND, 1964. Republished in edition of PSI Classics of the Counterinsurgency Era, 2006.

Gates, Robert. *From the Shadows: The Ultimate Insider's Story of Five Presidents and How They Won the Cold War*. New York: Simon & Schuster, 1996.

Gates Robert. *Duty: Memoirs of a Secretary at War*. London: Virgin Digital, 2014.

Ghani, Ashraf, and Clare Lockhart. *Fixing Failed States: A Framework for Rebuilding a Fractured World*. Oxford University Press, 2009.

Gopal, Anand. *No Good Men Among the Living: America, the Taliban and the War through Afghan Eyes*. New York: Metropolitan Books, 2015.

Gregg, Heather Selma. *Building the Nation: Missed Opportunities in Iraq and Afghanistan*. Nebraska: Potomac Books, 2018.

Grenier, Robert. *88 Days to Kandahar: A CIA Diary*. New York: Simon & Schuster, 2015.

Gray, John. *Black Mass: Apocalyptic Religion and the Death of Utopia*. London: Allen Lane, 2007.

Harnden, Toby. *Dead Men Risen: The Welsh Guards and the Defining Story of Britain's War in Afghanistan*. London: Quercus Books, 2011.

Hastings, Michael. *I Lost My Love in Baghdad: A Modern War Story*. New York: Pocket Books; 2008.

———. *The Operators: The Wild and Terrifying Inside Story of America's War in Afghanistan*. London: Orion Publishing, 2012.

Hillier, Rick. *A Soldier First: Bullets, Bureaucrats, and the Politics of War*. New York: Harper Collins, 2010.

Horn, Bernd. *No Lack of Courage: Operation Medusa, Afghanistan*. Toronto: Dundurn Press, 2010.

Johnson, Chris, and Jolyon Leslie. *Afghanistan: The Mirage of Peace*. London: Zed Books, 2013.

Kaplan, Fred. *The Insurgents*. New York: Simon & Schuster, 2013.

Kelley, Jill. *Collateral Damage: Petraeus/Power/Politics and the Abuse Of Privacy*. Kelley Publishing LLC, 2016.

Kilcullen, David. *The Accidental Guerrilla: Fighting Small Wars in the Midst of a Big One*. London: Hurst Publishers, 2009.

Kolenda, Christopher D. *The Counterinsurgency Challenge: A Parable of Leadership and Decision Making in Modern Conflict*. Mechanicsburg, PA: Stackpole Books, 2012.

Koontz, Christopher N., ed. *Enduring Voices: Oral Histories of the U.S. Army Experience in Afghanistan.* Washington, D.C.: U.S. Army Center of Military History, 2008.

Kissinger, Henry. *Diplomacy.* New York: Simon & Schuster, 1994.

Lamb, Christina. *Farewell Kabul: From Afghanistan to a More Dangerous World.* London: William Collins, 2015.

Lartéguy, Jean. *The Centurions.* London: Penguin, 2015.

———. *The Praetorians.* New York: Penguin, 2016.

Loyn, David. *Frontline: Reporting from the World's Deadliest Places.* London: Michael Joseph, 2005.

———. *In Afghanistan: Two Hundred Years of British, Russian and American Occupation.* London: Palgrave Macmillan, 2009.

Malkasian, Carter. *War Comes to Garmser: Thirty Years of Conflict on the Afghan Frontier.* London: Hurst Publishers, 2013.

Mann, James. *The Obamians: The Struggle Inside the White House to Redefine American Power.* New York: Penguin, 2011.

Martin, Mike. *An Intimate War: An Oral History of the Helmand Conflict, 1978–2012.* London: Hurst Publishers, 2014.

Mattis, Jim, and Bing West. *Call Sign Chaos: Learning to Lead.* New York: Random House, 2019.

McChrystal, General Stanley. *My Share of the Task: A Memoir.* New York: Penguin Publishing Group, 2013.

McChrystal, General Stanley, Tanbum Collins, David Silverman, and Chris Fussell; *Team of Teams: New Rules of Engagement for a Complex World.* New York: Penguin, 2015.

McChrystal, General Stanley, Jeff Eggers, and Jason Mangone. *Leaders: Myth and Reality.* New York: Portfolio Penguin, 2018.

Mazzetti, Mark. *The Way of the Knife: The CIA, a Secret Army and a War at the Ends of the Earth.* London: Scribe Publications, 2013.

McMaster, H. R. *Battlegrounds: The Fight to Defend the Free World.* New York: Harper-Collins, 2020.

Nasr, Seyyed Vali Reza. *Islamic Leviathan: Islam and the Making of State Power.* Oxford University Press, 2001.

Nagl, John A. *Learning to Eat Soup with a Knife: Counterinsurgency Lessons from Malaya and Vietnam.* University of Chicago Press, 2005.

Neumann, Ronald E. *The Other War: Winning and Losing in Afghanistan.* Nebraska: Potomac Books, 2009.

Obama, Barack. *A Promised Land.* London: Penguin Books Ltd, 2020.

Packer, George. *Our Man: Richard Holbrooke and the End of the American Century.* London: Jonathan Cape, 2019.

Powell, Jonathan. *Talking to Terrorists: How to End Armed Conflicts.* London: Bodley Head, 2014.

Prucha, Francis Paul. *The Sword of the Republic: The United States Army on the Frontier, 1783–1846.* New York: Macmillan, 1977.

Richards, General David. *Taking Command*. London: Headline Publishing Group, 2014.

Richter, Paul. *The Ambassadors: America's Diplomats on the Front Lines*. New York: Simon & Schuster, 2020.

Ricks, Thomas E. *Fiasco: The American Military Adventure in Iraq*. New York: Penguin, 2007.

———. *The Gamble: General Petraeus and the Untold Story of the American Surge in Iraq*. New York: Penguin, 2009.

Riedel, Bruce. *The Search for Al-Qaeda: Its Leadership, Ideology and Future*. Washington, D.C.: Brookings Institution, 2010.

———. *Deadly Embrace: Pakistan, America, and the Future of Global Jihad*. Washington, D.C.: Brookings Institution, 2012.

Robinson, Paul, and Jay Dixon. *Aiding Afghanistan: A History of Soviet Assistance to a Developing Country*. London: Hurst Publishers, 2013.

Rubin, Barnett R. *Afghanistan: What Everyone Needs to Know*. Oxford University Press, 2020.

Rucker, Philip, and Carol D. Leonnig. *A Very Stable Genius: Donald J. Trump's Testing of America*. Bloomsbury Publishing, 2020.

Rynning, Sten. *NATO in Afghanistan: The Liberal Disconnect*. Palo Alto, CA: Stanford University Press, 2012.

Sanger, David E. *Confront and Conceal: Obama's Secret War and Surprising Use of American Power*. New York: Crown Publishers, 2012.

Sayle, Timothy Andrews, Jeffrey A. Engel, Hal Brands, and William Inboden. *The Last Card: Inside George W. Bush's Decision to Surge in Iraq*. Cornell, 2019.

Schroen, Gary C. *First In: An Insider's Account of How the CIA Spearheaded the War on Terror in Afghanistan*. Random House Publishing Group, 2005.

Snodgrass, Guy M. *Holding the Line: Inside Trump's Pentagon with Secretary Mattis*. New York: Sentinel, 2019.

Sorley, Lewis. *A Better War: The Unexamined Victories and Final Tragedies of America's Last Years in Vietnam*. Boston, MA: Harcourt, 1999.

Steele, Jonathan. *Ghosts of Afghanistan: The Haunted Battleground*. London: Portobello Books, 2011.

Stein, Janice, and Eugene Lang. *An Unexpected War: Canada in Kandahar*. Toronto: Viking Canada, 2007.

Stewart, Rory and Gerald Knaus. *Can Intervention Work?* New York: W. W. Norton & Company, 2012.

Strick, Alex van Linschoten, and Felix Kuehn. *An Enemy We Created: The Myth of the Taliban / Al-Qaeda Merger in Afghanistan, 1970–2010*. London: Hurst Publishers, 2012.

Studwell, Joe. *How Asia Works: Success and Failure in the World's Most Dynamic Region*. London: Profile Books, 2013.

Surkhe, Astri. *When More is Less: The International Project in Afghanistan*. London: Hurst Publishers, 2011.

Tootal, Stuart. *Danger Close: Commanding 3 Para in Afghanistan*. London: John Murray Press, 2010.

Tuchman, Barbara. *The March of Folly: From Troy to Vietnam*. Knopf, 1984.

Waltz, Michael G. *Warrior Diplomat: A Green Beret's Battles from Washington to Afghanistan*. Nebraska: Potomac Books, 2014.

West, Bing. *The Wrong War: Grit, Strategy and the Way Out of Afghanistan*. New York: Random House, 2011.

Wright, Donald P. with the Contemporary Operations Study Team. *A Different Kind of War: The United States Army in Operation Enduring Freedom, October 2001–September 2005*. Fort Leavenworth, KS: Combat Studies Institute Press, 2010.

Woodward, Bob. *Bush At War*. New York: Simon & Schuster, 2002.

———. *Obama's Wars*. New York: Simon & Schuster, 2010.

———. *Fear: Trump in the White House*. New York: Simon & Schuster, 2018.

NOTES

INTRODUCTION

1   McChrystal, Stanley; *My Share of the Task—A Memoir [MYSOT];* Penguin Publishing Group; 2013; p351.

2   Author interview.

3   Landler, Mark; *New York Times;* January 1, 2017; https://www.nytimes.com/2017/01/01/world/asia/obama-afghanistan-war.html.

4   Obama, Barack; *A Promised Land;* Penguin Books Ltd; 2020; pp564–565.

5   *Midshipman* is a navy (and marine) term for officer cadet.

6   Some five hundred people were raped and murdered in a Vietnamese village.

7   http://www.foreignaffairs.com/articles/138459/fred-kaplan/the-end-of-the-age-of-petraeus.

8   https://www.foreignaffairs.com/articles/afghanistan/2013–08–12/limits-counterinsurgency-doctrine-afghanistan.

9   Author interview with head of Moby Group and founder of TOLO TV, Saad Mohseni.

10 Rynning, Sten; *NATO in Afghanistan—The Liberal Disconnect;* Stanford University Press; 2012; p136.

11 Waltz, Michael G.; *Warrior Diplomat;* Potomac Books; 2014; p203.

12 Boudreau, Brett; *We Have Met the Enemy and He Is Us;* NATO Stratcom Centre of Excellence; 2016.

13 Author interview with William Byrd, 2004.

14 Sedwill, Mark; former NATO senior civilian representative in Kabul; evidence to House of Lords Select Committee; October 14, 2020.

15 Tuchman, Barbara; *The March of Folly;* Knopf; 1984.

16 Johnson, Chris and Leslie, Jolyon; *Afghanistan—The Mirage of Peace;* Zed Books; 2013; Kindle loc 463.

CHAPTER I: NOT BUILDING A NATION

1   McChrystal; *MYSOT;* p96.

2   Ibid.; p77.

3   Dao, James; *New York Times;* June 1, 2002; http://www.nytimes.com/2002/06/01/world
    /new-us-commander-at-helm-in-afghanistan.html.

4   Wright, Donald P. with the Contemporary Operations Study Team; *A Different Kind of
    War—The United States Army in Operation Enduring Freedom, October 2001–September 2005;*
    Combat Studies Institute Press; Fort Leavenworth; 2009.

5   Franks, Tommy; *American Soldier;* Harper Collins; 2009; p324.

6   Congressional Research Service; July 2009; https://fas.org/sgp/crs/natsec/R40682.pdf.

7   McChrystal; *MYSOT;* p76.

8   Author interview with McChrystal.

9   Ibid.

10 Franks; p315.

11 Author interview with General Sir Nick Carter.

12 Author interview.

13 McChrystal; *MYSOT;* p77.

14 Loyn, David; *Frontline—Reporting from the World's Deadliest Places;* Michael Joseph; 2005;
    pp61–62.

15 Schroen, Gary C.; *First In;* Random House Publishing Group; 2005; p187.

16 Ibid.; p162.

17 Riedel, Bruce; *Deadly Embrace Pakistan, America, and the Future of Global Jihad;* Brookings
    Institution; 2012; Kindle loc 897.

18 Schroen; p173.

19 Woodward, Bob; *Bush At War;* Simon & Schuster; 2002; Kindle loc 2775.

20 Franks; p313.

21 Ibid.; p314.

22 Ibid.; p311.

23 Grenier, Robert; *88 Days to Kandahar;* Simon & Schuster; 2015; p60.

24 Grenier; p166.

25 The details in this account come from Dam, Bette: *A Man and a Motorcycle—How Hamid
    Karzai Came to Power;* Ipso Facto; 2014.

26 Blehm, Eric; *The Only Thing Worth Dying For;* Harper Collins; 2010; p155.

27 Coll, Steve; *Directorate S—The C.I.A. and America's Secret Wars in Afghanistan and Pakistan,
    2001–2016;* Penguin; 2018; p99.

28 Grenier; p163.

29 Deposed by his cousin Daoud Khan in 1973.

30 Blehm; p273.

31 Pentagon press conference; December 6, 2001.

32 *A Different Kind of War;* p113.

33 Pomfret, John and Chandrasekaran, Rajiv; *Washington Post;* November 17, 2001; https://
    www.washingtonpost.com/archive/politics/2001/11/17/report-taliban-set-to-pull-out-of
    -kandahar/aa2eae8a-091c-4b69-a3ca-c5b5cc8cce8c/.

34 Chayes, Sarah; *Punishment of Virtue—Inside Afghanistan After the Taliban;* Portobello; 2007; p57.

35 Ibid.; p77.

36 Dam; Kindle loc 2187.

37   *Afghanistan—Post-Taliban Governance, Security and U.S. Policy;* Congressional Research Service; https://fas.org/sgp/crs/row/RL30588.pdf.

38   Author interview.

39   Dam; Kindle loc 402.

40   Author interview.

41   Dobbins, James F.; *After the Taliban—Nation-Building in Afghanistan;* Potomac Books; 2008; p108.

42   Ibid.; p103.

43   Ibid.; p109.

44   *Washington Times;* Monday April 7 2008; https://www.washingtontimes.com/news/2008/apr/7/bush-a-convert-to-nation-building.

45   Dobbins; *After the Taliban;* p13.

46   Dobbins, James F. and others; *America's Role in Nation-Building: From Germany to Iraq;* RAND; 2003.

47   U.S. manual on stability operations FM 3–07; https://fas.org/irp/doddir/army/fm3–07.pdf; 2008.

48   Dobbins; *After the Taliban;* p105.

49   Hanagan, Deborah Lynn; *NATO and Coalition Warfare in Afghanistan 2001–2014;* King's College London; August 2017; https://kclpure.kcl.ac.uk/portal.

50   Dobbins; *After the Taliban;* p107.

51   Gall, Sandy; *War Against the Taliban—Why It All Went Wrong in Afghanistan;* Bloomsbury; 2012; p67.

52   Haass, Richard N.; *Newsweek;* July 18, 2010; https://www.newsweek.com/haass-time-draw-down-afghanistan-74467. This was the same size of force employed by the Soviet Union in the 1979 invasion, a far less permissive environment than was faced after the Taliban.

53   *A Different Kind of War;* p114.

54   Berntsen, Gary; *Jawbreaker—The Attack on Bin Laden and Al Qaeda: A Personal Account by the CIA's Key Field Commander;* Crown; 2005; Kindle loc p14.

55   *Tora Bora Revisited;* Senate Foreign Relations Committee report; November 30, 2009.

56   Mattis, Jim, and West, Bing; *Call Sign Chaos—Learning to Lead;* Random House; 2019; p74.

57   Mattis and West; p74.

58   *Tora Bora Revisited;* Senate Foreign Relations Committee report; November 30, 2009.

59   *A Different Kind of War;* p112.

60   Berntsen; p307.

61   *A Different Kind of War;* p135.

62   The 1991 operation against Saddam Hussein's seizure of Kuwait.

63   *A Different Kind of War;* p134.

64   *Air Force Magazine;* April 1, 2005; https://www.airforcemag.com/article/0405anaconda.

65   Stein, Janice, and Lang, Eugene; *An Unexpected War—Canada in Kandahar;* Viking Canada; 2007.

66   Interview with Alastair Leithead on *BBC Newsnight;* 2007.

67   McChrystal; *MYSOT;* p77.

68   Farrell, Theo; *Unwinnable—Britain's War in Afghanistan, 2001–2014;* Bodley Head; London; 2017; p99.

69   Lamb, Christina; *Farewell Kabul—From Afghanistan to a More Dangerous World;* William Collins; 2015; pp130–153.

70   McChrystal; *MYSOT;* p77.

71   Giustozzi Anthony; cited in *Corruption in Conflict—Lessons from the U.S. Conflict in Afghanistan;* Special Inspector General for Afghanistan (SIGAR); 2016; p18.

72   *Corruption in Conflict;* SIGAR; p18.

73   Human Rights Watch report; 2002; p7; https://www.hrw.org/reports/2002/afghan3 /herat1002.pdf.

74   Interview with the author for BBC News, 2014.

75   Afghanistan Independent Human Rights Commission report.

76   *New York Times;* June 19, 2002; http://www.nytimes.com/2002/06/19/world/commander -sees-at-least-another-year-in-afghanistan.html.

77   Farrell; p100.

78   Ibid.; p98.

79   McChrystal; p77.

80   *A Different Kind of War;* p193.

81   Ibid.; p194.

82   Ibid.; p226.

83   Stockton, Nicholas; *Strategic Coordination in Afghanistan;* Afghanistan Research and Evaluation Unit, August 2002; p1.

CHAPTER 2: THE FOG OF AID

1   Witnessed by the author.

2   Author interview for BBC program; https://www.bbc.co.uk/sounds/play/b037s8mk; August 4, 2013.

3   Ibid.

4   Dobbins, James, F.; *Preparing for Nation Building;* Survival; 2006; https://www.tandfonline .com/doi/abs/10.1080/00396330600905486.

5   The Clinton administration had good intentions, with a presidential order, PDD 56, in 1997, designed to deliver better civil-military coordination in future conflicts. But it was never fully implemented.

6   Kitfield, James; "Pox Americana?"; *National Journal;* April 6, 2002, p. 986.

7   https://www.nato.int/docu/review/2006/issue2/english/art2.html.

8   *Washington Post;* February 10, 2003; https://www.washingtonpost.com/archive/opinions /2003/02/10/role-reversal-and-alliance-realities/eb4531b4-43aa-493d-b28e-c4a375c6b4df/.

9   *A Different Kind of War;* p231.

10   Dobbins; p139.

11   Franks; Kindle loc; p311.

12   Nathan, Laurie; *Local Ownership of Security Sector Reform—A Guide for Donors;* January 2007; https://www.lse.ac.uk/international-development/Assets/Documents/PDFs/csrc -background-papers/Local-Ownership-of-Security-Sector-Reform-2007.pdf.

13   Rubin, Barney, Hamidzada, Humayun, and Stoddard, Abby; *Afghanistan 2005 and Beyond: Prospects for Improved Stability;* Clingendael; 2005; https://www.jstor.org/stable/resrep05388.11.

14   Author interview with Karimi.

15   Nancy was an inveterate smoker. When she died in Kabul in her nineties, still working, a packet of cigarettes was found behind the radiator in her office.

16 All Karimi quotes author interview.

17 Author interview with Vendrell.

18 Author interview with Vendrell.

19 Bush, George W.; *Decision Points;* Virgin Books, 2010; p194.

20 Author interview with Barmak.

21 Author interview with Hanif Atmar.

22 Lamb; p140.

23 CNN.com; Jan 21 2002; https://edition.cnn.com/2002/WORLD/asiapcf/east/01/20
    /afghan.donors/.

24 Author interview with Afghan government adviser.

25 *U.S. Assistance to Afghanistan 1950–1979;* 1988; DEVRES Inc. http://catalog.acku.edu.af
    /cgi-bin/koha/opac-detail.pl?biblionumber=15855.

26 Author interview with William Byrd, USIP.

27 Lamb; p140.

28 Loyn, David; *In Afghanistan;* St. Martin's Press; 2009; p210.

29 Quarterly Report; Special Inspector General for Afghanistan Reconstruction; July 30 2014;
    https://www.sigar.mil/pdf/quarterlyreports/2014–07–30qr.pdf.

30 Paris Declaration; 2005; https://www.oecd.org/dac/effectiveness/34428351.pdf.

31 Interview with the author for the BBC, 2004.

32 Ghani, Ashraf; Lockhart, Clare, and Carnahan, Michael; *Closing the Sovereignty Gap: An
    Approach to State-Building;* Working Paper 253; ODI; London; September 2005.

33 Author interview with Guggenheim.

34 Government Accountability Office; *Afghanistan Reconstruction;* GAO 05 742; July 2005; p37.

35 GAO; p37.

36 I am grateful to Astri Surkhe for this image.

37 Lamb; p143.

38 Byrd, William A.; *Economic Management in Afghanistan;* Afghanistan Analysts Network; Au-
    gust 2015.

39 *A Different Kind of War;* p244.

40 Koontz, Christopher N., editor; *Enduring Voices—Oral Histories of the U.S. Army Experience in
    Afghanistan;* Center of Military History, U.S. Army; 2008; p25.

41 Ibid.; p5.

42 Ibid.; Robin Fontes; p456.

43 Author interview with Karzai.

44 *Enduring Voices;* p25.

45 Farrell; p135.

46 GAO; p51.

47 Author interview with senior USAID official.

48 Perito, Robert; *The U.S. Experience with Provincial Reconstruction Teams in Afghanistan;* United
    States Institute of Peace; October 2005; https://www.usip.org/publications/2005/10/us
    -experience-provincial-reconstruction-teams-afghanistan-lessons-identified.

49 The principal nations were Canada in Kandahar, UK in Helmand, Netherlands and Austra-
    lia in Uruzgan (to the north of Helmand), Turkey in Kabul, Norway in Meymaneh in the

northwest, Italy in Herat in the west, and Germany in Mazar in the north. U.S. troops were already in the first PRT, at Ghazni in the east.

50   Farrell; p139.

51   Rynning; p6.

52   Associated Press; February 10, 2003.

53   Hillier, Rick; *A Soldier First, Bullets, Bureaucrats, and the Politics of War;* Harper Collins; 2010; Kindle loc 3559.

54   Hillier; Kindle loc 3586.

55   Ibid.; Kindle loc 3533

56   Speech to the Conference of Defense Associations Institute; February 22, 2008; cited in Saideman, Stephen, and Auerswald, David; *NATO at War;* 2009.

57   https://www.mccaffreyassociates.com/wp-content/uploads/2020/01/AfghanAAR-072004 .pdf; referenced by Boudreau, Brett; *We Have Met the Enemy and He Is Us.*

58   *Enduring Voices;* p115.

59   Interview with member of Ghani's team.

60   Kaplan, Fred; *The Insurgents;* Simon & Schuster; 2013; Kindle loc 5685.

61   GAO; p57.

62   British Special Operators retain their original regimental designation while serving in the Special Air Service (SAS) or Special Boat Squadron (SBS). Involvement in these services is never disclosed.

63   Harnden, Toby; *Sunday Telegraph;* January 29, 2006; https://www.telegraph.co.uk/news /uknews/1509071/British-troops-will-be-targets-in-Afghanistan.html.

64   *U.S. Assistance to Afghanistan 1950–1979;* 1988; DEVRES Inc. http://catalog.acku.edu.af /cgi-bin/koha/opac-detail.pl?biblionumber=15855.

65   Gall, S.; p85.

CHAPTER 3: THE BIGGEST WARLORD

1   Lamb; p147.

2   Neumann's father was ambassador to Afghanistan in 1967–1973. In a closet in the embassy, he found a pamphlet written by his mother with advice to diplomatic wives in Kabul.

3   Author interview.

4   Author interview with Karzai.

5   Author interview with Karzai.

6   The Allied Rapid Reaction Corps was a mobile NATO facility.

7   Butler, Ed; *Setting Ourselves Up for a Fall in Afghanistan;* Royal United Services Institute Journal; February/March 2015.

8   Butler; RUSI Journal.

9   Butler; RUSI Journal.

10   Butler; RUSI Journal.

11   Fergusson, James; *Taliban—The Inside Story of the World's Fiercest Guerrilla Fighters;* Bantam Press; 2010; p135. His description of "an enemy we created" became the title of Alex Strick von Linschoten and Felix Kuehn's book arguing that the Taliban and al-Qaeda did not have strong links in the late 1990s.

12   Butler; RUSI Journal.

13 Fergusson, James; *A Million Bullets—The Real Story of the British Army in Afghanistan;* Transworld; 2008.

14 Lamb; p264.

15 Richards, David; *Taking Command;* Headline; 2014; p185.

16 Butler; RUSI Journal.

17 Fairweather, Jack; *The Good War—Why We Couldn't Win the War or the Peace in Afghanistan;* Jonathan Cape; 2014; p175.

18 Fergusson, James; *A Million Bullets;* p156.

19 Author interview with Toner.

20 Forsberg, Carl, and Kagan, Kimberly; "Consolidating Private Security Companies"; Institute for the Study of War; May 28, 2010.

21 Fairweather; p162.

22 Ink spots had their origin in the French general Louis Lyautey's tactics to secure Madagascar and Morocco early in the twentieth century.

23 Lamb; p286.

24 Author interview with Richards.

25 Horn, Bernd; *No Lack of Courage—Operation Medusa, Afghanistan;* Dundurn Press, Toronto; 2010; p62.

26 Ibid. p84.

27 Author interview with Richards.

28 In addition, fourteen crew members died on the first day of the battle, when a UK Royal Air Force Nimrod reconnaissance aircraft crashed; there was no indication of enemy action involved.

29 Richards; *Taking Command;* p254.

30 BBC interview.

31 Richards; *Taking Command;* p238.

32 Author interview with Neumann.

33 The story has been optioned for a feature film.

34 Author interview with Richards.

35 Although the PAG did not outlast him, Richards liked to quote a 2009 RAND report saying that a mechanism such as a PAG should be a "sine qua non" of counterinsurgency operations in the future.

36 Interview with member of Karzai staff.

37 Richards, David; *Wars in Peace;* Royal United Services Institute Journal; 2014; xii.

38 Richards; *Taking Command;* p200.

39 Ibid.; p211.

40 Author interview with Neumann.

41 Richards; *Taking Command;* p254.

CHAPTER 4: THE HEART OF THE BEAST

1 Churchill, Winston S.; *The Story of the Malakand Field Force;* 1898.

2 Allen, Charles; *Soldier Sahibs;* John Murray; 2000; p217.

3 Kilcullen, David; *The Accidental Guerrilla—Fighting Small Wars in the Midst of a Big One;* Hurst; 2009; p93.

4   Donahue, Pat, and Fenzel, Mike; *Combating a Modern Insurgency;* Military Review;
    2008; https://www.armyupress.army.mil/Portals/7/militaryreview/Archives/English
    /MilitaryReview_20080430_art007.pdf.

5   Ostlund, William B.; *Operating Enduring Freedom VIII; Military Review;* July/August 2009;
    https://www.armyupress.army.mil/Portals/7/military-review/Archives/English
    /MilitaryReview_20090831_art004.pdf.

6   Author interview. Eight years into the war, this was the first involvement by USAID's Of-
    fice of Transition Initiatives, which helps build peace and democracy.

7   Malkasian, Carter, and Meyerle Gerald; *Provincial Reconstruction Teams;* Strategic Studies
    Institute; 2008.

8   C-SPAN; May 20, 2007; https://www.c-span.org/video/?198551–1/reconstruction
    -jalalabad-afghanistan.

9   C-SPAN; op. cit.

10 Kilcullen; p108.

11 Ibid.; p67.

12 *Restrepo* movie.

13 Junger, Sebastian; *New York Times;* April 20, 2010; https://www.nytimes.com/2010/04/21
    /opinion/21junger.html.

14 Land feud between two families in American Civil War; now subject of a TV miniseries.

15 Wanat; *Combat Action in Afghanistan;* Combat Studies Institute Press; 2008.

16 Author interview with Nuristani.

17 Author interview with Neumann.

18 West, Bing; *The Wrong War—Grit, Strategy and the Way Out of Afghanistan;* Random House;
    2011; p22.

19 West; p26.

20 Author interview with Atmar.

21 Martin, Mike; *An Intimate War—An Oral History of the Helmand Conflict, 1978–2012;* Hurst
    2014.

CHAPTER 5: RACK 'EM AND STACK 'EM

1   SIGAR interview with McNeill; Afghanistan Papers; *Washington Post;* Dec 9 2019;
    https://www.washingtonpost.com/graphics/2019/investigations/afghanistan-papers/
    documents-database/.

2   Richards; *Taking Command;* p281.

3   Afghanistan Papers.

4   Lamb; p380.

5   http://www.icosgroup.net/static/reports/Knife_Edge_Report.pdf.

6   Afghanistan Papers.

7   Wikileaks; *Guardian;* December 2 2010; https://www.theguardian.com/uk/2010/dec/02/
    wikileaks-cables-afghan-british-military.

8   Waltz; p205.

9   Chivers, C.J.; *New York Times;* April 8 2007; http://www.nytimes.com/2007/04/18/world/
    asia/18afghan.html.

10 http://archive.defense.gov/Transcripts/Transcript.asp?TranscriptID=3980.

11 Afghanistan Papers.

12   Gates, Robert; *From the Shadows—The Ultimate Insider's Story of Five Presidents and How They Won the Cold War;* Simon & Schuster; 1996; p139.

13   Gates Robert; *Duty;* Virgin Digital; 2014; Kindle loc 3656.

14   Ibid.; Kindle loc 3717.

15   Ibid.; Kindle loc 3662.

16   Waltz; p205.

17   Gall, Carlotta; *New York Times;* May 13, 2007; https://www.nytimes.com/2007/05/13 /world/asia/13AFGHAN.html.

18   It would not be until a McChrystal directive in 2009 that ISAF would stop putting out body counts.

19   BBC News; July 30 207; http://news.bbc.co.uk/1/hi/world/south_asia/6921713stm.

20   Pentagon briefing; February 6, 2008.

21   Afghanistan Study Group; https://www.researchgate.net/publication/235104691_Afghanistan _Study_Group_Report_Revitalizing_Our_Efforts_Rethinking_Our_Strategies.

22   Afghanistan Papers.

23   Baker, Peter; *New York Times;* October 14 2009; http://query.nytimes.com/gst/fullpage. html?res=9F0CE7DD1E3CF937A25753C1A96F9C8B63.

CHAPTER 6: COIN

1   Mattis and West; p154.

2   Speech to the World Economic Forum, Davos; January 23, 2008.

3   Author interview with senior officers. In her opening submission to the Senate Foreign Relations Committee, on October 19, 2005, Rice had talked of the need to move toward "clear, hold, and build." But it was clear that her concept was different from the counterinsurgency doctrine as it would emerge. She saw counterinsurgency then as "marrying our civilian reconstruction and development efforts with our military operations." There was no sense that the military themselves needed a new mindset.

4   Birtle, Andrew J.; *U.S. Army Counterinsurgency Operations Doctrine 1860–1941;* Center of Military History United States Army; 1997; p35.

5   *Small Wars Manual;* FMFRP 12–15; 1940; p29. https://www.marines.mil/Portals/1 /Publications/FMFRP%2012–15%20%20Small%20Wars%20Manual.pdf

6   Gates; *Duty;* Kindle loc 2563.

7   e.g., Filkins, Dexter; review of Thomas Rick's *The Generals* in *The New Yorker;* December 17, 2012.

8   Gates; *Duty;* Kindle loc 2112.

9   Ibid.; Kindle loc 2082.

10 Ibid.; Kindle loc 2161.

11 Letter to Princeton colleague; Broadwell, Paula; *All In—The Education of David Petraeus;* Penguin; 2012; p68.

12 Broadwell; p67.

13 Petraeus, David H.; *The Lessons of History and the Lessons of Vietnam;* Parameters; U.S. Army War College; autumn 1986.

14 Broadwell; p67.

15 Petraeus Ph.D.; Princeton; 1987.

16 Broadwell; p153.

17   Galula, David; *Counterinsurgency Warfare: Theory and Practice;* RAND; 1964; p63.

18   Mattis and West; p154.

19   McChrystal; *MYSOT;* p129.

20   Mattis and West; p124.

21   McChrystal; *MYSOT;* p131.

22   Packer, George; "The Lesson of Tal Afar"; *New Yorker;* April 10, 2006.

23   Sorley, Lewis; *A Better War—The Unexamined Victories and Final Tragedies of America's Last Years in Vietnam;* Harcourt; 1999; p199.

24   Loyn, David; *In Afghanistan—Two Hundred Years of British, Russian and American Occupation;* Palgrave Macmillan; 2009; p121. The phrase was first used by Sir Robert Sandeman in Baluchistan, on the Afghan frontier, in the 1870s.

25   In the Petraeus doctrine, this became "The Host Nation Doing Something Tolerably Is Normally Better than Us Doing It Well."

26   Mattis and West; p154.

27   Ricks, Thomas; *The Gamble;* Penguin; 2009; Kindle loc 579.

28   Eikenberry, Karl; *Foreign Affairs;* September/October 2013.

29   Galula; *Counterinsurgency Warfare;* introduction by Nagl, John A. in PSI Classics edition; 2006; viii.

30   Petraeus author interview. He used the phrase three times in the interview.

31   Frederick Kagan of the American Enterprise Institute, quoted in Gamble; Kindle loc 1909.

32   Pentagon Press Briefing; October 1, 2008.

33   Author interview with senior U.S. officer on background.

34   Ibid.

35   McKiernan, David; Atlantic Alliance speech, November 2008; https://www.atlanticcouncil .org/commentary/transcript/transcript-general-david-mckiernan-speaks-at-councils -commanders-series/.

36   Interview with the author for BBC News; May 27, 2009.

37   Eide, Kai; *Power Struggle Over Afghanistan;* Skyhorse; 2012; p118.

38   Cockburn, Patrick; *Independent;* September 15, 2008.

39   http://www.nato.int/isaf/docu/mediaadvisory/2008/09-september/ma080904–053.html.

40   Author interview with Umer Daudzai, Karzai's chief of staff.

41   Gall, Carlotta; *The Wrong Enemy;* Penguin 2014; p103.

42   Eide, Kai; *Power Struggle Over Afghanistan;* Skyhorse; 2012; p60.

43   North, Oliver; *Report from a Forgotten War;* Creators Syndicate Inc.; August 28, 2008.

44   Gall, Carlotta; *New York Times;* September 7, 2008; https://www.nytimes.com/2008/09/08 /world/asia/08afghan.html.

45   Eide; p61.

46   Ibid.; p70.

47   Ibid.; p72.

48   Murphy, Brett; *USA TODAY;* January 1, 2020; https://eu.usatoday.com/in-depth/news /investigations/2020/01/09/reporters-notebook-afghanistan/2820013001.

49   Eide; p69.

50   Ibid.; p68.

51   Author interview with Karzai.

52 Author interview wit Daudzai.

53 Author interview with Karzai.

54 Woodward, Bob; *Obama's Wars;* Simon & Schuster; 2010; p70.

55 Neumann, Ronald E.; "Failed Relations between Hamid Karzai and the United States"; United States Institute of Peace; May 2015; www.usip.org/sites/default/files/SR373-Failed -Relations-between-Hamid-Karzai-and-the-United-States.pdf.

56 Gates; *Duty;* Kindle loc 8379.

CHAPTER 7: OBAMA'S WAR

1   https://obamawhitehouse.archives.gov/issues/foreign-policy/presidents-speech-cairo-a -new-beginning.

2   This was best expressed by Henry Kissinger, in his famous line that "the conventional army loses if it does not win; the guerrilla wins if he does not lose."

3   Dobbins, James, Jones, Seth G., Crane, Keith, and Cole DeGrasse, Beth; *The Beginner's Guide to Nation-Building;* RAND; 2008; p38.

4   Eikenberry, Karl; *Foreign Affairs;* September/October 2013.

5   Gates; *Duty;* Kindle loc 3973. Jones had been Supreme Allied Commander Europe when ISAF took over the whole of Afghanistan in 2006 and knew the country well.

6   Malkasian, Carter; *War Comes to Garmser—Thirty Years of Conflict on the Afghan Frontier;* Hurst; 2013; p127.

7   Waldman, Matt; *Sun in the Sky;* 2010; https://assets.publishing.service.gov.uk/media /57a08b0c40f0b652dd000a78/DP18.pdf.

8   *New York Times;* July 15, 2008; https://www.nytimes.com/2008/07/15/us/politics/15text -obama.html

9   Obama, Barack; *A Promised Land;* Penguin Books Ltd.; 2020; Kindle edition; p414.

10 *Insurgencies and Countering Insurgencies;* FM 3–24; December 15, 2006; https://armypubs .army.mil/ProductMaps/PubForm/Details.aspx?PUB_ID=83748.

11 Gates; *Duty;* Kindle loc 3870.

12 McChrystal; *MYSOT;* p286.

13 Gates; *Duty;* Kindle loc 6014.

14 Ibid.; Kindle loc 6599.

15 Waltz; p218.

16 Lute interview; George W. Bush oral history project; p37; https://millercenter.org/the -presidency/presidential-oral-histories/george-w-bush-oral-history.

17 Waltz; p220.

18 Author interview.

19 Riedel; Kindle loc 1680.

20 It is hard to find the original source of this. It was widely repeated and became the title of a book by Carlotta Gall.

21 https://obamawhitehouse.archives.gov/the-press-office/remarks-president-a-new-strategy -afghanistan-and-pakistan.

22 Fair, C.Christine; *Time For Sober Realism—Renegotiating U.S. Relations with Pakistan;* The Washington Quarterly; 2009, Issue 2; https://www.tandfonline.com/doi/abs/10.1080 /01636600902775680.

23 Gates; *Duty;* Kindle loc 6179.

24 *Lessons from the U.S. Civilian Surge in Afghanistan, 2009–2014;* Graduate Policy Workshop; Woodrow Wilson School, Princeton University; January 2016 https://spia.princeton.edu /sites/default/files/content/591f_Final_20160208.pdf.

25 Waltz; p238.

26 Ibid.; p240.

27 Meacheam, John; Obama interview; *Newsweek;* May 25, 2009; https://www.newsweek.com /qa-obama-dick-cheney-war-and-star-trek-79715.

28 Woodward; *Obama's Wars;* p83.

29 Gates; *Duty;* Kindle loc 6118.

30 Ibid.; Kindle loc 6120.

31 Ibid.; Kindle loc 3716.

32 Kaplan, Fred; *Slate; August 4 2008; https://slate.com/news-and-politics/2008/08/finally-the -army-is-promoting-the-right-officers.html*

33 Casey himself had been moved out of Iraq in 2007 in favor a "new strategy" introduced by Petraeus. But it did not damage his career.

34 Pentagon press conference; October 3, 2008.

35 McKiernan, David; ISAF commander's counterinsurgency guidance 2008.

36 Farnan, Paul; *Washington Post;* May 25, 2009; https://www.washingtonpost.com/wp-dyn /content/article/2009/05/24/AR2009052401995.html.

37 Gates; *Duty;* Kindle loc 6131.

38 Ibid.; Kindle loc 3670.

39 McChrystal; *MYSOT;* p279.

40 Barnett, Thomas P.; *Esquire;* April 2008.

41 Gates; *Duty;* Kindle loc 6146.

42 Author interview.

43 U.S. CENTCOM's unclassified executive summary; June 18, 2009; https://www.hsdl.org/ ?view&did=35748. In contrast to the Azizabad incident early in his command, McKiernan was able to send U.S. investigators to the scene the following day.

44 Ignatius, David; *Washington Post;* May 15, 2009; https://www.washingtonpost.com/wp-dyn /content/article/2009/05/12/AR2009051203039.html.

45 Kaplan, Fred; *Slate;* May 11, 2009; https://slate.com/news-and-politics/2009/05/the-ouster-of -afghanistan-commander-david-mckiernan-could-make-or-break-the-obama-presidency.html.

46 Sullivan, Charles S. "Duff"; *The Air Commanders' Perspectives;* Air University Press; November 2014.

47 Department of Defense press conference; May 12, 2009.

48 Author interview.

49 Associated Press; April 10, 2009.

50 Department of Defense press conference; May 12, 2009.

CHAPTER 8: OWNING THE VILLAGES

1 Second Battalion, 504th Parachute Infantry Regiment, 82nd Airborne Division.

2 McChrystal; *MYSOT;* p295. He failed to close the garden.

3 Martin, David; "McChrystal's Frank Talk on Afghanistan"; *60 Minutes;* CBS; September 24, 2009; https://www.cbsnews.com/news/mcchrystals-frank-talk-on-afghanistan.

4   Kaplan, Robert D.; *Atlantic;* March 9, 2010; https://www.theatlantic.com/magazine /archive/2010/04/man-versus-afghanistan/307983/.

5   McChrystal; *MYSOT;* p150.

6   *60 Minutes;* September 24, 2009.

7   McChrystal; *MYSOT;* p380.

8   Brand, Matthew C.; *General McChrystal's Strategic Assessment;* Air University Press; 2011.

9   McChrystal; *MYSOT;* p277.

10 Author interview with McChrystal.

11 McChrystal; *MYSOT;* p288.

12 Franks; p280.

13 Rose Garden speech; March 27, 2009; https://obamawhitehouse.archives.gov/the-press -office/remarks-president-a-new-strategy-afghanistan-and-pakistan.

14 Obama; *A Promised Land;* p417.

15 Woodward; *Obama's Wars;* Kindle loc 4012.

16 Ibid.; Kindle loc 2573.

17 Packer, George; *Our Man—Richard Holbrooke and the End of the American Century;* Jonathan Cape; 2019; p472.

18 Obama; *A Promised Land;* p418.

19 Woodward; *Obama's Wars;* Kindle loc 2172.

20 Gerson, Michael; *Real Clear Politics;* September 4, 2009; https://www.realclearpolitics.com /articles/2009/09/04/in_afghanistan_no_choice_but_to_try.html.

21 Author interview with Petraeus.

22 McChrystal; *MYSOT;* p344

23 Obama; *A Promised Land;* p558.

24 Gates; *Duty;* Kindle loc 6589.

25 Coll; p366.

26 Woodward; *Obama's Wars;* p146.

27 *Offense and Defense;* Army Doctrine Publication 3–90; Headquarters Department of the Army; 2019.

28 McChrystal; *MYSOT;* p350.

29 Brand, Matthew C.; *General McChrystal's Strategic Assessment;* Air University; p13.

30 McChrystal speech in London; January 9, 2019; https://www.youtube.com/watch?v =3CbvkfAhnNI.

31 McChrystal; *MYSOT;* p352.

32 Woodward; *Obama's Wars;* Kindle loc 2747.

33 MacAskill, Ewan; *Guardian;* November 12, 2009; https://www.theguardian.com/world /2009/nov/12/obama-us-troops-afghanistan-kilcullen.

34 Author interview with Petraeus.

35 Author interview with Eggers.

36 *60 Minutes;* CBS; September 24, 2009.

37 Spillius, Alex; "White House angry at General Stanley McChrystal speech on Afghanistan"; *Daily Telegraph;* October 5, 2009; https://www.telegraph.co.uk/news/worldnews/barackobama /6259582/White-House-angry-at-General-Stanley-McChrystal-speech-on-Afghanistan.html.

38   Obama; *A Promised Land;* p559; and Gates; *Duty;* Kindle loc 6562.

39   Woodward; *Obama's Wars;* p175.

40   Landler, Mark and Zeleny, Jeff; *New York Times;* November 12, 2009; https://www.nytimes.com/2009/11/13/world/asia/13eikenberry.html.

41   Gates; *Duty;* Kindle loc 6772.

42   Hastings; *Rolling Stone;* June 22, 2010.

43   Gates; *Duty;* Kindle loc 8762.

44   This was the same figure calculated by McNeill's staff in 2007 when the Petraeus/Mattis FM 3–24 manual came out; see chapter 5.

45   Woodward; *Obama's Wars;* p325.

46   McChrystal; *MYSOT;* p345.

47   Gates; *Duty;* Kindle loc 6828.

48   Obama; *A Promised Land;* p563.

49   Woodward; *Obama's Wars;* p327.

50   Ibid.; p290.

51   West Point speech; Dec 1 2009; https://obamawhitehouse.archives.gov/blog/2009/12/01/new-way-forward-presidents-address.

52   McChrystal; *MYSOT;* p361.

53   *LA Times;* November 22, 2008.

54   Malkasian; *War Comes to Garmser;* p125.

55   Chandrasekaran, Rajiv; *Little America—The War Within the War for Afghanistan;* Bloomsbury; 2012; p63.

56   Gates; *Duty;* Kindle loc 6046.

57   Chandrasekaran; p65.

58   McChrystal; *MYSOT;* p313.

59   Ibid.; p310.

60   Elliott, Justin; *Muckraker;* April 2, 2010; https://talkingpointsmemo.com/muckraker/gen-mcchrystal-we-ve-shot-an-amazing-number-of-people-who-were-em-not-em-threats.

61   Author interview with Karzai.

62   McChrystal; *MYSOT;* p372.

63   Ibid.; p372.

64   Author interview with McChrystal.

65   Author interview with Carter.

66   McChrystal; *MYSOT;* p368.

67   Farrell; p311.

68   Chandrasekaran; p143.

69   SMA had an extraordinary capacity to get into diplomatic events and had photographs with several of the ISAF commanders.

70   Author interview with USAID official.

71   Reported by the author for BBC News.

72   *Investing in the Fight: Assessing the Use of the Commander's Emergency Response Program in Afghanistan;* RAND; 2016.

73   Author interview with McChrystal.

74   Author interview with McChrystal.

75   McChrystal; *MYSOT;* p328.

76   Among the lessons learned by the deployment was the unintended economic impact on Clarksville, Tennessee, and Hopkinsville, Kentucky, the two towns neighboring the camp, when fifteen thousand people went away for a year.

77   Raddatz, Martha; ABC News; July 6, 2010; https://abcnews.go.com/WN/Afghanistan /major-general-john-campbell-escalating-violence-war-afghanistan/story?id=11094971.

78   Subject of a feature film: *The Outpost.*

79   Army AR 15–6 investigation report; October 6, 2009.

80   Junger; *New York Times;* April 20, 2010.

81   George W. Bush Oral History Project interview.

82   Farwell, Matt, and Ames, Michael; *American Cipher—One Soldier's Nightmare in the Afghanistan War;* Wildfire; 2019; Kindle loc 609.

83   Tunnell, Harry D.; *Red Devils;* Combat Studies Institute Press; 2004; p52

84   *Military Times;* March 23, 2013; https://www.militarytimes.com/2013/03/27/report -blames-lapses-on-stryker-commander-532-page-report-finds-colonel-ignored-doctrine -proper-procedure-in-leading-undisciplined-bct.

85   Chandrasekaran; pp152–161.

86   *Military Times;* March 23, 2013.

87   Author interview with Carter.

88   Malkasian; *War Comes to Garmser;* p166.

89   McChrystal; *MYSOT;* p317.

90   *Christian Science Monitor;* April 8, 2010; https://www.csmonitor.com/World/Asia -South-Central/2010/0408/US-military-offers-sheep-in-apology-for-Afghanistan -deaths.

91   Mazzetti, Mark; *The Way of the Knife—The CIA, a Secret Army and a War at the Ends of the Earth;* Scribe; 2013.

92   Human Rights Watch; Oct. 31, 2019; https://www.hrw.org/report/2019/10/31/theyve -shot-many/abusive-night-raids-cia-backed-afghan-strike-forces#_ftnref48.

93   Hastings, Michael; *The Operators—the Wild and Terrifying Inside Story of America's War in Afghanistan;* Orion; 2012; p32.

94   Packer; p521.

95   Obama; p742.

96   Starkey, Jerome; *The Times* (London); June 23, 2010; https://www.thetimes.co.uk/article /mcchrystal-ready-to-hand-obama-resignation-letter-mf8b3nrvmng.

97   Author interview with Medley.

98   Gates; *Duty;* Kindle loc 8706.

99   The phrase was by Robert Shaplen, the *New Yorker* correspondent in Saigon, and used by Lewis Sorley as the title of his book on the last years of the Vietnam War.

100 Kelley, Jill; *Collateral Damage—Petraeus/Power/Politics and the Abuse Of Privacy;* Kelley Publishing; 2016; Kindle loc 959.

101 Broadwell; p3.

CHAPTER 9: THE BELL CURVE AND THE ANACONDA

1   Boot, Max; Commentary; quoted in Fisher, Max; *Wire;* June 23, 2010; https://www
    .theatlantic.com/international/archive/2010/06/with-mcchrystal-out-how-war-may
    -change/345107/.

2   Kaplan, Fred; *Slate;* April 28, 2011; https://slate.com/news-and-politics/2011/04/petraeus
    -to-cia-panetta-to-defense-and-other-shrewd-moves-by-president-obama.html.

3   Klein, Joe; *Time;* June 24, 2010; http://content.time.com/time/magazine/article
    /0,9171,1999418,00.html.

4   Ricks, Thomas E.; *Fiasco—The American Military Adventure in Iraq;* Penguin; 2007; Kindle loc
    5679.

5   Historian Conrad Crane quoted in *Washington Post;* January 7, 2007; https://www
    .washingtonpost.com/archive/politics/2007/01/07/iraq-will-be-petraeuss-knot-to-untie
    -span-classbankheadgeneral-known-to-see-peace-as-still-possiblespan/90e91b77-aeab-40a8
    -a139–9976ca3bda6d/.

6   Kelley; Kindle loc 838.

7   Ricks, Thomas, E; *Foreign Policy;* June 23 2010; https://foreignpolicy.com/2010/06/23/daves
    -back.

8   Associated Press; June 24, 2010.

9   Broadwell; p55.

10 *Christian Science Monitor;* June 23, 2011; https://www.csmonitor.com/USA/Politics/2010
    /0623/Gen.-David-Petraeus-nod-reopens-issue-of-withdrawal-deadline.

11 Donnelly, Thomas; blog post quoting Arthur Herman; American Enterprise Institute;
    June 2011.

12 This gave Fred Kaplan the title of the book *The Insurgents*.

13 Broadwell; p38.

14 Broadwell; p70.

15 Japanese for "umbrella"; the name was conferred as falling parachutists looked as if they had
    umbrellas in the occupation of Japan after World War II.

16 Broadwell; p106.

17 General Jack Keane was standing alongside him, and his swift actions in staunching the
    blood gave the two a strong bond. The surgeon who operated was Bill Frist—later Repub-
    lican senator from Tennessee and Senate majority leader.

18 Broadwell; p33.

19 Ibid.; p33.

20 Ibid.; p66.

21 Packer; p532.

22 Broadwell; p70.

23 Ricks, Thomas E.; *Washington Post;* June 27, 2010; https://www.washingtonpost.com/wp
    -dyn/content/article/2010/06/24/AR2010062402982.html.

24 Broadwell; p7.

25 Author interview with former staff officer on background.

26 Ibid.

27 Broadwell; p53.

28 Coll; p487.

29   Kaplan, Fred; "The End of the Age of Petraeus"; *Foreign Affairs;* January/February 2013.

30   There were six lines of effort in the original Iraq Anaconda; the seventh came as U.S. forces redefined information warfare, so it merited its own category, separated from "Interagency," which was mainly international relations.

31   Author interview with senior U.S. officer.

32   https://www.afcent.af.mil/About/Airpower-Summaries.

33   Senate Armed Services Committee; confirmation hearing, June 29, 2010.

34   Chaudhuri, Rudra, and Farrell, Theo; *International Affairs;* RIIA; Vol. 87, No. 2 (March 2011), pp271–296; OUP; ps://www.jstor.org/stable/20869660.

35   Mattis and West; p211.

36   Ignatius, David; *Washington Post;* October 19, 2010; https://www.washingtonpost.com/wp -dyn/content/article/2010/10/18/AR2010101803596.html.

37   Packer; p533.

38   Shah, Taimoor, and Nordland, Rod; *New York Times;* November 16, 2010; https://www .nytimes.com/2010/11/17/world/asia/17afghan.html.

39   *Afghanistan—Annual Report 2010, Protection of Civilians in Armed Conflict;* United Nations Mission in Afghanistan; https://unama.unmissions.org/sites/default/files/engi_version_of _poc_annual_report_2011.pdf.

40   Trofimov, Yaroslav, and Rosenberg, Matthew; *Wall Street Journal;* November 18, 2010; https://www.wsj.com/articles/SB10001424052748704312504575618863799357110.

41   Senate Armed Services Committee hearing; March 18, 2011.

42   FM 3–24; p20.

43   *"Just Don't Call it a Militia";* Human Rights Watch 2011; https://www.hrw.org/sites /default/files/reports/afghanistan0911webwcover_0.pdf; p7.

44   Ibid.; p20.

45   Chaudhuri and Farrell.

46   Dhofar was different to Afghanistan in two vital aspects: the insurgents had no safe haven, and when the new ruler, Qaboos bin Said, took over in 1970, they had an incorrupt competent partner.

47   Senate Armed Services Committee; confirmation hearing, June 29, 2010.

48   Author interview with Lute.

49   Karzai interview; *Washington Post;* November 14, 2010; https://www.washingtonpost.com /wp-dyn/content/article/2010/11/14/AR2010111400002_2.html?sid=ST2010111305091.

50   Author interview with Karzai.

51   Author interview with Daudzai.

52   Partlow, Joshua and Habib Zahori; *Washington Post;* February 20, 2011; https://www .washingtonpost.com/wp-dyn/content/article/2011/02/20/AR2011022000276.html?tid =a_inl_manual.

53   Ignatius, David; *Washington Post;* March 16 2010; https://www.washingtonpost.com /opinions/the-bin-laden-plot-to-kill-president-obama/2012/03/16/gIQAwN5RGS_story .html?hpid=z1&tid=a_inl_manual.

CHAPTER 10: THE COUNTERINSURGENCY DILEMMA

 1   U.S. Embassy Kabul, "NSA Spanta," Kabul 5184 cable, October 2, 2010; cited in *Corruption in Conflict;* SIGAR; p4.

2   This casual antisemitism is common in a country where *Mein Kampf* is a bestseller.

3   Author interview for BBC News, 2008.

4   Schwartz, Moshe; *Wartime Contracting in Afghanistan;* November 14, 2011; https://fas.org /sgp/crs/natsec/R42084.pdf.

5   Author interview for BBC News, 2008.

6   Congress Committee on Oversight and Government Reform; September 12, 2012.

7   *Corruption in Conflict;* SIGAR; p35.

8   Feith, David; *Wall Street Journal;* May 11, 2012; https://www.wsj.com/articles/SB10001424 052702304451104577392281146871796.

9   Broadwell; p61.

10   *Corruption in Conflict;* SIGAR; p16.

11   Author interview with Karimi.

12   Roston, Aram; *Nation;* November 2008. https://www.thenation.com/article/archive/how -us-funds-taliban.

13   Wilder, Andrew, and Gordon, Stewart *Operationalizing Counter/Anti-Corruption Study;* Joint and Coalition Operational Analysis (JCOA); February 28, 2014; p12; JCOA study https:// www.hsdl.org/?view&did=756004.

14   *Corruption in Conflict;* SIGAR; p8.

15   JCOA study; p28.

16   Egel, Daniel and others; *Investing in the Fight: Assessing the Use of the Commander's Emergency Response Program in Afghanistan;* RAND; 2016.

17   JCOA study; p13.

18   JCOA study; p13.

19   Fishtein, Paul and Wilder, Andrew; *Winning Hearts and Minds—Examining the Relationship Between Aid and Security in Afghanistan;* Tufts University; January 2012; https://fic.tufts.edu /publication-item/winning-hearts-and-minds-examing-the-relationship-between-aid-and -security-in-afghanistan.

20   Book title by Astri Surkhe.

21   Author interview.

22   Insight of Sarah Chayes in *Thieves of State—Why Corruption Threatens Global Security;* 2016; W.W. Norton.

23   McChrystal; *MYSOT;* p304.

24   Loyn; *In Afghanistan;* p181.

25   Author interview.

26   Chandrasekaran; p108.

27   Author interview with Byrd.

28   Packer; p453.

29   *Corruption in Conflict;* SIGAR; p20.

30   Chandrasekaran; p182.

31   Author interview with Chretien.

32   Chandrasekaran, Rajiv; *Washington Post;* May 31, 2010; https://www.washingtonpost.com /wp-dyn/content/article/2010/05/30/AR2010053003722.html.

33   Packer; p474.

34 See Studwell, Joe; *How Asia Works;* Profile; 2013.

35 Malkasian; *War Comes to Garmser;* p234.

36 *Afghanistan in Transition;* World Bank; 2013; p76. http://documents1.worldbank.org
    /curated/en/221481468189862358/pdf/Afghanistan-in-transition-looking-beyond
    -2014.pdf.

37 Ibid.; p111.

38 WikiLeaks; *New York Times;* December 3, 2010; https://www.nytimes.com/2010/12/03
    /world/asia/03wikileaks-corruption.html.

39 *"They've Shot Many Like This"—Abusive Night Raids by CIA-backed Afghan Forces;* Human
    Rights Watch; October 31 2019; https://www.hrw.org/report/2019/10/31/theyve-shot
    -many/abusive-night-raids-cia-backed-afghan-strike-forces#_ftnref48.

40 Chayes; *Thieves of State;* p54.

41 WikiLeaks; *New York Times;* December 3, 2010.

42 *Fighting Corruption in Afghanistan—Solving the Institutional Puzzle;* Integrity Watch Afghani-
    stan; 2016; p8; https://iwaweb.org/wp-content/uploads/2014/12/Solving-the-Institutional
    -Puzzle.pdf.

43 Filkins, Dexter; *New York Times;* October 24, 2010; https://www.nytimes.com/2010/10/24
    /world/asia/24afghan.html.

44 Ibid.

45 Rosenberg, Matthew; *New York Times;* March 6, 2013; https://www.nytimes.com/2013/03
    /06/world/asia/afghanistan-convicts-21-in-kabul-bank-scandal.html.

46 *"This Week" with Christiane Amanpour;* ABC News; August 15 2010; https://abcnews.go
    .com/ThisWeek/week-transcript-karzai-khan-levitt/story?id=11454631.

47 Chayes; *Thieves of State;* p142.

48 Filkins, Dexter; "The Afghan Bank Heist"; *New Yorker;* February 3, 2011; https://www
    .newyorker.com/magazine/2011/02/14/the-afghan-bank-heist.

49 *Corruption in Conflict;* SIGAR; p42.

50 "Senator Lindsey Graham on the War on Terror"; Carnegie Endowment for International
    Peace; June 15 2011; https://carnegieendowment.org/files/0615carnegie-graham.pdf.

51 Ivo Daalder memo; cited by Gates; Kindle loc 2646.

52 Senate Armed Services Committee hearing; March 15, 2011.

53 Gates; *Duty;* Kindle loc 10024.

54 Ibid.; Kindle loc 10094.

55 Senate Intelligence Committee; June 23, 2011.

56 https://obamawhitehouse.archives.gov/the-press-office/2011/06/22/remarks-president
    -way-forward-Afghanistan.

57 Malkasian; *War Comes to Garmser;* p253.

58 Ibid.

59 Broadwell; p341.

60 Woods, Elliott D.; "The Kunar Nine"; *Prairie Schooner,* Vol. 87, No. 4 (winter 2013);
    pp13–28; https://www.jstor.org/stable/24639492.

61 Reuters; March 26, 2013.

62 Ricks; *Gamble;* Kindle loc 54.

CHAPTER II: PIVOT POINT

1   *Afghanistan—Annual Report 2011, Protection of Civilians in Armed Conflict;* United Nations
    Mission in Afghanistan; https://unama.unmissions.org/sites/default/files/unama_poc
    _report_final_feb_2012pdf.

2   Author interview with Karzai.

3   Author interview with Chretien.

4   Author interview with Chretien.

5   Richter, Paul; *The Ambassadors—America's Diplomats on the Front Lines;* Simon & Schuster;
    2020; Kindle loc 3441.

6   https://www.newsweek.com/tragedy-john-allen-petraeus-scandal-62869.

7   Burroughs, Edgar Rice; *A Princess of Mars;* A. C. McClurg & Company; 1917; reissued
    1968; p15.

8   Obama speech; June 22, 2011.

9   Author interview with Carter.

10 https://archive.defense.gov/news/Defense_Strategic_Guidance.pdf.

11 Rubin, Alissa J.; *New York Times;* October 20, 2012; https://www.nytimes.com/2012/10/21
    /world/asia/afghan-insider-attacks-on-wests-forces-corrode-trust.html.

12 The color-coding began in British war-gaming exercises and spread across NATO coun-
    tries.

13 Bumiller, Elisabeth; *New York Times;* February 2, 2012; https://www.nytimes.com/2012/02
    /03/world/asia/nato-focuses-on-timetable-for-afghan-withdrawal.html.

14 Haynes, Deborah; *The Times* (London); February 1, 2012; https://www.thetimes.co.uk
    /article/exit-is-on-track-amid-fears-of-false-start-kmpvj2cpd7s.

15 Bordin, Jeffrey; *A Crisis of Trust and Cultural Incompatibility;* May 12, 2011; https://nsarchive2
    .gwu.edu/NSAEBB/NSAEBB370/docs/Document%2011.pdf.

16 This abuse was made illegal under the Taliban during their rule and punishable by death.

17 *Washington Post;* August 17, 2012; https://www.washingtonpost.com/world/asia_pacific
    /deadly-insider-attack-that-left-3-us-marines-dead-was-work-of-an-afghan-teenager/2012
    /08/17/20916eca-e7b8-11e1-936a-b801f1abab19_story.html.

18 Pentagon press conference.

19 Sageman, Marc; "The Problem of Green on Blue Attacks in Afghanistan"; presentation to
    Foreign Policy Research Institute; May 29, 2013.

20 Coll; p605.

21 The camp was called Leatherneck in the American section, Shorabak in the Afghan section,
    and Bastion in the British section where the airfield was situated.

22 Bradshaw, Peter; *Guardian;* September 17 2012; https://www.theguardian.com/film
    /filmblog/2012/sep/17/innocence-of-muslims-demonstration-film.

23 Senate Armed Services Committee; March 22, 2012.

24 Rosenberg, Matt; *New York Times;* February 6, 2013; https://www.nytimes.com/2013/02
    /07/world/asia/general-allen-departing-afghan-war-commander-saw-as-much-diplomacy
    -as-combat.html.

25 Author interview with Karzai.

26 Clark, Kate; Afghanistan Analysts Network; February 10, 2013; https://www.afghanistan
    -analysts.org/en/reports/rights-freedom/general-allen-leaves-with-an-improved-report
    -card-on-civilian-casualties-and-torture/ dd citation.

27   *Afghanistan—Annual Report 2012, Protection of Civilians in Armed Conflict;* United Nations
      Mission in Afghanistan; UNAMA; 2012 civilian casualty report; https://unama.unmissions
      .org/sites/default/files/2012_annual_report_eng_0.pdf.

28   Clark, Kate; Afghanistan Analysts Network; February 10, 2013.

29   UNAMA; 2012 civilian casualty report.

30   Rubin, Alissa J., and Risen, James; *New York Times;* March 10, 2011; https://www.nytimes
      .com/2011/03/11/world/asia/11karzai.html.

31   Sahak, Sharifullah, and Rubin, Alissa J.; *New York Times;* May 14, 2011; https://www
      .nytimes.com/2011/05/15/world/asia/15afghan.html.

32   Senate Armed Services Committee hearing; March 22, 2012.

33   Ibid.

34   Nordland, Rod, Shah, Taimoor, and Rubin, Alissa J.; *New York Times;* December 4, 2011;
      https://www.nytimes.com/2011/12/04/world/asia/for-afghan-us-accord-night-raids-are-a
      -sticking-point.html.

35   Senate Armed Services Committee hearing; March 22, 2012.

36   D'Agata Charlie; CBS News; April 8, 2012; https://www.cbsnews.com/news/us-and
      -afghanistan-strike-deal-on-night-raids.

37   Senate Select Committee on Intelligence; Committee Study of the Central Intelligence
      Agency's Detention and Interrogation Program; December 13, 2012; https://fas.org/irp
      /congress/2014_rpt/ssci-rdi.pdf.

38   Treatment of Conflict Related Detainees in Afghan Custody; UNAMA; October 2011;
      https://unama.unmissions.org/sites/default/files/old_dnn/UNAMA/Documents
      /October10_%202011_UNAMA_Detention_Full-Report_ENG.pdf.

39   Interview by senior consultant for the Open Society Foundations, Rachel Reid. https://
      www.opensocietyfoundations.org/publications/remaking-bagram-creation-afghan
      -internment-regime-and-divide-over-us-detention-power.

40   Author interview with Karzai.

41   Geo TV interview; October 23, 2011; https://www.youtube.com/watch?v
      =YDFggTzQQLg.

42   Nordland, Rod; *New York Times;* November 5, 2011; https://www.nytimes.com/2011/11
      /06/world/asia/us-general-fired-over-remarks-about-karzai.html.

43   Epstein, Susan B., and Kronstadt, K. Alan; Congressional Research Service; June 7, 2011.

44   Senate Armed Services Committee hearing; September 21, 2011.

45   GEO TV interview, quoted in *Washington Post;* September 23, 2011; https://www
      .washingtonpost.com/world/national-security/pakistan-backed-attacks-on-american
      -targets-us-says/2011/09/22/gIQAf0q6oK_story.html.

46   Gall, C.; p191.

47   Chandrasekaran, Rajiv; *Washington Post;* May 14, 2012; https://www.washingtonpost.com
      /world/national-security/the-triage-commander-gen-john-allen-hastily-transforming-us
      -mission-in-afghanistan/2012/05/12/gIQAzbttKU_story.html.

48   Chandrasekaran, Rajiv; *Washington Post;* November 14 2012; https://www.independent
      .co.uk/news/world/americas/four-star-general-earned-obamas-trust-before-suffering
      -collateral-damage-from-petraeus-affair-8315554.html.

49   Cordesman, Anthony H.; *Failing Transition: The New 1230 Report on Progress Toward Security
      and Stability in Afghanistan;* Center for Strategic and International Studies; August 5, 2013;
      https://www.csis.org/analysis/failing-transition-new-1230-report-progress-toward-security
      -and-stability-afghanistan.

50   March 27, 2009; https://obamawhitehouse.archives.gov/the-press-office/remarks-president
     -a-new-strategy-afghanistan-and-pakistan.

51   Cordesman; *Failing Transition;* 2013.

52   Published in accordance with section 1230 of the National Defense Authorization Act for
     Fiscal Year 2008 (Public Law 110–181), amended.

53   For example: Cooper, Chester L., Corson, Judith E., Legere, Laurence J., Lockwood,
     David E., and Weller, Donald M.; *The American Experience with Pacification in Vietnam, Vol. 2:
     Elements of Pacification;* Institute for Defense Analysis; March 1972.

54   Cordesman; *Failing Transition;* 2013.

55   Upshur, William P., Roginski, Jonathan W., and Kilcullen, David J.; "Recognizing Systems
     in Afghanistan Lessons Learned and New Approaches to Operational Assessments"; *Prism*
     Vol. 3, No. 3; 6/12; Center for Complex Operations; https://cco.ndu.edu/Portals/96
     /Documents/prism/prism_3–3/prism3–3.pdf.

56   Ibid.

57   Ibid.

58   House Armed Services Committee hearing; February 27, 2013.

59   Kelley,; Kindle loc 984.

60   Sieff, Kevin; *Washington Post;* January 31, 2013; https://www.washingtonpost.com/world
     /asia_pacific/departing-us-general-in-afghanistan-weighs-gains-and-uncertainty/2013/01
     /29/ab9764ea-6a3d-11e2–9a0b-db931670f35d_story.html.

61   Reuters; February 10, 2013; https://www.reuters.com/article/us-afghanistan-nato
     -command/natos-afghanistan-force-gets-new-u-s-commander-idUSBRE91902P20130210.

62   SIGAR; *Corruption in Conflict;* p50.

63   UNAMA; civilian casualty report; 2012.

CHAPTER 12: TRIPLE TRANSITION

1   This was the battle where Captain Lloyd Williams yelled, "Retreat? Hell, we just got
     here."

2   Retired sergeant major Carlton Kent, quoted by Dan Lamothe; *Washington Post;* June 9,
     2014; https://www.washingtonpost.com/news/checkpoint/wp/2014/06/09/the-untimely
     -search-for-a-new-coalition-commander-in-afghanistan.

3   Author interview with Dunford.

4   Senate Armed Services Committee; April 16, 2013.

5   BBC; June 12, 2013; author interview; https://www.bbc.co.uk/news/uk-22867205.

6   https://www.worldbank.org/en/news/speech/2014/12/04/london-conference-on
     -afghanistan-2014.

7   In tactical terms this might mean that infantry on the ground were the "supported" force,
     their air cover would be "supporting."

8   Leiby, Richard; *Washington Post;* February 25, 2013; https://www.washingtonpost.com
     /world/asia_pacific/karzai-aide-details-alleged-abuse-by-us-special-forces/2013/02/25
     /d59f3f1c-7f53–11e2–8074-b26a871b165a_story.html.

9   Ibid.

10   Aikins, Matthieu; "The A-Team Killings"; *Rolling Stone;* November 6, 2013; https://www
     .rollingstone.com/interactive/feature-a-team-killings-afghanistan-special-forces/; and
     "Mapping Allegations of an American War Crime"; *Nation;* June 21, 2013; https://www
     .thenation.com/article/archive/wardak-investigation/.

11   Press briefing U.S. embassy in Kabul attended by the author; September 23, 2014.

12   Author interview with Karzai.

13   Loyn, David; *In Afghanistan;* p204.

14   Emirate was the title the Taliban claimed. It was a profoundly subversive title, as it denied the democratic foundations of the modern Afghan republic. The background to this incident is in full in chapter 13.

15   The question was asked by the author.

16   Rubin, Alissa J.; *New York Times;* May 14, 2013; https://www.nytimes.com/2013/05/14 /world/asia/general-says-us-not-to-blame-in-death-of-afghan-civilians.html.

17   Sieff, Kevin; *Washington Post;* March 2, 2014; https://www.washingtonpost.com/world /interview-karzai-says-12-year-afghanistan-war-has-left-him-angry-at-us-government /2014/03/02/b831671c-a21a-11e3-b865-38b254d92063_story.html.

18   Sieff, Kevin; *Washington Post;* January 28, 2014; https://www.washingtonpost.com/world /karzai-suspects-us-is-behind-insurgent-style-attacks-afghan-officials-say/2014/01/27 /a70d7568-8779-11e3-a760-a86415d0944d_story.html.

19   Rosenberg, Matthew; *New York Times;* January 26, 2014; https://www.nytimes.com/2014 /01/26/world/asia/government-dossier-accusing-us-in-carnage-amplifies-doubts-about -karzai.html.

20   Loyn, David; "Politics Without Parties—Afghanistan's Long Road to Democracy"; *Royal Society of Asian Affairs Journal;* January 29, 2019; https://www.tandfonline.com/doi/abs/10 .1080/03068374.2019.1567101.

21   Reuters; February 25, 2014; https://www.reuters.com/article/us-afghanistan-usa-obama -idUSBREA1O1B420140225.

22   Report by the author; BBC News; February 14, 2014; https://www.bbc.co.uk/news/world -asia-26166949.

23   Reuters;; June 2, 2014; https://www.reuters.com/article/us-usa-afghanistan -bergdahl/afghan-president-fumes-at-prisoner-deal-made-behind-his-back-source -idINKBN0ED0Z720140602?edition-redirect=uk.

24   General David Richards went onto the equivalent position in the UK.

CHAPTER 13: TALKING TO THE TALIBAN—I

1   Mashal, Mujib; *New York Times;* December 26, 2016; https://www.nytimes.com/2016/12 /26/world/asia/afghanistan-taliban-peace-talks.html.

2   Farwell and Ames; Kindle loc 8039.

3   Ibid.; Kindle loc 3909.

4   Langan, Sean; *Sunday Times;* October 22, 2017; https://www.thetimes.co.uk/article/bowe -bergdahl-the-homecoming-from-hell-world-exclusive-interview-rppkznvkj.

5   Ibid.

6   Farwell and Ames; Kindle loc 3024.

7   Dam, Bette; *A Man and a Motorcycle*; and Dobbins, James and Malkasian, Carter; *Time to Negotiate in Afghanistan;* Council on Foreign Relations; June 22 2015; https://www.cfr.org /node/162634.

8   Woodward; *Bush at War;* Kindle loc 586.

9   Strick, Alex van Linschoten, and Kuehn, Felix; *An Enemy We Created—The Myth of the Taliban / Al-Qaeda Merger in Afghanistan, 1970–2010;* Hurst; 2012; p251.

10   Ibid.; p251.

11   Rubin, Barnett; "A Tale of Two Skepticisms: Fighting and Talking with the Taliban during the Obama Years"; *War on the Rocks;* February 26, 2020.

12   Ibid.

13   Ibid.

14   Ibid.

15   Ibid.

16   See Strick and Kuehn; *An Enemy We Created;* particularly pp110–155.

17   UPI interview with Mullah Omar; June 14, 2001; https://100years.upi.com/sta_2001-06-14.html.

18   Author interview with Blanc.

19   Author interview.

20   Mashal, Mujib; *New York Times;* December 26, 2016; https://www.nytimes.com/2016/12/26/world/asia/afghanistan-taliban-peace-talks.html

21   Ibid.

22   *A Good Ally—Norway in Afghanistan 2001–2014;* Norwegian Ministry of Foreign Affairs and Defense; 2016; https://www.regjeringen.no/contentassets/09faceca099c4b8bac85ca8495e12d2d/en-gb/pdfs/nou201620160008000engpdfs.pdf.

23   *All Things Considered;* NPR; September 14, 2010.

24   Rubin; *War on the Rocks.*

25   Coll; p432.

26   Ibid.; p431.

27   The author was with Holbrooke. He traveled in a BBC armored vehicle.

28   Packer; p502.

29   Author interviews with Taliban; this was a consistent line over many years.

30   Strick and Kuehn; p250ff.

31   Rubin, Barnett R.; *Afghanistan—What Everyone Needs to Know;* Oxford University Press; 2020; p277.

32   Farwell and Ames; Kindle loc 3266.

33   Author interview with Taliban contact.

34   Clinton, Hillary; Asia Society speech; February 18, 2011; https://2009–2017.state.gov/secretary/20092013clinton/rm/2011/02/156815.htm.

35   Clinton, Hillary Rodham; *Hard Choices—A Memoir;* Simon & Schuster; 2014; p165.

36   Ibid.; p165.

37   Farwell and Ames; Kindle loc 4065. Campbell confirmed this in author interview.

38   12 Civ. 7039 (DC) (S.D.N.Y. July 15, 2013); *United States v. Noorzai.*

39   Author interview with Amerine.

40   Amerine whistleblower deposition; January 29, 2015.

41   *Military Times;* December 10, 2015.

CHAPTER 14: AFGHANISTAN'S WAR

1   Ahmed, Azam and Goldstein, Joseph; "More Aggressive Role by U.S. Military Is Seen in Afghanistan"; *New York Times;* April 29, 2015; https://www.nytimes.com/2015/04/30/world/asia/more-aggressive-role-by-us-military-is-seen-in-afghanistan.html.

2   In the Afghan system, there are two vice presidents.

3   Witnessed by the author.

4   *The Times;* August 20, 2009; https://www.thetimes.co.uk/article/kick-out-karzai-we-de-serve-a-second-chance-wnk8f3p0dfx

5   BBC interview by the author; June 6, 2014.

6   Radio Free Europe; December 2015; https://www.rferl.org/a/afghanistan-dostum-accused-abduction-rape-former-governor/28176244.html.

7   Jeong, May; "Death from the Sky—Searching for Ground Truth in the Kunduz Hospital Bombing"; *Intercept;* April 28, 2016; https://theintercept.com/2016/04/28/searching-for-ground-truth-in-the-kunduz-hospital-bombing.

8   Author interview with McCarthy.

9   *Reconstructing the Afghan National Defense and Security Forces—Lessons Learnt from the US Experience in Afghanistan;* SIGAR; September 2017; https://www.sigar.mil/pdf/lessonslearned/sigar-17-62-ll.pdf.

10 SIGAR High Risk List; January 2017; https://www.sigar.mil/pdf/spotlight/2017_High-Risk_List.pdf.

11 Pentagon press conference; October 3, 2014.

12 Senate Armed Services Committee hearing; February 12, 2015.

13 SASC hearing

14 Author interview.

15 Raghavan, Sudarshan; *Washington Post;* December 27, 2015; https://www.washingtonpost.com/world/asia_pacific/a-year-of-taliban-gains-shows-that-we-havent-delivered-top-afghan-official-says/2015/12/27/172213e8-9cfb-11e5-9ad2-568d814bbf3b_story.html.

16 Author interview.

17 *MSF Internal Review of the Kunduz Hospital Attack;* November 2015; https://www.msf.org/afghanistan-msf-releases-internal-review-kunduz-hospital-attack.

18 *MSF Review*

19 *MSF Review*

20 *New York Times;* October 3, 2015; https://www.nytimes.com/2015/10/04/world/asia/afghanistan-bombing-hospital-doctors-without-borders-kunduz.html?searchResultPosition=1.

21 Jeong; *Intercept.*

22 Author interview with member of Campbell's staff.

CHAPTER 15: ENDURING COMMITMENT

1   McMaster, *Battlegrounds—The Fight to Defend the Free World*; HarperCollins; 2020; Kindle loc 2316.

2   Nicholson, John W.; BBC interview; March 12, 2018.

3   Senate confirmation hearing; Federal News Service; January 28, 2016.

4   *National Interest;* June 3, 2016; https://nationalinterest.org/print/feature/keep-troop-levels-steady-afghanistan-16450.

5   *National Interest;* September 14, 2016; https://nationalinterest.org/feature/forging-enduring-partnership-afghanistan-17708.

6   All quotations in this account taken from Rucker, Philip, and Leonnig, Carol D.; *A Very Stable Genius;* Bloomsbury Publishing; 2020; pp131–138.

7   Sevastopulo Demetri and Dyer Geoff; *Financial Times;* April 3, 2016; https://www.ft.com
    /content/0f397616-f9b8-11e5-8e04-8600cef2ca75.

8   Snodgrass, Guy M.; *Holding the Line;* Sentinel; 2019; p61.

9   Snodgrass; p102.

10 Garamone, Jim; DOD News; December 8, 2015; https://www.jcs.mil/Media/News/News
    -Display/Article/633454/dunford-praises-afghans-progress-in-tough-fight/.

11 Senate Armed Services Committee hearing; February 17, 2017.

12 Logan, Lara; "Ending America's Longest War"; *60 Minutes,* CBS; November 25, 2017.

13 Elliott, David; *New York Times;* September 16, 2017; https://www.nytimes.com/2017/09
    /16/opinion/trump-afghanistan-vietnam-war.html.

14 Press conference in Kabul with Ash Carter; DODDOC; July 12, 2016.

15 Lamothe, Dan; *Washington Post;* October 30, 2016; https://www.washingtonpost.com/news
    /checkpoint/wp/2015/10/30/probably-the-largest-al-qaeda-training-camp-ever-destroyed
    -in-afghanistan/.

16 Tarzi, Amin; "Islamic State—Khurasan Province"; *The Future of Isis;* ed. Feisal al-Istrabadi,
    Sumit Ganguly; Brookings Institution Press; 2018; p124.

17 Pentagon press conference; September 23, 2016.

18 *Islamic State Khorasan;* CSIS; 2018; https://www.csis.org/programs/transnation-
    al-threats-project/terrorism-backgrounders/islamic-state-khorasan-k

19 Petraeus, David, and O'Hanlan, Michael; *Wall Street Journal;* May 23, 2016.

20 CNN; February 7, 2018; https://edition.cnn.com/2018/02/06/politics/us-b-52-bomber
    -afghanistan-record/index.html.

21 Osman, Borhan; *New York Times;* May 9, 2017; https://www.nytimes.com/2017/05/09
    /opinion/the-wrong-enemy-in-afghanistan.html.

22 Press conference in Kabul; author's notes; April 13, 2017.

23 Gowen, Annie and Salahuddin, Sayed; *Washington Post;* June 4, 2017; https://www
    .washingtonpost.com/world/in-tense-kabul-hundreds-of-anti-government-protesters
    -demonstrate-near-blast-crater/2017/06/04/3b857c38-48a4-11e7-8de1-cec59a9bf4b1
    _story.html.

24 This is a direct similarity to the Amanullah government that Noorzai's great-grandfather
    served as foreign minister where tribal dress was banned at government meetings.

25 Maiwandi recovered and was appointed to head the National Environmental Protection
    Agency, a cabinet post.

26 Mashal, Mujib; *New York Times;* December 19, 2016; https://www.nytimes.com/2016/12
    /19/world/what-in-the-world/being-an-afghan-general-is-nice-work-if-you-can-get-it
    -and-many-do.html.

27 SIGAR; report to the U.S. Congress; July 30, 2020.

28 Nordland, Rod; *New York Times;* April 6, 2016; https://www.nytimes.com/2016/04/07
    /world/asia/afghanistan-helmand-opium-poppy.html.

29 Rasmussen, Sune Engel; *Guardian;* April 30, 2017; https://www.theguardian.com/world/2017
    /apr/30/it-feels-like-groundhog-day-us-marines-return-to-helmand-province-afghanistan.

30 Haqqani, Husain; *New York Times;* July 6, 2017; https://www.nytimes.com/2017/07/06
    /opinion/to-win-afghanistan-get-tough-on-pakistan.html.

31 Senate Armed Services Committee; February 17, 2017.

32 Logan, Lara; "Kabul Under Seige While America's Longest War Rages On"; *60 Minutes,*
    CBS; June 3 2018.

33 ANI; February 18, 2018; https://www.aninews.in/news/world/asia/no-terror-outfit
-camps-exist-on-pakistan-soil-gen-bajwa201802180856310001/.

34 Senate Armed Services Committee hearing; February 27, 2017.

35 Rowlatt, Justin; Afghanistan Fighting the Forever War; BBC; March 12, 2018.

36 Pentagon press conference; May 30, 2018.

37 Senate Armed Services Committee; September 22, 2016.

38 BBC News; January 25, 2019.

39 BBC News; September 16, 2019.

40 Pentagon press conference; May 30, 2018.

CHAPTER 16: TALKING TO THE TALIBAN—II

1 Author interview.

2 Mashal, Mujib; *New York Times;* March 29, 2018; https://www.nytimes.com/2018/03/29
/world/asia/afghan-helmand-hunger-strike.html.

3 Agence France-Presse; March 31, 2018.

4 Mashal, Mujib; *New York Times;* June 15, 2018; https://www.nytimes.com/2018/06/15
/world/asia/afghanistan-peace-march-.html.

5 Farrell, Theo, and Semple, Michael; *Ready for Peace? The Taliban After a Decade of War;* RUSI;
January 31, 2017; https://rusi.org/publication/briefing-papers/ready-peace-afghan-taliban
-after-decade-war.

6 CBC News; January 13, 2016; https://www.cbc.ca/news/politics/colin-rutherford-released
-afghanistan-taliban-1.3399377.

7 Author interview.

8 Rubin; *Afghanistan—What Everyone Needs to Know;* p284.

9 Khaama Press; February 24, 2016.

10 Rubin, Barnett; *New Yorker;* June 4, 2016; https://www.newyorker.com/news/news-desk
/what-the-u-s-strike-on-the-taliban-means-for-peace-in-afghanistan.

11 Craig, Tim, Olivo Antonio and Ryan, Missy; *Washington Post;* May 23, 2016; https://www
.washingtonpost.com/world/airstrike-on-taliban-leader-escalates-us-involvement-in
-afghan-war/2016/05/22/f26ced5a-2014–11e6-aa84–42391ba52c91_story.html.

12 Gall, Carlotta; *New York Times;* August 9, 2017; https://www.nytimes.com/2017/08/09
/world/asia/taliban-leader-feared-pakistan-before-he-was-killed.html.

13 Ibid.

14 Yusufzai, Rahimullah; *Arab News;* March 1, 2018; https://www.arabnews.com/node
/1256866/%7B%7B.

15 Barker, Memphis; June 17, 2018; https://www.theguardian.com/world/2018/jun/17
/taliban-refuse-to-extend-truce-with-afghan-forces.

16 Ibid.

17 Mashal Mujib; *New York Times;* September 2 2018; https://www.nytimes.com/2018/09/02
/world/asia/afghan-commander-us-john-nicholsonhtml.

18 Lawrence, J. P.; *Stars and Stripes;* August 17, 2019; https://www.stripes.com/news/middle
-east/a-decadelong-program-to-turn-the-tide-in-afghanistan-is-ending-long-after-military
-shifted-its-focus-1.594651.

19 Rubin; *Afghanistan—What Everyone Needs to Know;* p274.

20 Author interview with Afghan involved in the talks; it was Noorzai whom Colonel Jason Amerine had wanted to exchange for Bowe Bergdahl in 2014.

21 CBS News; March 14, 2019; https://www.cbsnews.com/news/afghanistan-us-envoy -zalmay-khalilzad-undermining-ghani-hamdullah-mohib-says/.

22 U.S. embassy in Kabul press release.

23 Ministry of Foreign Affairs, China; July 12, 2019; https://www.fmprc.gov.cn/mfa_eng/wjdt _665385/2649_665393/t1680481.shtml.

24 Congressional Research Service; July 15 2019; https://crsreports.congress.gov/product/pdf /IF/IF11270.

CHAPTER 17: ELECTION AND AFTER

1   Crane, Conrad C.; "Phase IV Operations—Where Wars are Really Won"; *Military Review;* May/June 2005.

2   Author interview.

3   Even when it was ruled that there would be tribal identity onto the cards, it included only the fourteen tribes named in the Afghan constitution, leaving eight aggrieved small minori-ties, who needed to side with an identity they did not own to be seen as citizens.

4   Jakes, Lara; *New York Times;* September 19, 2019; https://www.nytimes.com/2019/09/19 /world/asia/us-afghanistan-aid.html.

5   Thanks to Shazia Haya from the BBC bureau in Kabul for this research.

6   Author interview.

7   See Crile, George; *Charlie Wilson's War—The Extraordinary Story of the Largest Covert Opera-tion in History;* Atlantic Books; 2003.

8   Adili, Ali Yawar, Bjelica, Ruttig, Thomas; Afghanistan Analysts Network; October 22 2019; https://www.afghanistan-analysts.org/afghanistans-2019-election-20-even-lower-turnout -figures/.

9   George, Susannah; *Washington Post;* Febrruary 26 2020; https://www.washingtonpost.com /world/asia_pacific/afghanistan-us-taliban-peace-deal/2020/02/26/0cf11080–57d8–11ea -8efd-0f904bdd8057_story.html.

10 Ibid.

11 The event was witnessed by the author, invited as a guest at the inauguration.

12 Loyn, David; *In Afghanistan.*

13 Crane, Conrad C.; "Phase IV Operations—Where Wars are Really Won"; *Military Review;* May/June 2005.

14 Dobbins, James; Preparing for Nation-Building; *Survival,* Vol. 48, No. 3; 2006; https://doi .org/10.1080/00396330600905486.

15 TOLO News; February 9, 2020; https://tolonews.com/afghanistan/biden's-comments-rile -afghans-internationals.

16 Afghanistan Study Group report; February 3 2021; USIP; https://www.usip.org/programs /afghanistan-study-group.

17 Gall, C.; p27.

INDEX

Abdullah, Abdullah, 51, 305, 333, 357, 362, 382–93

Abizaid, John, 73, 172

Abrams, Creighton, 147, 216–17

Abu Risha, Abdul Sattar, 266

Accelerating Success, 69–70, 71

Achakzai, Abdul Raziq, 232

Afghan development zones (ADZ), 106, 124

Afghan Local Police (ALP), 232–34

Afghan National Army, 233–34
  casualties of, 340–41, 360–61
  desertions in, 62, 133, 344
  Taliban and, 341–44

Afghan National Security Council, 237, 337, 343–44

Afghan National Security Forces, 168

Afghanistan, x–1
  illusion of victory in, 16–21
  Phase One 2001–2006, 10, 25–57
  Phase Two 2006–2009, 10, 83–137
  Phase Three 2009–2011, 10, 139–262
  Phase Four 2011–2014, 10, 73, 263–327
  Phase Five 2015–2011, 11, 329–98
  war in north 2001, 2, 31–34
  war in south 2001, 3, 34–37
  weather in, 226–27

Afghanistan Reconstruction Trust Fund (ARTF), 72

AfPak, 117, 249, 251, 320, 321–22

Agha, Tayyib, 38, 320–21, 322

agricultural experts, 173–74, 251–52

Ahmad, Haji, 364–65

Ahmad, Mahmud, 32

Ahmad, Sardar, 302

Ahmadzai, Akmal Ghani, 363

Aikins, Matthieu, 297–98

airpower (air strikes), 16, 29, 34, 37–38, 39, 46–49, 278, 339, 356
  against Canada, 99–100
  civilian casualties from, 135–36, 160–62, 181, 261, 266, 290
  Kunduz hospital and, 344–46

Akhunzada, Mullah Haibatullah, 373

Akhunzada, Sher Mohammad (SMA), 94, 118, 125, 202

Alexander, Chris, 77

Ali, Hazrat, 46

Allen, John R., 13–14, 150, 245, 258, 259, 261, 264–90, 350, 398
  detention centers and, 280–81
  Karzai, Hamid, and, 266–67, 277, 279
  Obama and, 285–86, 290
  Pakistan and, 282–85

Allen, Kathy, 277, 289

ALP. See Afghan Local Police

Amanullah, King, 9, 361, 362

Amerine, Jason, 35, 37–38, 324–25

Amerkhel, Aminullah, 241–42, 243

Amos, James, 308

Anaconda strategy, 227–30, 316

Al-Anbar Province, 150

Annan, Kofi, 65–66

Anwar, Muhammad, 370

Arg, 7–9, 50, 63, 66, 85–86, 363

Arghandab Valley, 39, 210

Army Field Manual 3–24, 129

Arroyo, Israel, 217, 231

ARTF. *See* Afghanistan Reconstruction Trust Fund

A-Team, 33–34

Atmar, Muhammad Hanif, 69, 103, 116, 201, 375, 382–83

Atrafi, Auliya, 369

Australia, 152, 272

Authorization for Use of Military Force,
      54–55
Auxiliary Police, 235
Axis of Evil, 61–62
Aynoddin, 273
Azizabad, 160–61

B-52 effect, 52
Back, Gerhard, 77
Bagram Air Base, 28–29, 39, 54, 185
   Obama at, 281, 305
   Parwan Detention Facility at, 280–81,
      306–8, 314
Bajwa, Qamar Javed, 367
Baker, James A., III, 149
Bala Hissar, 41, 42
Bales, Robert, 276–77, 323
Baradar, Mullah, 373
Barakzai, Nisar, 362
Barmak, Wais, 40, 65–66, 70
Barno, David, 73–76, 79, 80, 146, 149–50
Bashardost, Ramazan, 242–43, 334
Basir, Abdul, 275–76
Bauguess, Larry, 128–29
"bear hunting," 28
Bell, Gertrude, 266
Benghazi, 342–43
Bergdahl, Bowe, 208–9, 308, 311–13, 320, 321,
      322, 325, 326
Berger, Louis, 72
Bernsten, Gary, 45
A Better War (Sorley), 146–47
Biden, Joe, 11, 135, 162–63, 215, 258, 294,
      342
   CT and, 165–66, 193
   CT-plus and, 191, 194, 353
   withdrawal announcement from, 396–97
Bigeard, Marcel, 144–45, 148
bilateral security agreement (BSA), 298–300,
      305
bin Laden, Osama, 45, 47, 53, 251, 316,
      395
   killing of, 238–39, 268, 322
   in Pakistan, 117, 238–39, 322
Black Hawk Down, 14, 376
Black Watch, 197
Blair, Tony, 44, 87, 89, 119
Blake, James M., 40
Blanc, Jarrett, 317, 322, 323, 325–27
Blinken, Antony, 396
Bordin, Jeffrey, 271–72, 274
Bosnia, 41, 144, 172, 314
Bradshaw, Adrian, 285

British, 15, 39, 44–45, 55, 61, 74, 87–91,
      111–14, 147, 152, 285
   in Helmand Province, 89–97, 152, 197–200,
      234
   in Musa Qala, 101–3
   Operation Medusa by, 97–101, 197–98,
      231
   Operation Mountain Thrust by, 91–93
Broadwell, Paula, 224, 261, 289
Brostrom, Jonathan, 115
BSA. See bilateral security agreement
Buckley, Edgar, 61
Buckley, Gregory, 273
Buddha statue destruction, 52
Bundy, McGeorge, 189
Bush, George W., 14, 40, 46, 69, 149, 156, 213,
      313
   Axis of Evil of, 61–62
   Iraq and, 16, 30, 87
   Karzai, Hamid, and, 124–25, 161–62,
      175
   McNeill, D., and, 122–23, 136
   nation-building by, 42, 54
   9/11 and, 61
   al-Qaeda and Taliban and, 394–95
   war on terror of, 24, 61, 280, 282, 314
Butler, Ed, 88–92
Byrd, William, 70, 249

Cameron, David, 15
Camp Leatherneck, 198, 344
Campbell, John F. "JC," 28, 56, 150, 205–6,
      207, 261, 308–9, 324, 331, 336–39,
      343–47, 398
   Obama and, 338–39, 342
Canada, 76–78, 88–89, 152
   air strike against, 99–100
   hostage from, 372
   Operation Medusa and, 98–101, 197–98,
      231
Canadian Battalion (CANBAT), 77
Carter, Ash, 342, 343
Carter, Nick, 39, 201, 210, 221, 268, 397
   ISAF and, 232
   Petraeus and, 235–36
Category IV intelligence, 208
Cavoli, Chris, 109
CENTCOM. See Central Command
Center for Strategic and International Studies,
      355
Central Command (CENTCOM), 29, 30, 46,
      73, 97, 131, 172, 180, 198, 244
   Petraeus and, 218–19, 234, 260

Central Intelligence Agency (CIA), 30, 31, 32, 45, 50, 78, 172, 175, 213, 254, 280, 316–17, 398
  bin Laden and, 238–39
  CT of, 33, 171, 211
  McChrystal, S., and, 186
  Petraeus and, 258, 261
  Sherzai and, 35, 36
  warlords and, 52, 244–45
The Centurions (Lartéguy), 144
CERP. *See* Commander's Emergency Response Program
Chandrasekaran, Rajiv, 252
Chayes, Sarah, 56
Cheney, Dick, 171, 174
Chretien, Marc, 203, 218, 251, 267, 268
Churchill, Winston S., 109
CIA. *See* Central Intelligence Agency
civilian casualties, 278–79, 290, 302–4, 323
  from air strikes, 135–36, 160–62, 181, 261
  in battle for Kabul, 357–58
  from meteor strikes, 276
  by Taliban, 80, 301–2
  at wedding parties, 51, 157–61, 358
Civilian Casualty Tracking Cell, 160
CJTF-Mountain, 48
Clapper, Jim, 131
Clark, Wesley, 181
Clarke, Michael, 271
Clifford, Clark, 189
Clinton, Bill, 14, 60–61
Clinton, Hillary, 175, 249, 258
  Eikenberry and, 194, 266
  Pakistan and, 284, 322
  Taliban and, 315, 321, 322–23
Cohen, Eliot, 149
COIN. *See* counterinsurgency
Coll, Steve, 191
Combat Fitness Test, 308
Commander's Emergency Response Program (CERP), 19–20, 203, 209, 245–47
Cone, Robert, 131
conflict resolution cell, 316
Conway, James, 197
COP Keating, 206–7
Cordesman, Anthony, 286–87, 289
CORDS program, 259
corruption, 20, 242–49, 364–65
  COIN and, 241–56, 315
  Karzai, Hamid, and, 254–56, 361
  USAID and, 249–53
  of warlords, 243–47

counterinsurgency (COIN), 16, 129, 141–63, 178–79, 217, 269
  corruption and, 241–56, 315
  in Iraq, 145–46, 150, 176, 187–88
  McChrystal, S., on, 187–88, 192–96, 217–18
  McKiernan, D., and, 150–60, 166–67, 177–78
  McNeill, D., and, 129–33
  Obama and, 165–67, 173–83
  Petraeus on, 24, 143–51, 190, 241–62
  in Vietnam, 14, 144, 146–47
Counterinsurgency Warfare: Theory and Practice (Galula), 145
counterterrorism-plus (CT-plus), 191, 194, 353
counterterrorist tactics (CT), 165–67, 193, 337, 343
  of CIA, 33, 171, 211
  Dunford, J., and, 293, 297, 351
COVID-19, 393
Cowper-Coles, Sherard, 124
Craddock, Bantz, 131
Crane, Conrad C., 147, 381, 394–95
Crellin, Brent, 100
cricket, 22, 369
Cripwell, Richard, 273–74
Crocker, Ryan, 266–67
Crumpton, Hank, 33, 46
CT. *See* counterterrorist tactics
CT-plus. *See* counterterrorism-plus
Cubbison, Douglas, 114
Cunningham, James, 298–99, 341–42
customs revenues, 79

Dailey, Dell, 45
Daoud, Muhammad, 94, 212
Daudzai, Muhammad Umer, 161, 237
David McKiernan, 8
Davis, Dickie, 74
Davis, Skip, 152
Dawlatzai, Esmatullah, 233
Dayton Accords, 172, 314, 319
DEA. *See* Drug Enforcement Agency
Defense Intelligence Agency (DIA), 186
Dempsey, Marty, 292
Department for International Development (DFID), 57
detention centers, 279–81. *See also* Parwan Detention Facility
  prisoner releases from, 306–8
DFID. *See* Department for International Development

DIA. *See* Defense Intelligence Agency
Dickinson, Scott, 273
disarmament, 64–65
Dobbins, Jim, 37, 40, 45, 60, 167, 395–96
Docherty, Leo, 96–97
Donahue, Pat, 110
Dostum, Abdul Rashid, 33, 68, 74, 335–36
drones, 155, 165, 170, 187, 307
    against Mansour, 372–73
    in Pakistan, 284, 372–73
Drug Enforcement Agency (DEA), 155, 325
Dunford, Ellyn, 292
Dunford, Joseph F., Jr., 12, 146, 246, 289,
        291–309, 323, 377, 396
    BSA and, 298–300
    CT and, 293, 297, 351
    NATO and, 293, 295
    Obama and, 293–95, 309
    prisoner releases and, 306–8
    Trump and, 351–52, 353, 354
Dupree, Louis, 64, 67
Dupree, Nancy Hatch, 64, 67
Durand Line, 283, 393
Dutton, Jim, 188
DynCorp, 94

Eggers, Jeff, 193
Eid cease-fire, 373–76
Eide, Kai, 150–51, 156, 159, 163, 204
XVIII Airborne Corps, 27–28, 29–30
eighty secure districts plan, 106
Eikenberry, Karl, 16, 62, 79, 146, 216, 254
    Clinton, H., and, 194, 266
    Karzai, Hamid, and, 194, 237, 266
Eisenhower, Dwight, 290, 332
Elizabeth, Queen, 61
Equality for Peace and Democracy, 397
expeditionary advisory packages, 351

Facebook, 297, 333, 386
Fahim, Muhammad Qasim, 32, 33, 34, 39–42,
        50, 62, 74, 397
Faizi, Aimal, 304
Fallon, William "Fox," 131, 180
Farkhunda, 21–22
Farnood, Sherkan, 255
Federal Bureau of Investigations (FBI), 186,
        255, 325
Fenzel, Mike, 110
Fergusson, James, 89
Ferozi, Khalilullah, 255
1st Brigade, 82nd Airborne, 56, 110
Five Pillars (magic carpet), 73–76

Fixed Failed States (Ghani, Ashraf), 305
Fixing Failed States (Loyn), 9, 332
Flournoy, Michèle, 172, 176, 178, 247
food aid, 59–60
Four-Hundred-Bed hospital, 243, 340, 357
Fox, David, 38
France/French, 62, 153, 271
Franks, Tommy, 29–30, 33, 34, 46, 49, 57,
        62–63, 73
Fraser, David, 98, 100
Freakley, Ben, 88, 91–92, 95, 98–99, 107
Freedom's Sentinel, 338
Fuller, Peter, 282

Galbraith, Peter, 204
Gall, Carlotta, 373
Galula, David, 145
Galvin, Jack, 143–44, 223, 224
Gandamack Lodge, 251, 302
GAO. *See* Government Accountability Office
Garmser, 94–95, 197, 253, 273
Gates, Robert, 18, 130–32, 136, 142, 150, 163,
        174, 258
    Helmand Province and, 199, 257
    McChrystal, S., and, 190, 193–94, 216
    McKiernan, D., and, 175, 179, 182
    Mullen and, 182–83, 190
    Obama and, 169–70, 257
    Petraeus and, 175–76, 182, 190
    terms sheet by, 195
General McMahon (fictional character), 218
General Orders 100, 141–42
Germany/Germans, 15, 51, 62, 130, 320, 322,
        362
Gerson, Michael, 190
Ghafour, Mullah, 119, 123
Ghamsharik, Haji Zaman, 46, 47
Ghani, Ajmal, 363, 382
Ghani, Ashraf, 7, 8–9, 67, 69, 71, 236, 305,
        331–40, 358–61, 363, 394, 398
    Abdullah and, 362
    Campbell and, 337–39
    Eid cease-fire and, 374–76
    in election of 2019, 382–93
    IS and, 354–55
    Khalilzad and, 378–80
    Pakistan and, 366–67
    warlords and, 333, 361–62
Gilani, Ali Haider, 366
Gilchrist, Peter, 79
Government Accountability Office (GAO), 75
Graham, Lindsey, 162, 256
Graham, Mark, 99

Grant, Ulysses S., 221–22, 226
Green Berets, 33–34, 36, 171–72, 297–98
Greene, Harold, 275
green-on-blue attacks, 270–77
Gregory, David, 222
Grenier, Robert, 32–36
Grossman, Marc, 321–22
Ground Zero, 66, 70
Guantánamo Five, 308, 313, 322, 326
Guggenheim, Scott, 71

Haass, Richard, 45
Habibullah, King, 363
Hagel, Chuck, 305
Hagenbeck, Franklin, 48
Hamad, Jalil, 60
Hamilton, Lee, 149
Haq, Abdul, 35, 397
Haqqani, Husain, 366
Haqqani network, 155, 208, 227, 283, 285,
    312, 319, 322, 347, 358
Harem Serai, 363, 398
Hashemi, Qais, 370
Hastings, Michael, 213–15, 217–18
Hayes, James, 232
Hazara, 52, 53
HEART 9/11, 269
Hekmatyar, Gulbuddin, 361
Helmand, Haris, 381–82
Helmand Province, *5, 6,* 15, 80–81, 88,
    210–11, 257
  British in, 89–97, 152, 197–200, 234
  corruption in, 251–53, 364–65
  McChrystal, S., on, 197–200
  McNeill, D., in, 133–35
  Nicholson, J., and, 364–65
  night operations in, 279
  opium poppy in, 89, 94
  Taliban in, 89–97, 288, 344, 364–65
  voting security in, 204
High Peace Council, 320
Hillier, Rick, 76–78, 88–89, 104
Hitler, Adolf, 36, 62
Hoar, Joseph, 291
Hodges, Ben, 210
Holbrooke, Richard, 163, 172–73, 189, 204, 282
  corruption and, 251–52
  Karzai, Hamid, and, 237, 334
  McChrystal, S., on, 215, 216
  Taliban and, 314–15, 318–19, 321
  USAID and, 249–50
Hollande, François, 271
Horner, Nils, 302

Human Rights Watch, 53, 233
Hunter, Duncan, 325
Huntington, Samuel, 8, 216
Hussein, Saddam, 17, 29, 43, 62, 75

I Lost My Love in Baghdad (Hastings), 214
ICRC. *See* International Committee of the
    Red Cross
IEDs. *See* improvised explosive devices
Ignatius, David, 182, 190
improvised explosive devices (IEDs), 100, 129,
    142, 170, 201–2, 209, 217, 231–32
Ingram, Mike, 217
Innocence of Muslims (film), 276
intelligence, surveillance, and reconnaissance
    (ISR), 17, 113
Inteqal, 296–97, 305
International Committee of the Red Cross
    (ICRC), 160
International Security Assistance Force (ISAF),
    18–19, 50, 76, 88, 206, 212, 232
  aid workers at, 105
  Allen, J., and, 258, 269
  green-on-blue attacks and, 273–74
  in Kabul, 42–45, 62, 86–89
  McKiernan, D., and, 78, 179
  McNeill, D., and, 129–33
  media at, 235–36
  NATO and, 94, 337
  NGOs and, 124
  Nicholson, J., and, 349
  warlords and, 86–87
Iqbal, Muhammad, 366
Iran, 21, 61–62, 79, 373
Iraq, 14, 17, 56, 76, 160, 395
  in Axis of Evil, 61–62
  Bush and, 16, 30, 87
  COIN in, 145–46, 150, 176, 187–88
  IS in, 294, 356
  McKiernan, D., in, 43, 169, 176
  Petraeus in, 122, 145–47, 187–88, 221, 225
  Small Wars Manual in, 142
Iraq Study Group, 149
IS. *See* Islamic State
ISAF. *See* International Security Assistance
    Force
Ishchi, Ahmad, 336
ISI, of Pakistan, 32, 64, 116, 299, 373
Islamic State (IS), 169, 294, 334, 354–57, 358,
    367
ISR. *See* intelligence, surveillance, and
    reconnaissance
Italians, 14–15

Jalaluddin Haqqani, 111
Jan, Abdul Rahman, 202, 211
Jawad, Said Tayeb, 66
Al Jazeera TV, 301
John Carter (fictional character), 267
Johnson, Lyndon B., 189, 334
Jones, James, 116, 117–18, 133, 167, 190
Jones, Terry, 238
Jouvenal, Peter, 250–51
Junger, Sebastian, 207

Kabul, 4, 19–20
    Allen, J., in, 258, 259, 269
    apartment blocks in, 22
    battle for, 357–58
    CIA in, 175
    Dobbins in, 40
    Fahim in, 41–42
    ISAF in, 42–45, 62, 86–89
    Karzai, Hamid, in, 39–40
    Khalizad in, 378
    Kratzer in, 57
    Lute in, 235
    McChrystal, S., in, 186–87
    McKiernan, D., in, 151–52, 179
    9/11 in, 11
    Northern Alliance in, 40
    Pakistan and, 366–67
    Petraeus in, 222, 224, 226–27
    riots in, 85
    Rumsfeld in, 106–7
    Russia and, 42
    SAR in, 215
    Schroen in, 31
Kabul Bank, 255
Kahlizad, Zalmay, 37
Kandahar, 5, 6, 35, 36, 39, 185
    Operation Medusa in, 97–101, 197–98, 231
    Petraeus and, 231–32
    Taliban in, 7–8, 30, 37, 97–101, 231–32,
        288–89
Kandahar Strike Force, 213, 254
Karimi, Sher Muhammad, 63–64, 245, 337, 344
Karimi, Zia, 337
Karzai, Ahmed Wali (AWK), 213, 253–54
Karzai, Hamid, 9, 10–11, 16, 18, 35, 37–40, 45,
        74, 76, 85–87, 114, 163, 200–204, 236,
        298, 335, 397
    Allen, J., and, 266–67, 277, 279
    Biden and, 162–63
    BSA and, 299–300
    Bush and, 124–25, 161–62, 175
    civilian casualties and, 302–4

corruption and, 254–56, 361
detention centers and, 279–81
Eikenberry and, 194, 237, 266
Fahim and, 39–40, 41, 50
Holbrooke and, 237, 334
McChrystal, S., on, 200–205
McNeill, D., and, 124–25, 134–35
meteor strikes and, 276–77
Obama and, 204, 281–82, 299, 305–6, 323
Pakistan and, 35–36, 117, 282
Petraeus on, 227, 236–37, 265
prisoner releases and, 306–8
Richards and, 103–4, 107
Taliban and, 38, 205, 300–301, 313, 319–20,
        322–23
wedding party bombing and, 51, 157, 160
Karzai, Hekmat, 371
Karzai, Yar Muhammad, 278
Karzai Twelve, 74
Kayani, Ashfaq, 153, 154, 282–85
Keane, John M. "Jack," 27, 29, 149, 150
Kearney, Dan, 112
Kelley, Jill, 218, 289
Kelly, Robert, 257
Kennedy, John F., 131, 171
Kerry, John, 204, 333
Key Terrain Districts, 195
KHAD secret police, of Russia, 274
Khairkhwa, Khairullah, 313
Khakrezwal, Akrem, 39
Khalifa, Umar, 366
Khalilzad, Zalmay, 18, 21, 74–75, 204, 378–80,
        382, 396
Khan, Bismillah, 274–75
Khan, Daoud, 393
Khan, Hafiz Saeed, 355
Khan, Hemad, 261
Khan, Ismail, 33, 53, 74, 79
Khar, Hina Rabbani, 283
Khogyani, Abdul Majid, 297
Khorasan, 355–57
al-Khurasani, Abu Muslim, 355
Khyber, Iqbal, 364
Kilcullen, David, 112, 262, 288
Kirk, Mark, 350
Kissinger, Henry, 62
Knowlton, William A., 223
Korengal Valley, 111–14, 207
Kosovo, 28, 41
Koster, Sam, 223
Kratzer, David E., 56–57
Krulak, Victor C., 131
Kuehn, Felix, 314

Kunar Province, 207
Kunduz hospital, 344–46

Langan, Sean, 312
Lartéguy, Jean, 144
Lashkar-e-Taiba, 155, 366
Lavoie, Omer, 101
Lavrov, Sergey, 367
Lawrence, T. E., 73, 147, 266
Lessons in Disaster (Bundy), 189
Levin, Carl, 135
Libya, 16, 395
Lincoln, Abraham, 222, 332, 334, 351
Local Defense Initiative, 235
Lockhart, Clare, 305
Lodin, Azizullah, 254
Loftis, John Darin, 275
Logan, Lara, 346
Longuet, Gérard, 271
Loya Jirga tent, 49–52, 299–300
    of Ghani, Ashraf, 361
    Taliban and, 314, 319–20
Ludin, Mullah Attaullah, 333–34
Lute, Doug, 170–71, 172, 191, 195, 208, 211,
    235, 315–16, 320

MAAWS. *See* Money as a Weapons System
MacArthur, Douglas, 8, 180–81, 185
Macedonia, 130
magic carpet (Five Pillars), 73–76
"Magnificent Seven," 203
Maiwand Battery, 101–2
Maiwandi, Schah-Zaman, 360–61, 363
Malkasian, Carter, 198, 210, 253, 259–60
Malmstrom, Eric, 114
Mangal, Muhammad Gulab, 203
Manning, Chelsea (Bradley), 187
Mansour, Mullah Akhtar, 316, 371–73, 398
Mao Zedong, 145
The March of Folly (Tuchman), 23
Marchanti, Robert, 275
Marine Task Force 58, 36, 46
Marshall, George, 54
Marshall Plan, 69
Martin, Mike, 96
Mashal, Mujib, 370
Massive ordinance Air Blast (MOAB), 356
Massoud, Ahmed Shah, 31–32, 65, 305
Mattis, Jim, 36, 46, 141, 145–46, 149, 286, 352,
    353, 354
Mauladad, Haji, 369
McCaffrey, Barry, 78
McCain, John, 162, 165, 225, 235, 294, 341

McCarthy, Pat, 339, 343
McChrystal, Annie, 214–15
McChrystal, Herbert J., Jr., 15
McChrystal, Stanley A., 8, 15, 27–29, 39, 50,
    143, 180, 185–206, 377, 397
    COIN and, 187–88, 192–96, 217–18
    corruption and, 244, 248
    detention centers and, 280–81
    fitness regime of, 185
    Gates and, 190, 193–94, 216
    Ghani, Ashraf, and, 332
    Hastings and, 213–15
    Helmand Province and, 197–200
    in Iraq, 187
    Karzai, Hamid, and, 200–205
    Obama and, 169, 189–90, 192, 193, 195,
        196, 215
    Operation Mostarak and, 200–204
    Petraeus on, 146, 150, 224
    population-centered counterinsurgency of,
        217
    PRT and, 55–56
    resignation of, 215–16
    Special Forces and, 206, 213
    Taliban and, 191–92, 216, 318
McColl, John, 44–45, 55
McDonough, Denis, 342
McDonough, John, 211
McKiernan, David, 8, 18, 43–44, 113, 165,
    176–77, 188, 397
    COIN and, 150–60, 166–67, 177–78
    end of career of, 180–83
    Flournoy and, 176, 178
    Gates and, 175, 179, 182
    in Iraq, 43, 169, 176
    ISAF and, 78, 179
    in Kabul, 151–52, 179
    Obama and, 167, 168, 170, 175
    opium poppy and, 155–57
    Pakistan and, 153–55
    wedding party bombing and, 157–60
McKiernan, Michael, 182
McMaster, H. R., 146, 176, 244, 349, 352
McNamara, Robert, 315
McNeill, Clarence "Boone," 136, 152
McNeill, Dan, 12, 13, 18, 27–30, 49–50, 54,
    55–56, 121
    Bush and, 122–23, 136
    COIN and, 129–33
    in Helmand Province, 133–35
    Karzai, Hamid, and, 124–25, 134–35
    Musa Qala and, 118–19, 124–28
    NATO and, 130–33

McNeill, Dan (*continued*)
    Pakistan and, 21, 128–29, 135
    wedding party bombing and, 51
McRaven, Bill, 212–13
Médecins sans Frontières (MSF), 344–46
Medley, Dominic, 215–16
Mehsud, Hakeemullah, 307
Mehsud, Latif, 307–8
Mendenhall, Joseph, 131
Metcalfe, Daniel T., 269–70, 273
meteor strikes, 276–77
Military Operations Other Than War, 15–16
militias, 232–34
Miller, Austin Scott, 376–77
Miller, Stephen, 352, 353
Milley, Mark, 347
mine-resistant vehicles (MRAPs), 142–43
MOAB. *See* Massive ordinance Air Blast
MOD, 63–64
Mohammad, Haji, 59
Mohammed, Khalid Sheikh, 53
Mohib, Hamdullah, 375, 378–79
Mojaddedi, Sibghatullah, 7, 135
Molinie, Guilhem, 345
Money as a Weapons System (MAAWS),
    246–47
money burning, 68–72
Mr. Pink, 160–61
Mr. White, 160–61
MRAPs. *See* mine-resistant vehicles
Muhammad, Din, 270
Muhammad, Haji Nazar, 86
Muhaqiq, Muhammad, 358
mujahideen, 20, 31, 40
    Karzai, Hamid, and, 86–87
    Russia and, 41–42, 393–94
Mullen, Mike, 151, 176–77, 180, 182–83, 190,
    283, 397
Murdoch, Rupert, 261
Murphy, Brett, 160
Musa Qala, 101–3, 118–19, 124–28, 368, 370
Musharraf, Pervez, 32, 116, 123, 153, 282
Muslim Brotherhood, 41
Muttawakil, Wakil Ahmed, 314
"mutually hurting stalemate," 367–68
My Lai massacre, 14, 223

N2K, 111
Najibullah, Mohammad, 8, 42
Nangarhar Province, 157
Naqib, Mullah, 37, 38
National Directorate for Security (NDS), 213,
    280, 307, 375

National Geospatial-Intelligence Agency
    (NGA), 186
National Security Council (NSC), 11, 186,
    268
National Solidarity Program, 72
nation-building, 42, 43, 54, 88, 395
NATO, 8, 11, 44, 97, 215–16, 286
    aid from, 76–78
    British and, 90–91
    Dunford, J., and, 293, 295
    Freedom's Sentinel and, 338
    green-on-blue attacks and, 272
    ISAF and, 94, 337
    Joint Force Command of, 77
    Karzai, Hamid, and, 236
    McNeill, D., and, 130–33, 152
    nation-building by, 88
    9/11 and, 61–62
    Operation Mostarak and, 203
    Petraeus and, 235, 256
    Taliban and, 317–18
    Trump and, 352
Natsios, Andrew, 60
Navy SEALs, 157, 238–39, 268
NDS. *See* National Directorate for Security
Nelson, Brendan, 272
Neumann, Ron, 86, 102–3, 108
New Ansari, 254–55
New Zealand, 152
NGA. *See* National Geospatial-Intelligence
    Agency
NGOs. *See* nongovernmental organizations
Nicholson, John W. "Mick," 109–11, 112,
    227–28, 347, 373
    battle for Kabul and, 358
    Helmand Province and, 364–65
    IS and, 356–57
    "mutually hurting stalemate" and, 367–68
    on 9/11, 349
    Obama and, 350–51
    Pakistan and, 366–67
    Trump and, 351, 353–54, 377–78
Nicholson, Larry, 190
night operations, 278–79
9/11, 10, 27, 53
    Authorization for Use of Military Force
        and, 54–55
    Bush and, 61
    CIA after, 30, 31
    disinformation campaign after, 316
    first responders at, 269
    in Kabul, 11
    NATO and, 61–62

Nicholson, J., on, 349
  Pentagon building on, 13
  revenge for, 8
  warlords and, 314
nongovernmental organizations (NGOs), 19,
    57, 66, 71, 124, 135
Noorzai, Daud, 362–63, 381
Noorzai, Haji Bashir, 324–25, 378
Norgrove, Linda, 238
North Korea, 61–62
Northern Alliance, 32, 34, 37, 40, 65, 233, 397
Norway, 317–18
NSC. See National Security Council
nuclear weapons, of Pakistan, 172, 366
Nuland, Victoria, 159
Nur, Atta Muhammad, 33, 74, 335, 360, 362
Nuristani, Muhammad Tamim, 113, 114

Obaidullah, Mullah, 64
Obama, Barack, 8, 10, 12, 162, 163
  Agha and, 321
  Allen, J., and, 285–86, 290
  Anaconda strategy and, 228
  at Bagram Air Base, 281, 305
  Bergdahl and, 311–12
  Campbell and, 338–39, 342
  CIA and, 213
  COIN and, 165–67, 173–83
  CT and, 343
  Dunford, J., and, 293–95, 309
  Gates and, 169–70, 257
  Holbrooke and, 319
  Jones, J., and, 167
  Karzai, Hamid, and, 204, 281–82, 299,
    305–6, 323
  Lute and, 172, 208
  Mansour and, 373
  McChrystal, S., and, 169, 189–90, 192, 193,
    195, 196, 215
  McKiernan, D., and, 167, 168, 170, 175
  National Security Council and, 11
  Nicholson, J., and, 350–51
  Nobel Peace Prize to, 196
  NSC and, 268
  Omar and, 322
  Pakistan and, 173, 299
  Petraeus and, 167, 218–19, 224, 234–35
  Powell and, 193–94
  al-Qaeda and, 188, 191
  redeployments by, 207–10
  responsible end of, 259
  surge of troops from, 23, 96
  Taliban and, 315, 321, 368

Obama's Wars (Woodward), 237
OEF. See Operation Enduring Freedom
Omar, Mullah, 38, 227, 308, 316, 319, 322,
    326, 371
opcon (operational control), 107
Operation Anaconda, 48–49
Operation Enduring Freedom (OEF), 44, 55,
    56, 78, 87–88, 107
  to Freedom's Sentinel, 338
  Gates and, 179
Operation Jawbreaker, 31, 33, 45, 244–45, 362
Operation Lariat Advance, 176
Operation Medusa, 97–101, 197–98, 231
Operation Moshtarak, 200–204, 231
Operation Mountain Thrust, 91–93
Operation Panther's Claw, 197
operational control (opcon), 107
opium poppy, 20, 60, 63, 81, 89, 94, 155–57
O'Rourke, Kevin, 269–70, 273
Osman, Borhan, 356
Ostlund, William B., 110
Owens, Kevin, 187

P2K, 111
PAG. See policy action group
Pakistan
  Allen, J., and, 282–85
  bin Laden in, 117, 238–39, 322
  British and, 285
  Bush and, 156
  CIA in, 172
  drones in, 284, 372–73
  Ghani, Ashraf, and, 366–67
  Haqqani network and, 283, 347
  Holbrooke and, 282
  ISI of, 64, 299, 373
  Islamic State and, 355
  Kabul and, 366–67
  Karzai, Hamid, and, 35–36, 117, 282
  McKiernan, D., and, 153–55
  McNeill, D., and, 21, 128–29, 135
  Nicholson, J., and, 366–67
  Northern Alliance and, 32
  nuclear weapons of, 172, 366
  Obama and, 173, 299
  Pashtun and, 111
  refugees and, 346–47
  Richards and, 115–17
  Special Forces and, 284
  Taliban and, 16, 32–33, 87, 153–55, 227,
    322
  Trump and, 365, 379
Paktia Province, 47–48

Panetta, Leon, 271, 276
Parhamovich, Andi, 214
Parker, Nick, 215
Parwan Detention Facility, 280–81, 306–8, 314
Pashtuns, 22, 33, 304–5
    corruption of, 247–48
    in Kandahar, 39
    Omar and bin Laden and, 316
    Pakistan and, 111
    Taliban of, 50, 64
    warlords of, 34–35
Pearl, Daniel, 317
Pech Valley, 112, 206, 207, 261
Pentagon building, on 9/11, 13
Pentagon Papers, 315
Perle, Richard, 75
Peshawar Accord, 42
Petraeus, David, 78–79, 397–98
    ALP and, 235
    Anaconda strategy of, 227–30, 316
    Big M of, 224–26
    bin Laden and, 238–39
    Broadwell and, 289
    Carter, N., and, 235–36
    CENTCOM and, 218–19, 234, 260
    CIA and, 258, 261
    COIN and, 24, 143–51, 190, 241–62
    corruption, on, 244
    eighty secure districts plan of, 106
    family of, 223
    on fragile and reversible, 256–60
    Gates and, 175–76, 182, 190
    in Helmand Province, 15
    image of, 221–22
    in Iraq, 122, 145–47, 187–88, 221, 225
    IS and, 356
    in Kabul, 222, 224, 226–27
    Kandahar and, 231–32
    Karzai, Hamid, and, 227, 236–37, 265
    as Malik D., 221–39
    Mattis and, 141, 145–46, 149
    McChrystal, S., and, 146, 150, 224
    NATO and, 235, 256
    Obama and, 167, 218–19, 224, 234–35
    political ambitions of, 261
    Vietnam and, 223
Pickering, Thomas, 133
policy action group (PAG), 104–6, 124
Popalzai, 35
"Pottery Barn Rule," 43
Powell, Colin, 14, 43, 193–94
prisoner releases, 306–8
A Promised Land (Obama), 168

provincial reconstruction team (PRT), 55–56, 74, 79, 171
Pry, Benjamin, 114
Public Protection Police, 235
Pugwash, 372
Pul-e-Charkhi jail, 333
Putin, Vladimir, 20, 367

Qadir, Haji, 50
al-Qaeda, 10, 17
    "bear hunting" of, 28
    Bush and, 394–95
    Dunford, J., and, 296
    Obama and, 188, 191
    OEF and, 78
    in Paktia Province, 47–48
    safe havens for, 296
    Taliban and, 315, 316, 321, 323, 378
    in Tora Bora cave complex, 45–49
    training camp of, 355
Quetta Shura, 320
Quran, 22, 183
    burning of, 275–76
    knife in, 210

Rabbani, Burhanuddin, 41–42, 282, 320
Rahimi, Abdul Salam, 362, 363–64, 380
Rahman, Amir Abdur, 398
Rakasans, 223–24
Ramms, Egon, 123
Ramslien, Alf Arne, 311, 317
Rassoul, Zalmay, 124, 323
Raziq, Abdul, 373
Red Mosque, 154
Red Team report, 271, 274
refugees, 34, 346–47
Reid, John, 89–90, 91
Resolute Support, 337, 338, 346
Restrepo, Juan "Doc," 112, 206
"Revolt of the Generals," 149
Revolutionary United Front (RUF), in Sierra
    Leone, 103
Rice, Condoleezza, 16, 42, 141, 159, 161
Rice, Susan, 312, 342–43
Richards, David, 87–88, 90–91, 93, 95, 108
    criticisms by, 119–20
    Karzai, Hamid, and, 103–4, 107
    McNeill, D., and, 123–24
    Musa Qala and, 101–3, 118–19
    Operation Medusa and, 97–101
    PAG and, 104–6
    Pakistan and, 115–17
Ricks, Tom, 190, 225

Ridgway, Matthew, 185, 226
Riedel, Bruce, 172–73, 192, 314–15
Rivera, Geraldo, 56
Rivera, Richard, 273
Robertson, George, 44
Rodriguez, David "Rod," 131, 182
Roosevelt, Franklin D., 332
Rubin, Barnett "Barney," 314–15, 320, 324, 373, 378
RUF. *See* Revolutionary United Front
Ruggiero, Frank, 320, 321
Rumsfeld, Donald, 10, 21, 38, 45, 54, 73, 121, 227
  airpower and, 29
  COIN and, 149
  Iraq and, 76
  in Kabul, 106–7
  light-footprint plan of, 30
  NATO and, 61
  "Revolt of the Generals" and, 149
Russell, Terrence, 312
Russia, 15, 243
  Bagram Air Base and, 29, 54
  IS and, 367
  Kabul and, 42
  KHAD secret police of, 274
  McKiernan, D., and, 176
  mujahideen and, 41–42, 393–94
  Stinger antiaircraft missiles and, 52
  Taliban and, 20–21, 34, 367, 379
  warlords and, 18
Rutherford, Colin, 372

SACEUR. *See* Supreme Allied Commander Europe
Saeed, Hafiz, 366
Sageman, Marc, 274–75, 276
Saleh, Amrullah, 50, 375
Salehi, Muhammad Zia, 254–55
Salt Pit, 280
SAR. *See* situational awareness room
Sarkozy, Nicolas, 153, 271
SAS. *See* Special Air Service
Saudi Arabia, 18, 31, 320
Sayyaf, Abdul Rasul, 33, 53
Scheffer, Jaap de Hoop, 132–33
Schoomaker, Peter, 12, 143
Schröder, Gerhard, 62
Schroen, Gary, 31–32, 33, 244–45, 362
Scotts, 197
Security Assistance Force, 44
Sedwill, Mark, 203
Shah, Muhammad Zahir, 37, 49

Shah, Zahir, 49
Shahim, Qadam Shah, 344
Shahrani, Nematullah, 157
Shalikashvili, John, 16
Sharif, Raheel, 346
Sherman, Matt, 316
Sherzai, Gul Agha, 35, 37, 38, 39, 97, 314
Shuja, Shah, 299
Sibghatullah Mojaddedi, *5, 7*
Sierra Leone, 103
SIGAR. *See* Special Inspector for Afghanistan Reconstruction
situational awareness room (SAR), 186–87, 215
Slim, William, 226
Small Wars Manual, 142, *145–46*
Small Wars Operations, 142
smartphones, 160, 333
  COIN and, 178–79
  of Mansour, tracking of, 372–73
Smith, Adam, 359
Smith, Gregory J., 237
Snodgrass, Guy, 352, 353
soccer, 22–23
social media, 19, 297, 333, 374, 386
SOF. *See* special operations forces
The Soldier and State (Huntington), 8
Somalia, 14, 41, 376, 395
Sopko, John, 364
Sorley, Lewis, 146–47
Spanta, Rangin, 241, 323
Special Air Service (SAS), 80
Special Forces, 38, 53, 78, 107, 108, 232
  CT and, 165
  Karzai, Hamid, and, 298
  McChrystal, S., and, 206, 213
  missing men and, 297–98
  on night operations, 279
  Pakistan and, 284
  in Tora Bora cave complex, 45
Special Inspector for Afghanistan Reconstruction (SIGAR), 255–56, 341, 364
special operations forces (SOF), 79, 171, 213, 398
Spotts, Robin, 365
Starkey, Jerome, 212
Steiner, Michael, 320
Stevens, Chris, 342
Stinger antiaircraft missiles, 52, 325
Stirrup, Jock, 234
Strategic Advisory Team, 77
Strick van Linschoten, Alex, 314

Stryker armored vehicles, 209
suicide bombings, 19, 22, 111, 282, 302, 316,
    357, 369
Sullivan, Jake, 396
Supreme Allied Commander Europe
    (SACEUR), 131, 290
Syria, 356

Tajik, 22, 33, 50
Taliban, 10, 11, 83–137, 398
    Afghan National Army and, 341–44
    in Anaconda strategy, 227–30
    at Bagram Air Base, 29
    Buddha statue destruction by, 52
    Bush and, 394–95
    casualties of, 371
    changing allegiance in, 38–39
    CIA and, 316–17
    civilian casualties by, 80, 301–2
    Clinton, H., and, 315, 321, 322–23
    coalition strategy against, 10
    corruption and, 242–49
    defeat of, 65–68
    Dunford, J., and, 301–2
    early elimination of, 16
    Eid cease-fire and, 373–76
    Fahim and, 40
    Germans and, 320, 322
    Ghani, Ashraf, and, 394
    green-on-blue attacks and, 272–73
    Haq and, 35
    Haqqani network and, 319
    in Helmand Province, 89–97, 288, 344,
        364–65
    Holbrooke and, 318–19
    Iran and, 373
    IS and, 356
    ISAF and, 18–19
    on Al Jazeera TV, 301
    in Kandahar, 7–8, 30, 37, 97–101, 231–32,
        288–89
    Karzai, Hamid, and, 38, 205, 300–301, 313,
        319–20, 322–23
    in Korengal Valley, 111–14
    Kunduz hospital and, 344–46
    Loya Jirga tent and, 319–20
    McChrystal, S., and, 191–92, 216, 318
    money burning and, 68–72
    morale of, 259
    in Musa Qala, 101–3, 118–19
    "mutually hurting stalemate" and, 367–68
    NATO and, 317–18
    Northern Alliance and, 32

    Norway and, 317–18
    Obama and, 315, 321, 368
    OEF and, 78
    Operation Medusa and, 97–101, 197–98, 231
    Operation Mostarak and, 200–204, 231
    Operation Mountain Thrust against, 91–93
    Pakistan and, 16, 32–33, 87, 153–55, 227,
        322
    in Paktia Province, 47–48
    of Pashtun, 50, 64
    as poorly educated, 63–64
    prisoner releases and, 306–8
    al-Qaeda and, 315, 316, 321, 323, 378
    reign of terror of, 30–31, 52
    return of, 16, 83–137
    Russia and, 20–21, 34, 367, 379
    on social media, 19
    strong influence of, 23
    talks with, 311–27
    talks with (II), 369–80
    Trump and, 354, 378–80
    unwillingness to talk to, 21
    warlords and, 17–18, 36, 52–53
    women's rights and, 30, 32
Tarzi, Mahmud, 362
Task Force La Fayette, 272
Task Force Spartan, 110, 115
Team America, 187–88
Templer, Gerald, 104–5
Ten Wars (Lute), 211
Tenet, George, 32
10th Mountain Division, 48, 92, 100, 110, 288
Teri Mangal, 128
terms sheet, 195
TF-2010, 244
TF-Nexus, 244
TF-Spotlight, 244
Tillerson, Rex, 352
time-phased force deployment, 168–69
Toner, Chris, 92
Tootal, Stuart, 89, 95
Tora Bora cave complex, 45–49, 333
Trout, Cliff, 342
Trump, Donald J., 11, 21, 146, 312, 351–54,
        376
    Nicholson, J., and, 377–78
    Pakistan and, 365, 379
    Taliban and, 378–80
TTP, 155, 307
Tuchman, Barbara, 23
Tunnell, Harry, 209–10
Turkey/Turks, 55, 336
Tweet of Damocles, 378

Umarzai, Lal Muhammad, 161
United Nations (UN), 65–66
USAID, 19–20, 60, 69, 71, 112
    corruption and, 249–53
    Five Pillars and, 75–76
    Operation Mostarak and, 203
    schools and, 73
    security for, 110–11
Uzbekistan, 29, 32, 33, 48

"Valley Forge of the Afghan Army," 62
Vendrell, Francesc, 50, 65
Vietnam, 131, 172, 189, 216–17, 223
    bombing pause in, 33
    COIN in, 14, 144, 146–47
    commanders from, 12–14
    CORDS program in, 259
    corruption in, 248
    Dunford, J., and, 291–92
    Holbrooke in, 319
    pacification in, 315
    Small Wars Manual in, 142
    Trump and, 352
Vuono, Carl, 223

Waltz, Michael, 174
Wanat, 114–15
war crimes, 53, 144
War Machine (film), 218
war on terror, of Bush, 24, 61, 280, 282, 314
Wardak, Abdul Rahim, 160, 201, 245, 274–75
warlords, 41, 50, 398. *See also* mujahideen
    airpower and, 39
    CIA and, 52, 244–45
    corruption of, 243–47
    digging in by, 51–53
    Five Pillars and, 74

funding of, 17–18
    Ghani, Ashraf, and, 333, 361–62
    ISAF and, 86–87
    at Loya Jirga tent, 49–52
    money burning and, 68–72
    9/11 and, 314
    Northern Alliance and, 233
    of Pashtun, 34–35
    prevention of return of, 17
    Russia and, 18
    Taliban and, 17–18, 36, 52–53
Warren, Elizabeth, 376–77
Washington Papers, 24
Waziri, Dawlat, 360
wedding parties, 51, 157–61, 358
Westmoreland, William, 216–17
Westside Boys, 103
WikiLeaks, 187
Wilder, Andrew, 247
winning hearts and minds, 147
Wolfowitz, Paul, 30, 61, 75
women's rights, 30, 32, 67–68
Wood, William "Chemical Bill," 155–57,
    162–63
Woodward, Bob, 195, 237
World Bank, 19, 69, 70, 72, 75, 78, 305, 332
    corruption and, 253
World Food Programme, 71
Worsley, Henry, 80–81

Yaqoob, Muhammad, 375

Zadran, Mullah Sangeen, 313
Zaeef, Mullah, 317
Zahir, Haji, 203, 212
Zorlu, Hilmi Akin, 55, 76
Zubaide, Mahfouz, 307